Diagnosis, Correction, and Prevention of Reading Disabilities

RUSSELL G. STAUFFER
Professor Emeritus, University of Delaware

JULES C. ABRAMS
Hahnemann Medical College

JOHN J. PIKULSKI
University of Delaware

Harper & Row, Publishers
New York, Hagerstown, San Francisco, London

Sponsoring Editor: Wayne E. Schotanus/George A. Middendorf
Project Editor: Richard T. Viggiano/H. Detgen
Designer: Helen Iranyi
Production Supervisor: Kewal K. Sharma
Compositor: American Book–Stratford Press, Inc.
Printer and Binder: Halliday Lithograph Corporation
Art Studio: Vantage Art, Inc.

DIAGNOSIS, CORRECTION, AND PREVENTION OF
READING DISABILITIES

Library of Congress Cataloging in Publication Data

Stauffer, Russell G.
  Diagnosis, correction, and prevention of reading
disabilities.

    Includes index.
    1. Reading—Remedial teaching. 2. Reading disability.
3. Reading—Ability testing. I. Abrams, Jules C.,
joint author. II. Pikulski, John J., joint author.
III. Title.
LB1050.5.S73   372.4'3   77–26610
ISBN 0–06–046418–6

Contents

Contents

Preface

In view of the obvious importance of the ability to read for every aspect of our personal and social lives, it is particularly unfortunate that year after year, for varied and sundry reasons, so many children are baffled and overcome by a society's ineptitude and inexperience. Whether we like it or not there is no denying that this is true. Not only is this unfortunate and abortive circumstance a reflection and drain upon our so-called prosperous society but also an affliction and adversity to each child who fails and, in turn, to his parents and friends.

Each year a very small proportion of children reaching compulsory attendance school age comprise a population requiring special clinical help. These are the children burdened with neurological and emotional disabilities that precipitate reading failure if and when early diagnosis does not lead to appropriate adjustment of instructional practices and learning expectancies. However, by far the larger number of children who become reading failures with varying degrees of disability are the result of pedagogical shortcomings. These children are indeed the unfortunate victims of a society that knows better. School boards, school superintendents, and principals are even more at fault in most instances than teachers. It is the incompetence of each, though, that burdens so many children with the label "failure."

The cry against lock-step methods of instruction has reverberated across the educational scene with marked fervor since the middle of the nineteenth century. The most widely used "in word" in the past decade has been the word *individualize*. Lip service is paid to this concept. Instructional practices refute the nobly voiced precepts. Even more shocking has been the mushrooming of commercially prepared "individualized" programs that represent lock-step procedures at their worst.

It is with all this in mind that this text on the *Diagnosis, Correction, and Prevention of Reading Disabilities* has been prepared. The text may not prove to be a panacea for all, but it should prove a boon to many.

We know that a normal child deprived of ability to read is a child handicapped for life. This is even more true of the child suffering from mental, physical, emotional, or multiple handicaps. Cutting off the handicapped from essential learning experiences robs them of the chance to develop the skills and coping capacities necessary for living, and this compounds the disabilities already there.

The child is a physical organism, functioning in a social environment, in a psychological manner. Reading, being a complex process of a total individual, may invoke any or all of these aspects, with cause and effect being closely interwoven. Learning is a dynamic process.

Teachers and reading specialists are often confused by newly introduced or invented terms that result from study of the reading process. While some of these terms represent diagnostic refinements, in some cases they are simply new labels for old, unvalidated ideas. Norm referenced testing, criterion referenced measures, maturational lag, learning disability, dyslexia, psycholinguistic functioning, and diagnostic-prescriptive techniques are but a few of the terms that are unknown or unclear to teachers and reading specialists. This text not only places these terms in perspective and notes their possible utility but also alerts teachers to their potential pitfalls and dangers.

Most texts dealing with the measurement of reading and reading problems stop short of giving the practitioner the information necessary to implement an effective, ongoing program of evaluation. This text elaborates on practical techniques well enough to allow actual application. Numerous, concrete illustrations are provided. A balance is maintained between those techniques and materials useful for classroom and group evaluation and between those applicable to cases of severe reading disability that require individual attention.

Just as the evaluation of "good" and "poor" readers is artificially separated, many texts fail to capitalize on the close relationships that can and should exist between teaching and testing. In *Diagnosis, Correction, and Prevention of Reading Disabilities,* the reader is shown how the most effective program of evaluation is one that is based upon the day-to-day observations of children as they learn to read.

R.G.S.
J.C.A.
J.J.P.

CHAPTER 1

Introduction

If the genesis of this text were to be traced to a single influence or inspiration, it would have to be to experiences that I had more than 40 years ago with two children.* One was a 12-year old girl who had repeated first and second grade and finally made it to fourth grade almost a total nonreader. The second was a 10-year old boy who, too, had been left back in first grade and then promoted from year to year to fourth grade. In a class of 33 children these two were standout failures, the girl more so than the boy. She was tall for her age and was showing early signs of pubescence. The lad, on the other hand, was small for his age and physically blended in with the class.

This was my first year of teaching. In many ways I was quite unprepared to teach reading in grades four, five, and six. I had had one year of student teaching as my apprenticeship, teaching algebra in the ninth grade. It had been a marvelous year, and under the supervision of Miss Brown I had learned much, but I was ill-prepared to teach reading and language arts at the intermediate-grade level and totally unprepared to teach remedial reading. In the midst of the depression of the 1930s I was fortunate indeed to obtain a teaching position of any kind, and I

---

* This chapter was written by Russell G. Stauffer.

tried to show my appreciation by being as diligent and inspiring as possible.

That year I learned many things about children, about reading programs, and about success and failure. In each of the three classes, I was allotted two different sets of basal readers and was instructed to divide each class into two groups. This was considered an advanced procedure, because prior to this year only one set of readers had been available and the top group proceeded through the grade level reader at a faster pace than the slow group. They would finish the reader by April and with great effort the slow group would "finish" by the end of the school term. By carefully pleading the case I was permitted by midyear to organize a third group, but only in the fourth grade. I had to teach this third group at the end of the school day, because I was told my schedule did not allow time for three groups. To stay after school was usually considered a punishment, so it had to be done on a voluntary basis and, as I discovered, only with parental admission.

Almost all teachers look back upon their first year of teaching as having been a year of liability. Neophytes in almost all endeavors tend to feel this way about their first year but, when one is influencing the lives of so many people, the awareness seems especially poignant.

CHILDREN'S VARIABILITY

In that first year I learned that children are different not only physically but also psychologically. Each year since then has reaffirmed this. Besides their affective and emotional variabilities, children differ widely in their rates and styles of learning and in their maturity and capacity.

That first year I learned that Pauline and Richard could read only a few words and did not know how to decode or unlock words they did not recognize at sight. Each year they had been reexposed to the same preprimers. This year, using a different series of preprimers did not make a bit of difference. Both children hated reading, yet both were willing to try again, largely, I believe, because I was their first male teacher. This, too, did not make a difference. I learned also that, as Bruno Bettelheim put it so well 15 years later, "love is not enough" (2).* It is true that his admonition was aimed primarily at parents, but a similar admonition can be directed at teachers with good intentions and particularly at remedial teachers.

Every school district has in its environs teachers who have retired or who stopped teaching, to raise a family or the like, who class themselves remedial reading teachers. Although these people have good in-

---

* Cited works are listed in the end-of-chapter Bibliography.

tentions and are no doubt fine classroom teachers, they just do not realize that repeating what was done in developmental basal programs is not the answer. They need to learn that "love is not enough." They need to learn that even the most thorough diagnosis and the facts provided thereby are not of as much value to instructing children as a thorough understanding of human variability: neurologically, psychologically, and pedagogically. They need to acquire the attitudes and insights necessary to attend a particular child's needs at a specific moment. The thousands of children that have been dealt with at the University of Delaware's Reading Study Center bear witness to this fact: Despite well-intentioned teaching, additional difficulties are too often created for children, because of the teacher's lack of an understanding and knowledge of how to deal with children's variabilities.

Gordon Allport put it well when he said that the outstanding characteristic of a person is his individuality (1). Each is a unique creation. All teaching, particularly remedial teaching, tends—for reasons that are enlarged upon in this text—to neglect this paramount fact of individuality. The range of genetic, structural, and biochemical variability requires us to expect temperament and motivation, rate and style of learning, and capacity to vary widely. The remedial teacher, or any teacher for that matter, must think seriously of the implications of the wide-ranging individuality for pedagogical and therapeutical handling. Rules of thumb will not do, because no one child is "normal."

At almost all levels of teaching and learning within the range of typical developmental rates of learning, from remedial rates at one end to the rates of the gifted at the other, instructional activities need to be structured around the concepts of action, interaction, and transaction (7). Each of the actions must be viewed as dynamic, as an interplay of acts and decisions that are functional. In other words, each must be a learning experience that is *purposive behavior* unified by the fact that the learner sets out with a problem and seeks a solution.

The basic concept of action is that of self-action. Children are constantly acting and learning, in the beginning at a sensori-motor-cognitive level, which is then augmented at a linguistic-cognitive level. It is such self-actions that must be utilized in an instructional environment made up of learning situations, structured by a teacher to provide the medium through which self-action can be expressed. In these structured situations children perform two types of actions: a sensori-motor overt type and an intellectual-decision-making, covert type. Cooperative pupil-teacher planning constitutes a big step toward attaining the scholarly skills of self-action.

The concept of interaction is that of group learning. Children not only interact with elements in a situation, they do so within the social-intellectual character of a group. It is in the environs of a group that an individual sees that different children react differently and may do so in ways that might have been overlooked. It is this kind of interacting and sharing that results in developing and maintaining a self-regulatory spirit.

On the other hand, transactions represent the use of language to internalize the actions and interactions, to objectify and obtain quality responses, and to communicate and share with others. This is what makes learning functional and durable.

It is almost self-evident that, if the "actions" defined are to result in maximal development of children, both individualized and group instruction are essential. This is true not only for developmental-type instruction but also for remedial instruction. Interestingly enough the range of human differences not only makes the wheels of society go around but also make learning in a classroom vital, exciting, and functional. Each student represents a tremendous reservoir of potential. What must be avoided is lock-step-type group instruction, as well as isolated tutor-type instruction. Most of the children tested in the Center and similar centers are the victims of Procrustean-type reading instruction. John I. Goodlad and Robert H. Anderson state it well:

> Certain time-honored practices of pupil classification, while perhaps not lethal, trap school-age travelers in much the same fashion as Procrustes' bed trapped the unwary. These practices are concomitants of our graded system of school organization. First, a certain amount of progress is held to be standard for a year's work. Then, the content of the work is laid out within the grade, to be "covered" and, to a degree, "mastered." The slow are pulled and stretched to fit the grade. Sometimes, because their God-given limbs lack enough elasticity, they are "non-promoted"—left behind, where presumably another year of stretching will do the trick. The quick are compressed and contracted to fit the grade. In time, they learn to adapt to a pace that is slower than their natural one. (4, p. 1)

CHILDREN'S INDIVIDUALITY

For "clinical work" purposes, distinction has been made between *nomothetic* and *idiographic* understanding (1). The distinction brings to focus the quandries of instruction, of counseling, of therapy. How to cope with the unique organization of each individual's bodily and mental processes is the question. The "work" is referred to as clinical because a single individual is studied and considered in an effort to bring about better achievement and improved adjustment. Nomothetic discipline, on the one hand, deals with broad, preferably universal laws or norms. Science prefers universals to particulars. Idiographic (not ideo-

4

graphic) discipline, on the other hand, deals with a person as a system of patterned uniquenesses.

Chapters 2, 3, 4, 5, and 6 of this text, prepared by Professor John Pikulski, detail the diagnostic procedures best used in a clinic, in addition to ways useful in a classroom. Clinical diagnosis is done with the intention of being idiographic. Tests are given, scores are plotted, evidence is confronted with evidence, and finally all is synthesized into a final report, in an effort to discover the complex personal pattern and the achievement patterns of the child being tested. Knowledge of group norms or actuarial data does not help very much, if at all. In addition, by virtue of the sacrosanct fact that reading is a process, determining a child's performance in a "reading situation" is in sharp contrast to the use of standardized tests that measure the products of reading in an atypical reading situation. Certainly the clinician must penetrate beyond the spotting of symptoms of inefficiency. Needed is a precise accounting of the acquired or unacquired capabilities that are essential when one reads for meaning. To manage the reading process requires ability to cope with language on a self-generating basis, so that the process varies in degree and kind according to (1) the purposes of the reader, and (2) the nature and difficulty of the material. In addition, command of the auxiliary aid of unlocking a word not recognized at sight represents essential skill attainment of a pedantic nature and must be measured primarily when the children are reading for meaning. Yet, oddly enough, most tests of word attack skill are done with words in isolation. To round out the picture, depending upon the children's degree of reading disability, skills related to concept attainment must also be appraised. To put all these pieces together to see what the subjects' cognitive and academic skill systems and their capacities are really like, to see a vitally interrelated mosaic of elements and test scores, requires a clinically trained person who has served at least a year, preferably two, of clinical apprenticeship.

When to all this is added the need to understand the children as unique individuals—their particular goals, their values, the directions of their strivings, together with their abilities and available energy—their ability to make judgments and deal with complexities becomes strikingly evident. Chapters 7, 8, 9, and 10, written by Professor Jules Abrams, add an insight and a sensitivity that calls for a psychological mindedness that goes well beyond intuition. The task is not easy. So many factors influence our success or failure. Indeed, one must be very guarded, lest the understanding is oversimplified. In addition, all of us are subject to the common sources of error: monopolistic stereotyping, projection, leniency, halo-judgments, and undue cautiousness. Even though the process and decision making is a complex one as Professor Abrams details it, we must face up to it.

THE TEACHER

In general, the wider the sampling, the greater the probability that the conclusions we draw are true. . . . For this reason the concept of *diagnostic teaching* holds high promise for accuracy in evaluation. . . . Teachers who instruct and observe children on a day-to-day basis obtain a wide sampling of reading behavior. This should make the classroom teacher's daily instruction and resultant observation of reading performance the most accurate form of reading evaluation.

Thus writes Professor Pikulski in his chapter, "Approaches to Evaluating Reading" (p. 54). Similar comments are made in other chapters.

It is true that in the University of Delaware Center situation, where we both diagnose and instruct, we generally conclude that if we could carefully integrate testing and teaching and start a program of remediation by immediate teaching, we could be far more productive. By and large this is what is done once the intensive diagnosis has been accomplished. The teaching, by skilled teachers diagnostically and pedagogically trained, causes our predictions about achievement to improve. This, combined with the frequent staff meetings described in Chapter 12, helps us to prescribe broader and more adequate instructional and therapeutical procedures. The teaching-testing-staffing process permits idiographic interpretations from which we form increasingly more insightful concepts of any particular child.

As a result, the concept of *empathy* (1, pp. 533–537) provides an important basis. Even though the term has broadened out to mean any process of successful understanding, if empathy helps to establish the "thou" of an individual, we come to know better how a person feels and thinks and acts. "There is no break between the strain, pride, sorrow, or playfulness which I feel empathically and the personality of the one I am seeking to understand." We must know the child as a mobile, spontaneous, intelligent, causal individual. In brief, we must locate the child in his world, discover his intentions, and adjust.

In the climate of a dynamically oriented approach to reading disabilities, any discussion of personality development is closely associated with ego development. The focus of dynamic clinical psychology has shifted from the emphasis on unconscious wishes, strivings, and impulses to the relatively autonomous function of the ego. . . . How one can speak of doing comprehensive evaluation of a child with reading difficulty and ignore the emotional factors is beyond our understanding.

Parents would not want to return day after working day to a position in which they failed constantly and knew that all of their peers knew that they failed. Teachers and principals would not care to do so either. If they were required by law to endure such failure, in a short time they would be emotional wrecks. Yet, the law requires children to attend school every day, even though instruction is not differentiated and nomothetic norms are made into standards. For these children school takes on the dread and anxieties of concentration camps.

Without question, the failure and knowledge of failure spills over into the home. Siblings either wish to help and try to do so or are embarrassed and annoyed. Parents try and try again and tend to run a gamut of Chicken Little to Pollyanna emotions. Medicine-show-type teachers claim specialist roles and amplify the circumstances. What child could avoid being filled with self-doubt and seek adjustment by devious means.

The marvel of it all is the fact that the 9-, 10-, and 11-year olds with a 4-, 5-, and 6-year history of failure retain as much poise as they do. The resiliency of children is amazing. If this were not so, society would be forced to act more positively and provide the needed help. Our need to refer a child to a psychiatrist is more the exception than the rule. When referral is warranted, the typical diagnosis is to join forces and provide therapy, as well as instruction. What the child needs more than anything else, more than an attentive ear, is to experience success.

Success is more likely in a center situation such as described in Chapters 11 and 12, first because of the quality of the teaching staff, and second because of the nature of the center's open-spaced circumstance. While it is true that instruction is to a large degree individualized in a semi-tutor circumstance, it is also true that the procedures detailed are based almost totally on pupil actions. The student acts upon his own experiences, either those acquired outside of the center or those structured in the center. He builds upon his own interests, his own language and his own motivation. He is provided with decision-making circumstances and required to make judgments and above all to act upon his judgments. Therapy is obtained through success, which is fostered by skillful teaching.

In addition, because there are present for instruction as many as 20 other children, the student realizes instantly that he is not the only one to have failed. He sees students of varying size and age. He not only responds to this physical evidence but also collaborates with the others. The attitude of a helping hand prevails. He works with others, reads to others, listens to others, and shares in their projects. Uniquely enough, in time he takes on teaching responsibility and helps others, as well as being helped by them. "How would you teach this skill to someone else?" is a challenge put to students over and over again.

This kind of instructional environment, based on pupil actions and interactions, is also premised on the efficacy of conscious planning. Gradually the pull of a child's image of the future asserts on his present conduct a power that results from the dynamic force of planning and intention. The cognitive and emotive forces become fused into intentions for the present but with a flavor of future orientation. The transition may be gradual, but it is nonetheless real and impelling.

The term *proception,* as used by Allport from the work of the philosopher Justus Buchler, is appropriate to our discussion (1). The term

> recognizes the fact that each individual carries with him his past relations to the world, his emotional dispositions, and his own expectancies for the future. These "proceptive directions" provide his potentialities for seeing, hearing, doing, thinking, making, and saying.

At every moment each student is conducting his own "ego-world" transactions and in his own way. Accordingly the constraints of the instructional situation are such as to provide environmental and pedagogical support gradually shaping pupils' self-esteem and self-acceptance so that they influence desire to achieve.

The teaching support is based on a close teacher-pupil relationship, stemming from the semitutor circumstance whereby two students share one teacher. This arrangement, though, is augmented by the interactions of all the teachers. Each instructor knows all the children, works with them from time to time, responds to their projects, shares in their creations. Each instructor attends the staff meetings regularly and is quite fully acquainted with each student's history and current instructional needs and achievements. In addition, group activities are deliberately scheduled. Directed reading-thinking activities are conducted with groups varying in number from two participants to six. In brief, esprit-de-corps pervades the entire center and embraces all the participants: students, instructors, supervisors, director, and secretaries. It is impossible to achieve such relationships unless there is some point of focus that is both individual and yet common to all, a point of anchorage. From a cognitive-emotive instructional point of view, the answer is identifying students' intentions, that is, their constellation of values and interests. These intentions are the dominating force that bind together students' lives and actions, their thought and development. In short, to instruct these children we must allow for both nomothetic and idiographic knowledge. Facts alone tell little. Needed is a balance, a method that is seasoned and perceptive.

SCHOOLS

Repeatedly throughout the text reference is made to the fact that the vast majority of the children who develop reading disabilities do so not because of neurological or psychological shortcomings but because of pedagogical failings. All concerned with education are responsible: school board members, superintendents, principals, and teachers (in that order). Instruction could be differentiated from the very beginning of a child's school life. The outcry against lock-step procedures has been voiced strongly since the 1880s (9). Preston Search led the protest then and innumerable authorities since then have voiced similar protests. Teacher's manuals either for basal readers or for the boxed-typed materials of the 1960s make "slaves and puppets" of teachers (8).

By and large our schools are staffed by able, creative, devoted teachers who sincerely wish to do that which is best. But their actions and deeds are controlled by delimiting mass-oriented instructions focused on rote parroting.

The problem is a national one. When over a four decade period one sees the number of failures increase rather than decrease, the situation becomes deeply shocking. Quite frankly the gnashing of teeth, the wailing and rubbing of hands, the expenditure of huge federal funds is disgusting and to a large degree fruitless. To the school authorities, who have the responsibilities, the bewildered and concerned American people should make only one demand and make it firmly: Get on with it.

> Almost all reading specialists and qualified educators will tell you that children who are likely to experience extreme difficulty in learning to read can be identified in first grade if not earlier in the preschool years. Even though this is so, most schools continue to devote most of their funds and their energies trying to cure or correct disabilities rather than to prevent them. (See p. 350.)

Ask superintendents or principals about standardized test achievement scores for their children, and they are quick to tell you a mean score and compare it with a mythical national monothetic norm, a norm that has become a standard. But embarrassed silence follows questions about the range of scores or the likelihood of skewed distributions.

When the twenty-fourth yearbook was written in the early 1920s, certain principals emerged that were and still are true (5).

> 1. No group has yet been found in which the individuals composing it possess equal amounts of any one ability.
> 2. Performances vary so greatly as to indicate that no single requirement is adequate as a stimulus to a majority of the group.
> 3. To study the development of the learning process it is absurd to set up as a standard a definite quantity of performance and expect each member of the group to accomplish just that amount and no other.

Coaching the laggards by providing remedial instruction is a name calling, segregationist way of not coping with the issue of individual differences. It results in habits of failure, or half-done work, of shirking, and of negative ego development. On the other hand "enriching the curriculum" for the bright is a skirting of efficiency of instruction and a denial of attitudes and practices that should be the mark of all teaching. Individual differences among children represent the wealth of society and the means by which society progresses; the only reason they are disturbing to our system of education is because the system is still caught up in lock-step procedures, augmented in recent years by boxed materials designed for the masses. Educators must stop paying only lip service to differentiated instruction and must practice what they preach.

> If we are sensitive to developmental needs we look at reading differently and we *go at it* differently. We go at it as creative guidance. The materials are not subject matter. They are the resources we use. (10, p. 166)

Teachers can help by achieving a wholesome classroom climate: one in which the classroom is viewed as a place for self-discovery; one in which all the children are respected for their uniqueness; one in which thought processes are honed and sharpened in the dynamics of a group, whereby minds meet the challenge of minds; and one in which children are listened to, as well as spoken to. The youngster who is only a failure endures a suffering that is real and calls for understanding and knowledgeable action. Pupils will develop feelings of being liked, wanted, accepted, and successful if they have been taught that way. Pupils who are self-reliant, self-directed, and responsible are those who have been a part of a classroom environment where they are free to make mistakes, to be creative, to be curious, to inquire, to struggle, to learn, and to change in their own way. They know what it means to work in an atmosphere that is challenging rather than threatening. If any one stage of a child's student life might be singled out as more important than any other, it must be the early childhood years, from ages 4 to 10. Why? Because it is during these years that the tone and tenor of a reader's life is set. A good start can and will make the difference.

It is not at all difficult to agree with Piaget's statement that the principal goal of education is to create students capable of doing new things, students who are creators, inventors, and discoverers (6). Cognitive functioning that pursues excellence requires just such performing. Reading performance in the pursuit of excellence makes similar demands. Each new word, each new phrase or clause, each new sentence, each paragraph, each page, each chapter requires the reader to create, to invent, to discover.

It is not at all difficult to agree with Piaget's second goal of education: to form minds that can be critical and can verify. If this is the grist of cognitive functioning, it certainly is of reading. The great danger today is of "slogans, collective opinions, ready-made trends of thought" transmitted either by voice or by print. The only way to resist is to do so individually. Each pupil must be taught to pursue excellence actively. Each pupil must learn to criticize, to tell what is verifiable, to distinguish between what is proven and what is not.

In this regard a statement entitled *Dimensions of Excellence in Education* (3), which was prepared by the Commission on Educational policy of the California Teachers Association, is ideal to use in measuring the excellence of reading instruction. The preservation of a free society and the fulfillment of its purpose depend upon each individual's ability to read and to listen and to do so critically. The commission's long deliberations led to an arrangement of its conclusions under six headings: capacity for inquiry, problem-solving competence, communication and computation skills, familiarity with organized disciplines, cultivated enjoyments, and democratic commitment. The first three dimensions have the flavor of processes and as such as particularly to the teaching of reading. The last three bear the quality of outcomes and as such help bring perspective to the processes and to make them more significant. In other words, the dimensions are mutually supportive.

Democratic commitment is viewed as having two facets. First, the individual achieves his own inner stability as he continuously learns to recognize his strengths and weaknesses and learns to understand and accept himself. The Greeks said "know thyself," and the Romans said, "control thyself." Today we frequently refer to these goals as self-fulfillment, self-realization, or self-actualization.

Second, the individual sees himself as a responsible member of society. He has a commitment to ideals, standards, ways of life, and to other persons. He has a concern for the social community, knows what his community expects of him, and has the capacity for effective action within the group. Now the Jewish maxim "give thyself" becomes pertinent, and "lessons embodying these principles could be expected to result in increased growth in personal self-direction and in capacity for moral decision" (3, p. 22). Undoubtedly, where each dimension plays a significant part in the educational process, excellence will result.

> The cliche, "If wishes were horses, beggars would ride" can be readily applied to the many who wish they could read but cannot. Wishing is not the answer. (See p. 357.)

SUMMARY OF THE BOOK

Chapters 2, 3, 4, 5, and 6 are devoted to diagnosis of reading disability and were prepared by Professor John Pikulski. In these chapters he discusses evaluation, its background and its utility as related to both the correction and prevention of reading disability. He frankly reviews what in our jointly formed judgment seems to be the merit and liability of intensive diagnosis as a guide for instruction purposes. Throughout he takes the position that all good teaching is diagnostic and that the best form of diagnosis could be best accomplished in the classroom where instruction is differentiated according to children's learning rate, maturity, and capacity for learning.

Chapters 7, 8, 9, and 10 are devoted to the relationships that exist between reading failure and emotional maladjustment and were prepared by Professor Jules Abrams. His attention to ego orientation and the influences of reading disability are directed toward determining the best possible way to help a child. Psychotherapy never taught anyone to read. By studying the interaction of neurological and psychological factors, one provides a better opportunity for treating the child as a whole. By focusing on ego functions attention is given to the essence of psychological life-perception, memory, cognition, thinking, action, postponement of gratification, repression, anxiety, integration, and syntheses.

Chapters 11, 12, 13, and 14 were prepared by Professor Russell G. Stauffer and are devoted to instructional procedures. Anyone engaged in analysis or in diagnosis knows how fascinating it can be to administer tests and diagram results and do so without contributing much to their true purpose (to differentiate instruction) and that far more important aspect, "what to do about it." It is true that sympathy can be readily offered, but this usually produces no more than self-pity and withdrawn defensiveness. What is needed are procedures that are sound and varied, flexible and tough, circumspect in thought and action, steady and courageous, addressed to a child's will to learn and based on an attitude of satisfaction through achievement. Instructional procedures are described in much detail, not only for use with children who have experienced failure, but also with children who have not.

BIBLIOGRAPHY

1. Allport, Gordon W. *Pattern and Growth in Personality*. New York: Holt, Rinehart and Winston, 1961.

2. Bettelheim, Bruno. *Love Is Not Enough*. New York: Free Press, 1950.

3. California Teachers Association. *Dimensions of Excellence in Education*. A Statement by the Commission on Educational Policy of the California Teachers Association, bulletin no. 10. Burlingame, Calif.: California Teachers Association, 1964.

4. Goodlad, John I., and Robert H. Anderson. *The Nongraded Elementary School*. New York: Harcourt Brace Jovanovich, 1959.

5. Gray, William S. "Essential Objectives of Instruction in Reading," in *Report of the National Committee on Reading: Twenty-fourth Year-*

Bibliography

book of the National Society for the Study of Education. Part 1. Bloomington, Ill. Public School Publishing Co., 1925.

6. Piaget, Jean. "Development and Learning," in Richard R. Ripple and Verne N. Rockcastle, eds., *Piaget Rediscovered.* A Report of the Conference on Cognitive Studies and Curriculum Development (March, 1964). Ithaca, N.Y.: Cornell University, School of Education, 1964.

7. Stauffer, Russell G. *Directing the Reading-Thinking Process.* New York: Harper & Row, 1975.

8. Stauffer, Russell, G. "Slave, Puppet or Teacher." *The Reading Teacher,* 24(1971):24–29.

9. Sutherland, A. H. "Individual Differences Among Children," in *Adapting the Schools to Individual Differences.* Twenty-fourth Yearbook of the National Society for the Study of Education, part 2 section 1. Bloomington, Ill: Public School Publishing Co., 1925.

10. Zirbes, Laura. *Spurs to Creative Teaching.* New York: Putnam, 1959.

CHAPTER 2

Evaluation: Background and Introduction

GENERAL CONSIDERATIONS

Historically, professionals from the field of medicine were responsible for the earliest systematic attempts to study reading problems. For example, one of the earliest names to appear in an historical account of developments in the area of reading disabilities is that of W. P. Morgan (8), a medical practitioner and oculist. Early attempts to explain serious reading problems frequently reasoned by analogy from cases of adults who had suffered traumatic brain injury. Early theorists such as Hinshelwood (6), an ophthalmologist, hypothesized the possibility of a failure of some areas of the brain to fully develop. Thus, in pioneer investigative efforts reading problems were associated with dysfunction of the brain or nervous system.

Perhaps because of the early association with the medical profession, reading problems and their diagnosis have taken on and retained a kind of "mystical" quality that educators often hold in awe. It is not uncommon for teachers to suspect a neurological basis for a reading disability. It is not unusual to find diagnostic facilities that almost always attribute a child's reading problem to a perceptual or neurological fault. In spite of substantial research and sophisticated technology, much remains unknown about the functioning of the neurological system; therefore, the mysticism remains and grows. While there are, in truth, some cases of reading disability that are related to neurological malfunctioning, there is no clear evidence to suggest that many of them are. The vast majority of reading problems appear to be the result of inadequate or inappropriate teaching procedures. Most of the children who are encountering difficulties in learning to read do not need to have an elaborate diagnostic evaluation performed. However, many educators and parents seem reluctant to accept straightforward reasons for the existence of a reading problem and continue to search for the exotic.

The author of these chapters takes the position that much of the activity undertaken in the name of diagnosis is unnecessary and that some of it is indeed detrimental to the well-being of the children involved. All too often children are subjected to numerous testing sessions in an effort to track down the reason for their reading disabilities. Various attempts are made to find out what is wrong with the disabled reader. Too often the entire diagnostic effort is aimed at finding a deficit in the child. Rarely is an effort made to critically analyze the instructional strategies being used in order to determine why they are failing. If more consideration were given to creating excellent circumstances for teaching reading, it seems very likely that fewer children would fail, and much of the time-consuming testing that is now undertaken would be unnecessary.

Accepting the position described in the last few paragraphs has certain disadvantages. Most prominently it will not allow the diagnostician to appear expert and all-knowing. Rather than talking about *the* cause of the problem, clinicians will be forced to talk about several possible causes; or perhaps the whole question of causality will seem irrelevant because the emphasis will be upon remediation. However, in all too many cases parents and often teachers, will prefer explanations that are direct, precise-sounding and resultantly oversimplified and misleading; it is difficult to convince parents and some teachers that professionals who maintain that they are able to locate a specific definite cause are often engaging in gross oversimplifications.

Is there, then, any legitimate purpose for a thorough diagnosis or for any diagnosis at all? Certainly. Two situations immediately present themselves. A lengthy diagnosis is called for when careful, well-planned, individualized teaching attempts have failed. The second reason is less professionally justifiable but nonetheless frequently compelling. Sometimes it is necessary to conduct a lengthy diagnostic evaluation simply to convince other professionals, parents, or state or federal officials that the course of action being pursued in a remediation program is the appropriate one. Unfortunately, in our society test scores, regardless of their source, are often given more respect than the judgment of a capable teacher who has had the opportunity to work with a child over a long period of time.

EVALUATION WITH A PURPOSE

It is not uncommon for staff members of a university reading center to receive phone calls from teachers or administrators who ask what reading tests they should be using. The caller often becomes puzzled when asked why the test is going to be administered. Responses such as: "we are required to" or "the principal said we should" are not unusual. There are a wide variety of reading tests available and the choice of which tests to use is dependent on the purpose of the evaluation. Thus, every testing program, ranging from individual diagnosis to national assessment, must begin with some stated purpose.

In some situations, the purpose for the testing may dictate the construction of new tests. For example, some states have now established general objectives or goals for reading achievement at various points in a child's school career. Frequently it is found that extant tests do not coincide with the general objectives or goals adequately or directly enough. The purpose for the testing dictates the creation of new tests which correspond closely to the stated objectives.

Teachers often have very different reasons for evaluating reading than the purposes existing for a state-wide testing program. In many cases, teacher purposes are very specific. For example, teachers may be faced with new students who were transferred to their classes in the middle of the school year. Their purpose for evaluating reading may be to determine if the new students can be placed in one of the three reading instructional groups that have already been established. These circumstances certainly do not call for the construction of a new group-reading test. Instead, the best solution would probably be to employ informal diagnostic procedures (see Chapter 4). Informal evaluation procedures would allow the teachers to carefully, yet quickly, sample the children's ability to read the materials that are being used to instruct the three different groups. Informal evaluation procedures also provide guidelines which help the teachers decide which materials seem best suited to the children's instructional needs.

The purpose for a reading evaluation may dictate some features of the testing. For example, only a group administered test would be a reasonable way to conduct a state testing program. Individual testing is appropriate for reaching a decision about the correct placement of an individual or a few children.

When clear purposes for testing exist, evaluation can be efficient and very useful. Wasted time and effort in evaluation occur when the reasons for the testing are vague or nonexistent.

COORDINATING TEACHING AND TESTING

Situations continue to exist where tests are chosen or constructed without reference to the goals and form of the instructional program. Likewise, tests continue to be administered, but the results of the tests are seldom, if ever, used to plan instruction. Both situations are wasteful and under most circumstances are intolerable, especially for the children involved.

The phrase, "test, teach, test" is one that appears often in educational literature. It makes good sense, because it would be inappropriate to spend time teaching something that students already know. In fact, pretesting to determine whether particular skills are in existence is used all too infrequently. Nevertheless, the phrase "test, teach, test" may inappropriately imply the primacy of testing. There are instructional situations where the first concern seems to be the test. As a result, the nature and content of the test dictate the nature of and content for the reading instruction. Truly, that is a case of the tail wagging the dog. Some wise educator once said, "Give me the power of evaluation, and I will dictate the curriculum." The statement summarizes succinctly the power inherent in testing and is especially significant when interest in "accountability" is aroused, as it periodically is. Pressures for test performance sometimes become so great that teachers literally "teach the test" in order for students to do well. In such cases, these teachers feel compelled to deliberately ignore cognitive and curricular considerations, which professionals continuously insist are of greater importance than test performance.

The above paragraphs should not be interpreted as denying the need for specialized diagnostic procedures, whole school evaluation programs or diagnosis by professionals from related fields such as psychology or neurology. Each of these and other evaluation procedures are necessary. Nevertheless, classroom teachers must be certain to:

    1. Use instructional activities as a means of obtaining continuous diagnostic information. The concept of diagnostic teaching continues to be an extremely valuable one.

    2. Refer children to a qualified reading specialist when it appears that an independent opinion or in-depth evaluation is needed.

    3. Refer children to specialists from related fields, such as psychology, optometry or ophthalmology, speech, pediatric neurology,

otology, or medicine when necessary. Teachers need to become familiar with symptoms of disorders in these areas and recommend evaluation when there appear to be limitations that obstruct a child's progress in reading achievement.

4. Play an active role in planning or revising programs or procedures used in the evaluation of reading achievement.

ACCOUNTABILITY

Education in general and the field of reading instruction in particular seem to face periodic emphases. One issue that is revived with a fair amount of frequency is the notion of accountability. In an oversimplified way it suggests that educators must be held responsible or accountable for their professional activities: for example, for teaching children to read. Unfortunately, accountability often tends to exacerbate the undue emphasis that can be placed on testing, because it is often concluded that only through test results can it be determined whether or not a teacher or reading specialist is performing up to professional standards.

Needless to say this approach evokes resistance. Teachers complain about situations in which testing is inappropriate or unnecessary, but complaining is rarely productive. Teachers need to suggest alternatives or supplementary procedures in order to avoid the abuses of inappropriate testing. For example, teachers sometimes complain that standardized survey tests do not reflect progress of seriously disabled readers, and this is a very legitimate complaint. However, few teachers produce anecdotal records or the results of teacher constructed tests to challenge and contradict the survey test results. There is obviously the need for far greater positive activity on the part of teachers in this regard. The concept of accountability cannot be avoided or sidestepped. Teachers and reading specialists can and should be able to insure that the concept is approached realistically and professionally.

DIAGNOSTIC LABELS

The goal of all evaluation and diagnosis must be to arrive at plans for improving reading achievement. All too often this does not appear to be the case. Instead, the purpose of evaluation appears to be merely to identify and label. Admittedly, labeling is sometimes a necessary administrative procedure for providing seriously disabled readers with the special help they need. However, labeling is sometimes used unnecessarily, and there is some evidence to suggest that it can have a negative effect on the children involved.

Diagnostic Labels

There are a number of dangers inherent in this labeling process. First, there is the danger that it can become an excuse for poor progress. For example, how can a teacher be expected to help improve the reading proficiency of a child who has "dyslexia"? Dyslexia often implies a neurological problem which is not amenable to treatment. Surely a teacher is likely to feel he or she has little potential for fostering progress with such a child. Second, there is the danger that a child who has been labeled will begin to think of himself as having a problem. A possible consequence is a lack of self-confidence. In turn, a fear of failure develops and interferes with achievement and ability to profit from instruction. Rosenthal and Jacobson (10), have popularized a construct called "the self-fulfilling prophecy." They presented some evidence to suggest that children who are specifically identified as having positive academic potential are treated differently by teachers and that these children achieve higher test scores than those who are not labeled as potential successes. It does not seem impossible that children who are given negative labels and who are expected to do poorly will receive less positive attention from teachers, have less self-confidence, and consequently achieve poorly.

There are those who would argue that, until you label a disorder, you cannot treat it. This may very well be true in medicine, where the diagnostic label "pneumonia" is determined by recognition of specific symptoms and carries with it a fixed prescription for treatment, but the same does not hold true in the field of reading disabilities. For example, it is not uncommon to hear that a child's reading problem is "caused" by minimal brain dysfunction. How helpful is it for a teacher to learn about this cause? What meaning does the label minimal brain dysfunction have for treatment? Bateman (2) explores this question in a thoughtful, clear manner. She cites evidence which suggests that there is no agreement on the constellation of symptoms or the treatment procedure for that diagnostic label. She concludes:

> It is as if many believe that separate programs have been developed, tested, and found efficacious for children who are "brain damaged," "emotionally disturbed," "dyslexic," "mentally retarded," and so on. Were it true, *which it is not,* then it would indeed be helpful to educators to have such categorical information. . . . What educators need to know about a child—minimal brain damaged or otherwise—is where to begin instruction (what tasks he needs to be taught) and how his performance changes as a function of specific instructional procedures (continuous assessment). (2, pp. 665–666)

Reservations about labeling grow very serious when the educational implications of terms like minimal brain damage are explored. However, there may be situations where the use of labels has medical implications. For example, there may be some cases where a child's behavior is so disruptive that a trial regimen of medication may be indicated. Under these circumstances the results of the labeling may not be detrimental. Nonetheless, even when a label has medical implications, we are still faced with the task of helping the child learn to read; unfortunately, labels almost never help in formulating an educational plan. In fact, the position taken here is that in trying to determine the cause or etiology of a reading problem, any attempt that simply results in a label is likely to be more detrimental than helpful. It may serve to divert attention from the educational decisions and considerations upon which teachers and reading specialists must focus.

CAUSES OF READING PROBLEMS

One of the concepts that became widely used in the 1940s and that continues to receive general acknowledgment is the principle of multiple etiology or pluralistic causation. Quite simply, it means that frequently there are many causes—a constellation of factors—that account for a reading disability. For example, one possible sequence of events that could contribute to the creation of a reading problem is the following: A child in first grade confuses and reverses letters during reading instruction activities; he or she seems unable to remember words. Depending on whom you consult, these difficulties may be declared to be neurologically based; may be seen as caused by inadequate environmental stimulation; or may be viewed as a normal manifestation of perceptual development. Thus, neurological or sociological factors or human individual differences appear to be possible initial contributors to the onset of a reading problem. However, it is possible that as a result of inappropriate group instruction, the child in the sequence we are describing may be faced with reading demands that are far too difficult. This, of course, may perpetuate or exacerbate the reading problem. Thus, pedagogical causes enter into the sequence. As a next step, the child may become aware of the fact that all or nearly all the others in the class are reading. This creates embarrassment and feelings of insecurity and inferiority. Simultaneously, the child's parents may begin to demand achievement, and this too creates significant discomfort for her or him. These stressful conditions add psychological causes to the list of etiological factors that are creating the reading problem.

By the time a child who has been exposed to a sequence of events such as those described above reaches third grade, diagnostically untangling the causes becomes almost impossible. Furthermore, one must keep asking, "How will determining the cause or causes affect a treatment plan?" In the plausible sequence just described, individual differences, maturational factors, neurological development, sociological considerations, pedagogical considerations, and psychological factors may all have interacted to create a reading problem.

SPECIFIC TERMS

One of the most frequently used terms in the field of reading disability is *dyslexia*. Vernon (13), in a brief review of the concept, traces it back to the work of Morgan (8) and Hinshelwood (6). Hinshelwood referred to the condition as word blindness and he attributed it to a congenital defect in the cerebral cortex. The Research Group on Developmental Dyslexia of the World Federation on Neurology defines dyslexia as:

> a disorder manifested by difficulty in learning to read despite conventional instruction, adequate intelligence and socio-cultural opportunity. It is dependent upon functional cognitive disabilities which are frequently of constitutional origin. (4, p. 11)

The basic definition suffers because of rather vague terms such as "functional cognitive disabilities" and because of a lack of certainty, for example, "*frequently* of constitutional origin." Indeed, it is difficult, if not impossible, to locate a clear, agreed-upon definition of dyslexia. Vernon summed up the situation well when she wrote, "The nature and causes of dyslexia are still extremely obscure" (13, p. 127). In a paper prepared for the second meeting of the federal government's attack on dyslexia, Adams provides a glimpse of the divided opinions that exist with respect to the use of the term (1). He found 32 definitions. From his review of the definitions by psychological and medical dictionaries, neurologists, psychiatrists, psychologists, and educators, Adams concluded that, "Its [dyslexia's] meaning is obscure and it has divided the efforts of professional men when collaboration would have been the better course" (1, p. 616).

There appears to be little purpose for this text to repeat an overview of the concept of dyslexia from a neurological point of view, as Critchley has done (4); nor does it seem necessary to belabor the definitional problems raised by Adams. Instead, two conclusions seem in order:

1. The term dyslexia is used in a variety of ways. Teachers and reading specialists would be wise to question anyone who uses the term as to the meaning they are attaching to it.

2. In our clinical experience, there appear to be three primary approaches taken to defining the term. Some parents and professionals use dyslexia simply as a descriptive term that becomes synonymous with a reading problem. Anyone who has difficulty in reading, even minor difficulty, is termed dyslexic. The second use

of the term reserves it for long-standing cases of reading disability that have not responded to intensive treatment. This use of the term revolves around severity and longevity of the reading problem. The third use of the term reserves it for those cases where there is the suspicion of a neurological basis for the problem. In some cases the neurological basis for the problem is defined from minimal evidence. In such cases it sometimes appears that a neurological explanation is accepted because no other "causes" can be located.

Another term that appears in the literature about reading disability is *primary reading retardation.* The term is used by psychiatrist Ralph Rabinovitch (9). He defines primary reading retardation as follows:

> The capacity to learn to read is impaired without definite brain damage being suggested in the case history or upon neurological examination. The defect is in the ability to deal with letters and words as symbols, with resultant diminished ability to integrate the meaningfulness of written material. The problem appears to reflect a basic disturbed pattern of neurological organization. (9, p. 74)

This definition of primary reading retardation is very much like the definition of dyslexia that implies a neurological basis for the reading problem. It should be noted that most definitions of dyslexia and the above definition of primary reading retardation evoke a concept similar to minimal brain damage. With all three terms there seems to be some evidence that neurological disorganization is responsible for the reading disability, but that evidence is not clear-cut. The minimal nature of the evidence of a neurological problem is emphasized in Rabinovitch's work by the fact that he includes a second category called "brain injury with reading retardation." In this category "the capacity to learn to read is impaired by frank brain damage manifested by clear-cut neurological defects." To complete his classification system, Rabinovitch uses the category "secondary reading retardation" to describe cases where the capacity to learn to read is intact, but where achievement in reading is not appropriate for the child's level of intelligence. The causes of secondary reading retardation are *exogenous,* outside the individual. Anxiety, depression, psychosis, and limited schooling opportunities are cited as examples of exogenous factors. The cause of primary reading retardation is *endogenous,* within the individual. It appears that endogenous causes are essentially neurological ones.

A somewhat more recent term applied to many children with severe reading problems is the term *learning disability.* The following definition proposed by the National Advisory Committee on Handicapped Children is a widely accepted definition of a learning disability:

Children with special learning disabilities exhibit a disorder in one or more of the basic psychological processes involved in understanding or using spoken or written language. These may be manifested in disorders of listening, thinking, talking, reading, writing, spelling or arithmetic. They include conditions which have been referred to as perceptual handicaps, brain injury, minimal brain dysfunction, dyslexia, developmental aphasia, etc. They do not include learning problems which are due primarily to visual, hearing, or motor handicaps or mental retardation, emotional disturbance, or environmental disadvantage. (7, p. 2)

This definition is sweeping in scope, and could be applied to many varied disorders which range in severity. This definition also includes many unclear terms. For example, what are "the basic psychological processes involved in understanding or using spoken or written language"? A second problem is that the term learning disabilities appears to be used in at least two different ways. Some practitioners maintain that it is a behavioral term in that it is applied to children who manifest behaviors such as reading or arithmetic disabilities. However, other practitioners use learning disabilities as an etiological term, that is, as the explanation for the cause of the problem. In the second use of the term, learning disabilities is evoked as the explanation for a reading problem. A child is said to have a reading problem because he has a learning disability. The next rather obvious questions are: "How does the learning disability cause the reading disability?" "What causes the learning disability?" When these questions are asked, a neurological basis for learning disabilities is often suggested. The reference to terms such as brain injury, minimal brain dysfunction, and developmental aphasia by the National Committee on Handicapped Children certainly appears to suggest a neurological basis for learning disabilities.

There appears to be a substantial amount of confusion as to how the term learning disability should be defined and applied. Bryan (3) outlines some of these problems. For example, he cites evidence suggesting the use of the term in a very restricted sense to apply to no more than 1 percent of the population, while others would apply the term to almost 50 percent of a school population.

A provocative view of the concept of learning disabilities is presented in the book *The Myth of the Hyperactive Child* by Schrag and Divoky (12). They trace, in a chapter entitled "The Invention of a Disease," the concept of learning disabilities from its essential obscurity before 1965 to its national prominence less than ten years later. They outline what they feel to be the roles played by parent pressure groups such as the Association for Children with Learning Disabilities (ACLD), pharmaceutical houses, university self-interest groups, and the schools themselves. The authors definitely represent a point of view, one with

23

which not everyone would agree; however, it may be needed to counter-balance some of the unbridled application of the term "l.d." to widely varying populations.

The dangers that can stem from labeling a child are not circumvented by the term learning disability, especially when it is interpreted to reflect a neurological problem. As with dyslexia, it seems that the only safe course of action at this point is for educators to constantly ask for definition and clarification whenever the term is used.

Another term that is rather vaguely defined, indiscriminately used and frequently related to reading or learning problems is *hyperactivity*. Eisenberg, in an introduction to a text dealing with the topic of hyperactivity, sums up very well the widely differing opinions about this condition.

> There are those who argue that the condition is the result of brain malfunction, who regard it as widespread and who recommend a vigorous program of medical and educational management for its remediation. There are others who contend that it is a myth invented by those who medicalize behavioral deviance; these critics stress the consequences of "labeling" and dismiss the proposed treatment as an altogether inappropriate response to normal or even "creative" variability. (11, p. x)

Much of the controversy surrounding the term hyperactivity has been about the consequences of labeling and the potential dangers of long-term use of drugs such as ritalin and dexadrine. Safer and Allen (11) provide an excellent summary of some of the research on the use of drugs; they draw the conclusion that the use of stimulant drugs, like the two mentioned above, is the single most effective way to treat hyperactivity. Schrag and Divoky (12) provide some strong arguments against the widespread use of drugs; they cite some shocking and disturbing statistics and case histories which strongly suggest that drug treatment is being used for a set of symptoms that cannot be reliably diagnosed.

There are a host of other terms, most of which have widely varying meanings. There are clear indications that terms related to reading disability are being used uncritically and imprecisely. Though there is a strong temptation to propose yet a new set of labels in an attempt to be clear and definitive; this is impossible, given our present state of knowledge regarding the measurement and causes of reading disabilities. Proposing new terms would seem destructive to an already confused field. Because of the varied ways in which diagnostic terms are used, an attempt will be made in the next few paragraphs to describe, as basically as possible, the forms of reading difficulties that exist.

Three dimensions are usually included in attempts to categorize or label reading difficulties. These include: grade placement, capacity level, and reading achievement level.

In considering the dimensions for grade placement, capacity, and achievement, perhaps the most common tendency is to ignore the troublesome concept of capacity and to draw comparisons between where a child is in terms of his grade placement and his reading achievement. While this is usually seen by teachers and parents as being very important, professionals in the field of reading usually stress comparisons between achievement level in reading and capacity level.

Traditionally, children's capacity levels have been, for the most part, their mental age as determined by intelligence tests. As you will read in greater detail in Chapter 3, a number of questions have been raised as to whether IQ tests, even individually administered ones, measure "capacity." Some have charged that IQ and hence the ability to measure capacity, is a myth. Ebel (5) approaches the question most realistically by saying:

> If you define it [IQ] in simple operational terms as a derived score on a particular kind of test, then there is nothing mythical about it. But if you define it as a measure of some latent trait that determines how rapidly a person can learn and places a limit on how much the person can learn, its real existence becomes much more debatable. (5, p. 87)

There is little doubt that even well-accepted measures of intelligence, such as the Wechsler Scales and the Stanford-Binet Intelligence Scale, are highly influenced by factors such as cultural background, langauge differences, motivation to achieve, educational opportunity, and many other considerations. There would appear, then, to be no absolute measure of potential for learning. However, it certainly would seem that a child who scores well on an intelligence test has good potential for learning. Nevertheless, enough questions have been raised to suggest that we must be very careful in interpreting the results of a child who scores poorly on an intelligence test, to insure that environmental or emotional factors have not adversely affected results.

In manipulating the dimensions of grade placement, intelligence test results and reading achievement level, the most commonly described and labeled situations are:

1. The children who are reading below their grade placement and below the level expected on the basis of intelligence test results.

2. The children who are reading at or above grade placement, but below a level expected from intelligence test results. These are usually brighter than average students who are doing only average work.

3. The children who are reading below grade placement, but at or near the level expected on the basis of intelligence test results. This may represent children who are not capable of learning as rapidly as most children their age. It may be that reading achievement is progressing at a very acceptable rate and that the children

are slow learners. The possibility also exists that the results of the intelligence test are simply not valid for the children and thus yield an artificially low level of expectation. It may be that some factor such as motivation, an unusual background of experience, or a language difference that is affecting performance on the intelligence test; a skilled psychologist should be able to interpret the test results to avoid misjudgment.

4. Children for whom grade placement, level of achievement expected from an intelligence test, and reading level all coincide. This would be the "normal," "average" children who do "normal," "average" work. Such children are relatively hard to find.

5. Children who are reading above their grade placement and the level expected from intelligence test results. Sometimes the term overachiever is used to describe these children. This category clearly demonstrates the limitations in the precision of extant devices for measuring reading or the capacity for learning. Overachievers would be children who are performing better than they are capable of performing.

With three dimensions, there are many other possible combinations, such as the children who are reading at the expected level for their grade placement and above the level expected from intelligence test results. However, listing all these combinations seems unnecessary. The five listed above are the ones that receive the most attention.

Rather than trying to label each of these combinations with specific terms, it would seem more parsimonious to simply describe them as was done above. This approach has some of the same limitations as do the more traditional terms like reading disability or reading retardation when they are given specific meanings. Describing the situation reduces, but certainly does not eliminate, the problems of terminology or measurement that will be discussed throughout the chapters dealing with evaluation.

No attempt will be made to use the terms reading disability or reading problem in a highly specific way in this text, because there is far from universal agreement on their meaning. Nor will an attempt be made to distinguish reading disability from reading retardation. In addition to the disagreement among textbook writers as to how these terms should be used, the terms are also defined differently, depending on the locality in which they are being used. Perhaps the present state of knowledge and the many disagreements in the field of reading mandate that each locality arrive at its own definition of what constitutes a reading disability. For example, does a child of average intelligence, who is essentially a nonreader at the end of first grade, have a reading disability? Unfortunately, in most schools, the child would be thought of as having a reading disability. However, if we paid more than lip service to the concept of individual differences, we would not begin the process of labeling so readily. Certainly success in initial reading experiences depends on more than measured intelligence and number of years in school. It seems reasonable to expect that not all children will learn to read by the end of first grade, not even all children of average intelligence. In practice a reading disability appears to exist when the school decides that the child is below an acceptable level of reading performance. In some schools not reading above grade level—only at grade level—is considered a problem; in other schools being a year below grade level is perfectly acceptable, because it is the most common state of affairs.

Finally, the terms corrective and remedial appear with a high degree of frequency in the field of reading. They are applied both to readers and to reading programs. The important dimension appears to be severity of retardation. Some use the term remedial to describe a child who is 2 years or more "behind in reading." It is not always clear as to whether the 2-year disparity is between achievement and grade placement or achievement and the level expected from intelligence testing. Children with less severe problems are classified as being corrective. The fundamental problem with this approach is that there is no evidence to suggest that grade levels represent equal units of growth. For example, a child in third grade reading at first-grade level is probably far more disabled than a tenth grader reading at eighth-grade level.

A more pragmatic, though more subjective distinction is to define corrective reading programs as those that treat reading difficulties as part of a classroom teacher's responsibility. The problem is such that individualized or small group instruction conducted by the classroom teacher appears sufficient to help a child achieve in reading. Remedial reading programs would be those operated by reading specialists. Remedial reading instruction is highly individualized, and often the specialist works with only one or two children at a time. Very specialized techniques may be necessary in order for the child to progress in the acquisition of reading skills. At the time of this writing it appears quite possible that in many areas the functions of the remedial reading specialist are being assumed by learning disability specialists. The reason for the shift seems related to the available sources of funding. In some cases special funds can be used for learning disability classes but not for remedial reading classes. This has created some controversy and problems in "territorial imperative." From this author's point of view, the major consideration is not what the class or specialist is called but rather the adequacy of educational programming. The primary and most frequent significant "symptom" exhibited by learning disabled children is difficulty in reading. Therefore, learning disability specialists should have extensive professional preparation in the field of reading and thus should be capable of providing an excellent program of reading instruction.

Throughout the chapters that discuss psychological development and its relationship to reading development, the importance of children's coming to see themselves as worthy, capable individuals has been stressed. As indicated at the beginning of this chapter, it seems very likely that attaching labels to children—such as l.d., reading disability, or remedial reader—could erode the development of positive self-perceptions. There is the related question that needs to be explored more carefully relative to how labeling children affects teacher attitude and behavior toward them. The work of Rosenthal and Jacobsen (10), certainly suggested a mechanism by which teachers might have a negative influence as a consequence of labeling. They refer to a phenomenon which has become known as the "self-fulfilling prophecy." It suggests that the level of performance and achievement that a child reaches is affected by the level of attainment expected by the teacher or other significant people in his or her life. If a child is expected by others to perform poorly, they may treat him or her in ways which encourage poor performance; this treatment, combined with a growing negative self-concept, results in failure. While more evidence is needed, sufficient questions exist to suggest that labeling might have a deleterious effect and that it should be used most cautiously. Teachers and specialists need to be willing to forego the satisfaction of feeling very skilled and erudite because they are able to apply labels to a constellation of symptoms. The focus must be upon functional, continuous diagnostic procedures that have implications for fostering achievement in reading. All activities done in the name of diagnosis or evaluation must be judged by the value they have in guiding the effective teaching of reading.

CONCLUSIONS

Teachers and reading specialists need to develop a realistic, pragmatic approach to the evaluation or diagnosis of reading problems. Much remains to be learned about the nature and causes of reading difficulties. However, there is a strong tendency for some professionals to imply or claim being able to diagnose with precision and certainty the nature and source of a reading difficulty. Interestingly enough, such professionals often keep finding the same cause for all reading problems. Depending on their biases, they are likely to see minimal brain damage, psychological interferences, perceptual deficits, or even learning disabilities as the cause of reading problems. In truth, reading problems appear to stem from many interacting factors, and we are frequently very limited in being able to clearly define the source of a reading problem. It is difficult to deal with this uncertainty and some professionals succumb to the temptation to engage in overly simplistic, falsely precise explanations. Labeling the child is frequently the result.

While extensive diagnoses aimed at determining the nature and cause of a reading problem are sometimes necessary, much more economy of time could be accomplished by focusing more attention on the nature of the reading problem (What kind of difficulty is the child having?) and on the type of instruction being given. Providing children with the type of educational program they need is the goal that should immediately be sought. When a well-designed instructional plan is unsuccessful, a more comprehensive diagnostic evaluation may be needed.

It is easy for teachers and reading specialists to feel both confused and intimidated by the vast number of terms that are used in the field of reading. The confusion is understandable; the intimidation unnecessary. When confronted by someone who bandies about terms like, m.b.d., l.d., dyslexia, and h.a. (hyperactivity), the most reasonable response is to say: "I understand that terms like _____ vary in meaning depending on the person using them. Could you tell me what you mean by _____ ?" The tone of the question should be one of honest inquiry and not one of negative challenge or threat, though do not be surprised if the person to whom the question is addressed acts threatened. Do not be surprised either if the explanation offered is incomplete, feeble, or essentially incomprehensible. However, the question must be asked if we are ever to move toward greater professional maturity and away from simplistic explanations that border on being fiction.

BIBLIOGRAPHY

1. Adams, R. "Dyslexia: A Discussion of Its Definition." *Journal of Learning Disabilities,* 2 (December, 1969): 616–633.

2. Bateman, B. "Educational Implications of Minimal Brain Dysfunction." *The Reading Teacher,* 27 (April, 1974): 662–668.

3. Bryan, T. "Learning Disabilities: A New Stereotype." *Journal of Learning Disabilities,* 7 (May, 1974): 304–309.

4. Critchley, M. *The Dyslexic Child.* London: Heinemann, 1970.

5. Ebel, R. "Educational Tests: Valid? Biased? Useful?" *Phi Delta Kappa,* 57 (October, 1975): 83–88.

6. Hinshelwood, J. *Congenital Word Blindness.* London: H. K. Lewis, 1917.

7. Kirk, S., and W. Kirk. *Psycholinguistic Learning Disabilities.* Urbana, Ill.: University of Illinois Press, 1972.

8. Morgan, W. P. "A Case of Congenital Word Blindness." *British Medical Journal,* 2 (1896): 1378.

9. Rabinovitch, R. "Dyslexia: Psychiatric Considerations," in J. Money. ed., *Reading Disability: Progress and Research Needs in Dyslexia.* Baltimore: The Johns Hopkins University Press, 1962.

10. Rosenthal, R., and L. Jacobson. "Teacher Expectations for the Disadvantaged." *Scientific American,* 218 (April, 1968): 19–23.

11. Safer, D., and P. Allen. *Hyperactive Children: Diagnosis and Management.* Baltimore: University Park Press, 1976.

12. Schrag, P., and D. Divoky. *The Myth of the Hyperactive Child and Other Means of Child Control.* New York: Pantheon Books, 1975.

13. Vernon, M. D. *Reading and Its Difficulties: A Psychological Study.* Cambridge, England: The University Press, 1971.

CHAPTER 3

Evaluation and the Prevention of Reading Problems

One of the notions in reading that receives widespread acceptance is that it would be far more economical, both psychologically and financially, to prevent reading problems from developing than to focus upon remedying problems that have already developed. There is also some agreement that most reading disabilities are preventable. Though a small portion of such disabilities are caused by neurological or psychological factors that are not readily amenable to treatment, many problems appear to develop because of an inappropriate match between the capabilities of children and the instructional demands that are placed upon them. In the jargon of the field of reading it is said that the child does not possess the necessary *reading readiness*.

Actually the term reading readiness has a variety of meanings and definitions. Many educators confine its use to the beginning phases of reading instruction, while others see it as a general concept, viable at all levels. Though the latter position is certainly valid, the former position is probably a better reflection of the common use of the term.

It is true, in a general sense, that readiness must exist for reading any piece of material. Most obviously, one must have some mastery of the vocabulary and concepts involved in a particular area in order to be able to read in that area. For example, many of you reading this chapter probably lack the readiness to read materials in a technical field such as biochemistry. However, it might be possible to struggle through some reading materials in biochemistry, especially if someone were available to provide help and if there were very significant interest in that area. Motivation and interest are powerful factors that have great influence on readiness to read.

Though reading failures can obviously occur at any level where there is an inability of a reader to cope with reading demands, most serious, long-standing, pervasive reading problems seem to appear during the initial phases of reading instruction; during grades one through three. It is less common to hear of readers who are successful in the primary (K–3) grades, but who fail thereafter. When failure does occur after the primary grades, some teachers and specialists contend that the failure occurred at that point because the child was exposed to reading materials that are not highly controlled in terms of vocabulary and skills. However, it seems that the "success" that such a child experienced in the primary grades was a very hollow one and that the reading failure would have become evident if the student had been encouraged to read widely, beyond a limited set of artificial materials designed to introduce a narrow set of reading skills. The sudden appearance of a reading problem when a child is asked to deal with a wide variety of reading materials is an excellent illustration of failure to develop the necessary readiness for the functional reading demands that will face children. A reading problem did not suddenly emerge. It was building during the primary grades through restricted, artificial reading instruction.

READINESS BEYOND INITIAL READING INSTRUCTION

The most functional form for assessing readiness at levels beyond the introductory phases of reading instruction is through the concept of diagnostic teaching. Important diagnostic information is continuously obtainable as teachers interact with students.

When students are working with controlled materials, such as basals, the question of readiness for reading a selection is usually not a difficult one to answer, because only a minimum number of new reading demands are made. The question of readiness for reading becomes a more challenging one when students are assigned content materials or when they work in an individualized research reading activity.

Perhaps the easiest approach to assessing overall readiness for reading a particular selection or a book is to introduce the topic and ask students to tell what they already know about it. The social studies teacher who is assigning a selection dealing with the Articles of Confederation can learn a great deal simply by announcing the topic and asking the children to predict what the content of the selection will be. This excellent procedure is the first phase of the D-R-T-A sequence and the purpose-setting phase of an I.R.I. The alert teacher may sometimes find that the pupils show little familiarity with the topic. On the basis of this diagnostic information, the teacher may decide that it is necessary to develop some general background or concepts of the group before independent reading on the topic is assigned. This does not mean teaching them about the Articles of Confederation. It may mean developing important concepts about how governments operate or developing a greater sense of the chronology of the time.

In a similar fashion, the readiness of a student to complete an individual D-R-T-A activity can quickly and efficiently be assessed. Do they have the ability to establish clear purposes for individual reading? Are they sufficiently familiar with the library? Do they know how to use appropriate reference materials?

All the above questions can be reduced to the following: The teacher needs to assess the demands that a reading activity will require and then needs to ask students a few questions designed to assess the extent to which they possess the skills needed to meet the demands.

READINESS FOR INITIAL READING INSTRUCTION

All too often readiness and reading instruction are discussed as if they were well-defined, agreed-upon entities. We are not at a point where readiness can be clearly defined or delineated. We can not quantify readiness sufficiently to be certain that one child has enough of it, or that one child has more of it than another. The correlations between readiness tests and reading achievement at some later point rarely exceed 0.70 and more frequently the correlations are in the neighborhood of 0.50. This means that less than half of what makes for success or failure in reading can be accounted for or predicted by readiness measures. Combining one readiness test with another rarely leads to much better prediction or predictions that exceed correlations of 0.70. (See Chapter 5 for a discussion of the meaning of correlations.)

There are two major factors that make prediction difficult. First, it appears that some children can compensate for weaknesses in one area of functioning because of strengths in another. One way of looking at reading readiness is to begin by assuming that there are a number of areas involved in it, such as auditory discrimination, language development, visual discrimination, and emotional adjustment. It might also seem that each of these areas needs to reach a critical level before a child can experience success in learning to read. This position, when evaluated in light of actual observation, is not tenable. For example, it is not uncommon to find a child who shows weaknesses in auditory discrimination tasks, but who has a good vocabulary and good oral expression, and who learns to read. (It might be added that one might need to reevaluate the judgment about poor auditory discrimination in a child with rich language development. How did the language become so well-developed if the child has difficulty distinguishing among the sounds which compose the language?) There appears to be no precise way to determine whether or not a child will be able to compensate for apparent areas of weakness.

The second major problem in reading readiness research is that it frequently fails to address itself to the way in which reading is taught. Certainly the demands may vary from one method of reading instruction to another. It becomes imperative that teachers and reading specialists begin to shift from asking, "is the child ready to read?" to asking, "from what kind of reading or reading-related instruction is the child ready to profit?" Much of the research and speculation in the area of reading readiness has been guided by the first question. Perhaps greater understanding and progress would occur if attention were shifted to a question such as: What is the child ready to learn, and how will this foster achievement in reading?

INFORMAL EVALUATION OF READINESS FOR INITIAL READING INSTRUCTION

The primary suggestion with respect to informal evaluation is that nonstressful, nonstructured reading instruction be introduced and the child's ability to respond to reading materials be observed. An ideal approach is the use of language-experience activities. For a full discussion of language-experience activities, see Stauffer (18). The type of information that may be obtained during such activities is outlined below.

1. One of the initial activities used in a language-experience sequence involves language and concept development. Typically the teacher presents some stimulus to a group of children in order to provoke thought and encourage discussion. During this discussion period, there is an opportunity to evaluate the following:

    a. *Powers of Observation.* How well do the children analyze the stimulus presented?

    b. *Vocabulary Development.* How well do they describe the stimulus?

    c. *Concept Attainment.* Are they familiar with the way the

34

stimulus works? Can they relate it to other things in the same class or category?

  d. *Motivation.* Is there an eagerness to participate?
  e. *Attention.* Is there a focusing upon the task for most of the discussion period?

After the discussion period the children are encouraged to dictate sentences which the teacher writes.

2. During the dictation, there is an opportunity for further evaluation:

  a. *All the Factors Listed Above Can Be Reevaluated.* The focus shifts somewhat and now the child's interest in print and writing can be assessed.
  b. *Ability to Recall Information.* Does the child remember ideas and vocabulary introduced by the other children or teacher during the discussion of the stimulus?
  c. *Ability To Deal with Logical Order, Sequence, and Relevance.* Does the child suggest story ideas that are related to the topic? Are they in a reasonable order?

After the contributions of the children are recorded, there is an opportunity for children to read the dictated story.

3. During the reading of the story, the full range of the children's individual differences will become apparent; therefore, there is an opportunity to evaluate:

  a. *Actual Reading Ability.* Do some children show the ability to read many words? Are some able to read the entire story?
  b. *Auditory Discrimination.* If the teacher gives two words and asks if they are the same or different, can the children respond correctly? Can they tell whether the words begin or end the same? Can the children offer illustrations of words that begin like one of the words from the story or give words that rhyme?
  c. *Visual Perception and Letter Recognition.* Can the children identify letters in the story? Can they find the same letter in two different places? Do they know about capital and lower-case letter forms?

4. After the story has been read, it is useful to provide the children with sheets of paper and pencils. There is now an opportunity for evaluating:

  a. *Fine Motor Skills.* Ask the children to do an illustration for the group story. What is their pencil control like? Ask the children who appear to have good motor control to copy the title from the group charts. How well do they perform this task, which calls for good eye-and-hand coordination?

b. *Ability to Write*. Which children are able to put their names on their papers?

The possibilities for evaluation through this approach are endless. Every conceivable form of readiness can be evaluated. In addition, skills are evaluated through actual reading related activities, rather than artificially, through some pencil-and-paper test. In addition the activity provides children with the opportunity to learn. They learn about the connection between speech and reading. A healthy concept of what reading is is developed. All the skills that are evaluated are also being taught. Hours are not being devoted to activities that teach the child nothing. Frustration is also avoided, because all children are not asked to do the same things. Some children read the whole story; others find their name, while still others participate only in the language development activities that are part of the sequence. Finally, the technique has the advantage of being able to be repeated. Instead of a one-time activity that is influenced by the events of a particular day, this procedure allows teachers to check their conclusions as often as necessary. As this happens it also allows for an assessment of the rate at which children learn and their ability to retain information over longer periods of time.

The procedures outlined above have what some consider to be a serious disadvantage. They are reliant on teacher observation and judgment. They place responsibility exactly where it belongs, with the teacher. Teachers who do not have the skills to conduct such activities should acquire them. Many teachers who do have the skills are reluctant to assume the responsibility for evaluation, but as noted previously in this text, the responsibility for teaching is a far more ominous one. Teachers who refuse to take the responsibility for evaluation and diagnosis should also surrender the responsibility for teaching and make room for those who will exercise full responsibility. The overreliance on artificial standardized procedures must be curbed if teaching is to ever achieve the full professional status it deserves.

ADDITIONAL INFORMAL MEASURES

Occasionally teachers who do obtain excellent information about readiness as they teach also feel the need for some supplementary, quantifiable information. The procedures suggested below are recommended.

Letter Knowledge Test

Knowledge of letter names is consistently a good predictor of success in reading. A group test can be administered in this area simply by arranging rows of four letters. About 20 rows is sufficient. These are then duplicated, and each child is given a copy. Children are directed to look at one row at a time as the teacher says the name of one of the four letters. The children are then expected to circle or underline the letter named by the teacher. This procedure is repeated for each row of letters.

Care must be taken to insure that children can follow the directions for the task. It is probably best to work with groups of six or eight children to insure proper supervision.

If even greater detail is desired regarding letter knowledge, the teacher can make a simple test by typing capital and lower-case letters in random order on a sheet of paper. Children can be shown this and asked to identify the letters. By having a duplicate copy, the teacher can keep a record of not only how many but also which letters children know. When administered individually, the task can become more diagnostic.

Listening Comprehension Activities

The procedures for constructing, administering, and interpreting a listening comprehension inventory are identical to those discussed in the next chapter, where the evaluation of listening comprehension is discussed in the context of informal evaluation procedures. Selections can be chosen from picture books designed to be read to children. The child's ability to answer questions will serve as a good reflection of general receptive language development, attention, and to some extent interest in reading.

L.C Test

Other Activities

Almost all of the activities listed in the discussion of language-experience activities lend themselves to use on an individual basis. Obtaining an individually dictated story from children and assessing their ability to respond to instruction using the story can provide a wealth of information. Working with a story for more than one day also provides an opportunity to assess rate of learning and long-term memory.

FORMAL MEASURES OF READINESS FOR INITIAL READING

Group Measure of Intelligence

Group pencil-and-paper intelligence tests, such as the California Test of Mental Maturity or the Lorge-Thorndike Intelligence Test, are sometimes used by schools to predict later reading achievement of students. Although these tests do show a moderate correlation with later achievement, their use for this purpose is not recommended. In a survey of this topic, one of the authors (13) reviewed studies which led to the conclusion that group intelligence tests did either only as well as, or in some cases more poorly than, the results of reading readiness tests in predicting reading achievement. Because the results of intelligence tests are often misunderstood or misinterpreted as a measure of a child's potential for learning, and because they may adversely affect a teacher's expectations for a student, the use of group intelligence measures to predict later achievement in reading is not recommended.

Individual Intelligence Tests

The article cited earlier (13) also reviewed the correlations between the Peabody Picture Vocabulary Test, the Stanford-Binet Intelligence Scales, and the Wechsler Preschool and Primary Scale of Intelligence. No study suggested a correlation of more than 0.60 between any of these instruments and later achievements.

Again, if the purpose is simply to predict which children will encounter difficulty in reading, there is little justification for administering an individual intelligence test. However, in the hands of a skilled psychologist the results of the intelligence test might serve as the basis for useful recommendations. The extent to which the results of individually administered intelligence tests may contribute to a child's general readiness for reading, then, is highly dependent on the psychologist's understanding of the process of reading and the factors that contribute to success in reading. There appears to be very wide variability in such understanding among psychologists.

READING READINESS TESTS

Tests which are specifically designed to measure readiness for beginning reading instruction are very popular. They are typically group administered and yield both an overall score and subtest scores. Frequently, subtests are included which measure visual perception, motor control, knowledge of the alphabet, and vocabulary development. The Gates-MacGinitie Readiness Skills Test, the Harrison-Stroud Reading Readiness Profiles, the Lee-Clark Reading Readiness Test, the Metropolitan Readiness Test, and the Murphy-Durrell Reading Readiness Analysis are among the most widely used measures for readiness for reading. Farr and Anastasiow (7) provide an overview and evaluation of some editions of all these measures.

Rather than discussing reading readiness tests in general, it might be profitable to look at one test in some detail to develop a clearer understanding of what readiness tests are like. The Metropolitan Reading Readiness Test was chosen because of its widespread use and because of its immediate availability. The 1964 edition is also fairly representative of what readiness tests are like. The test was revised in 1976 and became somewhat more complex. The 1964 edition had two parallel forms, A and B. It consisted of the following six subtests, which are very representative of the types of items used in readiness measures.

1. *Word Meaning.* Children look at a row of three pictures. The examiner (E) says a word that is the verbal label for one of the pictures. The child makes an X on the picture that is a representation of the word spoken by the examiner.

2. *Listening.* As the child looks at a row of three pictures, the E reads a few sentences that refer to several events that are depicted in one of the pictures. The child marks an X on the picture that best depicts the description offered by the E.

3. *Matching.* On the left side of the page is a visual design or a word; to the right of it are four designs or words which are similar in visual configuration to the one at the left. The task is to choose from the four last designs, the one that is like the one on the left side of the page. Of the 14 items in this subtest, 8 call for matching words.

4. *Alphabet.* The child looks at a row of four letters. The E says the name of one of the four. The child makes an X on the visual one that matches the one spoken by the E.

5. *Numbers.* The child, in response to statements read by the E, chooses answers which require a variety of math and math-related concepts, including counting ability and knowledge of numeral names, addition, subtraction, and monetary terms (e.g., dime, quarter).

6. *Copying.* At the top of a box are letters, numbers, or complex visual designs. The child is to copy the form in the remaining space of the box.

The Metropolitan also had a supplementary subtest called "Draw A Man." Figure drawings have been viewed as general measures of maturity since the work of Florence Goodenough in the 1930s. The child taking the Metropolitan was given 10 minutes to complete the drawing. The product was rated for number of details, proportion of the drawing, and the integration of parts.

Raw scores for the Metropolitan were converted to percentile ranks, stanine scores, or letter ratings. Letter ratings ranged from a high of A to a low of E. The accompanying descriptive categories are: superior, high normal, average, low normal, and low. There are also tables for converting each subtest raw score to a letter rating or quartile rank.

General scores on readiness tests or letter ratings could be used as guides for selecting children who might need special help and instruction in order to succeed in learning to read. In addition, teachers show a substantial amount of interest in using the subtest scores of reading readiness tests in order to diagnostically determine areas of relative strength and weakness. The manual for the Metropolitan Readiness Test implied that this can be done when they list as a suggestion for using the test results: "to identify specific areas in which a child (or group) appears to have attained a level of maturity or skill adequate for coping with first grade work" (p. 13). However, on the preceding page the manual pointed out:

> Ordinarily, the total score provides an adequate basis for classification and grouping of pupils, particularly with respect to the formation of instructional groups in reading. Efforts to attach significance to the subtest scores of individual pupils is not encouraged; the subtests are short and so the reliabilities of their scores are naturally lower than that of the total score.

Unfortunately far too many first-grade teachers who receive the results of readiness tests never read the manual and learn of some of the limitations or cautions. This is not to say that subtest scores must be ignored. They, like subtests from the WISC-R, can be looked at for possible implications with the constant recognition that the rating offered by the subtest may be inaccurate. The subtest score can serve as the means for setting forth a diagnostic hypothesis that can be checked through teacher observations.

The 1976 revision of the Metropolitan Readiness Test introduced a more complex form of a readiness test. To begin with, the test was divided into two levels. Level I is designed primarily for use in the beginning and middle of kindergarten. It is recommended for the end of kindergarten for children who would find Level II too difficult. Level II is generally recommended for end of kindergarten and beginning of first-grade level testing. There are two parallel alternate forms of both Levels I and II.

The types of subtests in Level I are quite similar to the 1964 edition of the Metropolitan Readiness Test. The only changes are that the word meaning and listening subtests are collapsed into one and a new subtest, rhyming, is added. The content of some of the subtests has been altered. In the new edition, scores from the letter recognition and visual matching subtests are summed to yield a "visual" skill score, and those from the school language and listening subtest and the quantitative language subtest are summed to yield a language-skill area score. The manual very appropriately recommends cautious diagnostic interpretation of the tests, primarily recommending focusing upon interpretation of the two skill area scores and total composite score. Even in the area score interpretations, the manual notes that differences of less than three stanines between the area scores are not significant.

Level II of the test includes a visual matching and a listening subtest, and a copying task. These three are somewhat similar to the Level I measure. Level II contains two quantitative subtests, quantitative concepts and quantitative operations, both of which are optional subtests. New subtests include:

1. *Beginning Consonants.* The child is shown a row of pictures. The teacher says a word, and the child must mark the picture whose name begins with the same sound as the spoken word.

2. *Sound Letter Correspondence.* The child looks at four letters or letter combinations (some words begin with blends) while the teacher says a word. The child must choose the letter or letter combination that represent the beginning of the spoken word.

3. *Finding patterns.* The child looks at a group of letters or letter-like symbols that appear to the left of the page, and must find these same forms within groups of letters or letter-like symbols that appear to the right. For example:

ite | light   biton   siten   rutes

Level II yields four skill area scores: auditory, visual, language, and quantitative (optional).

The letter-rating scores used in the 1964 edition are not used in the latest Metropolitan revision. This edition yields percentile ranks, stanine scores, and performance ratings. The possible performance ratings are low (stanines 1–3), average (stanines 4–6), and high (stanines 7–9).

It seemed useful to describe the two editions of the Metropolitan Readiness Test, because the 1964 seems more representative of the available readiness measures, and because the newest edition may represent a trend for the future. The de-emphasis on subtest scores, widespread cautions about interpreting differences between scores, and clear emphasis on taking the standard error of measurement of scores into consideration represent, in this author's opinion, positive trends. The manuals of the test also encourage teachers to use practice booklets that have been constructed by the publisher of the Metropolitan, in an effort to try to reduce the effect of test-taking skills or the lack of these skills. This too is seen as a positive step. The major reservation with respect to the new tests is that the content of Level II "looks" very challenging for use with end of kindergarten children; in some cases the tasks called for seem more like phonic mastery achievement tests rather than readiness measures. It would be unfortunate if kindergarten teachers begin to feel that they had to bring phonics programs into the kindergarten curriculum.

PREDICTIVE POWER OF READINESS TESTS

The Metropolitan Readiness Test and most readiness tests yield fairly good predictions of later achievement. In our own work at the University of Delaware, the Metropolitan (1964 edition) had a correlation of 0.61 with first-grade reading achievement scores. Similar correlations are reported in the manual for the Metropolitan (14).

It is interesting to observe that in one longitudinal study done at the University of Delaware (15), there was a correlation of 0.65 between the Murphy-Durrell Reading Readiness administered in kindergarten and the reading subtest of the Metropolitan Achievement Test administered in sixth grade. In general, many of the correlations between reading readiness tests and later reading achievement are in the range of 0.50 to 0.70. This is certainly far from perfect predictive power (it suggests that rarely are we able to predict more than 50 percent of the variance in reading achievement), but it is certainly interesting to see how stable these predictions can be.

Carefully used and cautiously interpreted, readiness measures can provide some useful information.

TEST BATTERIES

There are at least two very well known series of tests which aim to give an overall indication of readiness for school learning.

The Gesell Institute Behavior Tests

The Gesell Institute constitutes a very important influence in the fields of child psychology, early childhood education, and reading. Psychologists and others who involve themselves with this institute place a great deal of emphasis on the maturational or developmental level of a child. They maintain that much of the failure that occurs in schools is the result of overplacement, that is, asking children to engage in activities for which they are maturationally not ready.

The approach of the Gesell Institute would appear to be to identify the characteristics of particular age periods. "We would like the reader to begin to feel that each age has its own essence, that there is such an entity as five-year-oldness, seven-year-oldness, ten-year-oldness" (9,

p. 253). The work of the institute has produced extensive normative information of what average children do at each age level. The most important point is that a developmental examination is needed in order to determine a child's developmental age. A child who is seven years old chronologically may be only five years old developmentally. If this is the case, she or he supposedly will profit most from activities appropriate at five-year oldness.

The developmental examination is described rather fully in the book *School Readiness*. It consists of:

1. *A Child Interview*. Children are asked questions about such things as their age, birth date, number of siblings, and fathers' occupation. Particular kinds of responses are expected at various age levels.

2. *Pencil-and-Paper Tests*. Children are asked to write things such as their name, address, and numbers. Throughout the entire battery of tests the examiner must be a keen observer of how the children respond. Questions they ask, body posture, rate of response, and many other factors are considered in the final decision about the children's level of development.

3. *Form Copying*. The children are asked to copy six rather simple geometric forms, one at a time. The quality of the reproductions and the method of drawing along with observations are important. For example, in terms of method of drawing a circle, beginning at the bottom and proceeding clockwise ($\circlearrowright$) is considered less mature than starting at the top and moving counterclockwise. ($\circlearrowleft$)

4. *Incomplete Man*. For this part of the battery children draw a person or complete the drawing of a person. The exercise is a very popular way of assessing developmental maturity and appears in both intelligence and readiness tests (Stanford-Binet Intelligence Test, Metropolitan Reading Readiness Test, Goodenough-Harris Draw A Person Test). The number of parts correctly completed along with the method of completing the task are felt to be reflections of the children's developmental level.

5. *Tests of Right and Left*. Children are shown pictures of the two hands from the same person. One finger from the right hand touches another finger from the left hand. For some pictures children are asked to describe what is happening (e.g., the left index finger is touching the right little finger). For a second set of pictures they are to put their own hands in the position shown in the picture (e.g., they touch their left index finger with their right ring finger).

6. *Monroe Visual Tests*. There are two parts to this test. In

Visual 1, children are shown a form (e.g., D) and then choose the matching form from two on their answer sheets (e.g., D ◁). The task is a visual perception task that requires matching. The second task presents a series of four figures. Children are shown them for 10 seconds and then asked to make a copy of them from memory. In addition to the perceptual demands, this requires short-term memory.

7. *Naming Animals*. Children are simply asked to name as many animals as they can from memory. They are allowed 60 seconds for the task.

8. *Home and School Preferences*. Children are asked what they like to do best (a) indoors at school, (b) outdoors at school, (c) indoors at home, and (d) outdoors at home. A wide variety of answers are expected in response to these questions. From these responses evaluations of the children's interests are made.

The eight items listed above constitute the developmental battery of tests. Reading tests, vision tests, and psychological projective tests are valuable adjuncts to the battery, as is looking at the rate and pattern of the development of teeth. Though pattern of teeth development may seem like an unusual reflection of readiness for reading, proponents of this approach maintain that such development is a reflection of general rate of maturation. The book *School Readiness* should be consulted for a discussion of these variables.

The major difficulty with the Gesell battery is that it requires substantial training on the part of a developmental examiner. Few teachers or reading specialists are equipped to conduct the suggested evaluations. Though the work of Arnold Gesell dates back to 1911, there is still the need for refining and empirically investigating the theories and test procedures promoted by the Gesell Institute. The broad base of normative information that already exists provides an excellent foundation for further study.

The Jansky-DeHirsch Battery

The work of Katrina DeHirsch and Janette Jansky is summarized in two books: *Predicting Reading Failure* (4), and *Preventing Reading Failure* (10). The former work represents a preliminary study and, therefore, will not be discussed. It does contain some excellent summaries of the relationship between success or failure in reading and a variety of factors.

The purpose of the later study, published in 1972, was to develop two separate test batteries. One, a screening battery, can be administered to a large number of children. Its purpose is to "identify as many as possible of those children who are going to fail in the elementary grades." The purpose of the second, a diagnostic battery, is to "develop profiles of individual children's weaknesses and strengths, thus pointing the way to timely and highly specific intervention."

A wide variety of tests were administered to a group of over 500 kindergarten children. At the end of second grade about 400 of them were available, and their reading and spelling achievement was measured. The most predictive tests for reading achievement were a letter naming task, a picture vocabulary test (like the Peabody Picture Vocabulary Test), a word matching task (from the Gates Reading Readiness Test), the Bender-Gestalt Test, and a sentence memory test (from the Stanford-Binet Scales). These five tests were chosen as the screening battery. The correlation between these combined measures and later reading achievement was 0.66. The screening battery was able to identify slightly more than three out of four of the children who were not successful in reading at the end of second grade. It also identified as likely failures another 22 percent of the population, but this 22 percent did not fail.

The analysis of their results suggested that there were five areas that should be evaluated in a diagnostic battery. The five areas included: two types of oral language skills, pattern matching, pattern memory, and visual-motor organization.

The Jansky-DeHirsch approach has much merit in it. The distinction between screening and diagnosis appears a useful one. They have not overstated the potential of their approach and have not appeared to try to prematurely capitalize on its potential commercial value. It also appropriately places some decision-making responsibilities with local schools or school districts. For example, local educational agencies must define what constitutes failure in reading in their schools in order to use the battery.

The study needs to be replicated before the procedures are adopted. In an as-yet-unpublished study using 52 kindergarten children done at the University of Delaware, the correlation between the DeHirsch Screening Battery and first-grade reading achievement was a disappointing 0.41. Much more work needs to be done also in more clearly relating the results of the diagnostic battery to intervention strategies that would capitalize on the diagnostic profile derived from the history.

RELATIONSHIP OF SINGLE FACTORS TO READING ACHIEVEMENT

Several areas are typically discussed as part of reading readiness. This text has given greater attention to the test batteries, rather than evaluation of single areas, such as visual discrimination and auditory discrimination. Because reading readiness seems multifaceted, a test battery appears to hold greatest promise for progress. Many of the factors listed below have already been discussed in their relationship to reading disability; therefore, discussions will be kept brief.

Chronological Age

Age does not appear to be significantly related to reading. In the above-mentioned study conducted at the University of Delaware (14), the correlation between age in months and scores on a first-grade reading test was −0.04. In the Jansky-DeHirsch study, it was only 0.14.

Visual Discrimination

The problems involved in evaluating this area have already been discussed. Barrett (1) offers a comprehensive review of studies dealing with the relationship of prereading visual discrimination and first-grade reading achievement. His review suggested that tasks requiring visual discrimination of letters or words are better predictors of later achievement than those calling for discrimination of pictures or geometric designs. It is also a generally accepted conclusion that letters and words are also the best vehicles for training visual perception. It appears quite likely that training done with pictures and shapes does not have a positive effect on reading achievement.

Auditory Discrimination

The relationship between auditory discrimination and reading is often taken for granted; however, the utility of auditory discrimination tests for predicting later reading achievement is relatively weak. Dykstra (6) found that in most studies the correlations between measures of auditory discrimination and later reading achievement were between 0.20 and 0.40. Dykstra's study also suggested that it is not safe to assume that the various auditory discrimination tests that are available are measures of the same skills. In his study, he found a correlation of only 0.30 between the auditory discrimination test of the Harrison-Stroud Reading Readiness Profiles and the Murphy-Durrell Diagnostic Readiness Test.

These cautions should be kept in mind when considering the implications of auditory discrimination tests for later reading achievement.

Neurological Factors

The neurological status of the child is often evoked as an explanation for the failure to profit from reading instruction. Bender (2) has suggested the term *maturational lag* to describe a condition in which "functional areas" of the brain develop at an uneven pace. These areas of the brain serve such complex functions as speaking, reading, and developing preference of one hand over the other. Actually, much remains unknown about the mechanism for neurological development, and therefore Bender's formulations remain quite speculative. Like the concept of minimal brain damage there is no clear-cut, well-defined evidence that development of "functional areas" of the brain or some other neurological mechanism is responsible for the behaviors associated with difficulty in learning to read. When applied to young children, Bender's concept of maturational lag does seem preferable to the concept of minimal brain dysfunction. The term *lag* does suggest that development will or at least can take place. It seems more optimistic than deciding that there is a dysfunction.

Lateral dominance is another concept that is closely associated with neurological functioning and reading. Lateral dominance refers to the establishment of one side of the body as the most frequently used side. For example, a person may show a preference for using his right eye, right hand, and right foot. One position (5) is that unless one side of the body is consistently dominant over the other, difficulties in reading and other cognitive and perceptual functions are likely to occur. If an individual is right-eyed, right-handed, and left-footed, he is not completely one-sided. This condition is labeled *crossed dominance*. However, research such as that done by Robbins (16) suggests that the existence of crossed dominance does not result in reading disability.

Another aspect of dominance involves the preferred use of one side of the body over the other. For example, most of us think of ourselves as left-handed or right-handed. Left-handed people prefer to use the left hand for tasks requiring strength or precision. There is some evidence to suggest that children who develop a preference for one hand over the other more slowly than expected, do appear more likely to encounter difficulty in learning to read (3). It seems quite possible that a child who takes longer to consistently use his right or left hand as the preferred one is developing at a slower rate neurologically. If this is the case, then the neurological development rather than the dominance of one hand over the other is responsible for the delayed development.

LANGUAGE DEVELOPMENT

The close relationship between language and reading achievement is usually readily acknowledged. It seems axiomatic that reading comprehension is directly dependent on knowledge of the meaning of words and the ability to understand sentence structure. Jansky and DeHirsch (10), and M. Stauffer (17) provide thorough summaries of the relationships of both oral language development and listening ability to reading achievement. However, further empirical evidence is needed to show the long-term benefits that might be derived from development of language in young children. Some of the studies have suggested rather minimal relationships between some aspects of language development and initial success in learning to read. It may be that factors such as memory, perceptual development, attention, and motivation play a highly important role in success in beginning reading and, because of this, the direct importance of language skills is less. It would, however, seem most unfortunate for teachers to place diminished emphasis on language development in kindergarten and the primary grades. Eventually whether or not a child can read with understanding is going to depend very directly on language and conceptual development. At the earliest levels of reading instruction, children's language skills are far more advanced than their abilities in word recognition. This will not be so beyond the primary grades. It is the eventual achievement in reading that must be kept in mind when considering reading readiness or beginning reading activities.

TEACHER JUDGMENT

So much of the literature has focused upon testing approaches to determine readiness for reading that the judgment of kindergarten teachers is often overlooked. In fact, it is not uncommon to hear kindergarten teachers complain because educational decisions for a child's first-grade program were made on the basis of a reading readiness test score or a score on an IQ test, rather than on the basis of their judgments. Certainly kindergarten teachers are in an excellent position to judge the developmental level of a child. There is also evidence to suggest that kindergarten teachers are accurate in their judgments (8, 11, 12). Additional procedures need to be developed for refining the ability of kindergarten teachers to predict success or failure in reading. However, sufficient evidence suggests that it is rather irresponsible to make plans for a child's first grade without giving heavy weight to the observations that a teacher has been able to make over the course of a year.

Some teachers are uncomfortable in making global judgments about readiness for reading and likewise have difficulty in communicating the results of their judgments to teachers who will be responsible for working with the children in subsequent years. For these reasons, the author and the reading staff of the Alexis I. duPont School District in Delaware devised a checklist for use by kindergarten children. This checklist (Figure 3.1) is completed by kindergarten teachers near the end of the year. In one study (14), it showed a good correlation (0.68) with first-grade reading achievement. In addition, teachers felt that the ratings in the various areas could be diagnostically helpful for program planning.

Teacher Judgment

Scale

Student's Name _____

Teacher's Name _____

Scale columns (left to right): Very significantly below average (1), Slightly weak (2), Adequate (Average) (3), Slightly above average (4), Outstanding (5)

Scale	Section	Item
1 2 3 4 5	I.	**Background of Experiences and Concept Development**
1 2 3 4 5		1. Familiarity with common experiences and ideas. Places (grocery, post office, travel experiences). People (policemen, truck drivers, farmers). Basic concepts (above, below, different, same, larger, in-between, twice).
1 2 3 4 5		2. Familiarity with children's stories, nursery rhymes.
1 2 3 4 5		3. Familiarity with numerical, social, scientific, political, etc., concepts (more, less, 10, a hundred, friends, family, how things work, weather concepts, president, elect.).
1 2 3 4 5	II.	**Listening Skills**
1 2 3 4 5		4. Ability to understand directions when given initially (get out the scissors, etc.)
1 2 3 4 5		5. Can repeat simple sentences or directions (understanding & memory).
1 2 3 4 5		6. Can repeat stories so as to reflect main ideas and important sequence.
1 2 3 4 5		7. Memorizes songs, poems, stories (either from home or school).
1 2 3 4 5	III.	**Oral Language Skills**
1 2 3 4 5		8. Vocabulary (number of different words he uses).
1 2 3 4 5		9. Maturity of sentence structure (complete sentences, sentence complexity).
1 2 3 4 5		10. Language facility (ability to use words freely, readily expresses self) and clarity of speech (does not distort speech sounds, absence of baby talk).
1 2 3 4 5		11. Ability to express needs, ideas, etc. (ability to combine the skills listed above).
1 2 3 4 5	IV.	**Thinking Skills**
1 2 3 4 5		12. Ability to predict outcomes (eg. on basis of title has idea of story contents, can finish a story once it's begun).
1 2 3 4 5		13. Approaches problems in systematic fashion (goes beyond trial and error).
1 2 3 4 5		14. Relates new ideas to past experiences and generalizes from one situation to another.
1 2 3 4 5		15. Sees sequence (eg. in series of pictures).
1 2 3 4 5	V.	**Interest in Reading**
1 2 3 4 5		16. Shows interest in being read to.
1 2 3 4 5		17. Enjoys looking at books.
1 2 3 4 5		18. Eager to learn to read.
1 2 3 4 5		19. Asks what letters and words mean.
1 2 3 4 5	VI.	**Social-Emotional Adjustment**
1 2 3 4 5		20. Relationship with other children (plays with others, is accpeted by co-workers as part of group).
1 2 3 4 5		21. Reactions to adult figures (can accept direction, respond to assigned tasks and is not overly dependent).
1 2 3 4 5		22. Ability to work independently and persist in a task, and take initiative.
1 2 3 4 5		23. Impulse control.
1 2 3 4 5		24. Positive self-image.
1 2 3 4 5		25. Ability to assume a leadership role.
1 2 3 4 5		26. Ability to set realistic goals.
1 2 3 4 5		27. Adequate home relationship (over protected, quarrelling with brothers & sisters).
1 2 3 4 5	VII.	**Auditory Discrimination Skills**
1 2 3 4 5		28. Can distinguish gross differences in sound (bell vs. cows moo).
1 2 3 4 5		29. Can identify and reproduce rhythm patterns (clapping hands).
1 2 3 4 5		30. Can distinguish between similar sounding words (tells if words are same or different, if rhyme or not, if begins same way or not).
1 2 3 4 5		31. Can give illustrations of particular sound elements (can give rhyming words, words that begin with same sound).
1 2 3 4 5	VIII.	**Visual Perception Skills**
1 2 3 4 5		32. Can see similarities and differences in pictures and simple geometric forms.
1 2 3 4 5		33. Can see similarities and differences in letters.
1 2 3 4 5		34. Can name individual letters.
1 2 3 4 5		35. Ability to recognize words.
1 2 3 4 5	IX.	**Fine Motor Skills**
1 2 3 4 5		36. Ability to grasp the pencil.
1 2 3 4 5		37. Consistently chooses to use the same hand.
1 2 3 4 5		38. Ability to copy letters.
1 2 3 4 5		39. Ability to write name.
1 2 3 4 5	X.	**Gross Motor Skill**
1 2 3 4 5		40. As displayed in playground activities and in walking, running, and skipping.
1 2 3 4 5	XI.	**Related Physical Factors**
1 2 3 4 5		41. Ability to use near and far point vision.
1 2 3 4 5		42. Ability to hear speech at a normal volume within a classroom situation.
1 2 3 4 5		43. General physical maturity (size, muscle development).
1 2 3 4 5		44. General health (overweight, underweight, pale, listless).
1 2 3 4 5		45. Attendance Record.

Overall rating of readiness for initial reading
1 2 3 4 5 6 7 8 9 10

FIGURE 3.1

The combination of teacher judgment and test data from a reading readiness test would probably serve as an excellent, efficient means of identifying first-grade children who need special help in learning to read. When teacher judgment and test scores are not in agreement for a particular child, it would seem best to rely on teacher judgment and then to engage in careful observation of the child as the opportunity to read is presented. It might also then be useful to employ some of the informal readiness procedures described in the first part of this chapter. It is also important to constantly recognize that young children sometimes show remarkable changes in behavior and skill development within a brief period of time. Therefore, there is, in all cases, the need for a teacher to constantly reassess a child's readiness to engage in some form of reading instruction.

CONCLUSIONS

The development of methods for the early identification of children who are likely to encounter problems in learning to read seems to be a very worthwhile activity. There is certainly much room for developing greater precision in the identification process, but there is also the danger that so much effort is put into identifying potential problems that the purpose of such procedures is forgotten. Wolfensberger summarized it well: "Early diagnosis is desirable when it leads to prevention, early treatment, or constructive counseling; it is irrelevant if it is purely academic and does not change the course of events; it is harmful if, in balance, child or family reaps more disadvantages than benefits" (19, p. 65). It is the unfortunate experience of this author to frequently find school personnel who are eager to embark upon a sophisticated-looking diagnostic, early identification program without having a program of effective intervention mobilized. Identification of potential reading failures without effective intervention leads only to labeling with all of its potential negative consequences.

The use of test batteries which employ a variety of tasks seems a more promising approach to evaluating readiness than does attempting to assess single areas such as visual or auditory perception. A combination of teacher judgment plus reading readiness test scores seems a very efficient way of screening for potential reading failures. Informal readiness evaluation procedures and teacher observation likewise seem an efficient way of collecting needed diagnostic data. Through the use of language-experience stories a teacher can evaluate all areas of functioning that are important for success in reading.

The greatest potential for preventing reading problems would seem to be in providing excellent programs of reading instruction which consider and adjust to the wide range of differences found among young children. In the process of initiating an excellent reading program, the alert, capable teacher has more than sufficient opportunity for diagnostic observations that can effectively guide that program.

BIBLIOGRAPHY

1. Barrett, T. "The Relationship Between Measures of Prereading Visual Discrimination and First Grade Reading Achievement: A Review of the Literature." *Reading Research Quarterly,* 1 (Fall, 1965): 51–76.

2. Bender, L. "Specific Reading Disability as a Maturational Lag." *Bulletin of the Orton Society,* 8 (May, 1957): 9–18.

3. Cohen, S., and G. Glass. "Lateral Dominance and Reading Ability." *The Reading Teacher,* 21 (January, 1968): 343–348.

4. DeHirsch, K., J. Jansky, and W. Lanford. *Predicting Reading Failure.* New York: Harper & Row, 1966.

5. Delacato, C. *The Diagnosis and Treatment of Speech and Reading Problems.* Springfield, Ill.: Thomas, 1963.

6. Dykstra, R. "Auditory Discrimination Abilities and Beginning Reading Achievement." *Reading Research Quarterly,* 1 (Spring, 1966): 5–34.

7. Farr, R., and N. Anastasiow. *Tests of Reading Readiness and Achievement.* Newark, Del.: International Reading Assoc., 1969.

8. Fesbach, S., and H. Adelman. "An Experimental Program of Personalized Classroom Instruction in Disadvantaged Area Schools." *Psychology in the Schools,* 8 (1971): 114–120.

9. Ilg, F., and L. Ames. *School Readiness.* New York: Harper & Row, 1964.

10. Jansky, J., and K. DeHirsch. *Preventing Reading Failure: Prediction, Diagnosis, Intervention.* New York: Harper & Row, 1972.

11. Keogh, B., and L. Becker. "Early Detection of Learning Problems: Questions, Cautions, and Guidelines." *Exceptional Children,* 39 (September, 1973): 5–11.

12. Keogh, G., and C. Smith. "Early Identification of Educationally High Potential and High Risk Children." *Journal of School Psychology,* 8 (1970): 285–290.

13. Pikulski, J. "Assessment of Pre-Reading Skills: A Review of Frequently Employed Measures." *Reading World,* 8 (March, 1974): 171–197.

14. Pikulski, J. "Predictive Power of Individual and Group Tests for First Grade Reading Achievement." Unpublished paper. Newark, Del.: University of Delaware, 1975.

15. Pikulski, J. "Predicting Sixth Grade Achievement by First Grade Scores." *The Reading Teacher,* 27 (December, 1973): 284–287.

16. Robbins, M. "Delacato Interpretation of Neurological Organization." *Reading Research Quarterly,* 1 (Spring, 1966): 57–78.

17. Stauffer, M. "Comparative Effects of a Language Arts Approach and Basal Reader Approach to First Grade Reading Achievement." Unpublished doctoral dissertation. Newark, Del.: University of Delaware, 1973.

18. Stauffer, R. *The Language-Experience Approach to the Teaching of Reading.* New York: Harper & Row, 1970.

19. Wolfensberger, W. "Diagnosis Diagnosed." *Journal of Mental Subnormality,* 11 (1965): 62–70.

CHAPTER 4

Approaches to Evaluating Reading [I]

The purpose of this and the following chapter will be to outline major approaches taken to evaluating reading. The purpose will not be to serve as a catalogue of tests which describes or evaluates existing reading tests; instead, the intended goal will be to describe general procedures and fundamental concepts that will have longstanding value. Individual tests come and go; general principles of evaluation can be applied to many tests and many testing situations.

DIAGNOSTIC TEACHING

Testing is simply a sampling of behavior under conditions of some degree of control. In testing we usually want to make generalizations about a fairly large area of behavior by sampling just part of that behavior. For example, in trying to determine if children have the ability to associate visual symbols for digraphs with the sounds these digraphs most frequently represent, we do not check to see if they can recognize all the words that contain digraphs. Typically, we check to see whether they can correctly represent a few letter-sound associations, and on the basis of our observations of their behavior, we generalize about their ability to correctly represent all or most digraphs.

The smaller the sampling of behavior, the greater the likelihood that conclusions or generalizations about a fuller range of behavior will be wrong. If we check only pupils' ability to read words containing the initial digraph "sh," we might be in error if we generalize to "ch" and "th." If we checked these digraphs only in initial positions in words, we might be in error to generalize to ability to correctly produce the correct response when these digraphs appeared at the end of syllables or words.

In general, the wider the sampling, the greater the probability that the conclusions we draw are true. If we wish to generalize about children's ability to read fourth-reader level material, the more samplings we make of their reading of fourth-reader level material, the safer the generalizations. Following the vocabulary used in testing, the greater the sampling of behavior by a test, the more reliable the test is likely to be. The reliability of a test, which is discussed later, is a reflection of the extent to which a test yields consistency of results. For the reasons just listed, the concept of *diagnostic teaching* holds high promise for accuracy in evaluation. Every time a teacher instructs students and observes their interaction with a piece of written material, there is the potential for the evaluation of reading. Teachers who instruct and observe children on a day-to-day basis obtain a very wide sampling of reading behavior. This should make the classroom teacher's daily instruction and resultant observation of reading performance the most reliable and hopefully the most accurate form of reading evaluation.

Despite the fact that teachers are probably in the best position for evaluating reading, often they are very reluctant to assume that responsibility. Many teachers are very unsure of their ability to teach, observe, and consequently evaluate reading. They are far more willing to trust the judgment of an "outside expert" (almost anyone but themselves) or to trust the results of a reading test. While both "outside experts" and reading tests are extremely valuable contributors to the diagnostic process, the results from both are usually based on very limited samplings of behavior. Both "expert" opinions and test results must be compared with the day-to-day classroom behavior of a reader.

Instruction and evaluation of reading are complex activities, and even the best-schooled specialist does not have all the answers as to how such evaluations should proceed. Even the specialist may be uncertain about the accuracy, meaning, and implications of some test results. It is to be expected that teachers need to be tolerant of some of these same uncertainties. However, given their repeated opportunities for observation, teachers are by far in the best position to draw conclusions about a child's reading skills. Not to do so is an abdication of their professional responsibilities. A teacher incapable of making diagnostic observations is certainly incapable of meeting the challenging demands of teaching.

Teachers, classroom and special, must also feel free to question the results of the so-called experts. They should never be intimidated by the results from precise-sounding, newly-invented tests. If test results, based on some unknown test, are given to a teacher, it is a primary obligation for that teacher to ask for explanations. What is the instrument? How it is administered? What evidence exists to indicate that it is a valid measure? A critical, informed, and inquiring mind is essential. Venezky (12) reported that there were over 150 published tests of reading. Certainly teachers and reading specialists cannot be expected to be familiar with all of them. Too often educators refrain from questioning test results because they fear their questioning will be interpreted as a reflection of ignorance.

No doubt, some teachers lack some of the necessary skills to evaluate reading. They must not accept this as their final state. They must obtain the skills that will allow for a fuller utilization of the diagnostic opportunities that both instruction and testing provide for them.

RECORD KEEPING

As indicated above, a teacher who is a keen observer of behavior is in an excellent position to evaluate reading, but in order to make full use of those observations, it is necessary for that teacher to keep accurate and fairly complete records. Such records will allow that teacher to professionally discuss and plan for a reader's needs.

The form that record keeping takes can be quite individual to each teacher. Some teachers prefer to organize the record keeping according to children. Each child's name appears on a separate notebook sheet and periodic notations are made regarding reading skill development. This plan is excellent for recording useful data for individual planning and for holding conferences regarding individual children.

Such records are less efficient for planning group activities. For the latter, some teachers prefer to organize records around specific skills. Skills to be mastered appear across the top of a sheet, and the names of individual children appear down the side of the sheet. As children master a skill, the teacher places a check mark in the appropriate skill column. At a glance, a teacher can use these records to organize group skill work or direct small groups of children to the same acquisition or reinforcement activity. The potential problems of this approach center around determining the criterion for mastery of a particular skill and deciding how detailed to become in listing skills.

No system works for all teachers. But it is important to begin with some organizational form, and then systematically vary it until it works. It should be kept simple. Too many teachers enthusiastically begin elaborate record-keeping systems only to become discouraged with the complexity of these systems and with the amount of time that record keeping requires. By aiming to do too much record keeping, they end up doing none. It is more appropriate to begin with a very simple scheme and to elaborate upon it as the need for additional information becomes apparent.

INFORMAL EVALUATION

The concept of informal evaluation has many of the positive characteristics of diagnostic teaching. In addition, it introduces some systematic procedures for more closely observing and recording a variety of reading behaviors.

Organized informal reading evaluation procedures began to develop in the early 1920s. Rather full discussions for preparing and administering informal word recognition tests and informal reading inventories appear in the work of Betts (3, 4). Beldin (2) concisely traces the development of informal diagnostic procedures. The following suggestions are adapted from the work of and the presentations made by Dr. Emmett Betts, Dr. Marjorie Johnson, Dr. Roy Kress, and Dr. Stanley Rosner (3, 4, 6).

Informal procedures were designed to give classroom teachers and reading clinicians needed diagnostic techniques that were practical to administer, that yielded information that could be used as the basis for planning a reading program, and that allowed for diagnosing specific skill needs of individual children. Informal evaluation continues to enjoy considerable popularity and might receive even more widespread use if it were better understood by classroom teachers.

The primary characteristic of informal diagnostic procedures is that they use testing materials that represent samplings from material that is used for teaching reading or that is being considered for instructional use. As indicated earlier, testing should be seen as a sampling of behavior, and informal procedures suggest that the best way to determine whether children will be able to profit from instruction with particular instructional materials is to ask them to read a small portion of those materials. While there are some guidelines as to how to choose that material and how to guide and evaluate readers' performances, informal procedures give the teacher considerable flexibility in conducting the diagnostic process, hence the term "informal." Informal evaluation procedures have a wide range of uses. Some of the most frequent uses include: grouping children for instruction, diagnosing specific skill needs, monitoring progress in reading, and establishing "functional" reading levels.

FUNCTIONAL READING LEVELS

No one does or can read all books in the same way or with the same degree of proficiency. Certainly this is true also of children who are receiving systematic reading instruction. As a guide we can think of a pupil learning to read as having three reading levels. The term *functional reading levels* refers to all three levels described below. A fourth level, a hearing comprehension level, is closely related to the other three.

Independent Reading Level

Materials that are at children's independent reading level can be read by them with ease. No teacher guidance is necessary. After reading the material, the children have essentially complete mastery of it. No significant word recognition problems are encountered during the reading, and full comprehension of the material occurs. When recommending books for free reading or when giving homework assignments, teachers should suggest and use materials that are at children's independent reading level.

Instructional Reading Level

It is assumed (but needs to be empirically verified) that children will make optimum progress in reading if they are somewhat challenged by the materials they are asked to read; however, the level of challenge must not be overwhelming. Materials that are at children's instructional level are supposed to provide an optimum level of challenge; that is, they are neither too easy nor too difficult. Reading materials provide challenges in terms of the concepts, vocabulary, and skills they require. Readers bring to a reading situation some capabilities in each of these three areas. When materials are appropriate for instruction, there is a definite gap between the capabilities of the reader and the conceptual, vocabulary, and skill demands of the reading material. However, that gap is not a large one, so that with the help of a teacher, the reader can master the demands of the material. Initially, children will encounter some difficulty with word recognition and/or comprehension; but when the materials are read with the guidance and pacing of a teacher, mastery is achieved at the conclusion of the reading. The final performance and degree of mastery of the material is similar to that achieved by the independent reader, but the methods for achieving those ends are different in that teacher guidance and pacing are needed.

Frustration Level

Materials that are at a child's frustration level are definitely too demanding. Even if the readers are guided by a teacher's help, they cannot meet the challenge of the materials. The vocabulary, concept, and skill demands that are made by materials are far too challenging for them. There is almost no potential for success or mastery. Materials at this level should definitely be avoided. Even when the help of a skilled teacher is available, there is little probability of success. Materials that are too challenging are frustrating to teachers, as well as pupils.

The meaning of the functional reading levels might be made clearer through a concrete illustration. The following interpretations could be made if a child's functional reading levels were established as: independent level at third-reader level, instructional level at fourth-reader level, and frustration level at sixth-reader level.

> 1. Pleasure reading and independent homework assignments should be made from materials that are written at approximately a third-reader readability level.
> 2. Classroom reading instruction, under the guidance of a teacher, should focus on fourth-reader readability level material.
> 3. Materials of sixth-reader readability and beyond should be avoided, because it seems unlikely that the guidance and help of a teacher will allow the student to succeed.

What about fifth-reader level materials? The best answer seems to be that under some circumstances children may be able to cope with demands at that level, but not routinely. For example, if the fifth-reader materials are in a field that is well known to the reader or if much teacher help and supervision is available, there may be some potential for success.

Classroom and clinical experience, however, suggests that teachers show a strong tendency to use material that is too challenging in its demands. Though empirical evidence is lacking, some authorities in reading contend that about 95 percent of the students in this country are being asked to work with material that is beyond their instructional level. It does not seem unlikely that students who are continuously required to deal with frustration-level materials will begin to develop very negative attitudes toward reading. Once such negative attitudes are developed, the potential for progress in reading may become very limited.

Hearing Comprehension Level

Though this is not a reading level per se, it is closely related to the three levels just described. Students' hearing comprehension levels are established through materials similar to those used in establishing the three other levels. Children's hearing comprehension levels are defined as the highest level at which they can adequately comprehend material that is read to them. The thinking skills employed when listening to someone who is reading are quite similar to the skills utilized when reading that material oneself. Reading, however, adds the additional requirement of being able to efficiently transfer visual symbols into language equivalents. Because of the close parallels between listening and reading, it is often diagnostically very informative to establish a hearing comprehension level.

The hearing comprehension level is also sometimes interpreted as being an estimate of the level of reading achievement at which students should be functioning. The assumption is that if children can adequately understand materials that are read to them, they have excellent potential to read and understand materials of similar difficulty. A comparison of a child's hearing comprehension level and instructional level, as established on an I.R.I., is often interpreted as an index of the extent to which the child is reading up to his or her capability. Thus, a child would be considered achieving well if his or her hearing comprehension and instructional levels were both at second-reader level. However, a child with a hearing comprehension level of fifth and an instructional level of second would be considered to be 3 years retarded in reading. The procedures for establishing a hearing comprehension level are outlined later in this chapter.

When cautiously interpreted, the hearing comprehension can give a good reflection of a child's language skills, thinking abilities, attention and concentration, interest in reading-related materials, and even motivation. Because these factors all contribute heavily to success or failure in reading, they can give important clues regarding likely progress or nonprogress in reading.

The Unit of Measurement

Although there are many ways to report the results of reading tests, most teachers appear to rely on a unit called the *grade score*. Informal evaluation makes widespread use of this unit of measurement. Previously, an example was given of children reading at fourth-grade level or being instructional at fourth-grade level. Sometimes this is spoken of as fourth-*reader* level. For the most part, the terms grade level and reader level are used interchangeably; both involve serious difficulties and limitations. While both give a general idea of readers' proficiency, both are lacking in precision. For example, authorities in the field of reading can specify neither the skills that must exist in order to label children as fourth-grade readers nor the level of complexity at which these skills must be developed for the fourth-reader-level designation. On one test, depending on the choice of materials and testing procedures, a child might be evaluated as a fourth-grade level reader while on another test, the same child might be categorized as a fifth-grade-level reader. Even wider variations are possible, depending on the nature and complexity of the materials, as well as the procedures used for testing.

The unit reader level is most often associated with basal readers. Students reading at fourth-reader level would be judged capable of profiting from instruction that used books designed for fourth grade. However, there are many basal reader series, and most are not uniform in difficulty. The vocabulary, concept, and comprehension and word recognition skill demands made by a fourth-level book of one series may be quite different from those made by another series. Even revised or new editions of a basal reader produced by the same publishing company may change dramatically in terms of the skill demands made at a specific level. Barnard and DeGracie (1) provide some empirical evidence on this point. They analyzed the rate of new vocabulary introduction used by eight popular basal reader series published during the 1970s. They concluded that there were significant differences between series, both in the rate of vocabulary introduction and in specific vocabulary introduced. In another comparison they provided some evidence that basals of the seventies are more difficult than basals of the sixties. "Students are expected to decode more words by the end of first reader than students of a decade ago" (p. 179).

It must be pointed out that, beyond sixth-grade level, the concept of reading grade level or reader level becomes particularly vague and of limited utility. Until sixth grade, graded series of materials, which are specifically designed for developmental reading instruction, do provide at least rough reference points against which other materials can be compared. Beyond sixth grade, however, the nature of the material or the content of the reading material will probably play a decisive influence on the reader's performance. For example, children who are very interested in science may have read significant amounts of material in this area and may have developed rich science vocabularies. This may permit them to deal successfully with science materials at an eighth-grade readability level; while limited interest, vocabulary, and concepts for most social studies topics may allow them to succeed only with sixth-grade level readability materials.

Yet another approach that might be taken to the concept of reader level or grade level is related to the concept of readability. This text has already used phrases such as "material that is at fourth-reader level of readibility." There are specific formulas and graphs that are used to calculate the readability of material (see pages 151–154). While this approach seems far more scientific, it too is limited. The estimate of the readability of materials will vary, depending on the formula employed and the section of the material chosen to be analyzed. In addition, readability formulas fail to consider such important factors as reader interest in the materials or the rate at which the author introduces new ideas into the material. Thus, while a readability approach seems precise on the surface, it too has very serious limitations.

Still, the concepts of reading grade level or reader level are not useless. They do provide general reference points, but one should not be deluded as to the precision of these units. If a child is diagnosed as reading at second-grade readability level, the classroom teacher may or may not find that the child can deal with the second-grade level materials that are available in that classroom. Again it appears that the classroom teacher is in the best position to make such a judgment, and that the results of any evaluation must be critically considered by the person responsible for a child's ongoing instructional program.

INFORMAL WORD RECOGNITION TESTS

Another form of informal evaluation is the informal word recognition test. This can be used with any book, series of books, or reading program that includes a listing of new words. If the purpose is to be as diagnostic as possible with regard to a child's word recognition skills, informal word recognition tests of increasing difficulty can be constructed by using a series of books in which the vocabulary increases in level of difficulty.

Constructing Informal Word Recognition Tests

SELECTING THE WORDS. If the instructional materials are specified as graded in difficulty, start with the lowest-level book. Consult the back part of the book for the section containing new words. If the designated difficulty of the book is preprimer or primer, 20 words should be selected. If it is designated as first-reader level or beyond, 25 words will represent a good sample. Choose the words as randomly as possible. For practical purposes, choose every *n*th word (*N*th is used because in some cases you might use every fourth word; in others, every eighth word, or every twentieth word. The designation *n* means any number can be placed before the "th.") To determine *n,* count the total number of words and divide this by 20 if you are working with a preprimer or primer book, and by 25 if it is a first reader or above. Round out to the whole number that is below the decimal. For example, if there were 70 words at preprimer, you would divide 70 by 20. You should then round out the answer, 3.75, coming up with 3. Thus, you would take every third word. If there were 345 words at third-reader level, you would divide 345 by 25. The answer, 13.8, should be rounded out to 13. Every thirteenth word would therefore be chosen.

If a complete, graded set of word recognition tests is desired, one can begin with the lowest-level book and construct tests for each book to the highest one that might be used in a program. For example, for a first-grade teacher, word recognition tests for the preprimer to fourth-reader level may be sufficient. For a reading specialist who sees children of different ages, it is more appropriate to have tests ranging from pre-primer through sixth. Most word recognition tests do not go beyond sixth-reader level, because it is felt that all basic word recognition skills are taught by sixth-reader level. Beyond sixth-reader level, readers' abilities to recognize words without outside help is not only dependent almost entirely on the extensiveness of their listening and speaking vocabularies, but also on the application of previously taught skills.

PREPARING TEST FORMS. For ease of administration, it is best to prepare a student's and an examiner's form. The student's copy is used for showing the child the words. The procedure for doing this is described in the next section. Only a few copies of the student's form should be produced, because it can be used over and over again. The examiner's forms should be produced in greater quantity, because a new copy of it is required for each student.

Students' copies at preprimer and primer levels are best prepared using a primer typewriter, if one is available. The words are numbered and presented in columns. The only other information on the student's copy is the name of the book. A student's copy is illustrated in Figure 4.1. It is a preprimer list of words and was prepared with a primer typewriter.

THE FORM OF THE TEST. Examiners' copies should be labeled as to book and level of difficulty; words should be in column form and numbered; to the right of each word two blanks should be provided; the headings for the two columns of blanks are "Flash" and "Untimed." The meaning of these two terms will be explained shortly. An examiner's copy is shown on page 64.

In addition to the student's and teacher's copies of the tests, the only other testing materials needed are two 3″ × 5″ index cards and a pencil.

Administering Informal Word Recognition Tests

The child is usually seated beside the examiner, on the side opposite the examiner's dominant hand in order to facilitate recording. Thus, the child would be to the examiner's left if the examiner were right-handed. The child's copy is placed face down in front of the child. The

Student's Copy of
Informal Word Recognition Test
(Name of book from which list was taken.)

1. we
2. little
3. was
4. have
5. with
6. her
7. said
8. work
9. cars
10. ride
11. see
12. I
13. is
14. you
15. a
16. likes
17. black
18. in
19. pet
20. and

FIGURE 4.1

examiner's copy is positioned so that she or he can conveniently make notes on it.

The following directions can be given to the child:

I am going to show you some words between these two cards. You will only see a word for a very short time, so look carefully. Tell me the word as soon as you see it.

These directions can be varied, because this is not a standardized test. They should be modified in order to make them clearer or to better suit the examiner or child. However, it is advised that the directions be kept brief and simple. Explaining more of the procedure may make the child confused or anxious.

After the directions have been given, the examiner turns the child's copy face up, and, putting one card in each hand, covers the first word with the card in the left hand and places the card in the right hand directly above, higher on the paper. The lower card is dropped just far

Examiner's Copy
of
Informal Word Recognition Test

Primer Level			First–Reader Level		
Stimulus	Response		Stimulus	Response	
	Flash	Untimed		Flash	Untimed
1. will	_____	_____	1. all	_____	_____
2. she	_____	_____	2. they	_____	_____
3. my	_____	_____	3. bus	_____	_____
4. put	_____	_____	4. sat	_____	_____
5. away	_____	_____	5. first	_____	_____
6. baby	_____	_____	6. grain	_____	_____
7. no	_____	_____	7. garden	_____	_____
8. went	_____	_____	8. box	_____	_____
9. at	_____	_____	9. your	_____	_____
10. ball	_____	_____	10. hot	_____	_____
11. want	_____	_____	11. some	_____	_____
12. good	_____	_____	12. wish	_____	_____
13. read	_____	_____	13. but	_____	_____
14. looked	_____	_____	14. magic	_____	_____
15. he	_____	_____	15. there	_____	_____
16. man	_____	_____	16. yellow	_____	_____
17. what	_____	_____	17. night	_____	_____
18. take	_____	_____	18. lives	_____	_____
19. did	_____	_____	19. fish	_____	_____
20. ran	_____	_____	20. over	_____	_____
Percent			21. smiled	_____	_____
Correct	_____	_____	22. lunch	_____	_____
			23. cry	_____	_____
			24. stood	_____	_____
			25. happy	_____	_____
			Percent		
			Correct	_____	_____

enough to expose the first word, and then the upper card is almost immediately brought down to cover it. The word is exposed for slightly less than a second in this procedure, which is called the flash presentation of the word. If the child correctly identifies the word within about three seconds, the next word is exposed in similar manner, and so on to the completion of the list. The procedure can then be repeated with more challenging lists.

If the child incorrectly identifies a word or fails to identify the word in approximately three seconds, the upper card is moved a little higher on the sheet, thus reexposing the misidentified or unidentified word. The child is told: "Take another look at this one and tell me what it is."

As the child looks at the word, the examiner makes the appropriate recording (scoring notations are listed in the next section) under the flash column, waits for the child to respond to the word during the re-exposure (called the *untimed exposure*), and then records any other responses the child makes.

Some children are reluctant to give a response unless they are confident they will be right. Certainly this is important to note. However, if the child produces no responses on the word recognition test, possible interpretations of the results will be very limited. For example, if the word is "chair" and the child makes no response, the source of the difficulty is completely unknown. However, if the child says "care" for "chair," likely strengths and weaknesses in phonic skills can be specified. Therefore, when words are exposed on the untimed exposure, children should be encouraged to "guess."

Beginning and Ending Testing

Notations. In the flash exposure, the following responses can be made and would be recorded using the listed notations:

1. A correct response: No notation made.
2. No response: 0
3. Substitution of incorrect word: Write in the word child said or a phonetic representation for nonwords (e.g., for "chair" child says "care").
4. Hesitation for 1–3 seconds and then a correct response: +1

In the untimed exposure the following notations can be used:

1. Gives a correct response: √
2. Says he or she does not know: DK
3. No response: 0
4. Substitution of an incorrect word: Write in the word the child said or its phonetic representation.

A blank space in the untimed column indicates that the word was correctly identified in the flash presentation.

Calculating the Score. A simple percentage is calculated based on total number of words correctly identified. Separate scores are calculated for the flash and for the untimed exposures. Only blank spaces are counted in the flash column; blank spaces and check marks are counted in the untimed column. For example, for lists containing 20 words, the total number of words correctly identified in that list is multiplied by 5, and this yields the percentage score; for lists containing 25 words, a percentage score is equal to the total correct multiplied by 4. If 22 words were correctly identified on a flash presentation of a third-grade list, the percentage score would be 88 percent. If two additional words were correctly identified on the untimed presentation, the score would be 96 percent. Thus, although the child was not able to immediately identify three of the words, he or she did identify two of the three when given additional time. All items correctly identified in the flash presentations also receive credit in the untimed column. A flash score of 100

Informal Word Recognition Tests

Second-Reader Level			Third-Reader Level		
Stimulus	Response		Stimulus	Response	
	Flash	Untimed		Flash	Untimed
1. plow			1. pour	O	spar
2. room	O	every thing ✓	2. branch	O	✓
3. everything	O	✓	3. candle	O	candy
4. horns	horn	✓	4. watch	O	want
5. sell			5. stronger		stranger
6. been	barn	barn	6. enough		DK
7. flew	+/		7. main		✓
8. please	O	✓	8. discover		DK
9. strong			9. wishéd		✓
10. head	O	heed	10. journey		DK
11. wood			11. block		blow
12. sleep			12. teeth		✓
13. leave	+ /	butter fly	13. rich		✓
14. beautiful	O		14. anything		✓
15. exciting	ex	ex/sit/ing	15. bounce		bottle
16. hill			16. driving		✓
17. coat	O	✓	17. clothes		DK
18. suddenly	sunny	sunny	18. pencil		DK
19. gray			19. unhappy		✓
20. eating	eat	✓	20. chased		DK
21. deer	DK	✓	21. cottage		
22. found	find	funny	22. foolish		DK
23. nice	O	✓	23. east		✓
24. isn't	O	DK	24. shoot		shot
25. clowns	O	castle/ climb	25. pile		✓
Percent Correct	28 +2	68	Percent Correct		44

percent would automatically dictate an untimed score of 100 percent. Examples of the notation system and scoring are shown on the preceding page.

Interpreting Results

If the purpose of testing is to evaluate children's word recognition skills with reference to one book, then the whole testing process involves just one list that is constructed from the vocabulary of that book. Likewise, only one list is used if the purpose of the word recognition test is to determine students' mastery of the words in a book that they have just completed. If a more comprehensive assessment is sought, a series of word lists, sometimes ranging from preprimer to sixth-reader level, is used. If such thoroughness is desired, all children should be tested by starting with the easiest list. Children for whom the first list is too easy will be able to respond to an entire list in less than a minute; as a result of starting with an "easy" list, they usually build some confidence in dealing with the task. However, if time is very limited or if there is substantial evidence to suggest a fund of well-developed word recognition skills, testing can begin with the most difficult list. This abbreviated procedure is recommended for use only when the examiner anticipates that the child will attain a perfect or near perfect performance on the flash presentation of the highest level of the test.

Johnson and Kress (6) suggest that testing on an informal word recognition test should be discontinued when a student scores less than 50 percent on the flash exposure for two consecutive lists or when a student scores less than 25 percent on any one list. A somewhat more subjective, but actually very good procedure, is to discontinue testing when the examiner has gained sufficient information to satisfy the purposes for which the testing is being done. If the purpose is to estimate a child's instructional level, then testing can be discontinued when the child scores less than 75 percent on two flash presentations. If the purpose is to be as diagnostic as possible with regard to word analysis skills, testing should be continued until the child is making very few responses or is overtly frustrated. The more responses the child makes, the less risk the examiner takes of drawing inappropriate conclusions about specific strengths or weaknesses in word recognition development.

In order to obtain a fuller picture of a child's ability to recognize individual words, it is sometimes beneficial to make adjustments in the testing procedures. For example, if a child achieved a flash score of 20 percent on a third-grade list of words and an untimed score of 80 percent at this same level, there are only a minimum number of word attack errors for the examiner to interpret; but the flash score suggests that going to a fourth-grade list would result in substantial failure for the child when words are exposed for very brief periods of time. An obvious strategy that might be adopted is to discontinue the flash presentation and present words only on an untimed basis. Little would be learned from the flash presentation, because the third-grade list offered substantial evidence of a very weak sight vocabulary.

Another variation that often yields useful results is to give children the entire list of words at a level difficult for them and to ask them to read only those that they think they might know. Interpretation possibilities increase, because additional responses are made; unnecessary frustration is avoided. In addition, a great deal is often learned about some dimensions of the psychological make-up of children. Some children make many reasonable attempts at words with which they are somewhat familiar; other children attempt only words that they are sure that they know. Thus, there is a fairly good reflection of each child's ability to risk being wrong.

A final suggestion is to conduct what might be called a diagnostic inquiry after all testing on the word recognition lists is concluded. The basic purpose of the inquiry phase is to determine the amount of direction a child needs in order to correct an error made on the test. For example, one child identified the word "hope" as "hop" during the untimed portion of the testing. After all the necessary lists were administered, the examiner printed this word on a separate sheet and asked the child to make another attempt to pronounce it. The child looked at the word, announced that he had "said it wrong on the test," and then indicated that it should be "hope," because the silent "e" at the end called for a long "o" sound. Clearly, much valuable information was gained as a result of this brief inquiry. Interpretation of the child's knowledge of vowel sounds and vowel generalizations is far different than if, when asked to reconsider the word, the child had tried "hep" or "hap." During the diagnostic inquiry the examiner attempts to guide the student to the recognition of a word through good instructional procedures. Only a few words should be chosen by the examiner, otherwise this phase of the testing becomes too time-consuming. Words should be chosen for which the child demonstrated some potential for recognition; they also generally should be words that follow phonic and structural generalizations, rather than words that are irregular, because the primary use of the inquiry is to draw safer conclusions about word attack skills that a child possesses.

Interpreting Results

Two major reasons for administering an informal word recognition test are usually given: (1) for screening purposes, to decide whether a book is appropriate for independent reading or as instructional material, and (2) to gain a comprehensive picture of a child's strengths and weaknesses in word recognition. A less frequently cited, but quite valid reason is to check word recognition mastery of a book that a student had recently completed.

Interpreting Results for Screening. The flash scores are used as the primary criteria when a word recognition test is used as the means for estimating a child's instructional or independent reading levels. Flash scores are better predictors of a child's ability to read meaningful materials. (This will be explained more completely below.)

In general, if children can immediately recognize approximately 90 percent of the new words from a book, they will be able to read it independently for pleasure. No instructor or teacher help is likely to be needed. The most difficult list where a score of 90 percent accuracy is achieved would be a child's estimated independent level.

If children can immediately recognize approximately 75 percent of the "new words" from a book, the material is suitable for use when instructing them. The most difficult list at which 75 percent is attained would be a child's estimated instructional level.

If less than 50 percent of the words are recognized in the flash presentation, the materials from which those words were obtained is very likely to be too difficult. This would be the child's estimated frustration level.

"Screening" means that an attempt is being made to establish rough divisions that are not necessarily precise. Making the decision to encourage a child to read a book independently or with instructional help can be done rapidly through informal word recognition tests, but word recognition tests involve a word-in-isolation check and are an artificial method for measuring reading achievement. If time permits, an informal reading inventory will yield much fuller diagnostic information. Informal reading inventories are discussed later in this chapter.

Diagnostic Interpretations. Children's performance in the flash exposure is a reasonably good reflection of their *sight vocabulary:* those words which they can easily and immediately identify. Where graded word recognition lists are used, it may be said that children show an adequately developed sight vocabulary at points where they score 90 percent or better in the flash column; well-developed sight word ability should allow for effective instruction where the scores are between 75 and 90 percent; and marked weaknesses in sight vocabulary are suggested by scores between 50 and 75 percent. Flash scores below 50 percent suggest that children would encounter so many unknown words that they could not cope successfully with the material, even if given constant teacher help.

After commenting on the children's sight vocabulary, it would next be appropriate for the diagnostician to compare the flash and untimed scores at those levels where a child begins to encounter difficulty. If there is little difference between the two, weaknesses in word analysis is suggested. If the untimed score is 20 or more points higher than the flash score, the difference suggests that development of word analysis skills is more accelerated than development of sight vocabulary.

Perhaps the most important part of the interpretation of the word recognition test involves an attempt to isolate strengths and weaknesses in word analysis skills: for example, the extent to which children can effectively employ phonic structural analysis, and the extent to which they can use meaning clues. Some questions that a diagnostician should ask include:

1. Are the children attempting to give meaningful responses? In a word recognition test, children are asked to deal with individual words and are denied the use of sentence and paragraph context clues. This testing technique is deliberate, because the intent is to isolate and identify those skills used effectively, as well as those which need to be improved. Some children actively try to supply real words on a word recognition test, while others give nonsense words. When context aids are unavailable and when children do not recognize a word at sight, the only effective approach is for them to use phonic and structural clues to approximate the correct response and then to modify that response as necessary to produce a meaningful word. Children's failure to do so is diagnostically significant. The possible interpretations are: (a) they are not approaching reading as a meaningful task; they are too mechanical in their attempt to recognize words, and (b) their vocabularies (listening and speaking) may be limited. In order to make a meaningful word they must have heard that word before and remembered it.

2. Are the children using phonic skills or structural analysis skills systematically? Some children, especially those who have encountered problems in reading, become so anxious that they do not seem able to apply skills that they possess. Such children often look quickly at a word and "guess," sometimes making several rapid "guesses." Usually, they look at the word for only a fraction of a second. For example, in response to the word "horse," children may say "house, home, hold" in rapid succession. Yet, if they looked more carefully at the word, they might have noticed the "r" in the middle of the word; this could have been sufficient for them to correctly identify the word. With such children, it is often possible to obtain a more efficient performance by redirecting their attention to the word and asking them to look at it for a minute or two before attempting to pronounce it.

3. What are the children's approaches to analyzing words they can not immediately identify? Some children use very inefficient, self-defeating techniques, such as a spelling approach. They say the names of the

individual letters of the word and try to use letter names as a means of word identification. This is very inefficient, not only because it is time-consuming but also because letter names are not good sound clues to pronunciation. Another frequently used approach is to try to attach sounds to each letter and then to blend the discrete sounds and form a word. Some children are skilled in associating letters and sounds but are unable to blend sounds together.

Sometimes children use a more global phonic approach and try to find syllables and groups of letters to which they can respond. In addition, there are those who seek out meaningful units such as prefixes, suffixes, or inflectional endings. The manner of approaching words that are not known at sight should be observed and noted so that, where needed, recommendations can be made for a more efficient, balanced use of word analysis techniques. For example, it would be helpful to know that children use a spelling approach to reading, so that more efficient word analysis techniques can be introduced.

4. Can specific areas of weaknesses and strengths be observed? For phonics, the general question should be: Does it appear that the children have mastered the major elements? For structural analysis: Do the children appear familiar with common prefixes, root words, and inflectional endings? This type of diagnosis is dependent upon the diagnostician's being familiar with the major word analysis skills.

A Word of Caution. It is important to remember, especially in diagnosing specific skill weaknesses, that conclusions are being drawn from a small number of responses. Given a different set of words, the children's responses might yield different interpretations. For example, the conclusion might be drawn that children can deal with the diphthong "ou" because they identified the word "house." However, if on another word recognition test they said "moose" for "mouse," and "loose" for "louse," the interpretation would be very different. "House" may have been recognized as a sight word.

Conclusions from the results of a word recognition test should be stated cautiously, because children who use context clues effectively might not need some of the instruction that seems suggested by the test results. Both student and teacher time is too valuable to be spent on specific skill instruction that is not really needed. There are at least two alternatives for determining whether or not the skill is needed. A reading inventory can be administered to gather confirming or contradictory evidence. The other alternative is to tentatively accept the conclusion from the testing and then to present some instruction on the apparently needed skill, keeping open the possibility that the lesson may be quickly terminated because it is not needed. The first phase of the teaching might be and should be an extension of the diagnosis.

INFORMAL READING INVENTORIES

An *informal reading inventory (I.R.I.)* is composed of a series of paragraphs of increasing readability difficulty, selected from books that are graded and controlled in terms of level of difficulty. Ideally, the I.R.I. paragraphs are chosen from materials that are being considered for use in an instructional program. Most discussions of I.R.I.s usually advocate choosing the paragraphs from basal readers, which are controlled along a number of dimensions; however, the paragraphs can be chosen from any materials that are being considered for instructional use.

An I.R.I. will allow the teacher or diagnostician to: establish children's independent, instructional, and frustration reading levels; establish their hearing comprehension level; evaluate their oral reading proficiency; assess their functional use of word recognition skills; evaluate their understanding of materials read; and observe their ability to relocate information read previously. More specific information about evaluative and diagnostic information to be derived from an I.R.I. will be set out in the paragraphs which follow.

Choosing or Constructing an I.R.I.

As with most aspects of evaluation, many decisions about I.R.I.s must be based on the purposes for doing the testing. If the purpose is to evaluate children's reading in order to place them in a reading group or at a fitting level of a specific instructional program, the I.R.I. materials should be taken from these potential instructional materials. However, if the purpose is to diagnostically sample children's reading skills without reference to a particular program, an I.R.I. can be constructed from any well-written, controlled series of materials. Because of the grade sequence and language controls, basal readers are usually most suitable. Where comprehensive evaluation without reference to a particular instructional program is sought, published informal reading inventories or inventories prepared by local universities or colleges might also be used. Information about existing I.R.I.s can often be obtained by contacting a local university or college.

It is appropriate to be critical of any informal inventory that is prepared by someone else or that is published. Some are hastily done and use poor questions or materials of dubious value. Because the inventories are informal and not standardized, any user has the liberty of making changes. However, changes should not be made in the text of the material to be read by the child, because doing so may affect the difficulty of the passage, making it either more or less challenging. The ways in which I.R.I.s are best modified are through changing comprehension questions or replacing poorly chosen selections.

Most basal readers also have informal reading inventories that are prepared by the publisher. These are suitable materials with which to begin. Procedures for administering these prepared materials might be altered in order to suit the examiner's purpose. Questions which seem poor can be replaced or rewritten. Many teachers complain about weaknesses in prepared informal inventories, but have the erroneous impression that modifications cannot be made.

If a decision is made to construct a new I.R.I., two sets of paragraphs should be chosen from each book in a series. For example, second-grade teachers using a basal reader program might find it useful to have selections ranging from preprimer through fourth grade. If school reading specialists' purposes are diagnostic and they work in a clinical setting with children who range widely in grade placement and who cannot possibly be matched with the instructional program, an I.R.I. should be constructed from all levels in a series.

Paragraphs usually should not be taken from approximately the first five selections in the book. These frequently repeat and review words and skills from the previous level. Also, the selections should not be chosen from the last third of the book. In a carefully sequenced book there is a constant increase in skill demands, and one purpose of the evaluation is to determine whether the children could profit from instruction at that level. The practice and instruction the children will receive in working with the beginning parts of the book should allow them to meet the increased demands of the materials that follow.

Two selections should be chosen from each level. One of the selections will be read by the children orally, the other silently. Wherever possible, intact paragraphs should be chosen. Requiring children to stop reading in the middle of a paragraph is most unnatural. The length of the two selections should be approximately equal. It is also helpful to have both selections come from the same story. If this is not done, it is difficult to draw comparisons between performance in silent and oral reading. The length of the paragraphs chosen should vary, depending on the designated level of difficulty of the book. General guidelines to follow with regard to word length of the I.R.I. selections are:

Preprimer	=	50– 60
Primer	=	60– 75
First	=	75–100
Second	=	100–125
Third	=	125–150
Fourth	=	150–175
Fifth–Sixth	=	175–200
Seventh–Ninth	=	200–225

When choosing selections for the I.R.I., the following additional guidelines should be followed:

1. Avoid selections containing many unusual proper nouns.

2. Avoid selections that seem dependent on very specific or unusual areas of interest.

3. Avoid choosing paragraphs from the middle of a story if they depend heavily on the earlier story context.

4. Attempt to find selections that contain concepts and vocabulary that appear representative for that book from which it was chosen.

5. Try to find meaningful paragraphs of material that fit the guidelines for length suggested above; the length guidelines can be violated somewhat if a more meaningful reading unit results.

6. Be sure that the selection has enough content to permit the construction of reasonable questions.

After selections have been chosen, questions for checking reading comprehension should be written for each selection. It is generally recommended that 5–8 questions be used at levels preprimer through first and that there be 10 questions for each selection at each level thereafter. It has traditionally been recommended that questions be categorized as factual, inferential, vocabulary, or background of experience. This text recommends elimination of the background-of-experience questions, because in most cases they are non-reading-dependent. This means that they could be answered as well or almost as well by children who have not read the material as by those who have. All comprehension questions in an I.R.I. should be reading dependent. This does not imply that the evaluation of children's background of experience should not take place as part of testing procedure. This can, in fact, be done very effectively in the purpose-setting phase of the inventory, which will be described later in this chapter. For similar reasons, vocabulary questions should be asked only if the meaning of an unfamiliar word can be gleaned from the context of a sentence or paragraph.

The best advice for a teacher using an I.R.I. would be: Write the kinds of questions that you use to evaluate comprehension in instructional settings. Along with this, of course, goes the responsibility for asking relevant, intellectually stimulating questions that do not call upon the children to repeat unessential details. It is hoped that questions used in instruction or testing would meet these criteria.

For diagnosticians and for teachers who wish to prepare quality questions, the following guidelines are suggested:

1. Do not make more than one-third of the questions direct recall questions.

2. Ask questions that ask the children to think about:

   a. The confirmation, denial, and relevance of predictions they made before reading the story.

   b. The prediction of logical outcomes on the basis of information given.

   c. The main idea of the selection.

   d. Cause and effect relations.

   e. The recognition of chronological order or logical sequence.

   f. The evaluation of the accuracy of the information.

   g. The application of information to other concepts or situations.

   h. The purpose or purposes the author had for writing the selection.

   i. The feelings being experienced by the characters in the story.

Where possible, it is excellent to include a question about a vocabulary item that the children are unlikely to know, but which is defined in the context of the story. Under these conditions it is possible to avoid vocabulary questions which are non-reading-dependent or which encourage guessing. Yes-no or two-choice-answer questions are never acceptable. For example, the question: "Was the boy happy or sad?" is very unacceptable, because the children taking the I.R.I. have a 50 percent chance of being right simply by guessing.

Careful attention should be given to the way in which questions are worded. Occasionally the form of the question is so complex that the children are unable to understand what the examiner is asking. A general guideline in this area is to keep the level of complexity of language used in the writing of the question parallel to the complexity of the material that the children are asked to read.

After questions have been written, they should be labeled as to the type of skill they require (e.g., recalling facts, evaluating predictions, determining the main idea). It is helpful to include the suggested correct response after each question. However, caution should be exercised in the use of the suggested answers. Children sometimes give accurate, insightful answers that the writer of the I.R.I. did not anticipate as a possibility. Each child's response to each question must be carefully evaluated.

An oral rereading question is included after the comprehension questions for the selections that are to be read silently. The oral rereading question should require the child to locate and reread orally a specific line or two. Such questions frequently begin with: Find and read out loud the part that tells . . . An example is provided in the sample selections from an I.R.I. that are included on pages 77–78.

Preparing Materials for Testing and Recording

READING MATERIAL. It is probably best to use the actual book from which the I.R.I. was constructed as part of the testing material. The child should read the selections directly from these books. In order to save time, the examiner should place bookmarks in the books to mark the pages containing the selections chosen for use in the I.R.I. At one or two levels, the bookmark might be omitted, in order to check the students' ability to use the table of contents to find the right page when given the title of the story by the examiner. Some examiners feel that it is cumbersome to use books in the testing, because as many as a dozen books may be necessary when little information exists about the reading skill of a child and when a comprehensive reading evaluation is required. However, using the books avoids the necessity of preparing special student copies of the I.R.I. selections and allows full use of typographical, picture, or other graphic clues that are part of the original reading material. The advantages do appear to outweigh the disadvantages.

INVENTORY FORM. The following illustration of an informal reading inventory is in the form that is appropriate for the examiner. This is used by the examiner to record responses as the children read or answer questions. There is also space for recording any other relevant behaviors. Completed recording copies are very helpful for reviewing children's performance, keeping records, and allowing others to obtain a fuller understanding of children's reading performance.

Fourth Reader Level

Selection Taken From: *Adventures*
Total Number of words = 135
(0.74 per word)
Frustration Level: 14

ORAL READING SELECTION

People probably wanted to fly as soon as they first saw birds. One of the earliest things that people wrote stories about was flying. There is a fable, or made-up story, about how a man had magic wings. He used the wings to fly close to the sun. There are also true stories about how people made great kites or large wings, and they held onto the kite or wings and jumped off high places as they tried to fly.

The first people to invent an airplane that worked were Orville and Wilbur Wright. The first plane wasn't very much like airplanes of today. The first airplane had room for only one person and looked like a great big wing. It flew for only 12 seconds and then fell hard onto the soft, sandy beach.

COMPREHENSION QUESTIONS

(Fact)   1. What two things did people first try to use to fly? (wings and kites)

(Fact)   2. What did the story say made people want to fly? (watching birds)

(Vocabulary)   3. What is a fable?   (story, made-up story)

(Fact)   4. Who were the first people to invent an airplane that worked?   (Orville and Wilbur Wright)

(Inference)   5. Why might you think that the people who invented the airplane were related?   (same last name)

(Inference)   6. What did the story tell about that would make you think the first people who tried to fly were brave? (jumped off high places)

(Inference)   7. What reason could you give to help prove that the inventors of the first airplane thought carefully about where they would fly it?   (soft, sandy beach)

(Fact)   8. What were two main problems with the first airplane?   (only one person; flew only 12 seconds)

ORAL REREADING

Read the sentence that tells how far gliders can fly.

SILENT READING SELECTION

At one time people only dreamed of flying, but now there are many ways to travel in flight.

While airplanes are the most common vehicle for air travel, helicopters are useful if someone is flying a short distance. They also can land in a very small space. They usually can carry only a few people.

Gliders are planes that have no engines. They depend on the wind in order to fly. A very good glider pilot can go for hundreds of miles.

When a country needs to send someone into space, only a rocket will do. Rockets are the fastest way to fly and go the farthest. They are very expensive to operate and need pilots with special training.

COMPREHENSION QUESTIONS

(Main Idea)   1. What would be a good title for the story you just read? ("Vehicles for Flying," "Forms of Air Travel," etc.)

(Vocabulary)   2. What is a vehicle? (device for travel)

(Fact)   3. What was the major disadvantage of a helicopter that was listed in the story? (carries few people)

(Fact)   4. What is the name of the plane that has no engine? (glider)

(Fact)   5. What is the fastest way to travel mentioned in the story? (rocket)

(Fact)   6. What two advantages were given for rocket travel? (speed and distance)

(Inference)   7. Which form of air travel is affected most by the weather? (gliders)

The examiner's form should contain the following features:

1. The name of the book and page numbers from which the selection was chosen should be cited.

2. The number of words included in each selection should be indicated. (Also dividing 100 by the total number of words and listing it will make calculating the oral reading score easier. This needs to be listed only for the oral selection.)

3. The number of errors that would place a child at a frustration level should be listed. (This will help the examiner determine when testing should be discontinued.)

4. All selections that are to be read orally should be double spaced, because the examiner will need room for recording. Selections to be read silently may be single spaced, except for the portion to be orally reread. (The child will be reading from the book or a specially prepared copy of the selection. Therefore, the double spacing will not identify the passage that is to be orally reread. Only the examiner has access to the recording copy.)

5. Space should be provided for recording answers to comprehension questions.

SUMMARY SHEET. When an I.R.I. is administered in order to gain a fairly complete picture of the children's reading skills, it is usually helpful to summarize the results of their performance on the inventory. The format on this page is suggested and may be modified to meet specific needs.

I.R.I. And Word Recognition Test Summary

Subject's   Date _____

Name _____ Examiner _____

Grade _____ Age _____ Source of I.R.I. Material _____

School _____ _____

Word Recognition Test   Informal Reading Inventory

Level	Flash	Untimed	Oral Reading	Oral Comp.	Silent Comp.	Average Comp.	Hearing Comp.
Primer							
First							
Second							
Third							
Fourth							
Fifth							
Sixth							
Seventh							
Eighth							
Ninth							

Functional Reading Levels: Skills Needs:

Independent _____

Instructional _____

Frustration _____

Hearing Capacity _____

Comments on Established Levels: Recommendations:

Conclusions about oral rereading:

Administering and Recording an I.R.I.

WHERE TO BEGIN. If the purpose of the evaluation is to determine whether or not a child can deal with a particular book, there is no question as to where testing begins. The sequence for one phase of an I.R.I. is simply followed for the sample chosen from the book. However, if the purpose is to place the child in one of several books or to establish all three functional reading levels and a hearing comprehension level, a decision must be made as to which level or which book should serve as the starting point for testing. If material that is too easy is used as the starting point, it may result in more testing than necessary. In addition, it may fatigue the child and lead to less than optimal results. On the other hand, starting with materials that are too difficult may discourage the child unnecessarily.

If a word recognition test has been given before an I.R.I. administration, it gives valuable suggestions regarding a starting point. It is recommended that an I.R.I. be started at a level equivalent to the highest level where the child attained a flash score of about 90 percent on the informal word recognition test.

If word recognition test results are not available, teacher comments, standardized test scores, and any other available information should be used to decide whether testing should start at, above, or below the child's grade placement. If the initial decision is a bad one, the examiner should not feel obliged to proceed with an entire phase of the inventory. For example, if oral reading is very definitely at a frustration level, it may be unnecessary to give the comprehension questions or silent reading portion of that level of the inventory. In circumstances such as these, the next step might be to go three or four levels lower and then try to administer the inventory. Initiating the testing at a wrong level will not be disastrous if the examiner uses good judgment and moves to an appropriate level as efficiently as possible.

The steps below are followed for each level evaluated in an I.R.I. They are repeated for each reading level the teacher or diagnostician wishes to evaluate.

STEPS IN ONE CYCLE OF AN I.R.I.

1. *Setting Purposes.* Children are given minimal clues about the selection they are to read orally at sight. In most cases, it is best to have them work directly from the books from which the selections were chosen. Some of the techniques that are used include:

> a. Have them find the title of the selection in the index; ask them to predict what the story will be about.
> b. Have them make such a prediction after looking at the title as it precedes the selection.
> c. Have them predict on the basis of one or more illustrations.
> d. Tell them the topic that will be discussed in the selection and have them predict. (E.g., this story is about frogs; what do you think it might tell you?)
> e. Use combinations of the above.

During this portion of the inventory, the examiner must encourage children to think divergently: to use minimal information to arrive at creative possibilities. The attitude must be that there are no wrong answers. Children should be encouraged to combine their background of information with the minimal clues that they receive from the selection.

2. *Oral Reading.* After the child has given his prediction, the examiner should say: "Read this out loud [indicating the portion of the book to be read], and see if the story is about what you thought. Read it very carefully, because I will ask you many questions about it."

As the child reads the selection orally, the examiner has the task of recording all responses. The following notations are suggested for recording the child's oral reading in context:

   a. A line through a word (~~boy~~): omission.
   b. A caret with a line above (the ^*big* boy): insertion.
   c. A line through a word with another word written above it: (the ~~boy~~ *ball*): substitution.
   d. A word circled (boy) the examiner provided the student with the word.
   e. Printer's symbol for inversion (asked he): word order reversed.
   f. Check mark above the marked error (~~boy~~ *ball*✓): spontaneous correction.

The six notations above are used to indicate errors to be counted when calculating the accuracy of oral reading score. The notations below are used to record qualitative aspects of oral reading. They are not counted when calculating the oral reading in context score; only the six errors listed above are counted in the calculation.

   a. Word or phrase underlined (the boy): repetition.
   b. Punctuation mark X'd out (The girl likes school✗ She is . . .): punctuation disregarded in reading.
   c. Arrows up or down (↑ or ↓): inappropriate rising or falling inflection.
   d. Vertical lines (the/ boy /went /home): pauses.
   e. The notation w × w: pauses are prolific (word-by-word reading).
   f. The abbreviation f. p.: finger pointing.
   g. The abbreviation h.m.: head movement.
   h. The abbreviation v.: vocalization or whispering during silent reading.

Children should be encouraged to do as much as possible of the oral reading on their own and to make guesses where they are unsure of a word. However, after about five seconds, an unidentified word should be provided for the children, in order to avoid unusually long delays and in order to avoid frustration. Words provided by the examiner are circled.

The following passage shows recording and explanation of one passage from an I.R.I.:

Number of words = 42
Frustration = 4 or more errors

My Cat

I have a pet. My pet is a ~~little~~ cat. She likes to run and play. ~~She~~ *He* likes to play with a/ball.
One day my cat ran (away) I looked and looked for her. She was in the *hiding* car.

Explanation: Sentence 2: the word "little" was omitted. Sentence 4: The word "he" was substituted for "she." The child hesitated before the word "ball." Sentence 5: Examiner gave the word "away." Child repeated the entire sentence. Sentence 7: "She was" was
‸ repeated and "hiding" was inserted into the text.

Oral Reading Score: Ninety percent (4 scoreable errors including 1 omission, 1 substitution, 1 examiner aid, and 1 insertion. Repetitions and pauses are noted but scored as errors; $38/42 = 90.48$). Scores from any portion of an I.R.I. should always be rounded to a whole number. Decimals imply a level of precision that does not exist in informal evaluation.

3. *Oral Comprehension.* Oral comprehension refers to the children's understanding of the I.R.I. paragraphs that they read orally. For both oral and silent comprehension the questions are asked orally by the examiner. As soon as children complete the oral reading of the selection, the book is removed and placed face down on the desk or table and they are asked, "Were your predictions right?" In some cases, this may constitute the first comprehension question, but it should be asked even if not specifically included in the list of comprehension questions. Children's predictions should always be respected; asking about them is one way of conveying this respect.

The questions should then be asked in order. Answers should be recorded if they are incorrect, if there is some question as to whether they are correct, or if they can provide information that can be used in reporting the results. If children give the expected factual recall information, a check mark can be used to convey this, because there is little of worth to be derived from writing it down.

4. *Reestablishing or Establishing Purposes.* If the selection that is to be read silently is related in content to the selection read orally, the questions, "What do you think will happen next?" or "What else might the selection contain?" can quickly reestablish purposes. If the silent selection is not related to the one read orally, the procedure outlined for setting purposes for oral reading should be followed. The last question in the oral selection could ask children to predict outcomes; this is a sufficient purpose for reading the silent selection.

5. *Silent Reading.* Children should be told to read the selection silently, in order to find out if their predictions are correct and in order to be able to answer examiner questions. Their silent reading should be observed. Such possible signs of frustration as lip movement, vocalization, finger pointing, and eye regressions should be noted; however, these are not always signs of frustration or difficulty. In some cases they represent behaviors that children have retained beyond a level where they need them.

If children ask for the pronunciation of a word during silent reading, they should be asked what they think it is, and they should be encouraged to attempt it. However, a great deal of time should not be spent with this activity. If serious difficulty is being encountered, it is best to tell children what the word is. Any words provided to children are circled.

Where children are proficient readers or where speed of reading is a primary diagnostic consideration, the amount of time used by children during silent reading should be recorded. This is done most easily by using a stopwatch.

6. *Silent Comprehension.* This step of the testing proceeds exactly as did the check of comprehension for the selection read orally. The only difference is that the questions are about selections children read silently.

7. *Oral Rereading.* After all the questions relating to the silently read selection have been asked, the book containing the silent selection is returned to the children and the oral rereading question is asked. The examiner should note children's manner of locating the sentences in question. For example: Did they slowly reread all the material? Did they quickly skim the material until they located the information? Did they remember its location and very rapidly find it? Did they read information that did not answer the question? Did they read relevant but insufficient material? Did they read more material than was necessary to answer the question?

All errors made in the oral rereading should be recorded using the same notation system that was employed for oral reading.

Terminating or Proceeding with Testing

The above steps constitute one complete cycle of an informal reading inventory. After completing it, examiners must decide, based on the purposes for testing, whether they have sufficient information, whether they need to move to easier material, or whether they need to proceed to more challenging selections. The same decision must be made at the conclusion of any additional cycles. If the purposes of the evaluation are to establish an independent instructional and frustration level, as well as to obtain full diagnostic information, it is not uncommon to need to use five or sometimes even more cycles. If the purpose was to determine whether a particular book is or is not suitable for an individual child, one cycle is sufficient.

Evaluating Hearing Comprehension

After the examiner has obtained sufficient information regarding children's reading performance to satisfy the purposes of the evaluation, a hearing comprehension evaluation may be conducted. The procedures are very similar to those used in an I.R.I.

MATERIALS. It is commonly recommended that the first level beyond the children's frustration level, as determined by the I.R.I., be used as a starting place for the hearing comprehension evaluation. Thus, if children were frustrated by fourth-reader level material, the hearing comprehension test would be initiated using fifth-reader level passages. The materials used are those that would have been used for evaluating reading through the I.R.I. It is advised that an alternate I.R.I. be prepared from the same books that were used for the original inventory. The alternate selections can then be used if the children's hearing comprehension level is the same or lower than their instructional level in reading. For example, in the illustration above, the reading of the I.R.I. stopped at fourth and hearing comprehension testing was initiated at fifth. If such children did not meet the criteria for an acceptable hearing comprehension level at fifth, it would be profitable to try to establish whether they met it at fourth. It would be inappropriate to use the fourth-reader selection of the original I.R.I., because the children would have already read it and heard the comprehension questions. Hence, the need for an alternate set of paragraphs from the same materials used to construct the original I.R.I. would be needed.

ADMINISTRATION. An examiner might begin by saying to the child: "Now we are going to do something different. This time I will read the material to you, but you must listen carefully, because I will ask you questions about what I read to you." Purposes should then be set for listening. The procedures are parallel to those used for the purpose-setting phase of the I.R.I. The examiner provides clues and the child makes predictions.

The examiner next reads the oral reading selection to the child. The reading should be natural, careful, and accurate.

After the reading is completed, the purposes for reading should be briefly discussed. The examiner then asks the comprehension questions and records the child's responses. At the conclusion of this sequence, the examiner must decide whether to: (1) give the silent selection at the same reader level as an alternate hearing comprehension test, (2) give a more difficult passage, or (3) give an easier passage.

The silent selection is administered only if children's performance was marginal, that is, if they approached but did not quite satisfy the criterion of being able to answer 75 percent of the comprehension questions. If they clearly did not meet the criterion, a lower, easier selection should be given. It is not profitable to go lower than the children's instructional level in reading when evaluating hearing comprehension. This will be explained in the interpretation section later in this chapter. If the criteria were met or exceeded at the level where the children were tested, a more challenging level of material should be administered next. Testing at various levels continues until the highest possible hearing comprehension level is established.

Interpreting the Results
The information to be derived from each phase of the I.R.I. is discussed in the order in which it occurs during the administration.

PURPOSE SETTING. The diagnostic potential of the purpose-setting phase of the I.R.I. is all too frequently overlooked or minimized; yet, it is one of the richest sources of clues as to why children might be having problems with reading. The children's ability to form predictions on the basis of limited clues gives valuable information about:

1. *Background of Information.* Some children will display little familiarity with the topic about which they will be reading. They simply will not have encountered it either in their home or school experiences. This will certainly limit their understanding and even their ability to recognize words in the selection.

2. *Vocabulary.* The richness or poverty of the children's vocabulary for the topic can readily be assessed.

3. *Verbal Fluency.* This refers more to volume than to quality of language. People who are very fluent can use words with great facility. However, verbally fluent children sometimes use this

skill to effectively avoid new learning. Their long, elaborated answers are sometimes substantively empty.

4. *Willingness to Risk.* Some children find it very difficult to make predictions, because, either by training or personality, they are afraid to give an incorrect answer. They are unable to appreciate the fact that there are no right or wrong answers for this phase of the I.R.I.

5. *Skill in Divergent Thinking.* Children who are very capable use as much of the available clues and combine them in a creative way. Some children are willing to risk, but have serious difficulty with the thinking requirements of this task.

6. *Interests.* When several levels of an I.R.I. are used, is is sometimes possible to find topics that are of special interest to children being evaluated. These can be useful in planning a program for them.

7. *Motivation.* Even at this phase of the inventory, the eagerness of children to read and to participate in the one-to-one testing activity begins to manifest itself. Learning something about children's motivation to learn and read should be possible, and this information is needed in order to make useful recommendations.

8. *Use of Book Parts.* Depending on the method used to set purposes, it is possible to gain some information as to the children's ability to deal with the glossary and with interpretation of pictures, graphs, charts, and titles. Through varied approaches to purpose setting, information about several of these can be obtained as testing proceeds.

ORAL READING. It is best to begin by looking at the scores children achieved in the oral reading in context performance. Some of the following questions can be asked: Do the scores reflect an essentially error free, highly efficient performance (98–100 percent)? Are they adequate for instructional purposes (95–97 percent)? Do some weaknesses (91–95 percent), or serious difficulties (90 percent or less) exist? It is appropriate to look at the oral reading performance at all levels of the I.R.I. that are administered and to note where difficulties begin to appear.

Immediately after looking at the oral reading scores, the quality of the oral reading should be evaluated. For example, it is possible for children to achieve a 95 percent accuracy score in oral reading and for this to represent an unacceptable performance. This could occur if the reading were slow and labored, consisted of many repetitions, hesitations, and spontaneous corrections. By the same token, it is possible for a 90 percent accuracy score to really be part of a very acceptable performance.

Consider this illustration. The sentence to be read was:

The boy went back to the house to get the money.

The child read it as:

The boy went home and got the money.

Marked, it would look this way:

The boy went back ~~to the~~ ~~house~~ *home and got* ~~to get~~ the money.

It is possible to find five scoreable errors: two omissions, two substitutions, and one insertion. If the total context of the story had indicated that the house to which he was going was his own, and if it also indicated that he was successful in getting the money, then the misreading involved very little shift in meaning. If one views the goal of reading as a search for meaning and comprehension, then omissions and substitutions in the example above are hardly serious errors. The overall quality of the oral reading performance needs to be taken into account when interpreting the numerical scores.

Goodman and Burke (5) have provided suggestions for analyzing oral reading errors. For example, they direct the examiner to ask himself if the miscue is a reflection of the children's dialect. The position taken in this text is that this would not constitute a reading error. For example, children who refer to a writing instrument as an "ink pin" in their everyday speech and who read the written form "p-e-n" as "pin" are not making a reading error. These children are taking a written sequence of letters, and transcoding them to a sequence of speech sounds that represent the concept that is common to both the written and spoken forms. Correct meaning is being attached to the printed symbols; there is a meaningful connection between "pen" as written, "pin" spoken, and the children's experience with an instrument for writing. Therefore, these children are not making an error in reading; they are using nonstandard language forms. An important consideration here is that the examiner must be able to distinguish a dialect reading of the material from oral reading errors.

It is also suggested that the examiner ask if the miscue results in any change of meaning. As in the illustration of the children's reading, the sentence about the boy obtaining money, the errors or miscues can actually be healthy, positive signs that the children are responding to meaningful thought units rather than segmented reading of individual words. Goodman and Burke also suggest that the examiner ask if the miscue is grammatically acceptable, which suggests that the children are using their knowledge of the way the language is constructed and that they are attempting to extract meaning from the printed materials. When errors are not grammatically acceptable, there is again the suggestion that the children are overly dependent on mechanical clues. Shifts in intonation—inappropriately raising or dropping the voice—may again reflect the children's failure to make full use of language and meaning clues.

Finally, it is suggested that miscues be analyzed as to the extent to which they resemble the actual word in graphic and sound dimensions. Do the substitutions look and/or sound like the actual printed word? If there is wide divergence here, it may mean that phonic and structural clues are being inadequately employed.

The above discussion is an oversimplification of Goodman and Burke, and the reader is encouraged to read their work for additional details. Perhaps the most important consideration is that children should demonstrate a balanced use of word description techniques; the questions outlined above help to determine when imbalances exist.

Another step in analyzing the oral reading performance should involve comparing the results of the oral reading in context with the results of a word recognition test, if both an I.R.I. and word recognition test were given. In comparing percentages, it is probably best to compare flash scores with oral reading in context scores. However, it is not possible to compare the percentages in an absolute way, because the word recognition test contained only words new to that level, thus making them more uniformly difficult than those found in I.R.I. selections. If children score 90 percent on flash at a level, the corresponding oral reading score on an I.R.I. should be 98 percent or 99 percent. For 75 percent flash, one would expect a corresponding oral reading in context score of about 95 percent, and a 50 percent flash score would compare to 90 percent on reading in context performance in an I.R.I. With these as reference points, it should be possible to draw some conclusions about whether or not sentence and paragraph context is helpful to the children. In some cases, children do comparatively better with words in isolation. Many times it appears that such children feel overwhelmed when faced with sentences and paragraphs to be read, and that anxiety interferes with their performance. Such children seem to feel capable of dealing with one word at a time but may feel that reading all the words in a sentence or paragraph is overwhelming.

COMPREHENSION. When several levels of an I.R.I. are administered, the examiner should begin by drawing generalizations about levels where the understanding was relatively complete (90 percent or better), adequate or strong (75–90 percent), weak (50–75 percent), or totally inadequate (less than 50 percent). Consistency or inconsistency in performance should be noted.

In comprehension, it is very important, but sometimes very difficult, to determine why children performed as they did. Some diagnostic questions that need to be examined include:

1. Were the children's backgrounds of experience for reading the story adequate?

2. Were their vocabularies adequate?

3. Did errors in word recognition seem primarily responsible for their difficulties in comprehension?

4. Did the children orally read meaningful units or was their reading word by word? (Unnatural, inappropriate intonational patterns are often a clue to difficulty. Also, children who are so overly dependent on phonic or word analysis skills that they take considerable time to sound out each word will often experience difficulty understanding the material. Children who have been overdosed with synthetic phonic drills fall into this category.)

5. Did the content of the material significantly influence their performance, either because of their background or interests?

6. Was their attention consistent during the reading?

7. Were they weaker in oral as compared with silent comprehension? This is not uncommon, especially beyond the primary grades. (Oral reading at sight is a rather unnatural act and reasonably proficient readers may find it difficult to produce the oral reading accuracy required by the testing and to simultaneously attend to the meaning of the passage.)

8. Were they better in oral reading as compared with silent reading? (Children who are inattentive or poorly motivated sometimes present such a pattern of performance. Inattentive children are forced, through oral reading, to deal with all parts of the selection. Children who are poorly motivated or children who are embarrassed by their slowness or problems in reading sometimes skip a great deal of the material that they are asked to read silently. Children in the early primary grades also sometimes do better with any oral reading task, because it is stressed so much in many programs of beginning reading instruction.)

9. Could they deal more efficiently with some types of comprehension questions as compared with others? (For example, some children can do an excellent job recalling details from the selection, but have difficulty with any questions that require drawing inferences or conclusions, or in making abstractions or applications from the material read. An attempt should be made to determine if there are any patterns to the children's performance in comprehension.)

In order to identify the sources or possible causes of a comprehension problem, it is necessary to compare the information gained from the purpose-setting phase of the inventory with the information in the comprehension phase. It is also diagnostically important to compare children's performance on a reading test with performance on a hearing comprehension test. Children who cannot answer main idea questions in reading or main idea questions in listening are not displaying a problem unique to their reading.

It is very important to know something about children's prior reading instruction. Some programs, for example, encourage only literal comprehension. This could be a ready explanation of children's problem with other types of comprehension skills. The results of the I.R.I. must be interpreted in the context of the children's previous educational experiences.

As suggested earlier, one should compare the relative effectiveness of oral and silent reading comprehension. Particularly beyond third grade, silent comprehension is a far more natural approach to reading. In fact, in a good instructional program, it should be that way from the very beginning. Because of this, the importance of the silent comprehension performance should be weighed much more than the oral. Certainly, this is so when the silent comprehension is superior. When oral comprehension is superior, it raises the question of whether children have been given appropriate reading instruction. It may suggest that the reading program overemphasized oral reading and that the children found silent reading and silent reading comprehension a new activity.

However, if the oral and silent reading passages are from the same story or selection, the resetting of purposes provides an excellent opportunity to evaluate how well the student can integrate and use new information in order to revise predictions about the content of the selection to be read.

RESETTING PURPOSES. The considerations and interpretations here are essentially the same as those in the original purpose-setting phase. When the oral and silent passages are related, the resetting of purposes might allow for a fuller evaluation of the reader's ability to use newly acquired information in order to predict the content of the selection to be read.

SILENT READING. Evaluators frequently fail to collect diagnostic information in that portion of the I.R.I. where the children read silently. All too frequently this time is used by the evaluator to score other portions of the inventory and to decide upon the next diagnostic steps to be taken. Yet, there is much valuable information that can be obtained.

The use of finger pointing, lip movement, head movement, and vocalization during silent reading should be noted. Often, these reflect frustration on the part of the reader. This is most likely to be the case when these behaviors had not been in existence when the children were asked to read fairly easy materials. However, the importance of these behaviors is often overestimated. They are of minimal importance with children below third grade. With children at third-grade level and beyond these behaviors can represent marked inefficiencies, and some effort should be made to eliminate them. Most will have the effect of making the reader proceed more slowly and sometimes in a word-by-word fashion.

During silent reading, the examiner can also observe, to some extent, the eye movements of the reader. Elaborate schemes for doing this have been described in texts about reading diagnosis, but simple observation seems best. For experimental purposes there may be some value in precise recordings of eye movements; for diagnostic purposes, it is sufficient to observe whether there are numerous and serious regressions or long pauses or fixations. Sometimes the eye movement pattern of the children suggests that they are not really reading the material.

Note should also be made of whether or not the children request help with word recognition during the silent reading. Some children are overly dependent upon outside help during silent reading; they ask for help with many words. At the other extreme are children who need, but will not ask for, outside help. In both cases, valuable clues are derived from the children's behavior during silent reading.

As noted earlier, the silent reading selections can be timed, but this need not be done unless some use and interpretation is made of this information. It is not diagnostically useful to set an average reading speed or standard for rate, because rate of reading is so highly dependent on the level of difficulty and nature of the material and the purposes for reading. It is particularly difficult to set standards of rate for students in elementary grades. Rate of reading is important, but more satisfactory results can probably be obtained by informally sampling from longer sections of material. In most cases, I.R.I. selections are too short to give adequate reflections of speed of reading.

ORAL REREADING. The most obvious observation to be made here is whether or not the reader was able to locate the information requested by the examiner. Some children find it difficult to locate specific information. There is also the opportunity to observe whether or not the children can separate the relevant from irrelevant information. Some children read far more material than is necessary to fully answer the oral rereading question. Such children seem to have difficulty keeping in mind the purpose for their oral reading.

The children's approach to locating the information requested should be noted. Some children, for example, read each word slowly until they reach the needed information. This is obviously inefficient. Others search haphazardly from place to place in the selection. The skilled reader is able to rapidly skim through the selection in order to complete the task. In oral rereading some children demonstrate excellent memory for the location of the information that they are asked to reread.

Finally, there is the opportunity to compare the quality of the readers' oral rereading with their oral reading at sight. Generally, one can expect the oral rereading to be more expressive, have fewer errors, and generally be qualitatively superior. However, if the material is at the children's frustration level or if the children are very disabled in reading, such improvement is not usually found.

Establishing Functional Reading Levels

The functional reading levels and hearing comprehension level were defined on pages 57–59. Although three functional reading levels can be estimated from the word recognition test, the primary criteria used to establish these levels are the Oral Reading in Context scores and the Comprehension scores. The comprehension score criteria are usually applied to the average of the oral and the silent comprehension scores. The numerical criteria are as follows:

LEVEL	WORD RECOGNITION; PERCENT ORAL READING IN CONTEXT		PERCENT COMPRE- HENSION
Independent	98 or above	and	90 or above
Instructional	95–97	and	75–90
Frustration	90 or less	or	50 or below

The hearing comprehension level is set as the highest level at which children answer at least 75 percent of the questions that are asked of them.

In order to establish an independent and instructional level, readers must meet the criteria in both word recognition and comprehension. For example, if a child had a word recognition in context score of 95 percent and a comprehension score of 55 percent at third-reader level, that could not be considered his or her instructional level. However, only one criterion needs to be met in order to establish a frustration level. If either the word recognition or performance score drops below the recommended criterion, a frustration level is established. For example, if the word recognition in context score were 86 percent and the comprehension score were 65 percent, the performance would be considered to be at a frustration level, even though the comprehension score is higher than expected for a frustration level.

Unfortunately, it is rarely possible to apply these numerical criteria in a simple, straightforward fashion. The quality of the child's reading performance must continuously temper the application of the numbers. It is possible for scores of less than 98 and 95 percent to really reflect independent and instructional levels and for scores that exceed these levels to mask qualities of the reading performance that would present serious obstacles to effective reading instruction. Therefore, it is suggested that diagnosticians begin by applying the criteria but then look at the quality of the reading performance. The extent to which there is consistency from level to level might also help in the decision of setting levels. Finally, where these considerations still do not make for clear decision making, looking at the scores from the informal word recognition test might help.

The following illustrations are provided as an attempt to clarify how the decisions can be made, but there is no substitution for experience with actual evaluations.

Case Example 1:   Age = 7–1   Grade Placement = 1.9

Informal Word
Recognition Test   I.R.I. Results

LEVEL	FLASH	UNTIMED	ORAL READING IN CONTEXT	ORAL COMPRE- HENSION	SILENT COMPRE- HENSION
Preprimer	60	85	90	80	70
Primer	35	80	84	50	60
First	—	65			

Qualitative Information. Oral reading was slow and expressionless. Examiner's help was needed with two words and there were three substitutions, all of which were graphically similar to the stimulus words. However, the substituted words were not syntactically or semantically similar to the ones in the text. The child appeared to overly employ a synthetic phonics approach to reading.

Levels Established. Independent Level = None Established
Instructional Level = None Established
Frustration Level   = Preprimer

Justification. Little justification is needed for setting the levels. The criterion for frustration level in word recognition in context was in evidence at the preprimer level. The criterion for a frustration level was not met with regard to comprehension; however, questions at the preprimer level often can be answered from background of information.

Case Example 2:   Age = 8–0   Grade Placement = 2.7

Informal Word
Recognition Test   I.R.I. Results

LEVEL	FLASH	UNTIMED	ORAL READING IN CONTEXT	ORAL COMPRE-HENSION	SILENT COMPRE-HENSION
Preprimer	90	100			
Primer	85	100	98	100	80
First	75	95	90	80	80
Second	60	75	90	70	60
Third	30	50			
Fourth	—	20			

Qualitative Information. Oral reading was smooth and fairly expressive; quality of answers to comprehension questions was good. At first reader level, examiner gave help with one word, an adjective was omitted and the name "Tad" was read "Ted" twice.

Levels Established. Independent Level = Primer
  Instructional Level = First
  Frustration Level   = Second

Justification. On the basis of numerical criteria, first-reader level should be a frustration level, but aside from the one word provided by the teacher, the word recognition errors are very minor. "Ted" was a very reasonable substitution, because it is a more common name for a boy than "Tad." Additional evidence of good word recognition ability is found in the flash score of the word recognition test, the very high score at primer level and the fact that the oral reading score did not drop at second-reader level. The good performance in comprehension at all three levels is also supportive of the decisions made regarding the levels. This case clearly illustrates the need to go beyond the numerical criteria; however, it is always necessary to provide good justification for disregarding these criteria.

Case Example 3:   Age = 14–2   Grade Placement = 9.1
Informal Word
Recognition Test   I.R.I. Results

LEVEL	FLASH	UNTIMED	ORAL READING IN CONTEXT	ORAL COMPRE-HENSION	SILENT COMPRE-HENSION
Fifth	100	100	99	80	90
Sixth	95	100	98	70	80
Seventh			99	50	55
Eighth			99	80	70
Ninth			98	40	30

Qualitative Information. Oral reading performance excellent. Responses to many questions quite confused. Eighth-grade selection dealt with science fiction, a favorite area for this student.

Levels Established: Independent Level = Fifth *but* highly dependent on topic and interest of student.

                        Instructional Level = Sixth

                        Frustration Level   = Ninth

Justification. Technically, the criteria for an instructional level are met at eighth-grade level; however, it appears that the results at that level are spuriously high. Performance at seventh level was very weak in comprehension and also at ninth level. Instructionally, it seems important that the child build better skills for dealing with a wide variety of materials, even those in which she is not especially interested. The large discrepancy between the instruction and frustration levels suggests that the student has a good reservoir of skills upon which to build. If this student is well motivated, the prognosis for rapid progress seems good. The independent level is qualified because it seems likely that if this child is interested in a topic she might be able to independently enjoy materials considerably more challenging than fifth-reader level. The child falls just short of the criteria for an independent level at fifth-reader level.

Case Example 4:   Age = 10–6   Grade Placement = 5.5
    Informal Word
    Recognition   I.R.I. Results

LEVEL	FLASH	UNTIMED	ORAL READING IN CONTEXT	ORAL COMPRE-HENSION	SILENT COMPRE-HENSION
Preprimer	100	100			
Primer	100	100			
First	95	100			
Second	100	100	97	85	100
Third	90	95	95	80	100
Fourth	80	90	90	55	80
Fifth	60	75	91	40	70
Sixth	40	60	84	30	50

Qualitative Information. Quality of oral reading good through fourth level. Labored and more word by word thereafter. Scores seem an accurate reflection of performance in comprehension.

Levels Established. Independent Level = Third

                        Instructional Level = Fourth

                        Frustration Level   = Sixth

Justification. The independent level was set at third because of the excellent comprehension score at that level and because comprehension during silent reading remained good through fifth-grade level. Analysis of word recognition errors at third revealed that they were not serious;

the flash score adds further evidence of good skills. The instructional level was set at fourth level, in spite of the fact that the average comprehension score is below the acceptable criterion because the silent comprehension score reflects a more realistic reading situation. Word recognition was adequate there.

In the four case examples the numerical criteria for word recognition in context and comprehension were used only as starting points for the establishment of functional reading levels. Qualitative observations of children's reading performance are essential for making diagnostically useful decisions. The examples also illustrate that the children's performance on the entire inventory was considered in the establishment of levels. The examiner did not confine himself to one level of the inventory. Nevertheless, the word recognition in context scores and the comprehension scores were the primary criteria taken into consideration. The results of the word recognition were used only in a supplementary way.

Reporting I.R.I. Results

CLASSROOM TEACHERS. For classroom teachers who use I.R.I.s the question of reporting is usually limited to reporting the results to parents. Teachers who use I.R.I. procedures for the first time are often extremely surprised by and pleased with the utility of the inventory for use during parent conferences. Parents can be made to readily understand the concepts of independent, instructional, and frustration reading levels when these are explained without recourse to excessive jargon. In some cases it is beneficial to actually show parents the completed examiner's recording of their child's performance on the I.R.I. Even though the parents will not understand the specific notations, they are often very impressed with the increasing number of notations as the level of the reading material increases. The record form serves as a graphic illustration of the difficulty the child encountered.

It is usually unnecessary for a classroom teacher to prepare a formal report of the I.R.I. results. The use of a summary sheet such as that illustrated on page 79 is usually sufficient if some notes are made in the spaces reserved for comments, skill needs, and recommendations. It is also very useful for the teacher to keep the completed examiner's form. As suggested above, it can be useful for parent conferences. In addition, it may be used as a point of reference for any future I.R.I. testing that is done. The comparison of an I.R.I. administered at the beginning of a school year with one given at the end of the year can be very reassuring to a teacher who wonders whether or not progress has been made. Day-to-day change and improvement are sometimes difficult to see; change over the course of a school year can be dramatic.

READING SPECIALISTS. Classroom teachers usually do not have time for extensive administration of individual I.R.I.s. In some schools the responsibility for giving an individual I.R.I. falls to the reading specialist, who must then report the results to the classroom teachers. Supplying written summaries of the results can be extremely time-consuming. It is, therefore, recommended that as a reading specialist assumes responsibility for giving I.R.I.s, the specialist conduct an in-service session or two which reviews:

1. The source of the I.R.I. materials.
2. The procedures for administering an I.R.I.
3. The notations used for recording a child's performance. (These should also be distributed in the form of a handout to each teacher.)
4. The scoring procedures.
5. The criteria for establishing functional reading and hearing comprehension levels.

While this may seem like a time-consuming venture, it is in fact time-saving. If teachers are familiarized with I.R.I. materials and procedures, the reading specialist can report the results of an evaluation far more effectively and efficiently. Informed teachers can be given a summary sheet, which lists scores and brief comments and recommendations. If teachers are not informed, the reading specialist will have to offer lengthy explanations for each child tested and will need to prepare a report.

READING CLINIC PERSONNEL. When an I.R.I. is part of a clinic's reading diagnostic procedures, a much more elaborate reporting form is necessary. At the University of Delaware Reading Center, where I.R.I. procedures are extensively used, the results are explained to the parents of all children evaluated. The teachers of these children are invited to call the clinic for a verbal report of the evaluation. This also provides teachers with the opportunity to ask questions. Reporting verbally to parents and teachers has the distinct advantage of allowing for elaboration and questioning as is needed to accomplish an understanding of the results.

In addition to the verbal report, a thorough written summary of the results is also prepared. It is made as comprehensive as possible and written in descriptive, somewhat redundant language, in order that it might prove useful to a potentially very diverse audience. Some parents request a written summary, so it must not be too technical; teachers often request the report, so it must be detailed enough to communicate to them; school psychologists, vision specialists, pediatric neurologists, family physicians, and social workers are among the many other groups that sometimes request the results of the evaluation.

GROUP INFORMAL READING INVENTORIES

Informal reading inventories are often thought to be impractical for the classroom teacher, because they are considered too time-consuming. This judgment is the result of a far too rigid, narrow concept of informal evaluation. It is the result of the myth that whenever an I.R.I. is administered, one has to end with the establishment of an independent, instructional, and frustration level. This is certainly not so. It has been pointed out that one phase or one portion of one phase may satisfy the immediate diagnostic question that the teacher has. Consider this question: Have the children mastered the materials in the book in which they have been receiving instruction? To answer this question, the procedure might be to have them orally read at sight several hundred words and ask no oral comprehension questions, and then to have them read a second passage silently and ask them a few (not necessarily 10) silent comprehension questions. This brief procedure could serve as a basis for making a diagnostic decision. The entire procedure would take less than five minutes. The advantages are that the test is really a sample of the actual instructional material, the testing activities are not inordinately artificial, there is substantial flexibility in the procedures, and the diagnostic, evaluation procedures are part of an ongoing instructional program, not an isolated activity between a child and some specialist.

Sometimes, however, the evaluation questions are more focused upon groups rather than individuals. For example: Which of three texts would be best for a class? Which children in a class are likely to need special instruction in use of a chosen text? What is the range of reading ability in a class? In addition there are circumstances, such as the beginning of a year, when spending 5 to 15 minutes with each child seems impossible. All these circumstances call for techniques whereby I.R.I.s are administered to groups rather than individuals.

The Diagnostic D-R-T-A

This procedure essentially calls for following the steps of a D-R-T-A. (See Stauffer, 10, 11, for a complete discussion of D-R-T-A procedures.) The following modifications, however, are recommended:

> 1. Use groups of no more than five or six children; very close observation is necessary.
> 2. Use selections of material that are no longer than two or three pages.

3. Prepare varied questions from the available material.

4. Keep the sessions as short as possible.

5. Remember that the emphasis is on evaluation rather than instruction.

The recommended procedure is as follows:

1. Group together five or six children who, based on available information, appear to have similar skills.

2. Have the group make predictions and set purposes. In addition to providing the information that is gathered in an individual I.R.I., it allows for the observation of each child's behavior as part of a group.

3. Have the children read the designated selection silently.

4. Observe the silent reading.

5. Ask each child as many comprehension questions as can be reasonably devised from so short a selection.

6. Decide on the next steps. For children who appear to have been able to handle the material independently, retest them as part of a group who will receive a group I.R.I. using more difficult material. For those who appear to be at an instructional level, no further testing is needed. Those who had too much difficulty with the material should be retested with a group that will be exposed to easier material. Continue making these decisions after each group.

The above procedures rely on silent comprehension performance and teacher observation. It could, of course, be supplemented with individual word recognition or oral paragraph reading. The diagnostic D-R-T-A should be viewed as a first step, which is followed by teacher evaluation during teaching. The concept of diagnostic teaching is central. Any decisions based on so small a sampling are bound to be in error sometimes. It is important that they do not lead to rigid instructional decisions. If the purpose was to form D-R-T-A instructional groups, each time a teacher directs the activity, he or she has the opportunity to make revised judgments and to place the child at a different level.

Written Question Inventories

This approach is probably not as suitable for primary grades, but may be more helpful for teachers at secondary levels. The recommended procedures here are:

1. Select a passage of approximately 500 words from somewhere near the end of the first quarter of a book.

2. Prepare a list of about 10 questions. Duplicate enough copies of the questions so that there is one for each student. Provide sufficient space for written answers after each question.

3. Precede the administration of the inventory by stressing that the purpose is not to grade students but to learn something about the book they will be reading.

4. If sufficient copies of the book from which the selection was chosen are available, these can be distributed to students. The silent reading of the material can then be directly from the book. If sufficient numbers of copies are not available, the selection can be retyped and duplicated. (Most publishers will readily give permission for limited duplication for this purpose.)

5. After the students have read the passage, they should so indicate by raising their hands or some other procedure. Books can be then turned face down as the teacher gives the student a copy of the questions. If duplicated, retyped copies are used, they can be exchanged for questions.

6. Students are given as much time as they need to write the answers.

7. If students are able to answer 70–90 percent of the questions correctly, they are considered instructional. Students above and below that range might be given additional written question inventories at higher or lower levels. Answers are regarded as acceptable as long as they reflect accurate understanding and interpretation of the content. Faulty grammar and spelling should not be considered essential for the reading evaluation.

These procedures do not duplicate the full range of information that comes from an individual I.R.I., but they still serve practical purposes. A third procedure that might be able to answer some of the same questions as a group I.R.I. is the cloze procedure. It is discussed in the next chapter.

PUBLISHED INFORMAL READING INVENTORIES

As stressed earlier, the core concept of informal evaluation is that it represents a sampling from potential instructional materials. This evaluation procedure stresses the close connection between testing and teaching. One of the authors (8) has outlined some of the hard-to-answer questions that arise when informal reading inventories are not based on potential instructional materials.

Basal Reader I.R.I.s

One form in which published I.R.I.s are found is as part of a basal reader system. The best of these do build the inventory from selections included in the basal readers and do maintain the close correspondence between evaluation and instruction. However, many teachers and reading specialists complain about the quality of these inventories. These teachers complain that there are poor questions and badly chosen selections. There is an obvious remedy: new questions or new selections that appear to be better can be substituted. Teachers and reading specialists who use I.R.I.s need to keep reminding themselves that it is perfectly acceptable to make such substitutions if the attempt is to improve the utility of the diagnostic instrument.

Other Published Inventories

In some situations, reading diagnosticians see children from many classrooms or schools that use a wide variety of instructional materials. Under these circumstances, it would be impractical to have a different inventory for each set of instructional materials, and use of a general informal reading inventory—such as the Classroom Reading Inventory (C.R.I.) by Silvaroli (9)—might be appropriate. It has three sets of graded selections, ranging in difficulty from preprimer to eighth-reader level. One set could be used for oral reading, the second for silent reading, and the third for evaluating hearing comprehension. Each selection is followed with from five to seven comprehension questions. The questions are labeled às being factual, inferential, or vocabulary. The test manual also includes word recognition tests and spelling inventories. The major advantage of the C.R.I. is its convenience and low cost. The author gives the user of the test permission to duplicate record forms for the test, rather than requiring the user to purchase all forms from a publisher.

The C.R.I., however, has a number of limitations. It includes: questions that are nonreading dependent, only a few comprehension questions that require higher order thinking skills, no information about the source of the paragraphs used in the test, and no attempt to supply minimal information about test reliability or validity.

Reliability and validity questions are approached by the author of the Standard Reading Inventory (7). This test utilizes many of the concepts of informal reading evaluation. It contains selections ranging from preprimer to seventh-reader level. There is an A and B form (alternate forms), each containing two selections at each level. The administration and scoring of the Standard Reading Inventory are rather complex, and several variables must be considered in establishing independent, instructional, and frustration levels. A number of teachers and clinicians have objected to the complexity of this inventory. Thus, while it attempts to come to grips with the questions of reliability and validity that are raised when I.R.I.s are built on materials other than those being considered for instructional use, it does not appear to be widely used.

CONCLUSIONS

Informal evaluation procedures have been described in great detail, because they are felt to be flexible and very useful. They can be effectively employed by classroom teachers and reading specialists. One often hears the statement that informal reading evaluation is only as good as the person conducting the evaluation, which is to say that the effectiveness of the technique is dependent on the skill of the examiner. There is no argument with this position. However, it seems very plausible for a skilled teacher to become quite efficient in the use of informal procedures.

Informal reading inventories and informal evaluation procedures should be flexibly employed. Procedures can be modified and abbreviated in order to efficiently answer diagnostic questions that may be posed. In some places an I.R.I. is seen as a very regulated, static set of materials. If informal evaluation becomes equated with a set of materials rather than a general diagnostic strategy, much of its power and utility is lost. However, in the hands of a skilled examiner, informal evaluation may be the most useful and accurate available approach to evaluating reading.

BIBLIOGRAPHY

1. Barnard, D. P., and J. DeGracie. "Vocabulary Analysis of New Primary Reading Series." *The Reading Teacher,* 30, 2 (November, 1976), 177–180.

2. Beldin, H. L. "Informal Reading Testing: Historical Review and Review of the Research," in W. Durr, ed., *Reading Difficulties: Diagnosis, Correction and Remediation.* Newark, Del.: International Reading Assoc., 1970.

3. Betts, E. *Foundations of Reading Instruction.* New York: American Book, 1950.

4. Betts, E. *The Prevention and Correction of Reading Difficulties.* New York: Harper & Row, 1936.

5. Goodman, Y., and C. Burke. *Reading Miscue Inventory.* New York: Macmillan, 1972.

6. Johnson, M. S., and R. A. Kress, "Task Analysis for Criterion-Referenced Tests." *The Reading Teacher,* 24 (1971), 355–359.

7. McCracken, R. A. *Standard Reading Inventory.* Kiamath Falls, Oreg.: Kiamath Printing, 1966.

8. Pikulski, J. "A Critical Review: Informal Reading Inventories." *The Reading Teacher,* 28 (November, 1974), 141–151.

9. Silvaroli, N. *Classroom Reading Inventory.* Dubuque, Iowa: Brown, 1965.

10. Stauffer, R. G. *Directing Reading Maturity as a Cognitive Process.* New York: Harper & Row, 1969.

11. Stauffer, R. G. *Directing the Reading-Thinking Process.* New York: Harper & Row, 1975.

12. Venezky, R. *Testing in Reading: Assessment and Instructional Decision Making.* Urbana, Ill.: National Council of Teachers of English, 1974.

CHAPTER 5

Approaches to Evaluating Reading [II]

In addition to informal evaluation techniques, there are two other major approaches to evaluating reading: criterion referenced measures and standardized reading procedures. The categories are not mutually exclusive. Informal reading inventories are sometimes viewed as a form of criterion referenced measurement; the Standard Reading Inventory is an attempt to attach norms (a characteristic of standardized tests) to a test that is essentially an informal reading inventory. In spite of some blurring of distinctions, it is useful to categorize evaluation procedures into one of these three headings. This chapter focuses upon criterion referenced measurement and standardized approaches.

CRITERION REFERENCED EVALUATION

The exact beginning of the use of the term *criterion referenced evaluation* (C-R) is somewhat obscured in educational testing history; however, there are definite references to the term in the early 1960s, and the term became educationally very prominent in the 1970s. Its popularity is attested to by the fact that a number of other terms have come to be regarded, at least by some, as synonymous. These include: domain

reference testing, edumetric testing, mastery tests, maximum performance tests, content reference tests, and objective referenced tests. The
point has been reached where there is diagreement as to how C-R measures should be defined, what form they should take, and what value
they have. There has been sufficient time for reading specialists to have
become excited, confused, and cynical about the use of C-R tests. In
short, there appears to have been a sufficient initiation period to allow
us to examine the concept and its use or misuse with some perspective.

Before a definition of the term C-R measurement is offered, it might
be helpful to read the following statements, in order to decide whether
they are the result of C-R measurement, norm referenced measurement,
or diagnostic testing.

> 1. Marie scored at the eighty-fifth percentile in reading vocab-
> ulary, at the eighty-eighth percentile in speed of reading, and
> at the eightieth percentile in reading comprehension.
> 2. Nancy can read without error a list of 20 one-syllable words
> which contain short vowel sounds.
> 3. John's grade score on the last reading test was 7.2.
> 4. Frank can identify 20 percent of the words on a list con-
> taining words which begin with consonant blends of the *l* family.
> 5. James' overall performance on the reading test placed him
> at the second stanine.
> 6. Linda can read a paragraph from a seventh-grade social
> studies book with 90 percent word recognition accuracy.
> 7. Alice's difficulty in comprehension is due to a limited back-
> ground of experience, combined with low-average intellectual func-
> tioning.
> 8. Ted has been making little progress in word recognition be-
> cause of perceptual difficulties.

Statements 2, 4, and 6 reflect criterion referenced measurement; 1, 3,
and 5, reflect norm referenced measurement; and statements 7 and 8
would probably be labeled the result of diagnostic testing.

Most attempts to define C-R testing usually begin by contrasting it
with norm referenced testing and sometimes with diagnostic testing.
With norm referenced evaluation the basic question asks how well an
individual performs in comparison with other individuals. Under most
circumstances a student's performance is compared with the group of
individuals who comprised the standardization population for the test
that is being administered. They are the "norm" against which he or she
is compared. As a result, the examiner can draw comparisons with local,
regional, or national groups, depending on the population to which the
individual is being compared. The focus throughout is upon interin-

dividual differences. The greater the variability among the individual performances, the better the test is evaluated in most circumstances, because then it is felt to be more discriminating. The term standardized test is often used synonymously with the term norm referenced test. (Standardized tests are discussed later in this chapter.)

The distinction between diagnostic tests and criterion referenced measures is largely a matter of emphasis, and many authorities would prefer not to make a distinction between them. However, some feel that in diagnostic testing the emphasis is upon an evaluation of an individual's strengths and weaknesses in skill areas with attention to the possible causes of problems that exist. The primary purpose is often to distinguish between individuals who do and do not have a certain deficiency. Criterion referenced testing is less concerned with definition of disability and does not emphasize the cause of problems.

Prescott (37) introduces another consideration that merits attention. He maintains that it is more accurate to discuss criterion referenced interpretation of test scores rather than criterion referenced tests. Some authorities suggest that a test can be administered and then interpreted either from a criterion or norm referenced point of view. This position suggests that there are, in fact, no identifying characteristics that separate the two types of test items. Some would hold that the only necessary characteristic of a criterion referenced test is that some standard be established for determining whether or not a particular skill has been achieved. In other words, the score necessary for passing must be set ahead of time without reference to the scores obtained by others taking the test.

Millman's definition of the term criterion is very different from that given in the last paragraph. He maintains that the criterion in C-R testing refers to "specific tasks a student must be capable of performing . . ." (27, p. 312). However, some users of C-R testing would employ the term *domain referenced testing* for a situation where specific, important learning tasks are identified but where no cutoff is defined as an acceptable level of performance. Two books by Popham (34, 36), an education text and a collection of readings, are recommended for readers who wish to pursue definitional problems of criterion referenced measurement.

Characteristics of Criterion Referenced Tests

Rather than attempting a final definition here, it seems more appropriate to try to enumerate several characteristics that have been declared by some to be essential to criterion referenced measures.

One characteristic is that there must be a clear definition of the task, objective, or skill that is to be measured. This is the most obvious and essential prerequisite for a criterion referenced test. According to Millman the term *criterion* refers to the specific tasks a student must master; a criterion referenced test, therefore, must be one where the items refer to such a clearly stated set of tasks. Consequently, criterion referenced measures do not attempt to be global measures of reading, but instead attempt to center on specific skills. Most advocates of criterion referenced measures maintain that the objectives must be stated in behavioral terms and tested in a fashion that allows for clear evidence of whether a skill has or has not been acquired.

For example, the objective "the child will develop a sight vocabulary" would be considered too broad by most. It tells little about the means for determining whether the objective has been met, the necessary level of proficiency, or the conditions under which the measurement takes place. The item would be much more acceptable if it were stated as: "Given a maximum exposure of one second per word, the child correctly reads 90 percent of the preprimer and primer-level words on a test constructed from the basal reader that is being used in his classroom." This revised statement is certainly more cumbersome, but one can be much clearer as to how sight vocabulary is to be measured and whether or not a student has accomplished the objective after the test has been administered.

The requirement that the task to be measured must be clearly defined does present problems at times. For example, would the item: "The student will be able to read a newspaper," be an acceptable one? Carver (5) cites this as an illustration of an important piece of information about a student's reading ability in his discussion of criterion referenced measurement. If one were to take a newspaper, select an article, and ask a student to read it, would it be a criterion referenced test item? In its present form, it probably is too much like a "general test of reading." However, practical information such as this can rather readily be transformed into a format that would allow for the designation of criterion referenced. A clearer specification of the source and length of the article, along with the definition of an acceptable level of performance, would certainly go a long way toward making this a "respectable" test item.

A second characteristic of criterion referenced tests is that items in such a test are used to determine mastery rather than to obtain a normal distribution. This requirement is one that clearly divides criterion referenced from norm referenced tests. Items are chosen for norm referenced tests so that the results form what is called a normal distribution. This means that writers of test items include many items that are of a moderate level of difficulty, some that are reasonably easy and a few that are very difficult. A test is considered to be a good one when the scores of a group of individuals distribute themselves normally. A graph showing number of items correctly identified by a group of students on a norm referenced test "should" look like Figure 5.1.

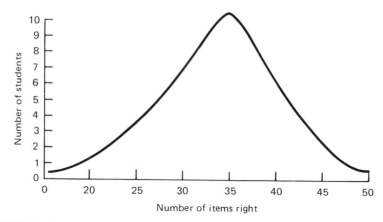

FIGURE 5.1

The anchor point for a norm referenced test is the middle or average. It is expected that most students will not do either very well or very poorly. Most are expected to be "average."

The situation is quite different in criterion referenced testing. Rather than looking for the normal distribution with the anchor in the middle, criterion referenced tests are anchored at the extremes and form a polarization or dichotomy. At one end are those individuals who have mastered the skill under consideration; at the other extreme are those individuals in whom the ability is absent. The results of a C-R test might look like Figure 5.2.

A criterion referenced test might be considered a poor one if there were many individuals who had some of the items right and some of them wrong. The purpose of a criterion referenced test is to try to determine whether a reader does or does not possess a specific skill.

In norm referenced measurement the goal for choosing items is to discriminate among and compare individuals; in criterion referenced measurement the goal of each item is the same: to determine whether a skill has or has not been mastered. Items are chosen because they are considered to be representative, essential skills needed by students. The goal of the teacher with regard to such a test is to have all students respond to all items with perfect or near perfect accuracy.

There is fairly good agreement on the part of test constructors that the criterion for choosing or retaining items for norm referenced and criterion referenced tests are very different.

A third characteristic of criterion referenced tests is this: The items should be representative of skills that are essential to learning to read. A primary validity question with regard to criterion referenced tests is the question of *content validity*. Content validity asks if the test items

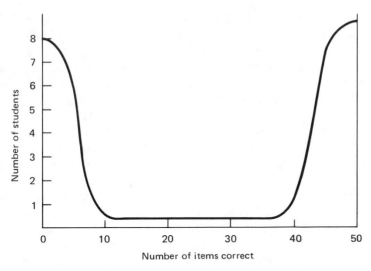

FIGURE 5.2

are an adequate sampling of the area of knowledge that they are supposed to be measuring. For example, a test that purports to be a general test of reading, but which includes items that depend only on word recognition and not comprehension would not possess content validity. All testing is simply sampling from a great body of behaviors, and test constructors must always face the question of whether the sample that they propose in a test is a fair and adequate sample. It should neither include irrelevant, nonessential items, nor should it fail to include a sampling of important items.

A major problem is that there is far from perfect agreement as to what are or are not the essential skills for reading. Because in criterion referenced testing the goal is mastery of a skill by all students, it is particularly wasteful in time and effort for a group of students to engage in achieving a minute goal that is not essential to some larger, practical goal.

Consider this item:

Objective: Given lists of three-syllable words divided into syllables, the reader determines the syllable stressed with 90 percent accuracy.

Directions to Student: Choose the word that has the accent on the wrong syllable.

1. a. em bar′ go
   b. his tor′ ic
   c. med i′ cine
2. a. re vol′ ver
   b. tur′ pen tine
   c. cer e al′

Critics of programs which list hundreds of behavioral objectives for reading have charged that many of these objectives are so limited as to be irrelevant to many readers. For example, might it not be possible for a child to be able to pronounce the word correctly without being able to locate a misplaced accent mark? Even very capable readers sometimes fail to correctly complete items like the ones just illustrated. Artificial and irrelevant activities should be avoided. When children are asked to read a word, do they not use a combination of skills, rather than just one? If this is so, stressing the ability to deal with a highly specific skill in isolation may be inappropriate and a waste of valuable instructional time.

Generating appropriate objectives has been a major problem. Popham (34) suggests that those used during the midsixties generated confusion, because they were so poorly defined that they permitted a wide variety of interpretations as to the types of test items that would evaluate them. Niles (29), voices a very different kind of reservation. She maintains that the emphasis on

> precise, measurable goals could result in dissecting reading into minutiae that are never synthesized into a meaningful process. Teachers could find themselves producing readers who can divide words into syllables with great accuracy or analyze a piece of writing for its main ideas but who cannot read in any global or important sense. (p. 106)

The tone of her article also suggests that through this dissection, we may be producing readers who never experience the warmth, excitement, and entertainment that can be a part of personal and recreational reading.

A fourth characteristic of criterion referenced testing is that the items should appear in an established hierarchy or should follow the sequence decided upon for reading instruction.

Prescott (37) is very firm regarding the first alternative. He writes,

> Basically, the criterion-referenced approach is of little value unless the assumption is made that mastery of one skill or bit of informtaion is essential for mastery of another skill or bit of knowledge of a somewhat similar character at a higher level of difficulty or complexity. (p. 352)

He goes on to acknowledge that there is no well-accepted hierarchy of reading skills. The various commercial reading programs follow different sequences. Many of the skills are not hierarchical in the sense of depending on previously acquired skills. Some children may use context clues effectively before demonstrating a knowledge of certain phonic skills, or vice versa. One could, therefore, conclude that given our present state of knowledge about the way people learn to read, using criterion referenced testing is inappropriate. In truth, if we insisted on a hierarchy that was well accepted, it would be necessary to at least temporarily abandon the concept of C-R testing. The more reasonable approach, however, seems to be to arrange the testing of skills in the order in which they appear in a program by which a child is being instructed. This suggests that testing operates most efficiently at this time when considered in relationship to a well-developed instructional program. The program need not be a published one. It can be totally teacher devised, but it does require that the teacher designing the program have some suggested sequence of skill development in mind.

If skills are sequentially arranged, there is much greater potential for determining necessary steps to overcome problems.

A fifth characteristic of criterion referenced testing is that the tasks to be accomplished must be evaluated in the context of a normal reading situation.

Johnson and Kress (21) in effect challenge the position that norm referenced tests can be used for criterion referenced interpretation. They maintain that a multiple-choice format is contradictory to the basic purpose for criterion referenced measures, which they say is finding out if the student can accomplish the task of reading.

Consider these illustrations:

Objective: Given a list of words, the reader will correctly identify the vowel sound with 90 percent accuracy.

Directions to Student: Choose the answer that tells what vowel sound is heard in the following words:

1. poke
   a. short e
   b. long e
   c. long o
   d. short o
2. pail
   a. short i
   b. long i
   c. long a
   d. short a

A number of reading authorities would prefer to have students read the words "pail" or "poke" as a way of evaluating student mastery of vowel sounds. An opposing point of view, however, suggests that some students might be able to read the two words as sight words and therefore not know the generalizations about "silent e" or "two adjacent vowels." Quite likely those in harmony with the Johnson and Kress position would ask if a student really needs to know these generalizations, so long as the word can be correctly identified. Bleismer (1) in advocating the greater use of more "natural" evaluation techniques, raises the question of whether it is not possible for children to be able to accurately syllabicate a list of 30 words and yet not be able to pronounce any of them. He asks if it wouldn't be a more valid procedure to observe what students do when they meet an unknown polysyllabic word in their reading material.

Advantages of C-R Measurement

One of the most frequent criticisms hurled at testing programs is that they have no goals. Reading tests are administered for the sake of administering reading tests. Because criterion referenced testing must begin with the specification for goals and objectives, it certainly can help to avoid needless testing.

Criterion referenced tests might also help to minimize some of the insidious comparisons that are made in schools. Norm referenced tests encourage comparisons between children, and while C-R tests will not eliminate comparisons, they do invite educators to place the emphasis on specific skills and on the question of the extent to which children have mastered the goals of an instructional program. Under these circumstances C-R tests might also help to emphasize the need to recognize individual rates of progress. Teachers, parents, and administrators might be led away from expecting all children who have completed second grade to be finishing at least a second-grade book or scoring at least 3.0 on a standardized test. Unfortunately, some schools have simply substituted the objectives they wish to see mastered for a particular level of a book for a score on a standardized test.

If C-R tests are used appropriately, they could also help to reduce or avoid the negative consequences that result from cultural differences among children. Language differences, background of experience, and other factors may penalize particular groups of children. Standardized test results often make such children appear inferior rather than different. In fact, the whole C-R movement, with an emphasis on progress achieved, could help to reduce the extent to which children are labeled. The emphasis could shift from using tests to define a child as a remedial reader or an l.d. to using test data to help plan an effective instructional program. C-R testing could help achieve the latter objective by employing evaluation tools more frequently, by trying to view learning to read in sequential steps, and by yielding test results that are very much related to the goals of instruction. C-R tests also have the advantage of allowing for revision by the user. Like informal tests, it is permissible to alter, add, and delete items so that the test best suits those taking and those giving it.

Criterion referenced measures generally are better measures to apply when one wishes to evaluate the effectiveness of a new program or of a programming change. Standardized measures tend to be global and rarely can evaluate the goals of a program. One of the outstanding features of C-R measurement is that the evaluation instrument can be built to reflect the programming goals. One is much more likely to see the positive benefits of a good program through well-designed C-R measurement than through a global norm referenced measure. It is difficult to see improvement resulting from instruction reflected in norm referenced tests. If a program has clearly defined goals and if the effectiveness of that program is to be evaluated, it would be most unwise not to use some form of C-R evaluation.

All these considerations contribute to the recognition of the advantages of C-R testing: (1) They force us to examine our goals for a reading program or to set some goals if they have not already been set. (2) They recognize the primacy of instruction over testing. (3) They serve as better measures of the effectiveness of educational programming. When they work well, C-R tests should correspond closely to the instructional program and exist simply to maximize the effectiveness of that program.

Limitations of C-R Tests

Many of the limitations of C-R tests have already been noted. All C-R tests fail to meet a few of the criteria discussed earlier in this chapter. There is no agreed-upon hierarchy of reading skills. Unnecessary items are often included and the presence of unessential items could encourage teaching skills that are unnecessary, thus not allowing for potentially more useful instructional activities. Most C-R measures use just a few items to measure a skill, so that it might be very unsafe to draw conclusions as to whether or not a child has mastered that skill. However, if the number of items per skill area is significantly increased, the tests become too long, and an inordinate amount of time is spent on testing. Some teachers involved in C-R programs complain that so much time is spent on testing that it disrupts the instructional program.

As was indicated earlier, a goal of criterion referenced measurement is to establish whether or not a child has mastered a particular skill. Some of the problems surrounding the concept of mastery have already been noted. There is also the question of what the criterion for mastery should be. Some C-R tests require a student to achieve 80 percent accuracy on a test before moving to a new learning task; other tests require 90 percent; some tests even require 100 percent. Some test manuals clearly indicate that the criteria for mastery are arbitrary. Teachers and specialists should recognize that this is the case. Experience with a particular C-R test may in fact lead a teacher to conclude that a somewhat higher or lower criterion would better serve the children with whom that teacher works.

Sax (41) puts this problem into excellent perspective:

The prespecified standards of proficiency required of students in criterion-referenced tests are not only arbitrary at any given level of instruction, but they are often meaningless, unrelated to the purposes of criterion referencing, and potentially hazardous to students. . . . If the domain is hierarchically arranged and the attainment of one skill is prerequisite to other more complex and essential skills, the teacher's goal should always be 100 percent mastery. . . . If the domain is largely unsequenced, the teacher can as easily establish one criterion as another with equally meaningless justification. (p. 262)

Because C-R tests demand that goals be clearly specified, a program that stresses such measurement could de-emphasize those aspects of reading that are not easily measured and concentrate on easily identifiable skills. Developing a desire to read, enjoying various literary forms, being able to empathize with characters in a book and being able to relate what is read to past and future experiences may be minimized if the C-R program centers around the measurement of only word recognition skills.

The final danger, previously stated, is that, as skills are listed, the process of reading becomes so minutely dissected that any pleasure, excitement, or even utility to be derived from it becomes almost extinguished as students plod through a long list of specific behavioral objectives that never blend to become the active, integrated process of reading.

Forms of Criterion Referenced Evaluation

C-R testing exists in three primary forms. First, there are published C-R measurement systems that are not keyed to any particular program. In general, they include a scope and sequence of skills and thus provide a framework in which skill development can take place. The Wisconsin Design for Reading and The Fountain Valley Design System are illustrations of this approach.

A second major approach is to develop a set of criterion referenced tests to accompany published instructional reading materials. Most of the newer or revised commercial reader systems include such testing materials.

Finally, there are those who use criterion referenced measurement within the framework of informal evaluation.

The second approach is highly specific to particular instructional materials, and therefore will not be discussed further.

Published C-R Measurement Systems (General)

A number of sets of criterion referenced materials are available. There is substantial interest from educational practitioners in these tests and the ways in which they might be used.

The Wisconsin Design for Reading Skill Development is one such program. Other illustrations include: Criterion Reading, The Fountain

Valley Design System, and Read On. New programs are always being developed. All are fairly complex, so only one, the Wisconsin program, will be described here. It was chosen primarily because of its availability and the fact that the author has seen it in use.

The Wisconsin Design for Reading Skill Development is primarily a "management system" for skill development. Its authors appropriately begin by limiting the claims that they make for the program. The teacher's planning guide notes that it is:

> limited to the word recognition skill development aspect of reading. . . . We have made no attempt to describe a total instructional program in reading, the assumption being that viable reading programs are best worked out at the local level. . . . Our assumption is that teachers must accept the responsibility for directing learning experiences which suit their pupils' characteristics and needs. (30, p. 2)

And again:

> Teachers who know their pupils are in the best possible position to guide instruction. For this reason the *Wisconsin Design for Reading* offers neither a definitive reading program nor specific instructional presumptions for any child or school; it offers possibilities. . . . Teachers, not the system or the materials, do the teaching. (p. 5)

The Wisconsin Design has attempted to identify essential skills in six areas: word attack, study skills, comprehension, self-directed reading, interpretive reading, and creative reading. At this time, specific behavioral, or *closed,* objectives have been identified for the first four areas. *Open objectives,* which are not evaluated through pencil-and-paper tests, are identified for the last two areas: interpretive and creative reading. Teacher observation of pupil behavior is necessary in the last two areas.

There are also seven major components to the design:

> 1. *The Outline of Reading Skills.* This is essentially a scope and sequence of reading skills for grades kindergarten through sixth and is similar to those produced by other commercial programs. All the other components of the design are keyed to this outline. The six skill areas are clustered according to grade level (K through 6).
>
> 2. *Statement of Objectives.* Behavioral objectives are written for each of the skills in the areas of word attack, study skills, comprehension, and self-directed reading.
>
> 3. *Guides to Informal, Individual Skill Observation.* These are designed to provide teachers with a flexible and continuous approach to the assessment of skill-related behaviors.
>
> 4. *Wisconsin Tests of Reading Skill Development.* These are

printed tests for specific objectives that are keyed to the outline of reading skills. They can be either individually or group administered.

5. *Individual Skill Development Records.* Pupil profile cards exist for each skill. Cards are preprinted with lists of skills and can be rapidly separated according to students who have and have not mastered particular skills.

6. *Teacher's Resource Files.* Selected published reading materials are keyed to a specific entry or skill in the outline. The teacher's manual suggests that the files are intended to serve as resources, not as prescriptions.

7. *Guidelines for Interpretive and Creative Reading.* These consist of a collection of guidelines for making observations of pupil performance and suggestions for directing pupil activities related to each skill. Resource materials for skill development are suggested.

At the time of this writing specimen sets of materials are available in the areas of word recognition, comprehension, study skills, and self-directed reading. Interested readers should consult these. The preceding description is meant only to provide a brief illustration of an independent C-R system and is not meant to be comprehensive. The Wisconsin Design has the advantage of being fairly widely used so that it can be observed in operation, is comprehensive in nature, acknowledges the importance of skills that cannot be easily measured, and clearly states the preeminence of a good instructional program over evaluation. Its limitations are that it too fails in varying degrees to reflect most of the five characteristics of criterion referenced tests listed earlier in the chapter.

Criteria for Evaluating Published C-R Materials

The following are suggested as guidelines for choosing published criterion referenced materials:

1. The material does not overstate what it can accomplish. No criterion referenced system can eliminate the need for an excellent instructional program or for well-prepared teachers. It should acknowledge the primacy of instruction over testing, and it should acknowledge the importance of reading skills that do not lend themselves to evaluation through published materials.

2. The scope and sequence of reading skills in the C-R program is approximately the same as or similar to the scope and sequence of the instructional program. This guideline suggests that, all other things being equal, the C-R test that accompanies

a set of instructional materials is probably best if those instructional materials are being used.

3. It avoids testing skills that do not appear necessary for reading, and it tests skills in as natural and applied a form as possible.

4. It provides an efficient record-keeping system. If the data from a C-R system are to be used to individualize instruction, the teacher must be guided to use a record-keeping system that is efficient. Otherwise, the test results will simply be filed away and not used.

The guidelines listed above are meant only to be a start for evaluating a published C-R program. It is a very heavy investment that should be made only after serious thought. Before embarking upon it, educators should try to locate some professional, published reviews of the program, and should definitely visit one or two schools where it is in operation. Talking with teachers who are using a C-R testing or management system when they are not in the presence of those responsible for instituting or directing the program can be extremely useful. It is important to obtain as much information as possible. Pros and cons should be investigated and an attempt should be made to determine how well the system will fit into the educational setting for which it is being considered. Actually, this procedure should be followed whenever a decision regarding any important educational change is to be made.

Alternatives to Published C-R Measures

The concept of criterion referenced evaluation should not be confined to published materials. The whole concept of informal reading evaluation discussed in the last chapter can be used in a criterion referenced way. It encourages those concerned with the evaluation of reading skills to decide on an optimal program of reading instruction, define necessary skill components, and choose materials. Portions of the instructional materials are sampled and a child's reading performance on these materials is then analyzed in terms of skills that are absent or present. The advantage of this approach is that it involves little financial outlay; evaluates reading in a very practical, ongoing way; provides close "fit" between evaluation and instruction; and can be introduced slowly, working on one phase of informal evaluation at a time.

Perhaps the most important form of C-R evaluation is the on-going evaluation that a classroom teacher should make in every instructional situation. Again, the old term *diagnostic teaching* seems appropriate. It avoids the unfortunate amount of student testing time that is sometimes used. It offers the opportunity for rechecking initial observations as the children work with new materials. It does require a record-keeping system that is practical and efficient and a teacher who establishes instructional objectives and who can determine whether or not these objectives are being met. Certainly it requires a professional of high caliber, but that should be exactly what a classroom teacher is. Surely we should be willing to designate responsibility for evaluation of reading skills to the person whom we expect to take on the more important and demanding job of teaching reading!

Conclusions Regarding C-R Testing

There is some tendency for professionals in reading to see C-R evaluation as all good or all evil. Obviously, such is not the case. Excessive, unnecessary testing has been done in the name of C-R evaluation. Programs have made specific skill development the only important goal, thus detracting from the concept of reading as an active, thinking, creative process; however, the concept of C-R evaluation cannot and should not be dismissed because of its misuse. In most respects it offers far more valuable information for instructional planning than does norm referenced evaluation. It needs to be put in a form that yields useful information to teachers. The form that it takes will need to vary from one instructional situation to another.

STANDARDIZED READING TESTS

In a 1968 article, Davis (7) cited evidence which indicated that at least 37 million standardized achievement tests were being administered to school-aged children each year. In spite of their widespread use, there is often confusion as to what standardized tests are and how their results can be used.

Characteristics of Standardized Reading Tests

In order for a test to be termed standardized it must possess at least the following characteristics:

1. *It Must Have Norms.* Standardized tests are norm referenced tests; that is, they tell how an individual who takes a test compares to others who have taken it. In order to "norm," or standardize, a test, the author or publisher of the test arranges to administer it to a group of individuals that seem to be representative of some total group. The smaller group to whom the test is actually given is considered a *sample* of the total group. For example, the author or publisher may want to know the average achievement of third graders in the United States, but he or she settles for testing 1000 third graders. It is often assumed that the 1000 are a representa-

tive sample of all third graders in this country. This sample then becomes the *norm group,* and their performance yields the normative information, or *norms,* against which the performance of anyone else who takes the test is compared.

2. *A Standardized Test Must Include Data Which Establish Its Reliability and Validity.* These concepts will be discussed more thoroughly later in this chapter. Basically, reliability is the extent to which a measurement instrument is consistent in the test results it yields. Validity is the extent to which a test really measures what it says it will measure.

3. *There Must Be Clear, Well-Defined Directions for Administering and Scoring.* Unless the directions are explicit enough for the administration of the test to be essentially the same for all who take it, confusion and unfair comparisons would result. For example, if one examiner limited a group of children to 10 minutes for completing a test, while another examiner gave another group unlimited time, both groups could not be compared to the norm group, because the second group would have an obvious advantage.

4. *It Usually Yields What Appears to Be a Precise Numerical Score Rather Than a Description of a Child's Performance.* The most typical forms for reporting scores will soon be discussed in this chapter.

Beyond these very general characteristics, standardized reading tests vary considerably among themselves. At least three kinds can be distinguished: survey tests, which are meant to be general measures of reading; group diagnostic tests, which aim to measure several components of reading in order to determine strengths and weaknesses; and individual diagnostic tests, which usually aim to provide a detailed, comprehensive diagnostic assessment through administering the test to only one child at a time.

Forms of Test Scores

RAW SCORES. Raw scores are usually the total number of items correct on a test. They usually have little meaning if reported, so they are usually converted or changed to one of the types of scores discussed below.

GRADE SCORES. These are probably the most popular form for reporting scores. They are frequently assumed to reflect a child's grade attainment in reading. For example, a child who achieves a grade score of 5.6 is sometimes said to have mid-fifth-grade reading skills. The last statement is inaccurate, because there is no agreement as to which skills should exist at fifth grade or the level of complexity to which these skills must be developed. Because the grade score does not tell which skills the child was able to demonstrate during the testing, the results have limited diagnostic utility. A more accurate, though admittedly more cumbersome interpretation of a grade score of 5.6 is: The child answered as many items correctly as the average score attained by mid-fifth-grade students who were part of the standardization population. Actually even this is probably not technically correct, because in most test construction procedures children's scores are obtained only at the beginning and end of the year and interpolated to all points in a year. Thus, in most cases, there were no average scores for children in the middle of fifth grade. However, the suggested interpretative statement is accurate enough for most practical purposes.

The interpretation of grade scores suggested above points out that the comparison is only in terms of number of items answered correctly (not *which* items are answered correctly) and that the score is based upon comparisons with a specific group of individuals, those in the standardization population.

PERCENTILES. Percentile scores give some information about how high or how low an individual's score was when compared with the scores obtained by the standardization population. Children whose percentile score is 63 did better than 63 percent of the standardization population; 63 percent of the scores were lower than theirs. By the same reasoning, 37 percent of the standardization population did better than they. Percentage scores are quite different. They usually tell what percent of the items were correctly identified. Percentage scores are not regularly used in standardized tests of reading, but are frequently used in teacher-constructed tests.

One major drawback with percentile scores is that the intervals or distances between various percentiles are not equal. For example, it would take far more growth in reading for students to move from the ninetieth to the ninety-fifth percentile than it would to move from the fiftieth to the fifty-fifth percentile. Because of this inequality, percentile scores should not be numerically manipulated. For example, they should not be averaged, nor should they be subtracted from each other in order to assess growth in reading.

STANDARD SCORES. Standard scores are mathematically and statistically the most acceptable form for reporting test results; however, standard scores are among the least popular ways of submitting test results to teachers. Some teachers have difficulty interpreting them because standard scores depend on two other statistics: the mean and standard deviation. Both of these statistics will be explained shortly. For the present, let us simply define a standard score as one where the raw score has been adjusted in terms of the mean and standard deviation. When numerically manipulating scores, standard scores should be used.

Among the most widely used standard scores is the *stanine,* which is an abbreviation for "standard nine." When this standard score is used, scores are converted into values ranging from one to nine. Stanine scores have a mean of five and a standard deviation of two. A stanine value of one is the lowest possible score, and a stanine of nine is the highest.

TEST CONCEPTS AND STATISTICS

Many teachers and reading specialists become instantly terrified upon meeting the term "statistics" or upon needing to interpret any numerical information. As long as this continues, they will be looked upon as intellectually limited and will remain unnecessarily dependent upon professionals from other areas. In most cases, teachers and reading specialists do not need to calculate statistics, but they do need to be able to interpret them. The explanations which are suggested in the next part of this chapter are meant to lead to a greater understanding of a few elementary statistical concepts that are essential to understanding reading test results.

Two primary branches of statistics are descriptive statistics and inferential statistics.

Descriptive Statistics

The primary purpose here is to summarize scores and to make them more manageable and understandable. For example, if we had the reading scores for 120 second grade students, looking at one score after another would be quite cumbersome, and we might be left with a very incomplete or even distorted picture of the overall performance after going through all these individual scores.

One of the simplest techniques might be to arrange the scores from highest to lowest. This arrangement can be called a *distribution.* We might go further and group scores in order to summarize our results. For example, instead of listing scores of 1.1, 1.1, 1.2, 1.2, 1.2, 1.2, 1.2, 1.3, 1.3, 1.3, 1.3, 1.3, 1.4, 1.4, 1.4, 1.5, 1.5, 1.5, 1.5, 1.5, 1.5, etc., which appear at the lowest end of our listing of scores, we might group scores between 1.1 and 1.5 and note that there are 20 scores which fall within this range. We might also find 35 scores in the range 1.6–2.0. This is the beginning of a frequency distribution. It groups data and

TABLE 5.1
Frequency Distribution for Reading Grade Scores

Grade Score	Number of Students
1.1–1.5	20
1.6–2.0	35
2.1–2.5	45
2.6–3.0	20

lists and the number of scores falling within each of the groups. The 120 second-grade scores might be summarized as in Table 5.1 and Figure 5.3.

It is often helpful to plot the results of a distribution or a frequency distribution and present the results in graphic form (called a frequency diagram).

Averages

In addition to grouping scores, it is frequently desirable to know something about the average performance of a group. The most frequently used descriptive statistic here is the *mean,* which is simply the average calculated by adding together all the scores and dividing by the number of scores.

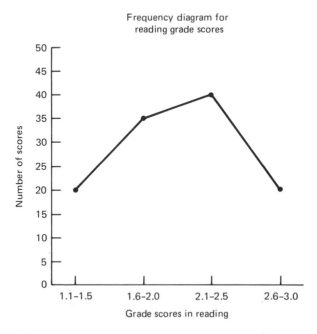

Frequency diagram for reading grade scores

FIGURE 5.3

Two other statistics are sometimes used to describe an average performance. The *median* is the score above which and below which 50 percent of the scores lie. The *mode* is the score which occurs most frequently. In a *normal distribution* (see p. 126) the mean, median, and mode all have the same value.

Measures of Dispersion

In addition to the information about the average performance, it is frequently helpful to know something about how "spread out" the scores are, that is, how variable they are. In working with a classroom of fifth graders, knowing that the average score is 5.3 may be helpful, but it would also be very important to know something about how variable these scores are. For example, at the simplest level, knowing that the reading scores ranged from 4.5 to 5.7 would help and would certainly have far different implication for a teacher than if the scores ranged from 1.5 to 8.5. In both cases, it would be possible for the mean to be 5.3.

A statistic called the *range* can be computed by subtracting the lowest from the highest number in the distribution of scores. One serious limitation of the range is that it is very much affected by extreme scores. In the example just cited, it may be that there was only one individual with a score of 1.5 and only one with a score of 8.5, all other scores could be very closely clustered around the mean of 5.3. This would not be reflected in the range.

A second measure of dispersion, and one which avoids some of the disadvantages of the range, is the *mean deviation*. It is computed by: (1) subtracting the mean score from each of the individual scores in the distribution, (2) adding each of these differences, ignoring the positive (+) or negative (−) value of the difference, and (3) dividing the sum by the number of cases.

The average deviation is not a frequently used statistic, because it is difficult to work with from a mathematical point of view. A statistic which is more mathematically acceptable and very frequently used is the *standard deviation* (S.D.). It is similar in logic to the average deviation. Its formula is:

$$\text{S.D.} = \sqrt{\frac{\text{The Sum of (Scores} - \text{Mean})^2}{\text{Number of Scores}}}$$

The S.D., therefore, is based on the extent to which individual scores deviate from the mean or average score. The S.D. describes a set of scores by telling how far they are spread out.

Tables 5.2 and 5.3 present two distributions which have the same mean but very different standard deviations. The S.D. for distribution *A*

TABLE 5.2
Illustration A: Standard Deviation

The Score (X)	The Score — The Mean (X − X̄)	Difference Squared (X − X̄)²
6.0	1.0	1.00
5.9	0.9	0.81
5.9	0.9	0.81
5.9	0.9	0.81
5.8	0.8	0.64
5.7	0.7	0.49
5.7	0.7	0.49
5.5	0.5	0.25
5.3	0.3	0.09
5.3	0.3	0.09
5.3	0.3	0.09
5.1	0.1	0.01
5.0	0.0	0.00
5.0	0.0	0.00
5.0	0.0	0.00
5.0	0.0	0.00
5.0	0.0	0.00
4.8	−0.2	0.04
4.8	−0.2	0.04
4.8	−0.2	0.04
4.8	−0.2	0.04
4.5	−0.5	0.25
4.5	−0.5	0.25
4.5	−0.5	0.25
4.5	−0.5	0.25
4.3	−0.7	0.49
4.1	−0.9	0.81
4.0	−1.0	1.00
4.0	−1.0	1.00
4.0	−1.0	1.00
Total = 150.0		**Sum of $(X − \bar{X})^2 = 11.04$**

(Table 5.2) is 0.6, or approximately half a grade level. The S.D. for distribution B (Table 5.3) is 2.5, or two and a half grade levels. The second distribution is far more spread out, as reflected by the fact that its S.D. is four times that of distribution A. Distribution A is a much more homogeneous population.

$$\text{Mean} = \frac{\text{Total of Scores}}{\text{Number of Scores}} = \frac{150}{30} = 5$$

$$\text{S.D.} = \sqrt{\frac{\text{The Sum of (Scores − Mean)}^2}{\text{Number of Scores}}} = \sqrt{\frac{11.04}{30}} = \sqrt{0.368} = 0.6$$

124

TABLE 5.3
Illustration B: Standard Deviation

The Score (X)	The Score — The Mean (X − X̄)	Difference Squared (X − X̄)²
8.3	3.3	10.89
8.2	3.2	10.24
8.2	3.2	10.24
8.0	3.0	9.00
7.5	2.5	6.25
7.4	2.4	5.76
7.1	2.1	4.41
7.0	2.0	4.00
7.0	2.0	4.00
7.0	2.0	4.00
6.5	1.5	2.25
6.1	1.1	1.21
6.1	1.1	1.21
5.9	0.9	0.81
5.8	0.8	0.64
5.6	0.6	0.36
5.3	0.3	0.09
5.0	0.0	0.00
4.1	−0.9	0.81
3.3	−1.7	2.89
3.2	−1.8	3.24
3.2	−1.8	3.24
2.8	−2.2	4.84
2.7	−2.3	5.29
2.1	−2.9	8.41
1.5	−3.5	12.25
1.4	−3.6	12.96
1.3	−3.7	13.69
1.2	−3.8	14.44
1.2	−3.8	14.44

Total = 150.0   **Sum of** $(X − \bar{X})^2$ = 182.83

$$\text{Mean} = \frac{\text{Total of Scores}}{\text{Number of Scores}} = \frac{150}{30} = 5$$

$$\text{S.D.} = \sqrt{\frac{\text{The Sum of (Scores} - \text{Mean})^2}{\text{Number of Scores}}} = \sqrt{\frac{182.83}{30}}$$

$$= \sqrt{6.09} = 2.47, \text{ or } 2.5$$

None of the above would have been reflected in the mean scores, because the mean for both distributions is exactly the same.

The median for distribution *A* (a point between the fifteenth and sixteenth scores; half of the scores are above and half below this point) is 5.0. The median for distribution *B* is higher than for *A*. While distribution *B* certainly has some very high scores, the median would fail to reflect the fact that there are some very poor achievers in distribution *B*. Distribution *A* has no one who scored below 4.0, while there are 11 scores below 4.0 in distribution *B*.

The standard deviation, then, is a very important fundamental statistic. It, plus some measure of central tendency, do a great deal to describe a distribution of scores.

The Normal Curve

The concept of the normal curve is very popular and useful in education. It is based on a mathematical equation that is impractical to discuss here. However, it has been found that many human characteristics closely approximate the form of a normal curve if very large numbers of subjects were measured. If a distribution of scores approximates the shape of a normal curve when it is plotted, the distribution is said to be normal. In a normal distribution, most of the scores are near the mean, and there are few scores which are extreme, that is, far from the mean. Scores in reading and other achievement tests often approach the form of a normal curve when large numbers of subjects are used.

It is very helpful to be able to assume scores will arrange themselves in a normal distribution, because mathematical normal distributions have a specified percentage of scores that fall within various standard deviations from the mean, as illustrated in Figure 5.4. The units of measurement for the standard deviation are always the units used by the measuring device. In reading, the measuring device may be a test and the standard deviation units may be, for example, grade scores or they may be standard scores.

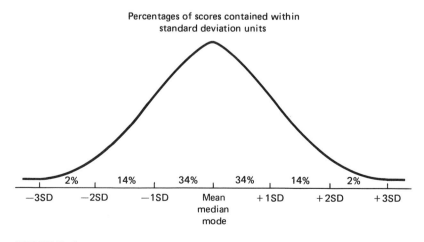

Percentages of scores contained within standard deviation units

FIGURE 5.4

Thus, in a normal distribution approximately 34 percent of all scores will fall between the mean and the distance to one standard deviation above the mean. Similarly, 34 percent of the cases will fall between the mean and distance to one standard deviation below the mean. Therefore, slightly more than two-thirds of the scores from a normal distribution will be within one standard deviation on either side of the mean. Between one standard deviation and two standard deviations, there are 14 percent of the cases, and only 2 percent between the second standard deviation and the third. Over 99 percent of the cases will fall between +3 standard deviations and −3 standard deviations.

There are a wide variety of ways in which this information can be used. For example, if we know that the word recognition scores for all the third-grade classes in a school have a mean grade score of 3.5, and if we know that the standard deviation is 0.8 of a grade score, we know that about 68 percent of the scores fall between 4.3 and 2.7. If, for example, we know that Jane obtained a word recognition score of 5.1, we could conclude that she scored well above the mean and that, in fact, she did better than approximately 98 percent of the students who took the test. (She is two standard deviations *above* the mean. Fifty percent of the cases are below the mean; she did better than they. Thirty-four percent of the cases are one standard deviation above the mean, she did better than they; likewise, she did better than the 14 percent who were between one and two standard deviations above the mean. Thus, 50 + 34 + 14 = 98). We can also say that she scored at about the ninety-eighth percentile.

The above are just two examples of the way an understanding of the mean, the standard deviation, and the properties of a normal curve allow us to make meaningful interpretations.

Standard and Transformed Scores

As indicated earlier, standard scores are raw scores that have been adjusted in terms of the mean and standard deviation. Knowing that one child achieved a raw score of 40 on test *A* and that another child achieved a raw score of 55 on test *B* tells us essentially nothing, because we know nothing about the number of items on each test, the difficulty of the two tests, and so forth. Knowing that the mean on test *A* is 30 and the mean on test *B* is 40 provides some additional information. We now know that both students scored above the mean, but we are still not in a position to discuss how well they did relative to each other. By adding the information that the standard deviation of test *A* was 5 and the standard deviation of test *B* was 10, we can begin to make comparisons through the use of standard scores. A standard score is computed by subtracting the mean score from the raw score and dividing the difference by the standard deviation. See Table 5.4.

TABLE 5.4

	Raw Score	Test Mean	Test Standard Deviation
Child A	40	30	5
Child B	55	40	10

$$\text{Standard Score} = \frac{\text{Raw Score} - \text{Mean}}{\text{S.D.}}$$

$$\text{Child A} \quad \text{Standard Score} = \frac{40 - 30}{5} = 2$$

$$\text{Child B} \quad \text{Standard Score} = \frac{55 - 40}{10} = 1.5$$

Thus, assuming that the standardization populations were similar for both tests, child *A* did relatively better than child *B*.

Standard scores can also be readily changed to percentile scores if one assumes that the scores obtained in the standardization were normally distributed. Many statistics texts contain tables indicating the percent of cases lying below a particular score (e.g., 35, pp. 386–395). For example, a standard score of 2 corresponds to a percentile rank of approximately 98; a standard score of 1.5 corresponds to the ninety-third percentile.

Some educators object to using standard scores, because these scores look very unusual to teachers and because they frequently require use of decimals. Standard scores can be transformed so that both the means and standard deviations can be set at any desired value. The procedure is to multiply the standard score by the desired standard deviation and add the desired mean value. For example, intelligence test scores frequently have means set at 100 and standard deviations set at 15. For the two scores discussed above, the procedure would be:

Child A: Transformed Score = $(2 \times 15) + 100$, or 130
Child B: Transformed Score = $(1.5 \times 15) + 100$, or 122.5 = 123

In some cases, transformed scores are desirable in order to communicate scores more effectively or in order to draw comparisons easily.

Correlation

DEFINITION AND EXAMPLES. Correlation refers simply to the extent to which two variables are related to each other. A score on some variable is a characteristic of a person or object being studied. For example, one might ask how performance on reading test *A* (variable 1)

TABLE 5.5

	Number Correct Botel Word Recognition	*Number Correct California Reading Test*
Harry	60	90
Alice	56	84
Sue	52	78
Tom	48	72
Jack	40	60

is related to performance on reading test *B* (variable 2) at second grade. In order to compute the extent to which a relationship exists (a correlation), it is necessary to have two pieces of information (in this case, scores) about each subject. Thus, each individual would need to take both test *A* and test *B*. Just as means and standard deviations are used to describe a distribution, correlation coefficients describe the relationship between two distributions.

Consider Table 5.5, in which hypothetical scores for five children are listed.

Notice that the relationship is what is called a *perfect* one. Harry answered the greatest number of items correctly on test *A* and on test *B*. Jack had the poorest performance on both tests. The ranking of each child is the same on both tests.

The relationship would be even clearer if the scores were plotted on a scattergram, as illustrated in Figure 5.5.

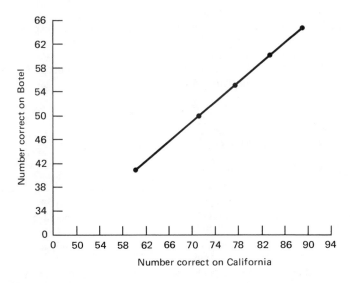

FIGURE 5.5

Students often find it helpful to actually calculate correlations in order to obtain a clearer idea of what a correlation is. Therefore, the data on the five students presented in Table 5.5 is used to calculate a correlation. Each step and all terms are explained.

There are several formulas that can be used to calculate correlation. The following, though ominous looking, is probably the best to use in developing a clearer concept of a correlation.

$$r = \frac{\dfrac{\Sigma XY - (\Sigma X)(\Sigma Y)}{n}}{\sqrt{\Sigma X^2 - \dfrac{(\Sigma X)^2}{n}}\sqrt{\Sigma Y^2 - \dfrac{(\Sigma Y)^2}{n}}}$$

Where:

r = The correlation coefficient.

X = Scores on one test (e.g., number correct on the Botel Reading Inventory).

Y = Scores on another test (e.g., number correct on the California Reading Test).

Σ = Greek letter sigma; in statistics it stands for "the sum of."

n = The number of pairs of scores under consideration (there are five pairs of scores in this illustration).

ΣX = The sum of the values of the X scores (the Botel in this illustration).

ΣX^2 = The sum of the squared values of X.

$(\Sigma X)^2$ = The sum of the values of X are squared.

[ΣY, ΣY^2 and $(\Sigma Y)^2$ are interpreted just as the corresponding X values.]

In using the above formula, it is helpful to arrange scores and to calculate values as shown in Table 5.6.

TABLE 5.6
Information Needed to Calculate a Correlation Coefficient

STUDENT	X	X^2	Y	Y^2	XY
A	60	3600	90	8100	5400
B	56	3136	84	7056	4704
C	52	2704	78	6084	4056
D	48	2304	72	5184	3456
E	40	1600	60	3600	2400
	$\Sigma X = 256$	$\Sigma X^2 = 13344$	$\Sigma Y = 384$	$\Sigma Y^2 = 30024$	$\Sigma XY = 20016$
		$(\Sigma X)^2 = 65536$		$(\Sigma Y)^2 = 147456$	

Substituting the values listed in Table 5–6 into the formula:

$$r = \sqrt{\frac{\dfrac{\Sigma XY - (\Sigma X)(\Sigma Y)}{n}}{\sqrt{\dfrac{\Sigma X^2 - (\Sigma X)^2}{n}} \; \sqrt{\dfrac{\Sigma Y^2 - (\Sigma Y)^2}{n}}}}$$

$$r = \sqrt{\frac{20016 - \dfrac{(256)(384)}{5}}{\sqrt{13344 - \dfrac{65536}{5}} \; \sqrt{30024 - \dfrac{147456}{5}}}}$$

$$r = \sqrt{\frac{20016 - \dfrac{98304}{5}}{\sqrt{13344 - 13107.2} \; \sqrt{30024 - 29491.2}}}$$

$$r = \sqrt{\frac{20016 - 19660}{\sqrt{236.8} \; \sqrt{532.8}}}$$

$$r = \sqrt{\frac{356}{(15.39)(23.08)}}$$

$$r = \sqrt{\frac{356}{355.2}}$$

$$r = 1.00$$

Correlations of 1.00 are essentially never found in education or in most social or behavioral science areas. A correlation of 1.00 is called a *perfect correlation,* because performance on one test can be perfectly predicted from performance on another. The higher a person's performance on one test, the higher the performance on the test that is perfectly correlated with it. It is also possible to have a perfect negative relationship ($r = -1.00$). The hypothetical data in Table 5.7 represent a perfect negative relationship.

Again the two variables are related, but in a very different way. Mark has the highest score in the first column and the lowest score in the second. Edna, who has the lowest score on the first variable, has the highest score on the second. Plotted, the relationship would look like Figure 5.6.

Once again, the relationship is a perfect one, but the slope of the line

TABLE 5.7

	Number of Word Recognition Errors	*Number of Comprehension Questions Answered*
Mark	40	8
Carl	32	10
Sid	25	12
Sandy	20	14
Edna	12	16

is reversed. Figure 5.4 shows a perfect positive relationship $(+1.00)$, while Figure 5.5 shows a perfect negative relationship (-1.00). Perfect negative relationships are just as useful and just as rare as perfect positive relationships. In a positive relationship, two sets of scores rise or fall simultaneously; in a negative relationship, as one set of scores increases, the other decreases.

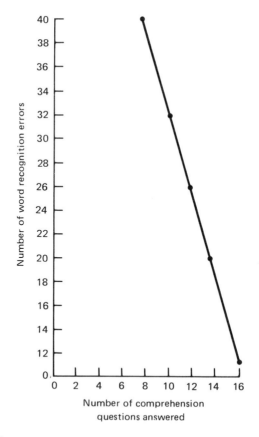

FIGURE 5.6

TABLE 5.8

	Number of Minutes on School Bus	Number Right on Reading Test
Marsha	10	50
Ed	10	40
Tim	10	30
Esther	10	20
Sally	10	10

In the middle of the continuum lies a situation where two sets of scores are totally unrelated. Consider this hypothetical relationship between scores on a reading test and number of minutes spent riding the school bus to school. All five of the children rode the school bus for 10 minutes, but they achieved very different scores on the reading test. Table 5.8 shows both sets of figures.

These scores are plotted in Figure 5.7.

The scores and *scattergram* illustrate a situation in which there is no relationship between performance on the two variables. All students ride the bus for 10 minutes, but they receive different scores on a reading test. The correlation between these variables is 0.0. It is rare to find such a clear cut correlation in education and in the field of reading.

INTERPRETING CORRELATIONS. Correlations of −1.00, +1.00, or 0.0 are easily interpreted, but what about 0.70? What is an

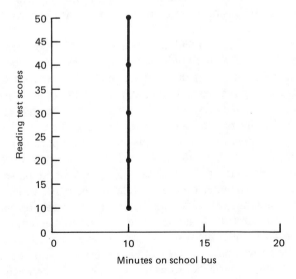

FIGURE 5.7

adequate correlation? What is considered high? These and a host of other questions could be raised about interpreting correlations.

There is a temptation to interpret a correlation as a percentage, but this is a completely inaccurate procedure. Correlations in their usual form are, in fact, very difficult to interpret. Perhaps the easiest and most appropriate way to understand a correlation is to square it and then multiply by 100. The number obtained from squaring the correlation is interpreted as the percent of the variance of one measure that is shared by the other measure. It is a reflection of the extent to which two measures vary (increase or decrease) together. For example, if the correlation were perfect ($r = 1.0$), it would mean that as one measure increases, the other to which it has been correlated always increases also. If the first measure decreases, the other also always decreases. A correlation of 1.0 when squared is still 1.0 and when multiplied by 100 is 100.

Thus, $r = 1.0$ is still 1.0 when squared and is 100 when multiplied by 100. It means that 100 percent of the variance (increase or decrease) in performance on one variable is accounted for by performance on another variable. We could predict perfectly that as one measure increases or decreases, the other will do likewise every time. In Figure 5–4, 100 percent of the variance in scores on test A is accounted for by performance on test B. That is why the score on test B can be predicted perfectly from the performance on test A and vice versa. There is complete overlap between the two variables. Notice that when -1.0 is squared, it becomes $+1$ and when multiplied by 100 is 100; again suggesting that 100 percent of whatever makes for failure on one variable also makes for success on the other. In Figure 5.5 whatever makes for success in comprehension is accounted for by measuring word recognition errors.

In one study, the correlation between the Metropolitan Reading Readiness Test and a first-grade achievement test was 0.66. We can conclude that 44 percent of the variance of the achievement test scores is accounted for by the reading readiness test. This could be interpreted as the proportion of the variance in the reading test that can be accounted for by the readiness test. The r^2 is sometimes called the *coefficient of determination* (39), because it is the proportion of the variance of one variable that can be determined by another variable. The utility and limitations of a correlation can be kept in perspective by squaring it. For example, even a correlation of 0.70, which is rather high for educational research, suggests that one measure can predict only about 50 percent of the variance that occurs in another. Quite obviously, 50 percent of the variance remains unaccounted for.

Correlation questions are also often concerned with the extent of shared variation or variance. Consider the r of 0.81 between the total reading score found between performance on the California Achievement Test and the total reading score on the Prescriptive Reading Inventory (25). The *r* squared is 0.656, and our interpretation would be that 66 percent of the variation on one reading test is shared by the other. In diagram form, it can be expressed as below:

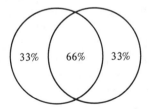

If each circle represents the total variance on each of the tests, we see that there is a 66 percent overlap between the two. Approximately 33 percent of the variance in each of the tests is not shared by the other. Thus, both tests have some unique variance; that is, individual's scores vary because of some factors that are unique to each test.

Notice that none of the above interpretations in any way implied causation. There is a constant tendency to want to say that one factor causes another. Some studies show rather high correlations (above 0.80) between intelligence and reading. There is a temptation, therefore, to say that high intelligence causes good reading. This is not an appropriate way to interpret correlations. In fact, it may be that people's ability to read "causes" them to do well on the intelligence test. It is also possible that some third factor, for example motivation, is a "cause" of the performance on both the intelligence and the reading test. A caution that frequently bears repeating is: Correlation does not imply causation.

In addition to interpreting the variance accounted for there are other ways of interpreting correlations. One is to ask the question: Is it likely that the correlation obtained is due only to chance or random factors? For example, if one tossed a coin, one would expect heads to appear on the basis of chance 50 percent of the time. Therefore, the probability of getting heads is really fairly high, simply on the basis of chance. However, the probability of getting heads twice in a row is only 1 out of 4, or 25 percent, so it is less likely that heads will come up on two consecutive coin tosses. The probability of getting ten heads in ten coin tosses is extremely unlikely; in fact, the probability is only 1 in 1024. Thus, if 10 heads appeared in 10 tosses, one would become very suspicious that something other than chance was influencing the results.

A somewhat similar approach can be taken in looking at correlations. A correlation of 0.10 almost certainly reflects no real relationship, but instead reflects a chance relationship; a correlation of 0.90 is most unlikely to be due to chance. What about correlations in-between?

As an illustration, one study found a correlation of 0.35 between the scores from the I.T.P.A. administered in kindergarten and first-grade reading scores. What is the likelihood that a correlation this high is due to chance? Tables in statistics texts allow one to answer that question. If, in the illustration above, the number of subjects were only 20, the correlation of 0.35 would not be considered significant. The probability is greater than 5 out of 100 (0.05 or 5 percent) that a correlation this high is due to chance. However, the original study from which these subjects were drawn used a total of 53 subjects and yielded a correlation of 0.36. The table in Guilford's book (17, p. 538) indicates that this high a correlation for this number of subjects would occur by chance less than 1 out of every 100 times ($p < 0.01$).

Level of probability is a form in which many statistics are reported. It is usually written as $p < 0.05$ or $p < 0.01$. The $p < 0.05$ means that a relationship of the magnitude obtained occurs, on the basis of chance factors, 5 times out of 100. The $p < 0.01$ means that the relationship can be expected to occur only 1 time out of every 100 because of chance.

In most educational research studies, if the probability level is greater than 0.05, it is usually concluded that the results are due to chance, rather than systematic factors. Again, consider the illustration of the correlation of 0.35 between I.T.P.A. and reading scores for 20 subjects. Because the probability was greater than 0.05 that the relationship was due to chance, the conclusion would be drawn that the I.T.P.A. does not predict later reading achievement.

Teachers often ask, "How high does a correlation have to be in order to be good?" Many statisticians take a noncommittal stance, which is appropriate, because the question is complex to answer. How "good" a correlation is depends on what is being measured and what the typical correlations in this area tend to be. For example, in alternate form reliability, one might expect an r of 0.90; in predicting first-grade reading achievement, a correlation of 0.70 or above is usually quite good. The uses to be made of the correlations is also an important consideration. For example, one could accept lower reliability correlations for tests to be used for making statements about groups of students than one would accept for diagnostic tests that will yield data about an individual. Cost may also be a factor. If a three hour, individually administered battery of tests in kindergarten yielded an r of 0.76, the correlation —and the test—might not be considered very worthwhile, because of the tremendous cost and time expenditures necessary to obtain the predictive information.

If pressed, some writers are willing to establish some general guidelines, such as: the reliability for a test whose scores are going to be used for individual (as opposed to group) evaluation should be approximately 0.90. Some suggest (14) that correlations from 0.20–0.40 are low; 0.40–0.70 are moderate; and anything above 0.70 is high. In the final analysis, however, the utility of a correlation must be judged on the basis of rather complex criteria.

Reliability and Validity

DEFINITIONS. The preceding discussions should lead to a better understanding of the concepts of reliability and validity, two concepts very central to tests and testing. *Reliability* is a measure of a test's stability; that is, the extent to which it offers consistent results. Examples from physical measurement are usually offered to create an understanding of reliability. For example, it would be very difficult to try to obtain the measurements of a room with a ruler of variable length that was continually giving different results. Certainly, struggling dieters wouldn't tolerate scales that yielded a different weight each time they stepped on them. The basic question with reliability, then, is: Does it consistently give the same results if nothing has happened to change the thing that is being measured?

Validity, on the other hand, goes a step further and asks if the test measures what it says it is measuring. Reliability is the more fundamental of the two concepts. It is essentially impossible to have a valid test unless it is reliable, but it is possible to conceive of a reliable test that is not valid. For example, suppose we decided that reading comprehension could be measured directly by measuring the circumference of the reader's head. We might be able to get consistent (i.e., reliable) results, but they would not be valid; the results would not be measures of reading achievement.

FORMS OF RELIABILITY. There are a number of ways in which the reliability of a test can be approached. For example, some tests have more than one form. As an illustration, the 1976 edition of the Metropolitan Readiness Test has a Form P and a Form Q. Both are assumed to be measuring the same thing and a person taking Form P should obtain essentially the same score from Form Q. This is called *alternate form reliability*. A high correlation should be found between scores obtained by the same individuals on the two forms.

A second form of reliability relates to the extent to which there is stability of results over time. If you are given the same test two weeks apart, and no appreciable learning has occurred, you would anticipate obtaining essentially the same score. This form of reliability is referred to as *test-retest reliability* and is a measure of the stability of test results.

There is also the question of the extent to which a test is internally consistent; that is, whether people do as well on one part of a test as they do on another. The way in which this form of reliability is assessed is to correlate performance in one-half of the test with performance on the other half. This is often referred to as *split-half* or *odd-even reliability,* because the most common procedure is to correlate the performance of a group of subjects on the odd-numbered test items with their performance on the even numbered items. Reading-test manuals that report split-half reliability usually refer to the Spearman Brown Formula or the Kuder Richardson Formula. Further elaboration of these formulas seems unnecessary for this text. It would appear sufficient to know that they are measures of internal consistency.

The final form of reliability to be considered is *interscorer reliability*. This reflects the extent to which different examiners could score the same tests and obtain the same results and arrive at the same interpretations. For example, interscorer reliability will probably be near perfect when different people score a multiple-choice standardized test, but less so when they record oral reading errors on an informal reading inventory.

JUDGING RELIABILITY. Test users would like to have some definite guidelines for evaluating the reported reliability coefficients that appear in test manuals. One guideline that is frequently suggested is that a test should have a reliability coefficient of at least 0.90 if the test is to be used to make decisions about individual children. Somewhat less rigor is demanded if the results are used to make decisions about groups of children.

The question of reliability is also important for interpreting subtests within a test. There is substantial interest in trying to diagnostically interpret subtests to find particular strengths or weaknesses in reading. At the simplest level, standardized survey tests often have subtests of word recognition and comprehension and many users would like to be able to separate word recognition problems from comprehension problems on the basis of relative performance on these subtests. This type of interpretation is inappropriate unless the subtests have high reliability. The reliability of the subtests should begin to approach an r of 0.90. Interpreting subtest scores which are less reliable is justifiable if the interpretations are used nondogmatically as starting points for more reliable evaluation. A later chapter discusses the interpretation of subtests from the Wechsler Intelligence Scale for Children (Revised Form) in tentative terms.

Another criterion that might be used is that the more forms of reliability that are reported in a test manual the better. In the opinion of the authors, there is an overuse of split-half reliability with the resultant exclusion of other forms of reliability being reported. A final suggestion is that reliability should be looked at realistically. It is rare to choose a test in a vacuum; comparisons are usually drawn between reliabilities of different tests that seem to satisfy the purposes for which a test is to be administered.

STANDARD ERROR OF MEASUREMENT. One of the most useful descriptive statistics for test users is the *standard error of measurement*. It is an estimate of the extent to which a score that an individual obtains on a test deviates from that individual's *true score*. The true score is a statistical concept which cannot actually be measured. Theoretically, it is the average of all scores that particular individuals would obtain on a test if they took that test an infinite number of times, and if their performance were not affected by factors such as practice. A true score would not include irrelevant, chance factors (e.g., guessing, physical alertness, and fatigue) that affect obtained scores.

The standard error of measurement is a way of estimating how closely a person's obtained score approximates her or his true score. The standard error of measurement is calculated from the reliability of the test and the standard deviation of the test. The formula is:

$$SeM = \text{Standard Deviation} \sqrt{1 - \text{Reliability}}$$

For a test with perfect reliability ($r = 1.0$), the *SeM* will be equal to zero, that is there would be no error. As the reliability becomes poorer, the standard error increases. For example, if the standard deviation is 15 and the reliability is 0.90, th *SeM* is 4.8, as illustrated in the example below. If the reliability is 0.70, the *SeM* becomes 8.3.

Example 1	Example 2
$SeM = 15 \sqrt{1 - 0.90}$	$SeM = 15 \sqrt{1 - 0.70}$
$= 15 \sqrt{0.10}$	$= 15 \sqrt{0.30}$
$= 15 \ (0.32)$	$= 15 \ (0.55)$
$= 4.8$	$= 8.3$

Many test manuals now report the standard error of measurement, so that the test user does not need to calculate it. It is important, however, to be able to interpret the standard error of measurement. Its interpretation is based on probability and the normal curve. Consider the example of a child who obtains a score of 105 on an IQ test with a standard error of measurement of 4.8. The standard error is interpreted much like a standard deviation. It is assumed that if the person retook the test over and over again, most of the scores (68 percent of them) would fall within (plus or minus) one standard error of measurement. In a normal curve, 68 percent of the scores are expected to be between the mean and one standard deviation above and one standard deviation below the mean. Similar assumptions are made about the relationship between a score and the standard error of measurement.

Following the examples given above, the standard error of measurement is added to the score and subtracted from the score. Thus, 105 − 4.8 = 100.2 and 105 + 4.8 = 109.8. The appropriate interpretation is that the chances are 68 out of 100 (roughly two out of three) that the true score for a person with an obtained score of 105 is somewhere between 100.2 and 109.8.

If there is the need to have greater certainty regarding a person's true score, one can add and subtract two standard error-of-measurement units to the obtained score. Remember, on a normal distribution this will include 95 percent of the cases. Thus, returning to the illustration, one can be 95 percent certain that a person with an obtained score of 105 has a true score between 95.4 and 114.6.

Whenever test scores are used to draw conclusions about a particular student's performance, the standard error of measurement should be taken into consideration. It is much more realistic to think that a child's score on a reading test is probably between 2.3 and 2.9 than to think of it as being 2.6. Using the standard error of measurement is one way of reducing the impression that testing of students is an exact, precise science.

VALIDITY. Just as there are several forms of reliability, there are several types of validity. One of the most frequently employed forms is called *concurrent validity.* It starts with the assumption that there is some established, acknowledged valid measure of some construct, such as reading. The results of a new, less well established test are correlated with the results of the established test, and if there is good agreement (a high correlation) between the two, the new test is considered valid. For example, the authors of the reading section of the Wide Range Achievement Test attempt to show one form of validity by correlating the scores obtained from it with the scores obtained from the New Stanford Paragraph Reading Test. The correlation between the two was 0.81. The authors concluded then that evidence of validity had been offered.

The difficulty in the use of concurrent validity in reading is that there is not good agreement as to which of the existing tests are valid. Authors of a new test are faced with the difficult task of trying to decide on a measure with which they should try to correlate their test of reading. Therefore, judgment must be used on the part of the test users or reviewers in weighing the concurrent validity information offered.

A second widely used form of validity is *predictive validity*. The question here is whether scores obtained at one point in time will predict some behavior at some later point in time. For example, will some screening device administered at the beginning of a school year predict reading achievement test results at the end of the year? Reading readiness tests are frequently subjected to predictive validity scrutiny.

Another form of validity is called *content validity*. It is less used in reading than in other school achievement areas, but probably deserves greater consideration. It asks if the test items are an adequate sampling of the universe that they are said to represent. For example, if a test purported to be a test of word analysis and included only items which were dependent on phonics, one might conclude that this was not a representative sample of items because it totally ignored inclusion of items requiring a knowledge of structural analysis. Content validity is usually dependent on the judgments made by "experts" and, therefore, is often not subjected to formal statistical analysis. The concept is, however, a valuable one and one that the test reviewer should try to apply when looking at test items. Are they a fair and adequate sampling of the area of reading that they say they are measuring? As pointed out previously in this chapter, the concept of content validity seems especially important for criterion referenced measurement.

Construct validity is another approach to validation and one that is more difficult to conceptualize and use. Helmstadter (19) points out that the human characteristics that we are usually interested in measuring (e.g., intelligence, psycholinguistic abilities, reading comprehension) are hypothetical constructs; that is, they are a proposed set of ideas which are used to explain why certain phenomena occur. For example, if people can answer questions after looking at a page of print, we conclude that they did so because of reading comprehension. In this sense, reading comprehension is the hypothetical construct which is used to explain the ability to answer questions. Construct validity asks the question of how well a test matches the construct it says it is measuring. To continue the example, we could propose that the construct of comprehension is composed of two parts: factual recall and interpretive recall. If a test were constructed to measure this particular construct of reading comprehension, we could expect that a person who could answer one factual question could also answer most other factual recall questions of similar difficulty and that a person who had great difficulty with interpretive recall questions would have consistent difficulty. If people tended to perform as expected on the test, there would be some validation of the construct of reading comprehension.

Construct validity is rather complex and, at times, difficult to separate from other forms of validity. More comprehensive discussions, such as that by Helmstadter, should be consulted for a more complete understanding of this form of validity.

TYPES OF STANDARDIZED READING TESTS

Group Survey Tests of Reading

Group survey tests are probably the most popular type of reading tests used in schools. Their purpose is to yield an assessment of overall or general reading achievement rather than a diagnostic assessment of strengths and weaknesses in reading skill development. Survey tests often have subtests of reading vocabulary and reading comprehension. Some also include subtests of study skills and speed of reading. Very frequently two or more subtest scores are combined to form a total reading score. Representative survey reading tests include the reading sections from The Stanford Achievement Test, the California Achievement Test, the Comprehensive Test of Basic Skills, and the Iowa Test of Basic Skills, as well as the Metropolitan Reading Tests and Gates-MacGinitie Reading Tests.

The Gates-MacGinitie Reading Tests will be briefly described as an illustration of a widely used, group-survey reading test. Its discussion does not imply an endorsement of it over others. It was chosen because it seems typical of this type of test and because of its availability.

The Gates-MacGinitie consists of six different levels, ranging from Level Primary A, for use at mid-first to second-grade level, through Level F for tenth, eleventh, and twelfth grades. In addition it includes a readiness test which is suggested for mid-kindergarten and beginning first grades; Level CS is designed to measure speed of reading for grades mid-second to end-third. The levels of the test designed for first to third grades have only two sections: vocabulary and comprehension. The levels designed for fourth through twelfth grades retain these two sections, and a speed and accuracy section is also included. The Level CS may be used, at the examiner's discretion, as a supplementary speed-and-accuracy test for some second- and third-grade students.

At the lowest levels (for grades one and two), the vocabulary subtest consists of a picture and four words for each test item. The reader must choose the word that identifies the picture. For grades four and beyond, each item consists of a stimulus word followed by five other word choices. The reader must choose from the five the one that is the nearest synonym for the stimulus word. The vocabulary subtest for third grade is a combination of the two formats.

The comprehension subtest for grades one and two involves choosing one of four pictures that best depicts what is described in a sentence or short paragraph. At third-grade level, students are to read a paragraph that is followed by two comprehension questions; they must choose the best of four one-word answers to the question. For fourth grade and beyond, the comprehension subtest is essentially a short cloze passage (see p. 154). Words are deleted from a paragraph, blank spaces inserted. The following illustrates the format:

> Comprehension can be   1   in a variety of ways. Standardized measures of   2   comprehension tend to be global in nature.
>
> 1. typed   measured   purchased   prevented
> 2. spelling   watching   reading   arithmetic

The student would be expected to draw a line under the word following the number 1 that best fits into the blank numbered 1.

The speed-and-accuracy subtests consist of very short paragraphs that end with a question or incomplete sentence. The student chooses from four choices the one that best completes the sentence or the one that best answers the question. The publisher distributes both a teacher's manual and a technical manual. The teacher's manual includes clear directions for administering the test, the time limits for the tests (15 minutes for vocabulary, 25 minutes for comprehension, and 5 minutes for speed and accuracy at most levels). Very general information for interpreting scores and tables for converting scores to the grade level, percentile, and standard score equivalents are also included.

The technical manual describes in adequate detail: how items were selected for the test, how the test was standardized (e.g., the tests were administered to a nationwide sample of approximately 40,000 students in 37 specially chosen communities), and evidence of reliability. It also includes a disappointing six sentence discussion of the test's validity. The technical manual also includes some extremely helpful tables that should aid a conscientious, informed test user to draw some useful and realistic conclusions about an individual's or a group's performance on the test. It is disappointing to note that the standard error of measurement for the various forms, levels, and subtests of this test are not all given, though one could calculate them from the available information. However, the technical manual is reasonably comprehensive and includes good examples of the kind of information that should be supplied by a test publisher.

The Gates-MacGinitie is an example of a general, group, standardized, survey reading measure that can be useful if cautiously interpreted. The manuals make no exaggerated claims for the test. For example, in a section dealing with the interpretation of grade scores, the teacher's manual points out:

> The grade scores given in the norms are simply average values; they do not indicate how well a given child should read. . . . [G]rade scores are

not very useful for assessing a child's position relative to others or his grade as he moves through the grades. (p. 5)

Many other cautions are offered. Nowhere do the authors suggest that grade scores should or can be used to plan a student's instructional program, nor do they suggest placing a student at a particular reader level on the basis of a grade score on this test.

Advantages and Limitations of Group Standardized Survey Tests of Reading

Recent editions of survey reading tests are for the most part very carefully and adequately standardized. They are also improved over earlier editions in the information they provide, which should allow test users to judge the reliability and validity of the test. The test manuals also provide very helpful information for interpreting test scores. For example, it is becoming common for the manuals to report the standard error of measurement, which allows for a more realistic estimate of the accuracy of the score.

There are some readily apparent limitations to standardized survey tests. They are not diagnostic. It is very speculative to try to draw conclusions based on the way a child responds to items in the test. This, of course, is not to imply that these tests should be diagnostic. At times the purpose of testing calls for some overall estimate of reading skills.

Most of the standardized survey tests are in multiple-choice format, which does allow a child to guess at items and as a result possibly achieve an inflated score. With multiple-choice tests having four possible answers, the correct answer can be chosen on 25 percent of the items simply by guessing. Thus, if there were 40 items, one might expect a child who guessed at all of them to achieve a score of 10. This is called a *chance score;* Fry (12) refers to it as an orangutan score and presents estimates of chance scores for several commonly used tests. The possibility of artificially high scores is most likely at higher grades where a chance score can yield a grade score of third or fourth. Substantial caution should be used in interpreting the results of survey reading tests taken by severely disabled readers. Similarly, such tests may underestimate the full reading achievement of very superior readers, because test items are primarily chosen so that most can be answered by average students. Only a limited number of challenging items are included in most standardized survey tests. Therefore, one can generalize that survey test scores need to be interpreted very cautiously for extremely good or extremely poor readers.

As pointed out in the discussion of forms of test scores, grade scores need to be interpreted with caution. Few test publishers claim that the grade score achieved in a survey reading test can be used to place an individual child in the appropriate level of a reading program. A child who achieves a grade score of 3.2 may or may not be able to function in a third-reader level book. One frequently hears the generalization that standardized survey tests particularly, and standardized tests in general, overestimate a reader's level of achievement (42). Our clinical experience suggests that this is true in most cases, but not always. Results will vary from one standardized test to the next and not all basal readers designated as a specific level are equally challenging. The strategies individual children use in taking tests will also influence results. Therefore, the best conclusions appear to be: (1) that teachers should be very alert to the possibility that standardized tests will overestimate a reader's instructional level, and, (2) that survey tests do not appear to be the appropriate form of testing to use in order to place a child in instructional materials.

Individual Survey Tests

These are a group of tests that are similar to group survey tests in that they simply survey reading skills and yield only global scores rather than diagnostic information; they are, however, individually administered. Two good examples here are the reading recognition and reading comprehension subtests of the Peabody Individual Achievement Test (PIAT) and the reading section of the Wide Range Achievement Test (WRAT). The PIAT also includes subtests to measure mathematics, spelling, and general information. The reading recognition subtest requires letter naming at the lower levels and identification of individual words without any time limit. The reading comprehension subtest is rather unusual. The subject reads a sentence or sentences, which are then removed. The subject must then choose from four pictures the one that is the best pictorial representation of the sentence or sentences read. In order to make the items increasingly difficult, the vocabulary becomes very challenging and sentence structure more complex. The later items in the test are very artificial sounding.

The manual (8) clearly indicates that the purpose of the PIAT is to provide "a wide-range, *screening* measure of achievement." The authors go on to point out that "when a more intensive study of an individual is required, these results can assist the examiner in selecting the more diagnostic instruments . . . or the more precise measure at a particular level of achievement." The test can be used for readers from kindergarten to twelfth-grade level.

Though the test has limitations, such as a rather artificial way of measuring comprehension and rather low reliability for some subtests, it would seem useful if used for its stated purpose, as a screening device.

In sharp contrast to the modest claims of the PIAT, the WRAT (20) makes very extravagant, far-ranging claims. This test, which has norms for ages 5–45 and above, has spelling, arithmetic, and reading subtests. The reading subtest consists simply of lists of isolated words that the subject is asked to pronounce within 10 seconds. No attempt is made to measure comprehension, because the authors of the test reject comprehension as being an essential part of reading. In spite of the very limited nature of the test, the first page of the manual makes 11 unsubstantiated, undocumented claims for the test, ranging from "the accurate diagnoses of reading, spelling, and arithmetic disabilities in persons of all ages," through "the assignment of children to instructional groups," to use in "validity studies to extract the essential adjustment factors underlying the learning of the basic media of communication." All of this through mere word pronunciation! The manual for this test is one of the best illustrations of claiming far too much for a very limited testing instrument. The WRAT does have the advantage of being rapidly and easily administered and scored. However, a test user without a background in reading could be very misled by the claims made for it.

Advantages and Limitations of Individual Survey Reading Tests

Tests like the two just cited are useful for screening individual children. In most cases they are highly correlated with group survey tests. Thus, if many children must be screened, group tests are preferable; when children are seen individually, tests like those just described are useful. They are often used as screening devices by professionals who are not principally responsible for reading evaluations, such as school psychologists, learning disability specialists, and speech therapists. The major limitations are that they yield data that is not very useful in program planning and that some professionals attribute far too much precision to these measures and use the results inappropriately. In our clinical experience we have also observed a tendency for the WRAT reading subtest to seriously overestimate a child's reading ability.

Standardized Group Diagnostic Tests

These tests attempt to assess particular skill strengths and weaknesses. For example, the Stanford Diagnostic Reading Tests include subtests for reading comprehension, vocabulary, auditory discrimination, syllabication, beginning and ending sounds, blending, and sound discrimination for the level of this test designed for grades two to four. A slightly different list of subtests exist for the level designed for grades four through eight. Other tests that might be classified as diagnostic are the New Developmental Reading Tests which purport to measure four different comprehension skills; the McCullough Word Analysis Tests and the Silent Reading Diagnostic Tests for various word recognition skills.

Advantages and Limitations of Standardized Group Diagnostic Tests

As with all group tests, the obvious advantage is that a large number of tests can be administered in a relatively short period of time. In order to be able to make accurate diagnostic conclusions from these tests, it is necessary to have information which suggests that: (1) the subtest scores are reliable; the correlations should be about 0.90 or above; (2) the various subtests should not show high correlations with each other; if they do, then it does not appear that separate or different reading skills are being measured. In some cases such information is not provided or the evidence provided is weak.

Individual Standardized Diagnostic Tests

Through the use of individual diagnostic tests and the observations of an examiner during the reading evaluation, a comprehensive, detailed analysis of a child's reading skills is possible. Some, such as the Gray Oral Reading Test and the Gilmore Oral Reading Test, focus on a particular aspect of reading; while others, such as the Spache Diagnostic Reading Scales and the Durrell Analysis of Reading Difficulty, attempt to yield overall scores for reading, as well as to measure some specific aspects of reading.

The oral reading tests were among the first tests systematically used to measure reading. The popular Gray Oral Reading Test is an outgrowth of the Oral Reading Paragraphs that were published by William Gray in 1915. The purposes of the Gray Oral Reading Test, as indicated in its manual, are two: (1) the provision of "an objective measure of growth in oral reading, . . . and, (2) "the diagnosis of oral reading difficulties" (16, p. 1). The extent to which the latter can be accomplished is highly dependent upon the background and prior skill of the examiner.

The Gray Oral Reading Test can be used with beginning readers through adult readers. There are four available forms of the test and each contains 13 paragraphs that range from preprimer to adult level. Each passage is followed by five literal recall questions. The test yields grade scores that are a reflection of rate of reading and number of oral reading errors. Standard errors of measurement, which are rather large, are reported throughout.

The Gilmore has two forms and is intended for use in first to eighth grade. Its more limited scope, old-style basal reader format, poor alternate form reliability, and blatant sex stereotyping combine to make it a test of very limited use.

The Durrell Analysis of Reading Difficulty is probably the most ambitious in terms of its diagnostic scope. It is designed for use with nonreaders through sixth-grade level. It appears designed primarily for use with children who are having difficulty in the area of reading. It contains the following subtests: oral reading, silent reading, listening comprehension, and word recognition and word analysis.

The oral reading subtest consists of eight paragraphs ranging from first- to sixth-grade level. Each paragraph is followed by seven literal comprehension questions. The subtest yields a grade score and position (i.e., high, middle, low) within a grade. Thus, oral reading could yield a grade of middle third. Though oral reading errors and comprehension errors are noted, the grade score is derived solely on the basis of time required to read the passage.

Paragraphs parallel to those for oral reading are used for silent reading. After students read the appropriate paragraphs silently, they are asked to tell the examiner everything they remember. Grade norms like those for oral reading are available and are again based exclusively on amount of time required to read the passage.

The listening comprehension subtest is a set of seven paragraphs available for reading to the children. The children's grade levels for listening comprehension are estimated on the basis of ability to answer factual questions about the selection read to them.

In the word recognition and word analysis subtest, four word recognition lists of 20 or 25 words are presented to children in both flash and untimed presentations. (These terms are explained on pages 64 and 65 of the last chapter, in the discussion of informal reading levels.) A grade score is yielded both for the flash and the untimed performance.

In addition to these main portions of the test, five additional subtests are available for nonreaders or those reading at first-grade level. They include: (1) naming letters, (2) identifying letters named, (3) matching letters, and (4) learning rate.

For children reading at third-grade level or below, the hearing-sounds-in-words primary subtest and the sounds-of-letters subtest can be used. Children who have trouble with the hearing-sounds-in-words subtest can be given a subtest called learning-to-hear-sounds-in-words.

Finally, there are visual-memory-of-words (intermediate), phonic-spelling-of-words, spelling, and handwriting subtests.

There are about ten different subtests on the Durrell (the total depends on what one counts as a subtest). The manual estimates that it requires 60–90 minutes for administration. In addition to the grade norms, there is a heavy reliance on checklists as a means of obtaining useful diagnostic information, which some practitioners see as the test's main strength.

The manual provides no information about reliability and validity; the information about the standardization population is also very inadequate. The manual states:

The Durrell Analysis of Reading Difficulty is designed primarily for observing faulty habits and weaknesses in reading which are pertinent to planning a remedial program. The checklists of errors are more important than the norms.

The statistical qualities of the test are very unacceptable by current standards. The materials that are part of the Durrell, however, might be useful to a very skilled reading clinician who could make good diagnostic observations; however, the merits of informal evaluation seem greater.

Advantages and Limitations of Standardized Individual Diagnostic Tests

The tests listed above allow the examiner to closely observe the child as the child is reading. They permit rather detailed analysis of reading performance and are the most appropriate type of standardized test for planning programs for children.

The diagnostic accuracy of individual tests tends to be highly dependent on the skill of the examiner. Putting such tests in the hands of an examiner who has had no training or who poorly understands the process of reading can result in very inaccurate conclusions and inappropriate recommendations. Teachers and reading specialists need to become familiar with the content of tests, the derivation of scores, and the terminology used by the test's author. For example, Spache uses the term *independent level* very differently from the way it is used in informal reading inventory procedures. He uses it to designate a level that is a higher readability level than the frustration level. On the Spache test, one might expect a child to score a frustration level of fourth and an independent level of fifth. This would be impossible when using an informal reading inventory according to the procedures discussed in the last chapter. Independent level is defined differently.

How to Choose a Published Test

The *Mental Measurements Yearbook* by Oscar Buros is now in its seventh edition (4). These yearbooks include descriptions of tests, their cost, publisher, and usually one or two critical reviews. They are an excellent starting point for obtaining names of tests, approximate cost, and some outside evaluation of their worth. The limitations of the yearbooks are that they sometimes do not include very recently published tests; and although an attempt is made to have the reviews done by competent, unbiased individuals, this is not always the case.

If choosing the test takes place well in advance of its planned use, a highly desirable procedure is to order specimen sets of the test, which contain some actual tests and test manuals. They are fairly inexpensive.

Read the manuals and evaluate the test along the dimensions listed below. If possible, give the test to several children and evaluate the results. If two or three tests are being considered, they might be administered to small groups of children and the results compared.

Test manuals should contain the following information, which will allow you to evaluate the test:

1. *Normative Information.* The major question here is related to how closely the normative population approximates the group with whom the test is to be used. One very interesting, positive feature of some tests is that they provide norms derived from several different populations. Tables may be provided so that a student's performance can be compared with a general, national population; an urban, large city population; college-bound students; and so forth.

2. *Data Regarding Established Reliability and Validity.* The more forms of reliability and validity reported, the better. Evidence about the extent to which they are, in fact, established must be weighed carefully.

3. *Directions for Administration.* These should be clear and suggest a manageable way to administer the test.

In addition to the above, there are several other considerations such as: How long does it take to administer the test? Is it administered individually or to a group? How much does it cost per student? How easily can it be scored? Is a scoring service available for the test?

Undoubtedly there are many other questions that deserve attention. However, the overriding question remains: How well does it satisfy the purpose that I have for testing? Often that question can be answered only after the test has been tried. Therefore, it does seem wise to trial-administer several tests to small numbers of readers, in order to evaluate the measures before making a commitment to large-scale testing.

Conclusions Regarding Standardized Reading Tests

All forms of testing have limitations and standardized procedures are no exception. Each form of standardized tests can be used in order to satisfy some testing purposes. The various mental measurement yearbooks are invaluable sources of information about standardized tests and should be consulted when the need arises for a test.

No attempt has been made to list all standardized tests or to describe them thoroughly. The emphasis has been upon providing the background information that should allow test users to better understand concepts that are typically part of standardized testing procedures.

READABILITY

The preceding sections have dealt with means of evaluating children's reading performance. Some attention was drawn to the need to carefully consider the materials used for the evaluations. This portion of the chapter focuses on the concept of readability, which tends to emphasize the evaluation of materials rather than people.

Reading materials quite obviously vary in their level of difficulty. For the last 50 years scholars have been attempting to find some way of summarizing and objectively reporting just how difficult a piece of reading material is. The level of difficulty of reading materials is commonly referred to as its *readability,* or the reading ability needed, and is expressed as a grade level. Thus, a book or piece of material whose readability is described as sixth-grade level is supposedly substantially more difficult than material whose readability is second-grade level.

Readability Formulas

One of the most common approaches to trying to calculate the readability of a set of materials is by means of readability formulas. These are typically applied to samples of the reading material under consideration. For the most part they rely heavily on word length, the number of words in a sample that lie outside some established word list, and sentence length. For example, the well-known formula for materials at intermediate grade levels, the Dale-Chall formula (6), is calculated on the basis of the number of words in samples of approximately 100 words that do not appear in the Dale list of 3000 words and the average sentence length in these samples. The formula itself requires: (1) counting the number of words in the sample, (2) counting the number of sentences in the sample, (3) counting all words that do not appear in the Dale list, (4) determining the average sentence length, (5) obtaining the Dale score by dividing the number of words not on the Dale list by the total number of words, (6) multiplying the average sentence length by 0.0496, (7) multiplying the Dale score by 0.1579, and (8) adding a constant of 5.3684. This yields a raw score. If several samples are taken, the raw scores are averaged and the average raw score is converted, through a table, to a grade score.

The above procedure is fairly complex and time-consuming. A similar procedure is followed for calculating the Spache formula, a frequently used formula for elementary-level materials. For those interested in the readability of adult material, the Flesch formula is probably the most frequently used. References for all three of these formulae are included in the bibliography at the end of the chapter (6, 11, 43).

Recently there have been several less-difficult and less-time-consuming methods for objectively calculating readability. For example, Williams (45) has devised a table for rapid determination of revised Dale-Chall scores and Safier (40) has suggested a shorter method for working out scores according to the Spache formula. Another popular approach to readability is the readability graph devised by Fry (13). This approach is discussed below. With it, the grade level of materials can be established with relative ease. It can be applied to a wide range of materials.

The Fry Procedure
Directions for its use are:

1. Select three 100-word passages from near the beginning, middle, and end of a book. All proper nouns are omitted in the calculations.

2. Count the number of sentences in each of the 100-word samples. Estimate the number of sentences to the nearest tenth. Average the number of sentences for the three samples.

3. Count the total number of syllables in each 100-word sample.

4. Plot on the graph (see Figure 5.8) the average number of sentences and the average number of syllables per 100 words.

5. The readability score is the number that appears above the line marked "Approximate Grade Level." For example, if the

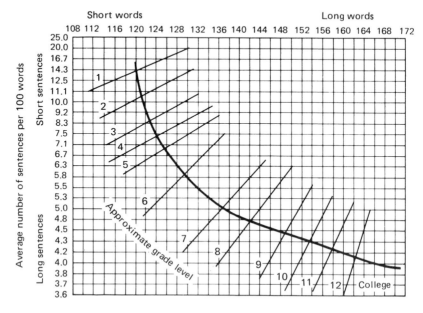

FIGURE 5.8

average number of syllables per 100 words were 136 and the average number of sentences were 5.5, the readability level would be Seventh Grade.

The Smog Procedure

A second procedure, which its author G. Harry McLaughlin (26), claims is even easier, allows for rapidly estimating the readability of middle-grade materials. Called the SMOG grading, its instructions are:

1. Count 10 consecutive sentences near the beginning of the text being assessed, 10 in the middle, and 10 near the end. Count as a sentence any string of words ending with a period, question mark, or exclamation point.

2. In the 30 selected sentences, count every word of three or more syllables. Any string of letters or numerals beginning and ending with a space or punctuation mark should be counted if you can distinguish at least three syllables when you read it aloud in context. If a polysyllabic word is repeated, each repetition is counted.

3. Estimate the square root of the number of polysyllabic words counted. This is done by taking the square root of the nearest perfect square. For example, if the count is 95, the nearest perfect square is 100, which yields a square root of 10. If the count lies roughly between two perfect squares, choose the lower number. For instance, if the count is 110, take the square root of 100 rather than that of 121.

4. Add three to the approximate square root. This gives the SMOG grade, which is the reading grade that people must have reached if they are to understand fully the text assessed.

Limitations of Readability Formulas

Even a superficial analysis suggests that it is quite possible that a readability formula may yield an inaccurate estimate. No provisions are included for measuring:

1. *Interest.* Some materials have a great deal of appeal and are easily read by many people in spite of long sentences and long words. In addition there is the fact that an article or book may be appealing to some and not to others. It is almost certain that it will be far more readable for those interested in its contents.

2. *Difficulty of Concepts.* Although there is some correlation between length of words and difficulty of concepts, the relationship is far from perfect.

3. *Density of Concepts.* A writer who repeats ideas and provides many examples to illustrate ideas will make printed material

easier to understand. This is not reflected in readability, as measured by the popular formulas.

4. *Organization of Material.* Some material is written logically and carefully, with each idea conclusively explained; whereas other authors present ideas haphazardly, with little internal organization.

5. *Use of Support Materials.* Some text material is made considerably easier to read through illustrations, charts, diagrams, and the like. By the same token, such support materials can make the reading more demanding.

Expanded Concept of Readability

Perhaps the greatest difficulty with formulas is that they take a very restricted view of readability, implying that the ease or difficulty with which materials are read is a function only of the material. A far more satisfactory concept of readability is one that sees it as an interaction between a reader and reading materials. Interest alone can make a supposedly frustrating book quite readable. Background of information and language abilities are two other strongly influencing factors. For these reasons, we should look beyond the formulas to better means of answering the question, "Will this child or will this group of children be able to read this book?"

Informal Evaluation and Readability

An informal word recognition test or parts of an informal reading inventory could be used to match a child and a book. If a word recognition list can be readily constructed, it may work well if there are a few children who need to be screened. For children who usually have good understanding of materials they read, perhaps the oral reading at sight phase of the I.R.I. will yield the desired information. In other instances, having the children read a section silently and asking them several questions about it may prove a suitable procedure. Informal reading inventories are most suitably samplings from potential instructional materials, and an astute evaluator will sample only far enough to satisfy the purposes of the testing. If you need to be as sure as possible about whether or not children will be able to read a book, you could do an entire informal reading inventory. But in most circumstances the consequences of an error in evaluation are not severe. Group reading inventories, of course, are another reasonable approach to readability.

Cloze Procedure

DESCRIPTION. A very interesting procedure for assessing whether a child or group of children will be able to meet the demands of reading materials is called the cloze procedure. Like informal measures, it has some face validity because the test is a sampling from potential reading materials. The name *cloze* is derived from a term used in psychology, *clozure,* which is the tendency to fill in gaps in order to see a completed entity. For example, most people who are asked what this figure is— ☐ —would report that it is a square even though part of the right end of it is missing. There is a tendency to try to interpret stimuli as meaningful wholes.

The cloze procedure has the particular advantage of being very easy to construct, quick to administer, and objective to score. However, because the procedure is relatively new, there is some disagreement as to the best way to construct it and the best criteria to apply to evaluate the results. At present, the best suggestions for constructing a cloze test appear as follows:

1. Select a passage of about 250 words. The passage should seem representative or typical of the content of the book. If the book becomes progressively more difficult, choose something between the first quarter and the first half of the book.
2. Keep the first and last sentences intact.
3. Beginning with the second sentence, omit every fifth word.
4. Replace the deleted words with blanks which are uniform in length. Number the blanks consecutively.
5. Prepare an answer sheet with numbers from 1 to 50 and with spaces to write the answers.

The following is an illustration of a cloze passage. It is suggested that the illustration be completed at this time.

Directions: On a separate answer sheet, numbered from 1 to 25, write the word that should be inserted in each of the blanks that follow.

TRENDS IN READING

Anyone who has worked in the field of reading for any length of time begins to wonder if anything "really" new is introduced. Often it seems as __1__ professionals in reading are __2__ involved in either rehashing __3__ ideas or trying to __4__ prove something that's so __5__ obvious that it needs __6__ proof. Reading also seems __7__ be a field that __8__ susceptible to fads and __9__, especially in trying to __10__ the causes of reading __11__. The search continues for __12__ perfect test that will __13__ many subtest scores that __14__ each carry a specific __15__ for remediation. It seems

155

__16__ at all times there __17__ someone or some group __18__ proclaims with certainty that __19__ cause of serious reading __20__ has at last been __21__. Failure to establish laterality, __22__ visual perception, insufficient phonic __23__, inadequate mothering are only __24__ few of the many __25__ that are periodically cited as "the" cause. Unfortunately the pronouncements never seem to result in the elimination of the problem and so the search goes on.

(It is generally recommended that 50 blanks be used; this abbreviated form was used to conserve space.)

Correct Answers:

1. if	14. will
2. constantly	15. prescription
3. old	16. that
4. experimentally	17. is
5. blatantly	18. that
6. no	19. the
7. to	20. problems
8. is	21. discovered
9. gimmicks	22. poor
10. understand	23. instruction
11. disabilities	24. a
12. the	25. factors
13. yield	

ADMINISTRATION. Because the activity is new to many children, it is often very valuable to do a practice exercise, perhaps on the board. A selection with at least 10 blanks should be used and the first and last sentences should be kept intact. For the practice session, materials should be chosen that will be fairly easy for those being evaluated. The following directions or modifications of them can be used:

Some words have been left out of these sentences. Our job is to try to fill in as many of the missing words as possible. The best thing to do is to try to read through all the sentences first. Some of the later sentences will give us clues about the earlier ones. Read the sentences silently.

After the children have had sufficient time to read the passage, individual children should provide possible answers. Any answers that are meaningful and syntactically correct should be accepted. The children should come to see that there are, at times, several possible choices for filling in the blanks. If there are some answers that are not reasonable (e.g., "she" instead of "he" when a boy's name is used as the referent), these should be discussed as to why they would not be good choices. Answers should be recorded on the board as they are discussed. This practice session can also be conducted very effectively by using an overhead projector.

After the introductory exercise, children should be provided with copies of the cloze materials and then should be encouraged to proceed by themselves in the same way they did as a group. They can be told that they will not be penalized for incorrect spellings and that they should use the word that they think fits best. There are no time limits for completing the procedure.

SCORING. Score as correct only exact reproductions of the missing word. Do not accept synonyms. (The reasons for not accepting synonyms are discussed below.)

For children scoring 50 percent or more, the material is judged as being at an independent level. For those scoring between 30 and 50 percent, it is at an instructional level. Scores of less than 20 percent reflect a frustration level. These criteria are based largely on middle-grade students (22, 33). Other authors suggest more stringent criteria. Because there is disagreement, the reader of this text is urged to adopt the just-cited criteria as starting points and then to modify them based upon practical experience with a particular population of readers or with a particular type of reading material.

LIMITATIONS. The cloze technique has encountered resistance from teachers and some reading specialists. Some maintain that it is a frustrating experience for children, because they find it very difficult. Cloze relies heavily on the use of language content and meaning clues, and it would seem very beneficial for readers to sharpen their skills in this area. Those who find it very frustrating should be given additional cloze passages, taken from easier materials, so that they may learn to more fully employ meaning clues. Some children object to the cloze because they are not "sure" that their answers are correct. One of the authors of this text has often spoken of the "tyranny of the right answer" (44), and it appears that this is the force at work in this case. Children need to come to understand that there are many acceptable answers, even when only one is scored right. Gomberg (15) reports very encouraging results in the using of cloze activities to encourage children with reading difficulties to express greater intellectual curiosity and to ask more spontaneous questions.

The second major objection to the cloze is the procedure of scoring only exact word reproductions and not synonyms as correct. The pro-

157

cedure currently used makes the scoring highly objective and reliable. If synonyms were counted as correct, there would be many difficult scoring problems, because it would be difficult at times to tell if the given work is really a synonym. In addition to the potential scoring problems, the other obvious consequence of accepting synonyms would be that the criteria levels would be raised. Research conducted by Bormuth (2) indicated a very high correlation between cloze scores obtained when only exact reproductions were accepted and when synonyms were accepted as correct. Because there is reasonably good evidence to suggest that similar results are obtained with the two procedures, accepting only exact reproductions seems wise, because it is an easier, faster, and more reliable approach.

MODIFICATIONS OF CLOZE PROCEDURE. A multiple-choice format was suggested for use in the cloze procedure by Ransom (38). Her reason for the suggestion was that it allowed young children to complete cloze procedures even when they would have had difficulty writing the responses. More recently, Guthrie et al. (18) suggested use of multiple-choice cloze procedure with a clinical population. They call this procedure the maze technique.

Multiple-choice format for the cloze procedure has both advantages and disadvantages. Its primary advantage is that children object to it less than they object to completing conventional cloze passages. Likewise, it requires less time to administer. Its disadvantages are that it is more time-consuming to construct, it has been subjected to far less research, and it appears to yield more varying results from one examiner to another.

To construct a multiple-choice cloze test, approximately every fifth or tenth word is omitted but three words are inserted in its place. One of the choices is the reinserted word that had been deleted, the second is a distractor which is the same part of speech as the omitted word, and the third choice is a word that is syntactically different from the omitted word. An example would be:

Flowers which must be planted every year are called annuals.

leaves

Those which survive winter are labeled perennials. Per-

old

     carefully   that

ennials are will   attractive since the gardener does

        obviously   goes

             anew

not have to start last   each year. However, annuals have

             which

| all | Tall | shall |

some advantages as well. They grow very rapidly and insect

| both | He | do |

               forethought

not require as much should   . Annuals always bloom

            cattle

   second

the first   year; perennials frequently do not.

   grow

One problem is that there are no guidelines as to how close in meaning the distractors should be to the correct choice. For example, the first choice in the example above would have been more difficult to make if the distractor "summer" were substituted for "leaves." One recent research study (33), suggests that the multiple-choice technique is not discriminating enough for use with regular classroom students. Its use, therefore, should for the present be restricted to clinic populations. For an excellent comprehensive discussion of readability consult Klare (24).

CLOZE FOR MASTERY TESTING AND INSTRUCTION. In addition to its use as a testing device, which can be used to approximate independent, instructional, and frustration levels, cloze has been suggested for other uses as well. When cloze is not being used to approximate functional reading levels, several modifications seem in order. For example, cloze has been suggested as a way of measuring mastery of the content of a course or for understanding of materials read by a student. For these purposes, words should not be randomly deleted at the rate of every fifth word. Instead, it would be much more meaningful to systematically delete key or important words. In addition, one would certainly want to accept synonyms as being correct. It is only when one wishes to use the criteria for establishing functional reading levels that only the exact reproduction of the deleted word is counted as correct.

Cloze has also been suggested as a teaching procedure (3, 32). Though the summarized research (23) is not particularly encouraging, the ease and economy with which cloze activities can be constructed continue to attract many users. Additional research is needed to clarify the potential value of cloze procedures, both for testing and teaching.

CONCLUSIONS

This chapter focused upon two major approaches to evaluating reading. Criterion referenced evaluation appears to have excellent possibilities for offering suggestions that can be used for program planning. The focus upon establishing goals and determining whether or not students have achieved these goals is a very fruitful way to approach evaluation. Unfortunately, C–R evaluation has sometimes resulted in an approach to reading that focuses upon specific skill development to the exclusion of the more cognitive and affective aspects of reading. In some programs, it has also resulted in excessive testing which detracts from time available for instruction.

Standardized tests generally yield information about how an individual compares with some group of individuals. There are some educators who would like to see all standardized testing eliminated. They maintain that it wastes time and encourages unfair comparisons. Unquestionably some of their objections are legitimate, but it is the ways standardized tests are used and not the tests themselves that generally are to blame. Teachers and reading specialists must develop the ability to evaluate tests and to learn to limit themselves to legitimate uses of these measures. This would almost certainly result in a diminishing of abuses.

In the field of reading a great deal of attention has been paid to the concept of readability, which focuses upon the evaluation of materials. Readability formulas, though probably the most popular approach to assessing readability, have numerous limitations. It is most viable to regard readability as the interaction between a reader and reading materials. Informal reading evaluation procedures, including the cloze technique, appear to be very promising approaches to a much more practical and expanded notion of readability.

BIBLIOGRAPHY

1. Bleismer, E. "Informal Teacher Testing in Reading." *The Reading Teacher,* 25 (1972): 268–272.

2. Bormuth, J. "Comparable Cloze and Multiple-Choice Comprehension Test Scores." *Journal of Reading,* 10 (February, 1967: 291–299.

3. Bortnick, R., and G. Lopardo. "An Instructional Application of Cloze Procedure," *Journal of Reading,* 16 (January, 1973), 296–300.

4. Buros, O., ed. *The Seventh Mental Measurements Yearbook.* Highland Park, N.J.: The Bryphon Press, 1972.

5. Carver, R. "Reading Tests in 1970 Versus 1980: Psychometric Versus Edumetric." *The Reading Teacher,* 26 (December, 1972), 299–302.

6. Dale, Edgar, and Jeanne Chall. "A Formula for Predicting Readability: Instructions." *Educational Research Bulletin,* 27 (1948): 37–54.

7. Davis, W. Q. "Functional Use of Standardized Reading Tests," in

A. Berry, T. Barrett, and W. Powell, eds., *Elementary Reading Instruction*. Boston: Allyn & Bacon, 1969.

8. Dunn, L. M., and F. C. Markwort. *Peabody Individual Achievement Test Manual*. Circle Pines, Miss.: American Guidance Service, Inc., 1970.

9. Durrell, D. *Durrell Analysis of Reading Difficulty: Manual of Directions*. New York: Harcourt Brace Jovanovich, 1955.

10. Farr, R., and N. Anastasiow. *Tests of Reading Readiness and Achievement*. Newark, Del.: International Reading Assoc., 1969.

11. Flesch, R. "A New Readability Yardstick." *Journal of Applied Psychology*, 32 (1948): 221–233.

12. Fry, E. Q. "A Readability Formula That Saves Time." *Journal of Reading*, 11 (1968): 513–516, 575–581.

13. Fry, E. Q. "The Orangutan Score." *The Reading Teacher*, 24 (1971): 360–361.

14. Garrett, H., and R. Woodworth. *Statistics in Psychology and Education*. New York: McKay, 1966.

15. Gomberg, A. "Freeing Children to Take a Chance." *The Reading Teacher*, 29 (1976): 455–456.

16. Gray, W. S. *Gray Oral Reading Tests: Manual of Directions*. Indianapolis: Bobbs-Merrill, 1963.

17. Guilford, J. *Fundamental Statistics in Psychology and Education*. New York: McGraw-Hill, 1956.

18. Guthrie, J. T., M. Seifert, N. Burnham, and R. Kaplan. "The Maze Technique to Assess, Monitor Reading Comprehension." *The Reading Teacher*, 28 (November, 1974): 161–169.

19. Helmstadter, G. C. *Principles of Psychological Measurement*. Englewood Cliffs, N.J.: Prentice-Hall, 1964.

20. Jastak, J. F., and S. R. Jastak. *WRAT Manual*. Wilmington, Del.: Guidance Associates of Delaware, Inc., 1965.

21. Johnson, M. S., and R. A. Kress. "Task Analysis for Criterion-Referenced Test." *The Reading Teacher*, 24 (1971): 355–359.

22. Jones, M., and E. Pikulski. "Cloze for the Classroom." *Journal of Reading*, 17 (March, 1974): 432–438.

23. Jongsma, E. *The Cloze Procedure as a Teaching Technique*. Newark, Del.: International Reading Assoc., 1971.

24. Klare, G. "Assessing Readability." *Reading Research Quarterly*, 10 (1974): 62–102.

25. Malley, J. "The Measurement of Reading Skills." *Journal of Learning Disabilities*, 8 (June–July, 1975): 377–381.

26. McLaughlin, G. H. "SMOG Grading: A New Readability Formula." *Journal of Reading*, 12 (1969): 639–646.

27. Millman, J. "Criterion Referenced Measurement," in W. J.

Popham, *Evaluation in Education.* Berkeley, Calif.: McCutchan Publishing Co., 1974.

28. Mavrogenes, N., C. Winkley, E. Hanson, and R. Vacca. "Concise Guide to Standardized Secondary and College Reading Tests." *Journal of Reading,* 18 (October, 1974). 12–22.

29. Niles, O. "Behavioral Objectives and the Teaching of Reading." *Journal of Reading,* 16, 2 (November, 1972): 104–110.

30. Otto, W., and E. Askov. *The Wisconsin Design for Reading Skill Development: Rationale and Guidelines.* Minneapolis, Minn.: National Computer Systems, 1972.

31. Pikulski, J. "Criteria for Instructional Levels for Disabled Readers." Unpublished paper. Newark, Del.: University of Delaware, 1972.

32. Pikulski, J. "Using the Cloze Technique." *Language Arts,* 53 (1976): 317–318.

33. Pikulski, J., and E. J. Pikulski. "Cloze, Maze, and Teacher Judgment." *The Reading Teacher,* 30 (April, 1977): 766–770.

34. Popham, W. J. *Educational Evaluation.* New York: Prentice-Hall, 1975.

35. Popham, W. J. *Educational Statistics: Use and Interpretation.* New York: Harper & Row, 1967.

36. Popham, W. J., ed. *Evaluation in Education.* Berkeley, Calif.: McCutchan Publishing Co., 1974.

37. Prescott, G. "Criterion Referenced Test Interpretation in Reading." *The Reading Teacher,* 24 (1971): 347–354.

38. Ransom, P. "Determining Reading Levels of Elementary School Children by Cloze Testing," in J. A. Figurel, ed., *Forging Ahead in Reading.* Newark, Del.: International Reading Assoc., 1968.

39. Roscoe, J. T. *Fundamental Research Statistics for the Behavioral Sciences.* New York: Holt, Rinehart and Winston, 1967.

40. Safier, D. "Notes in Readability." *Elementary School Journal,* 59 (1959): 429–430.

41. Sax, G. "The Use of Standardized Tests in Evaluation," in W. J. Popham, *Evaluation in Education.* Berkeley, Calif.: McCutchan Publishing Co., 1974.

42. Sipay, E. "A Comparison of Standardized Reading Scores and Functional Reading Levels." *The Reading Teacher,* 22 (October, 1968): 10–16.

43. Spache, G. "A New Readability Formula for Primary Grade Reading Materials." *Elementary School Journal,* 53 (1953): 410–413.

44. Stauffer, R. G. *Directing the Reading-Thinking Process.* New York: Harper & Row, 1975.

45. Williams, R. T. "Table for Rapid Determination of Revised Dale-Chall Readability Scores." *The Reading Teacher,* 26 (1972): 158–165.

CHAPTER 6

Factors Related to Reading Problems

This chapter will discuss factors which are frequently thought of as causes of reading problems. Harris (18) refers to factors such as faulty vision, hearing, and neurological functioning as correlates of reading problems. The terms correlates and contributors seem more appropriate to use in discussions of reading problems, because it is difficult to clearly isolate or specify the source or cause of the failure to achieve in reading. Diagnosticians who claim they can clearly delineate causes often reflect their personal biases as to why reading failure occurs. As a result of such biases, some diagnosticians almost always find a perceptual problem causing the reading failure; others almost always find a psychological cause.

In some cases of reading disability, there are discernible factors which contribute to or perpetuate the problem. Unquestionably, a child with a severe visual problem may continue to fail in reading unless necessary correction is made. However, in the vast majority of cases evaluated at the Delaware Center and other clinics throughout the country, there is no clear, single cause or outstanding contributor. The problem in learning to read often appears to be a manifestation of a combination of factors, much like the situation described in earlier chapters.

In some cases of reading disability, the teacher or reading specialist needs to do a thorough diagnosis; however, the question that must be kept in mind is: What implications do the results of the evaluation have for the plan of instruction? In some cases, the responsibility of the classroom teacher or reading specialist is limited to making observations or conducting screening procedures to determine whether or not referral to another professional, such as an ophthalmologist, neurologist, or psychologist is in order. It should be abundantly clear that a teacher or reading specialist cannot be an expert in all of the areas that might contribute to the existence of a reading problem.

This chapter begins with a discussion of intelligence and its relationship to reading. Low intelligence is not seen as a cause of a reading problem by many. In most classification systems, a child with less than average intelligence is expected to have less than average reading achievement. If a child with low intelligence has even lower reading achievement than expected, then the question remains as to why this is so. A large part of the chapter is devoted to the discussion of intelligence because it is an area that is frequently misunderstood by teachers and because it is felt that a diagnostic interpretation of the results of an intelligence test can help to shed light on the nature of a reading problem. Such an interpretation of intelligence test results can have implications for the correction of a reading problem.

INTELLIGENCE

Discussions about the relationship of intelligence and reading can be among the most frustrating, especially when they occur among people who have not agreed on a definition of each. Mention the word intelligence and your audience will appear to clearly understand what you mean; ask that audience for a definition of intelligence and often you will be confronted with a sea of blank faces.

Over fifty years ago, Boring (3) wrote: "Intelligence as a measurable capacity must at the start be defined as the capacity to do well on an intelligence test." In other words, intelligence is that which is measured by intelligence tests. Certainly this seems to be a kind of absurd tautology, but it is not. Most educators use the results of intelligence, or IQ, tests as the basis for drawing conclusion about a child's intelligence. However, Green maintains:

> First of all, I. Q. is not a synonym for intelligence. The I. Q., intelligence quotient, simply represents a numerical score earned on a test. That test does not measure the broad range of experience encompassed by all intellectual functions. (13, p. 90)

It appears, then, that intelligence has at least two meanings. One definition is limited in scope and defines intelligence in terms of IQ tests.

164

Green uses the term in a very broad sense to refer to a host of cognitive and adaptive skills. Educators should remind themselves of the two possible interpretations and avoid using the two interchangeably.

Green also points out the many limitations that IQ testing has. One of his conclusion is:

> San Francisco psychologists went to court to obtain a restraining order to temporarily halt the use of tests for classifying school children. Parents, teachers, and others who see tests being used in a harmful way should take similar action. (p. 92)

Intelligence tests and tests in general have been condemned by many. However, it is maintained in this text that the major problem lies not with the tests but with the mistaken or uninformed way in which test results are used. If the biases and limitations of IQ tests are known by teachers and educators in general, test results will not be used to set limits for what teachers expect from a child; the results will be used to try to understand factors which interfere with progress in reading.

By now almost everyone is familiar with the study by Rosenthal and Jacobsen (25) that suggested that teacher expectation can actually influence children's learning and level of performance. Many critics oppose intelligence testing because they fear what has been labeled the "self-fulfilling prophecy." Quite simply this suggests that people behave the way they are expected to behave. It is maintained that, if we perceive someone as bright and intelligent, we will respond to them as such and that this will stimulate them to act even brighter and more intelligently. If teachers perceive students as dull and incapable of learning, it is maintained that those students will not learn very well. Although the Rosenthal and Jacobsen study has been criticized because its basic premise seriously reflects on teacher insight, it did alert many teachers to the possibility of selective treatment of students on the basis of teacher expectations. Critics of intelligence tests maintain that IQ tests are primary vehicles for creating expectations of limited potential for learning.

IQ tests have been particularly criticized for penalizing poor, black, Spanish speaking, Indian, rural, and other minority group children. Williams (28) has been a forceful critic of the way IQ tests have been used with minority groups and cites himself as an example. At 15, his measured IQ was 82. His high school counselor advised that Williams become a bricklayer. Williams is now a highly respected psychologist with a Ph.D. from Washington University in St. Louis. IQ tests do appear to be biased against minority groups. Teachers, therefore, must know the content of IQ tests in order to discover the nature and extent of such biases.

The position is taken here that teachers can become responsible professionals with regard to interpreting intelligence tests. However, before that can happen they must know something about intelligence tests. Therefore, the use of and possible interpretation of the Wechsler Intelligence Scale for Children—Revised Form (WISC—R) will be discussed in some detail.

WISC—R

This is the most frequently administered individual intelligence test and one of the best intelligence measures available. However, it has limitations. As these are understood, it is felt that a greater understanding for the concept of intelligence and its measurement will be developed. The goal here is not to have teachers administer or be primarily responsible for interpreting the results of the WISC—R; however, it is hoped that the lengthy description which follows will help teachers and reading specialists to actually make use of the results of intelligence tests.

BACKGROUND FOR THE WISC—R. The WISC—R is one of three widely used Wechsler Scales. They were the early work of David Wechsler, which began with the publication in 1938 of the Wechsler Bellview Scale, which is no longer in use. In 1949, the Wechsler Intelligence Scale for Children (WISC) was published. It has been replaced by the WISC-R which appeared in 1974. The Wechsler Intelligence Scale for Children—Revised Form (WISC—R) is used with children between the ages of 6 years and 16 years, 11 months. There is also the Wechsler Adult Intelligence Scale (WAIS) (1955) for individuals 16 years and older and the Wechsler Preschool and Primary Scale of Intelligence (WPPSI) for young children between 4 years and 6½ years of age. The organization, content, and administration of all three currently used Wechsler Scales are similar, so that the discussion of the WISC—R should help in understanding the other scales, as well.

GENERAL DESCRIPTION. There are 12 subtests in the WISC—R. Six of them are classified as verbal subtests and six are performance subtests. Verbal subtests require an oral, verbal response from the subject, while in the performance subtests, the subject is required to actually work with materials and a much less verbal response is required. One of the subtests in each section is supplementary, and its results are not included in deriving the IQ score.

The WISC—R yields three IQ scores. A full scale IQ, which reflects the child's performance in all 10 key tests, a verbal IQ, which is derived from the five verbal subtests, and a performance IQ, derived from the five performance subtests. All three IQ scores have a mean of 100 and a standard deviation of 15.

The following is used as a classification scheme for the full scale, verbal, and performance IQ scores:

130 and above	Very superior
120–129	Superior
110–119	High average
90–109	Average
80–89	Low average
70–79	Borderline
69 and below	Mentally deficient

Each of the subtests also yields a score. The raw score is based on the total number of points a subject scores on a subtest. Like most raw scores, it has no immediate meaning. However, through tables based on a subject's age, raw scores can be converted to scaled scores. Subtest scaled scores have a mean of 10 and a standard deviation of 3.

WECHSLER'S DEFINITION OF INTELLIGENCE. Intelligence is defined as: "the overall capacity of an individual to understand and cope with the world around him" (27, p. 5). Wechsler stresses that intelligence is a multifaceted, global entity rather than a singular one. He goes on to point out that intelligent behavior may call for non-cognitive capabilities including "persistence, zest, impulse control, and goal awareness." This is important, because it strongly suggests that intelligence in its purer form cannot be measured and that its manifestation is dependent on personality factors, as well as on social and moral values. Teachers and reading specialists must keep in mind that some of these factors may seriously influence a child's performance on an intelligence test.

DESCRIPTION OF THE SUBTESTS. The subtests are administered in an order which calls for alternating verbal and performance subtests. For purposes of clarity, all the verbal subtests will be described first and then the performance subtests. Item examples are similar to those in the WISC—R, but were constructed by the author specifically for this chapter. It may be that they do not faithfully represent the true Wechsler items, and the reader is urged to become familiar with the actual test.

WISC—R VERBAL SUBTESTS

Information. This subtest measures background of information and long-term memory. It is highly dependent on general environmental stimulation and educational influences. To a lesser extent it is influenced by the extent to which an individual is intellectually curious and attentive to events and stimuli around him.

> *Item Examples:* How many months are there in a year?
> From what animal do we get eggs?
> How many pints are there in a quart?
> What is the capital of France?

Implications for Reading. Children who have a very limited background of information will probably have difficulty dealing with the concepts and facts presented in reading materials. Thus, these children are likely to have difficulty with the comprehension of reading materials. Obversely, children with a reading problem, especially beyond primary grades, probably fail to expose themselves to much of the background that is normally developed through both school and recreational reading. Thus, the reading problem contributes to a poor score on this subtest. This is probably not true with very young children. If children score very poorly on this subtest, it may mean that background of experience needs to be developed before reading demands are made upon them, or it may simply indicate that the children's background of experience is different from what is asked for on this subtest. This may suggest the need to find reading materials or techniques that can capitalize upon the experiences that they have had. The term "culturally different" may be particularly relevant when considering the implications for performance on this subtest.

Similarities. This subtest is designed to measure abstract reasoning, ability to categorize, and level of conceptualization attained by subject.

> *Item Examples:* In what way are a bat and a doll alike?
> A rope and string?
> A shirt and jacket?
> A car and train?

Implications for Reading. The nature of incorrect responses needs to be analyzed. Some children seem incapable of the active thinking required by this subtest and give no responses at all. Some children have difficulty focusing on the relevant aspects of a problem and so deal only with the very peripheral attributes of the items to be compared. For example, they give response such as "they're both things." Some analysis can also be made as to the approach that children take to comparisons. For example, if asked how a shirt and a jacket are alike, they could respond at a concrete level, saying that they both have buttons or sleeves; at a functional level, saying you can wear them both; or at an abstract, categorical level, saying they are both clothing. Children who do poorly on this subtest may have difficulty with reading comprehension beyond the level of literal recall. Recommendations might call for developing thinking skills by asking questions which require making comparisons and contrasts and seeing relationships. Opportunities for logically approaching problems should be introduced.

Arithmetic. This subtest measures the attainment of basic arithmetic concepts, mastery of basic computational processes, and arithmetic reasoning. It is dependent on long- and short-term memory. Attention and concentration are very influential factors.

> *Item Examples:* The child is shown a card with 12 apples. The examiner says, "Count these apples with your finger."
>
> Jim had three dollars and his mother gave him two more. How many dollars did he have altogether?
>
> 60 is ¾ of what number?
>
> If a woman walked a half mile in one hour and a quarter mile every hour after that, how far would she walk in four hours?
>
> *Note:* 1. This subtest is timed (30 seconds to 120 seconds, depending on the item.) For some children, this introduces a stress that reduces their efficiency; for others, it appears to motivate them to improve their performance.
>
> 2. The last three items on this test are read by the children. This represents the only place in the entire test where children are asked to read. However, if they cannot read the items, the examiner reads them while they listen.

Implications for Reading. Again, the implications for reading are multiple. "Bright" children who are unable to read sometimes channel their efforts into arithmetic. A high level of achievement may then be reflected on this subtest. It is important educationally to continue to provide opportunities wherein they can experience such success. On the other hand, a poor performance can suggest limitations in attention and concentration and, therefore, the need to keep instructional periods short. Limitations in attention and concentration may also reflect anxiety, which needs to be dealt with; if there is strong supporting evidence, psychological intervention or treatment may be recommended. If the anxiety is test or school specific, then techniques for overcoming this can be employed in school.

Vocabulary. Vocabulary development is usually considered to be among the best indicators of general, functional intelligence. Measures of vocabulary are felt to reflect learning ability, range of ideas, and general verbal skills.

Item Examples: What does spoon mean?
   What is a horse?
   What does antagonize mean?
   What does instinct mean?
   What does exacerbate mean?

Implications for Reading. There is an interaction between performance on the vocabulary subtest and reading disability that is similar to the interaction between the information subtest and reading disability. However, vocabulary development (as measured by this subtest) appears seriously affected by a reading problem only when the reading disability is very severe and longstanding. Everyday contacts seem to provide children with the vocabulary necessary to function in the initial phase of the test. Certainly a very poor score here has clear-cut implications for reading. Because reading is built upon aural and oral vocabulary, the better these are developed, the more likely reading instruction can be successful. Listening and speaking experiences should be recommended for children with weak vocabulary development. With intermediate and older children, some systematic vocabulary study might be recommended. As with the information subtest, it may be that the children have functional vocabularies that are different from the vocabulary tapped by this subtest. Cultural differences may be present, and if this is felt to be the case, appropriate recommendations should be made.

Comprehension. In this subtest, the skills measured vary with the nature of the question. Therefore, test question illustrations will follow the function being measured. Some factors include: Common-sense judgments (What should you do if you are lost?); societal value judgments (What should you do if you break someone's window? Why should people pay bills?); understanding the aim and workings of societal organizations (Why do we have post offices? What do we expect lawyers to do?) In addition, this subtest seems highly influenced by verbal facility. Children who can expand and elaborate upon answers usually do well. Children who are verbally restricted sometimes seem to "know" the answer but are unable to express it.

Implications for Reading. This subtest probably has more psychological than educational implications. Children's responses can reflect such things as impulsiveness, attitudes and values different from societal expectations, or inability to make independent decisions (overdependency). Limitations in background of information and verbal facility or fears of being wrong are more obviously related to reading achievement. Performance on this subtest requires particularly skilled interpretation; however, it could suggest the need for increasing verbal facility (helping the children to better express themselves verbally), helping them to risk being incorrect, or building additional background of experience.

170

Digit Span. This subtest measures short-term memory and attention and concentration. Although it is a supplementary test, it is usually administered to children with reading problems, because they are frequently found to have limited attention spans.

> *Item Examples:* In the first part of this subtest, the examiner says a series of digits (ranging from a series of three to a series of seven) at the rate of one per second. The child is asked to repeat them.
>
> In the second part, the examiner presents a series of digits (ranging from two to seven numbers per series) and the child is asked to repeat them backwards.

Implications for Reading. Many of the conclusions from the arithmetic subtest can be applied here. It is interesting to compare performance on these two tests. Children who do better on the arithmetic subtest than on the digit span subtest are frequently anxious, but seem capable of overcoming their anxiety if given a well-structured problem to which they must actively respond. Initiating a program of remediation with a great deal of structure for such children may be helpful. The structure can be reduced as the children gain confidence and become less anxious. Children who are intellectually limited and who have very limited thinking skills can sometimes do reasonably well on the digit span subtest.

WISC—R PERFORMANCE SUBTESTS

Picture Completion. In this subtest, children are shown a series of pictures from which some essential part is missing. They must name the missing item or point to where it should be. It measures attention to detail, ability to distinguish relevant and essential from irrelevant and unessential details, and sensitivity to environmental surroundings. It is a timed test in which children must respond within 20 seconds.

> *Item Examples:* A dog without a tail.
> A candle without a wick.
> Profile of a man without an ear.
> Picture of an electric lamp without a cord.

Implications for Reading. Children who cannot see the important missing item sometimes have difficulty seeing the relevant dimensions of a problem or a situation. Recommendations for development of skills along these lines may be called for. Children who perform poorly on this subtest may be inattentive to details (a skill that can be very important in word recognition). Both pictures and verbal activities could be used to help the children pick up important omissions.

Picture Arrangement. In this subtest children are presented with four or five pictures. They are presented in an order that does not represent a meaningful sequence. The children are then asked to rearrange the pictures into a proper sequence, a sequence that tells a story. This subtest measures: logical thinking skills, ability to see cause-effect relationships, ability to see chronological sequence and meaningfully integrated details. Performance is timed and bonus points are given for rapid performance. Thus, children who can analyze a situation quickly and respond rapidly do very well.

> *Item Examples:* A child would be shown four pictures in the following order: a person chopping down a tree (picture 1 = cutting tree trunk into pieces; 2 = person approaching tree trunk with axe; 3 = tree falling; 4 = trunk of tree cut ¼ of way through).
>
> The child would be expected to rearrange them so that the order is: 2, 4, 3, 1.

Implications for Reading. Many of the skills listed above are directly called for in reading comprehension. In reading we expect, for example, that children will be able to understand logical sequence and cause-and-effect relationships. Some of these same skills are called for in this subtest. If a weakness is indicated in these areas, then recommendations are rather straightforward. Impulsive children who do not attend to details and who are not self-critical do poorly here. They may be overly dependent on outside criticism and fail to critically review their performance. Helping them to become more self-critical in academic tasks may be necessary.

Block Design. Children are presented with four (and in later designs, nine) blocks and asked to reproduce a model that the examiner has constructed or a design presented in a picture. This subtest measures analytic and synthetic thinking skills, visual perception, visual-motor integration, and neurological integration. It is considered to be a very good measure of general intelligence.

> *Item Examples:* Using blocks that have sides that are red, white or half-red and half-white, the child is asked to reproduce Figure 6.1.

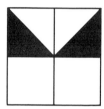

FIGURE 6.1

Implications for Reading. Poor performance on this subtest may suggest the need to consider building visual and visual-motor skills as reading activities are slowly and informally introduced. If there is supporting evidence from other sources, it may indicate the need for further evaluation of neurological functioning. Children who are impulsive and do not stop or who are unable to analyze a problem before becoming involved in its solution usually do poorly with this subtest. Development of analytic skills may be called for. Children sometimes begin to correctly deal with this task and then, after partial solution has been achieved, they either give up completely or destroy what they have accomplished to that point and start anew. More appropriate problem-solving strategies need to be developed. As with picture arrangement, bonus points are given for speedy performance.

As with most of the subtests, the results must be cautiously and expertly interpreted. As was indicated, cognitive, personality, or neurological factors or even some combination of the three could contribute to a poor performance.

Object Assembly. The subject is presented with puzzle-like pieces and asked to put them together to make something. objects include a boy, a horse, a face and a car. Many of the same skills required by block design are required here. Less emphasis is on analytic thinking skills and more is on seeing the relationship of parts to a whole. The implications for reading are very similar to those derived from Block Design. Bonus points are part of this subtest also.

Coding. In this subtest, Figure 6.2 is shown to the children:

1	2	3	4	5	etc to 10
N	\	⌒	:		

FIGURE 6.2

Followed by 50 numbers as in Figure 6.3.

2	3	5	6	2

FIGURE 6.3

The children must fill in the symbol that goes with each of the numbers (now in random presentation) in the empty boxes below the numbers. They have 120 seconds to complete as many of the examples as possible. This subtest is dependent on visual perception, motor speed, visual-motor integration, and ability to form rapid associations. It also requires consistent movement in left to right sequence.

Implications for Reading. The subtest may also give some clue regarding perceptual and/or motor limitations that may require some consideration. Persistence and motivation also affect performance. The positive or negative effects of working under a closely timed task might also be observed. Children who are overly detail-bound or overly perfectionist do very poorly here. They unnecessarily strive for perfect reproductions of the symbols. Such children may need help in more realistically evaluating their goals and achievements. In order to do well, children must learn some of the associations between the symbols and the numbers.

Mazes. This supplementary subtest is a typical pencil-and-paper maze. It requires the ability to plan ahead, anticipate outcomes and use visual-motor control.

Implications for Reading. A poor performance may suggest the need for helping children to develop better impulse control or it may be a reflection of neurological difficulties.

CONCLUSIONS. The above descriptions should lead to a number of conclusions. The WISC—R does not measure native potential; performance on the test can be influenced by such noncognitive factors as persistence or anxiety; and it is not culturally neutral. However, it and most measures of intelligence have reasonably high correlations with reading achievement. Correlations tend to be in the neighborhood of 0.50–0.60 in the primary grades, increasing to about 0.70–0.80 by junior high and high school. Most likely this high relationship reflects the strong probability that the same factors which influence performance on IQ tests also influence general school achievement, and specifically reading achievement.

The subtests of the WISC—R were described in some detail to show that there are educational strategies important for reading that may be suggested by children's performance on an IQ test. Some psychologists are opposed to the interpretation of subtest scores, because their reliabilities are rather low. The reliabilities are indeed low. However, this chapter suggests that subtest scores can provide a starting point that may prove either valid or erroneous. If the teacher who works with children on a day-to-day basis remains alert to the possibility that the interpretations from the subtest scores were in error, there is no danger. The results of an intelligence test should be looked at for diagnostic clues and for tentative hypotheses that may lead to a better understanding of children's problems. Intelligence tests should not be used to create teacher prejudices about what children can or cannot potentially do.

Other Measures of Intelligence

THE STANFORD-BINET INTELLIGENCE SCALE. Another popular measure of intelligence is the Stanford-Binet Intelligence Scale. Its norms were revised in 1972, and it is therefore a fairly current test. It is individually administered and non-reading-dependent. In the hands of a skilled psychologist it can yield very useful information, much like the WISC—R; in fact, many items on the two tests are similar. However, the Stanford-Binet is organized very differently from the WISC—R. Items are arranged according to age level rather than type of item. Thus, there are six items that are appropriate for a child who is functioning at a six-year old level; six others for the nine-year old level. There are no subtest scores. The total score yields an overall mental age which can be converted into an intelligence quotient. It is not possible to calculate a separate verbal and performance IQ with this measure. Beyond the ages of six or seven, its overall score tends to be more dependent on language skills than does the WISC—R overall score.

THE SLOSSON INTELLIGENCE TEST. This is a condensed form of the Binet Scales. It is organized in a similar way. Its author indicates that it can be administered by teachers, because it requires only minimal training. However, it should be used only by someone who has a thorough understanding of the concept of intelligence and the nature and limitations of IQ testing. The Slosson could serve as a useful screening device for reading specialists or special education teachers. Specialists should, however, discuss its possible use with a supervising psychologist. A full measure of intelligence administered by a psychologist should, however, be given in cases where a device like the Slosson suggests mental deficiency or when important decisions are to be made on the basis of the IQ test results.

THE PEABODY PICTURE VOCABULARY TEST (PPVT). This is an extremely easy measure to administer and score. The examiner says a word and presents the subject with a set of four pictures. The subject chooses the one picture which best depicts the word spoken. All items are of this type and so the PPVT is essentially a measure of receptive vocabulary. The Peabody yields an IQ, a mental age (M.A.), and a percentile score. Both the Peabody and Slosson show high correlations with the WISC—R (21). However, the PPVT too should be considered as a screening device. If it is thought of as a measure of children's vocabulary rather than as a measure of intelligence, it might be even more useful to a reading specialist. Vocabulary development has important implications for understanding reading difficulties, and the Peabody could provide some useful clues.

Group Intelligence Tests

All the IQ tests discussed thus far have been individual tests. Individual tests are administered to one person at a time by an examiner. Group tests are those which are given to a number of individuals at the same time by one or a small number of examiners. Group tests are almost always pencil-and-paper tests, in which the test material is presented in booklets or on sheets of paper. The person taking the test reads words or symbols and uses a pencil to record responses. The California Test of Mental Maturity, the Kuhlmann-Anderson Measure of Academic Potential, the Kuhlmann-Finch Scholastic Aptitude Tests, the Lorge-Thorndike Intelligence Tests, and the Pintner-Cunningham Primary Test are well-known illustrations of group IQ tests. Before trying to interpret the results of these tests for children with reading disabilities, it is important to determine whether or not reading skills are required by the test. The test—or that section of the test which involves reading—is completely invalid, useless, and grossly misused when applied to children with reading disabilities. As psychologists, teachers, and reading specialists have become more aware of the dangers inherent in testing, interpreting the results of reading dependent IQ tests as a measure of children's "potential" or "capacity" is becoming quite uncommon. Such interpretations, however, were made in the past. Measuring a disabled reader's intelligence by means of a test that required reading is one of the most blatant illustrations of a misuse of tests.

The results of group tests are sometimes used to defend the position that all schools in a district or all school districts in a state should not have equal average achievement scores. School administrators and teachers argue that expectations should vary according to the intelligence test results. Although the necessity for and value of such a procedure may be debated, it sometimes seems appropriate when unrealistic demands are made upon a school or school district.

Group tests are not recommended for the diagnostic study of an individual child's reading problem. Most conclusions or decisions to be made on the basis of an IQ test are too important to be based on a group test. The observations of a reading specialist using an individual screening test or the observations of a psychologist administering a full IQ measure need to be added to a test score. Such observations can be made only on the basis of administering an individual IQ test.

Expectancy Formulas

One of the most widely used activities in diagnostic procedures in the field of reading and learning disabilities is the calculation of what children can be expected to achieve. Most often the expectation is set on the basis of IQ or M.A. scores. For example, Harris (19), suggests the use of the following:

$$\text{Reading Expectancy Age (REA)} = \frac{2 \text{ M.A.} + \text{Chronological Age (C.A.)}}{3}$$

This means that the reading age that a child should be able to achieve at any given time can be calculated by multiplying the child's mental age by 2, adding the chronological age, and then dividing that total by 3. Before providing an illustration, it should be observed that M.A. can be rather quickly calculated if a child's IQ and C.A. are known. The conversion formula is:

$$\text{M.A.} = \frac{\text{IQ} \times \text{C.A.}}{100}$$

Also, it is helpful to know that most writers recommend that reading expectancy age (REA) can be changed to reading expectancy grade by subtracting 5.2 (children are assumed to start kindergarten on the average at about the age of 5 years, 2 or 3 months). When engaging in such calculation, one must keep in mind that age is usually represented as years plus months; for example, 5–6 means 5 years, 6 months. However, grade scores are usually years plus a part of 10 months. Therefore, it is recommended that all age scores be dealt with in terms of years plus tenths of a year; for example, a chronological age of 5–6 (5 years and 6/12ths of a year) would be represented as 5.5 (5 years and 5/10ths of a year).

AN ILLUSTRATION. Let us illustrate the Harris formula with a child who is 10 years, 8 months old with an IQ of 70.

First, the chronological age should be converted to years plus tenths of years: 8/12ths of a year is equal to 0.666 of a year. For ease of calculation this should be rounded to 0.7.

$$\text{M.A.} = \frac{\text{IQ} \times \text{C.A.}}{100}$$

$$\text{M.A.} = \frac{70 \times 10.7}{100}$$

$$\text{M.A.} = \frac{749}{100}$$

M.A. = 7.49, which can be rounded to 7.5

$$REA = \frac{2(M.A.) + C.A.}{3}$$

$$REA = \frac{2(7.5) + 10.7}{3}$$

$$REA = \frac{15 + 10.7}{3}$$

REA = 8.57, which can be rounded to 8.6

Thus, the formula suggests that the child should be reading at the level of a child 8.6-years old. In order to convert that to a grade expectancy, 5.2 is subtracted. Therefore, according to this method the child should be reading at 3.4, or approximately mid-third-grade level.

Formulas such as this have some utility in suggesting that a child with an IQ of 70—if it is derived from a "valid," individually administered, non-reading-dependent IQ test—should not be expected to be reading at mid-fifth grade, as his or her chronological age might suggest. In this sense, these formulas are useful.

At the other end of the continuum, we might look at the illustration of a very bright child.

Consider the following: C.A. = 12–10   IQ = 145

Following the same steps: 13–10 = 13–10/12s, or 13.8

$$M.A. = \frac{IQ \times C.A.}{100}$$

$$M.A. = \frac{145 \times 13.8}{100}$$

$$M.A. = \frac{2001}{100} \text{ or } 20.01 \text{ or } 20.0$$

$$REA = \frac{2(M.A.) + C.A.}{3}$$

$$REA = \frac{2(20.0) + 13.8}{3}$$

$$REA = \frac{53.8}{3} \text{ or } 17.93 \text{ or } 17.9$$

Grade Expectancy = 17.9 − 5.2 = 12.7

Again the formula may be useful in suggesting that children who have had an accelerated general development, as measured by IQ tests, should be achieving beyond which might be expected from their C.A.

However, there are limitations to the expectancy formula approach. To begin with, there is not agreement as to which formula should be used. In addition to the Harris formula, there is what might be called the mental age approach. This simply calls for subtracting a constant such as 5.2 from the child's mental age. The reading expectancy age and the mental age are identical. Proponents of this formula suggest that all children should be working up to their intellectual potential and that chronological age should not be used to dilute this expectation. A third approach is suggested by Bond and Tinker (2). Their formula weighs school experience as being equally as important as mental age:

Reading-Grade Expectancy Score (RES)

$$= \frac{IQ}{100} \times \text{Number of Years in School Beyond Kindergarten} + 1$$

For the child with an IQ of 70 who is 10.7-years old and in school for 4.5 years (in mid-fifth grade), the expected grade score would be calculated as follows:

$$\begin{aligned} \text{RES} &= \left(\frac{IQ}{100} \times \text{No. of Years in School}\right) + 1 \\ &= (0.70 \times 4.5) + 1 \\ &= 3.8 + 1 \\ &= 4.2 \end{aligned}$$

For this same child, the reading-grade expectancy would be 2.3 according to the mental age approach (M.A. − 5.2, or 7.5 − 5.2). Thus, the three formulas yield the following estimates:

Bond and Tinker = 4.2
Harris   = 3.4
Mental Age   = 2.3

Similarly, the child who is 13.8-years old with an IQ of 145 and who has been in school 7.6 years would have an expected grade score of: 12.0 (Bond and Tinker), 12.7 (Harris), or 14.8 (Mental Age).

It should be more than apparent that calculating an expectancy formula is far from the precise procedure often implied. The tentativeness of the procedure is placed in even better perspective when one realizes that different IQ scores and different reading scores can be obtained, depending on the measures used.

Another source of difficulty is that in spite of warnings to be cautious, teachers and specialists continue to think of a measured IQ as the outer limits a child can reach. If expectancy formulas are used to try to answer the question of whether children have reached their potential in reading (or any other area of achievement for that matter) the answer is clearly no, notwithstanding the results of any formula calculations.

The answer is no simply because it is inconceivable to think of anyone who has achieved their full potential in reading, or in any other area for that matter.

In most situations, the calculation of a grade expectancy is somewhat irrelevant. The important educational question is: What do the children already possess and what do they need next instructionally?

IQ Tests and Reading: Conclusions

Many cautions regarding IQ testing have already been voiced here. Others can be found in a recent publication (21). However, if teachers become knowledgeable about the instruments being used to measure intelligence, if they keep the limitations in mind, and if they use the results to formulate some tentative hypotheses that have educational relevance, then the tests can be diagnostically quite valuable.

Often intelligence tests are administered in order to provide children with special educational placement. Such placements are often necessary in order to provide the degree of individualization required for a slow-learning child to make progress. Even here the IQ test should not be used to formulate limited expectations for children. The tests could be in error. The goals for special education and regular classes are the same: to help each child learn as much, and as efficiently, as possible.

As indicated earlier, measures like the WISC—R may suggest some areas that need specific attention, such as building background information, helping children to express themselves more completely, working to build more accurate visual perception, and so forth.

VISION

At a superficial level, reading is a visual act, and therefore the visual efficiency of children with reading problems is often the first area that is suspect, particularly by parents. Historically the eye movements involved in reading were among the first considerations systematically researched. Woodworth (29) reports that in 1878 Emile Joval found that the eyes did not move across a line of print in a steady sweep but instead moved in a series of jumps with pauses between these jumps.

Because of the increased awareness by schools of the need for continuous screening of children's vision, vision problems rarely appear to be a major contributor to reading deficiencies referred to a clinic such as the one at the University of Delaware. However, this is not to suggest that the evaluation of children's vision is unimportant in a complete diagnostic evaluation. In certain cases, visual problems may be major contributors. Certainly, these must be detected.

Though the relationship between visual efficiency and reading has been studied over a long period of time, the results remain inconclusive. Various investigators seriously disagree with each other concerning the importance of visual problems as related to reading. The interested reader should consult summaries by Cleland (6) and Rosen (24) for fairly comprehensive reviews. However, in many respects, the question of the extent of the relationship is academic, because there is widespread agreement that, if they are very serious, visual problems can be important contributors to reading disabilities.

Types of Visual Problems

The field of vision is an extremely complex one and the forms of visual defects are far too numerous for a teacher or reading specialist to be familiar with all, or even most of them. Therefore, only a few of the most common problems will be mentioned.

Perhaps the most familiar visual problems are those involving defects in the structure of the eye. *Myopia,* or nearsightedness, is a condition in which a person can clearly see only objects that are close. The difficulty lies in seeing distant objects. *Hyperopia,* or farsightedness, is the obverse condition, in which there is difficulty in seeing objects at close range. Both these conditions are usually caused by a malfunctioning of the lens of the eye or by an unusually long or short distance between the lens and the fovea (that part of the eye which is most sensitive to visual stimuli). *Astigmatism,* a condition which results in blurred or distorted vision, is the result of irregularities in the lens of the eye.

Of the three conditions above, only myopia seems unrelated to problems in reading. However, even myopia could create problems with the child's ability to see various classroom group-media presentations and materials written on a blackboard. All three conditions can usually be corrected through the use of glasses or contact lenses.

In addition to problems related to the structure of the eye are problems stemming from the fact that both eyes must operate together in order to produce a single, clear image. The term *binocular difficulties* is used to describe conditions in which both eyes do not exactly focus the same images on the same part of the fovea. In certain cases, binocular difficulties are the result of defects in the operation of the muscles which control eye movement. If a reader is faced with blurred or double images, reading becomes very uncomfortable. Readers with binocular difficulties frequently find reading very fatiguing and, therefore, avoid it. In some cases, suppression of vision in one eye results as a means of avoiding fatigue and discomfort. Suppression of vision means that the person relies almost exclusively on the stimuli coming from one eye and ignores the stimuli from another.

Screening Procedures

The primary responsibility of the teacher or reading specialist is that of detecting symptoms of visual problems and making referrals for further evaluation. There is also the responsibility of making certain that the screening procedures that are used by a school or clinic are adequate.

In most school situations, the screening of vision is done by a school nurse so that teachers and reading specialists need not become familiar with all the details. They should, however, know what screening procedures are being used and should lobby for changes if they seem inadequate. For example, in the past most schools relied exclusively on the administration of the Snellen Chart as the visual screen procedure. The Snellen Chart measures a person's ability to see letters from a distance of 20 feet. A rating of 20/20 means that the person can see at 20 feet what a "normal" person can see at 20 feet. A rating of 20/40 means that a person can see at 20 feet what a "normal" person can see at 40 feet. A rating of 20/200 is often defined as blindness for legal purposes.

Exclusive reliance on the Snellen Chart is inadequate for detecting problems that might contribute to reading difficulty. It will not usually detect farsightedness, astigmatism, or binocular difficulties. In fact, the only visual disorder it usually detects is nearsightedness, a visual problem that appears to have little effect on reading.

Therefore, it is necessary at times for teachers or reading specialists to urge the adoption of more adequate screening procedures, such as the Keystone Vision Screening test, the Ortho-Rater, or the Titmus School Vision Tester. All three of these tests offer comprehensive visual screening procedures and are far more adequate than a test which measures the ability to see objects at a distance of 20 feet.

Making Referrals

In school situations, the primary responsibility of a teacher or reading specialist will be to observe symptoms and to refer children to the school nurse for a comprehensive screening evaluation. If problems are indicated by the screening procedures, the nurse usually takes the responsibility of notifying the parents and encouraging them to seek a professional examination by a vision specialist. In a reading clinic setting, reading specialists are trained to screen vision and to make referrals.

The teacher or reading specialist should look for the following potential indicators of vision problems: (1) unusual appearance of the eyes, including redness, tearing, bloodshot, or crustlike accumulations near the eye; (2) unusual habits, such as rapid blinking, twitching, facial contortions, and holding a book unusually close or far; and (3) complaints by the student about such problems as dizziness, fatigue, pain, nausea after reading, and distortion of what is seen.

For the teacher or reading specialist, the appearance of even a few symptoms would seem to warrant a screening by the school nurse. The nurse should then inform the person making the referral of the results. In some school districts, there is an unfortunate reluctance on the part of nurses to suggest that the child receive a professional visual examination. The apparent fear is that the parents will be told by the vision specialist that there is no serious problem and that the parents will, therefore, feel they wasted money on the examination. This fear of overreferral is often without basis and may result in a child not receiving needed visual attention. The nurse, or in some cases the reading specialist, needs to tell the parents that the child failed to perform satisfactorily on the screening procedure. The recommendation to the parents is that they obtain professional services to determine whether or not the child has a problem. There should be no suggestion that a serious problem has already been found; that type of determination should be the province of a professional vision specialist.

Teachers are sometimes confused by the differences among ophthalmologists, optometrists, and opticians. *Ophthalmologists* are M.D.s who have specialized in treating disorders of the eye. *Optometrists* are specifically trained vision specialists. They have the degree of doctor of optometry (O.D.). Optometrists primarily examine visual functioning and prescribe lenses when they are required. The ophthalmologist performs these same functions, but also treats diseases of the eyes and performs surgery as needed. *Opticians* are the professionals who fill prescriptions for lenses.

There is some disagreement among optometrists and ophthalmologists regarding the role that vision specialists should play in the treatment of reading and learning problems. In some localities, optometrists assume a very active role. These optometrists maintain that reading problems are often the result of faulty eye movement and poor eye coordination. They therefore recommend and carry out programs of *orthoptics,* or eye training, designed to increase visual efficiency. They feel this will, in turn, result in greater reading efficiency. While this may be the case, many have questioned the efficiency of such programs. Ophthalmologists stress that reading is far more a cognitive than a visual process and have gone on record challenging the procedures employed by some optometrists (9).

There is insufficient evidence to support or completely reject the programs advocated by optometrists. Certainly much depends on the individual child and individual vision specialist. In our clinical experience, however, we have encountered optometrists who appear to recommend costly glasses (often bifocals) or visual training when there appears to be no evidence which warrants such a recommendation. Therefore, caution should be exercised before commitment is made for such training.

Some related issues are discussed in the section dealing with visual perception later in this chapter.

HEARING

There are some striking parallels between vision and hearing as they relate to reading. Both are sensory activities, though superficially reading seems more a visual than an auditory act. However, because reading requires the association of sounds and written symbols, hearing is certainly a necessary prerequisite for reading. Persons with severe hearing deficits sometimes do become fairly proficient in reading, but only rarely and then only after extraordinary effort. It appears easier for a blind person to master braille than it is for a deaf person to learn a functional system of reading.

Vision and hearing are also similar in their relationship to reading, because there remains some uncertainty as to the extent to which a hearing loss affects progress in reading. As in most areas, wide individual differences exist. Some individuals with mild hearing losses experience great difficulty in learning to read, while others, with more severe losses, are successful.

There is fairly good agreement that certain types of hearing losses have a more detrimental effect on reading ability. Losses at the highest frequencies of human hearing tend to have the most negative effect. This will be discussed in the paragraphs that follow.

Screening Procedures

Screening procedures for hearing have some parallels to those in vision. They tend to be the responsibility of school nurses in schools and reading specialists in reading clinics. The primary responsibility of classroom teachers and school reading specialists are to observe symptoms of hearing problems, in order to refer children for screening evaluations and to lobby for adequate screening procedures.

Children who demonstrate speech problems should be thoroughly evaluated for possible hearing problems. This includes cases where the onset of speech seems unusually late. In addition, teachers should be alert to other possible indicators of hearing difficulties including: frequent requests for the repetition of directions; apparent inattention; unusual habits (for example, turning ears toward the source of sound); or physical abnormalities of the ear, including discharges and inflammations.

There is fairly wide agreement that an audiometer should be used to screen hearing. This is a device for presenting carefully controlled sounds to an examinee. Generally, the two dimensions that are controlled are the intensity of sound, which is roughly equivalent to loudness, and the frequency of sound, which is roughly equivalent to pitch of sound. Intensity is typically measured in decibel units, a fairly complex unit of measurement. It is important to know that "normal" hearing is said to be characterized by a 0 decibel loss. Children who demonstrate losses of 15 to 20 decibels on an audiometric screening should be referred for a professional evaluation. Losses of 25 decibels or more are rather serious and usually are accompanied by some distortion in speech.

Frequency of sound is roughly equivalent to pitch. The human ear is sensitive to sound frequencies between 20 to 20,000 cycles per second. Children who have difficulty hearing high frequency sounds (500 to 2,000 cycles per second) are likely to have difficulty with reading and probably with clarity of speech. High frequency sounds seem particularly important to reading, because most consonant sounds, which are critical to understanding speech, are high frequency sounds.

Educational Implications

Some authorities have suggested that children who have hearing losses do particularly poorly in reading if they are instructed with a method highly reliant on phonic skills. The argument goes that they become confused, because the hearing loss prevents the development of the auditory discrimination skills necessary for phonics. The recommendation, therefore, is that a method which stresses the development of sight vocabulary be used. This argument certainly has some logic to it, but as yet there is little objective evidence to support it.

PERCEPTUAL AND NEUROLOGICAL FACTORS

The term *perception* is probably one of the most poorly understood, overworked, and misused concepts in the field of reading. Teachers, psychologists, reading specialists, special education teachers, and parents glibly talk about how children's reading problems are the result of perception problems. Usually these people are unable to provide an adequate definition of perception or give a clear idea as to how faulty perception is determined. Before proceeding, it might be profitable to explore a very few basic definitions.

Perception is defined by Blankenship (1) as follows:

Perception is the thinking process which gives meaning to a sensation or stimulus; it is the knitting together of nerve impulses into a conscious impression of the external world. It is the understanding of that which is seen or heard or felt. Every perception is a complicated weaving together of the stimuli of past experiences, of interests and even desires. (1, p. 579)

A full exploration of the concept of perception is beyond the range of this book. However, the above definition makes several important points. Perception is receptive in the sense that it involves the taking in of sensations; it also involves some internal process of matching past experiences with the sensations in order to form the perception.

The definition also implies that there are two potential sources of difficulty in the process of perception. First, the definition indicates that perception involves the "knitting together of nerve impulses." If there is malfunctioning of the neurological system, it is quite possible that there will also be resultant difficulty in perception. A neurologically disturbed individual may have difficulty perceiving a *b* as different from a *d* because the neural messages are not being received properly or because the neural processes in the brain do not allow for adequate processing of the stimuli presented. However, perception is also dependent on a second factor, "past experience." It is also quite possible for a person to show *b/d* confusion if he has not had experience with these as distinct and different stimuli. In everyday life, objects are considered equivalent regardless of their orientation or directionality. A chair is seen as a chair regardless of whether it is seen from front, or back, or side; the direction it faces does not change what it is. If people have not been taught that the marks *b* and *d* are letters or if they have not been taught that the direction of the letters is important, there is no good reason why the two marks should not be seen as equivalent.

There are many questions that even neurologists cannot answer about the nervous system. Certainly educators cannot be expected to fully understand its workings. Therefore, it seems best that educators concentrate on the environmental influences on perception and avoid speculations on the workings of a child's nervous system. Evaluation of perceptual functioning is often the province of the school psychologist.

Measures of Perceptual-Motor Development

Notice that, although the discussion has been about perception, the heading has shifted to perceptual-motor measures. This is because most of the measures that are used to evaluate perception simultaneously evaluate motor skills. *Motor skills* are skills required for carrying out an act. *Gross motor skills* involve large muscle movements and are required for activities such as running, skipping, walking, swimming, and riding a bicycle. *Fine motor skills* require the precise, small muscle movements for writing, using scissors, drawing, and sewing.

Form Copying Tests

The most frequently used measure of perceptual-motor functioning used is the *Bender Visual-Motor Gestalt Test*. It consists of nine figures that are shown to a person one at a time. The examinee is asked simply to make a copy of them. Some are as simple as a row of dots; others are more complex, such as a circle and a diamond touching each other. Distortions in the subject's copy are taken to be indicators of a perceptual-motor problem. These results are often used to recommend a program of perceptual training. Even superficial analysis suggests that the difficulty may not be in the subject's accurate perception of the figure, but with the fine motor control necessary to reproduce the figure.

Zach and Kaufman (30), for example, found that there was no significant relationship ($r = -0.19$) between a child's score in the regular administration of the Bender Gestalt test, which requires copying the design, and an experimental version which did not require the use of motor skills. In the experimental version, the child was shown a Bender Gestalt figure and then had to select a copy of that figure from four choices, three of which were distortions of the figure. The experimenters point out that poor performance on the Bender Gestalt test may be ascribed to several different factors: perceptual deficit alone, perceptual deficit in conjunction with motor dysfunction, motor dysfunction alone, or inefficient coordination of visual and motor processes.

Tests such as the Beery-Buktenica Test of Visual-Motor Integration and the Winterhaven Perceptual Forms Test are similar in content and administration to the Bender Gastalt. They are subject to difficulties in *differential diagnosis*. A test which is high in differential diagnosis can effectively distinguish one problem from another. Most form copying tests do not allow distinguishing a visual-perception from a fine motor problem, except possibly through the careful judgments of the examiner administering the test.

A second measure that is frequently used to diagnose perceptual problems is the Developmental Test of Visual Perception (sometimes called the Frostig Test after its principal author). This test claims to be able to measure five separate areas of visual perception: eye-motor coordination, figure-ground relationships, consistency of shape, position in space, and spatial relationships. Many of these subtests also require fine motor skills and, therefore, the conclusions regarding perceptual difficulties must be drawn very cautiously. There is some evidence to suggest that this test is of very limited utility beyond first grade. Reviews of the literature by Olson (20) and Smith and Marx (26) led to the conclusion that there is inadequate evidence to suggest that the Frostig actually has the diagnostic ability to measure five separate visual perception skills. Most of the studies they reviewed suggested that the Frostig measures just one, general visual perception factor. Hammill (15) has also questioned whether the skills measured by the Frostig are significantly related to reading achievement. From his review of the literature he concluded that the bulk of the studies that met minimum criteria for acceptability suggested that performance on the Frostig was not related to performance on reading tests.

Some of the initial enthusiasm for the D.T.V.P. was due to the fact that a program designed to overcome the areas of visual perception deficiency also existed (11). Therefore, the testing on the D.T.V.P. was to have immediate implications for remediation, certainly a most desirable state of affairs. However, a review of the literature challenges the utility of the program and questions whether perceptual processes can actually be trained. As a result of their review, the investigators concluded:

> The results of attempts to implement the Frostig-Horne material and Kephart-Getman techniques in the schools have for the most part been unrewarding. The readiness skills of children were improved in only a few instances. The effect of training on intelligence and academic achievement was not clearly demonstrated. Particularly disappointing were the findings which pertained to the effects of such training on perceptual-motor performance itself. (16, p. 476)

At present there appears to be insufficient evidence that programs designed to train visual-perception processes have any significant effect on improving reading skills. Church notes that training with programs might have a negative effect on motivation. She observed, relative to the Frostig-Horne perceptual training program, that "while a few children find the workbooks to be enjoyable, many had to be continually encouraged or reprimanded to continue to work in the books" (5, p. 364). She also raised the question of what the children might be missing in their school experiences as a result of engaging in extensive perceptual training programs.

> Language development, crucial in a young child's life, is neglected when children are placed in a regimented situation whereby all children merely follow directions. Opportunities for intellectual interaction are nil under these conditions.

Conclusions and Implications
Regarding Visual Perception

There is a great deal of confusion regarding visual perception and its relationship to reading problems. The alert teacher or reading specialist must critically analyze the results of so-called tests of perception, because many appear to be simultaneously measuring other skills. The efficacy of visual perception training programs has been challenged.

Observing children during reading instruction sessions can provide many clues to perceptual difficulties. Do they confuse letters such as *b, d, p, m,* and *n?* Do they have difficulty visually moving across a line of print? Do they copy letters in reverse? These or other behaviors suggest possible perceptual weaknesses. They do not, however, immediately imply a neurological problem. Young children typically see letters such as *b* and *d* as equivalent and have difficulty distinguishing between them. A very important skill that children must be taught is to consistently approach letters and words from left to right. Directional confusion is a very common contributor to letter and word reversals. With respect to such confusions, the most immediate question facing a teacher or reading specialist is: What educational strategies can be used to avoid such confusions? If careful diagnosis by a reading specialist, psychologist, or neurologist suggests that there is a neurological basis for the confusions, the educational strategies used are usually not different from when the problem is not neurologically based. Finally, it should be kept in mind that children who are continually unsuccessful with the perceptual demands of reading may need additional time for their neurological system to achieve greater maturity. Unfortunately, the last statement is based on speculation, because not nearly enough is known about the development of neurological maturity. Nor can we accurately diagnose children in order to determine with certainty that they have achieved the neurological maturity necessary to meet the perceptual demands of reading. We find ourselves back into speculation and the use of jargon.

Auditory Perception Factors

It is probably more common to discuss auditory discrimination than auditory perception. In its most general terms, auditory discrimination involves being able to distinctly perceive similarities and differences among sounds. In its relationship to reading, the ability to perceive differences among speech sounds is of vital importance. Phonics involves the association of particular sounds with particular letters. It would be extraordinarily difficult to form appropriate associations between the symbols *l* and *r* if the sounds heard at the beginning of the words *rap* and *lap* were not distinguishable. In some Oriental languages, the difference between the two sounds is not a significant one and, therefore, the two words would be perceived auditorily as identical. If sounds are not clearly perceived or if functionally different speech sounds are not perceived as being different, confusion is likely to exist in word recognition and the use of phonics.

Groff (14) has pointed out that there is also a certain amount of logic and fact that suggest that most children are capable of making accurate distinctions among speech sounds. He cites the work of Carroll (4), which suggests that children can accurately produce all but seven of the phonemes necessary for dealing with speech. In working with children, it is rare to find that they are confused by similarities and differences of speech in their everyday activities. For example, if a child were sent to a toy corner and asked to bring back a doll, it is unlikely that the child would bring back a ball. Yet when asked if the two words, ball and doll, are the same or different on an auditory discrimination test, many young or reading disabled children respond incorrectly. It seems quite possible that children do not fully understand the directions for and concepts involved in responding to auditory discrimination tests.

As a result of his review of existing literature on the relationship of auditory discrimination and reading, Dykstra concluded:

> When comparisons are made between matched groups of "good" and "poor" readers, skill in auditory discrimination appears to be significantly related to achievement in reading. In other words, inferior auditory discrimination is a correlate of reading disability, even though present research does not warrant the inference of a cause and effect relationship. (7, p. 16)

In a more recent review, Hammill and Larsen (17) maintain that the relationship between auditory discrimination and reading achievement is artificially high because when children are separated into groups according to their reading achievement, they are inadvertently separated in intellectual ability, as well. The differences in intellectual ability may explain to a great extent the differences in performance on the auditory discrimination tests. Their interpretation of the results of studies that have investigated the relationship between reading achievement on a variety of auditory skills led them to question many of the assumptions made about the influence of auditory factors on reading achievement.

It seems quite likely that teachers, specialists, and researchers have used the term auditory discrimination without sufficient care. It also appears likely that auditory discrimination has been overused to explain the cause of reading disabilities. For example, it is not uncommon to find teachers ascribing an auditory discrimination problem to a child who has difficulty manipulating initial consonant sounds. If the teacher asks the child to give a word that begins like "boy," and the child says "toy," some teachers conclude that an auditory discrimination problem exists. Actually, the problem is probably more with the concept of what "begins like" means than with perception or discrimination. A clearer analysis and explanation of the kinds of auditory skills prerequisite for reading and more adequate ways of measuring these are needed. More information about the effects on reading achievement and of strategies designed to increase auditory skills is also needed.

In addition to these general questions regarding the relationship between auditory skills and reading, the relationship has been intensively studied in one particular group of children recently. The so-called disadvantaged or linguistically different child has been singled out as having auditory discrimination problems. It does seem that children who speak a dialect form of a language are more likely to do poorly on some phases of auditory discrimination testing. For example, there is evidence to suggest that some black children from some urban areas simplify consonant clusters at the ends of words so that only the first consonant in the word is pronounced. Thus, "past" would be pronounced like "pass," "went" would be pronounced as "when," and so forth. If these items were included in an auditory discrimination test, it is likely that pairs such as pass and past would be perceived as the same word spoken twice. The extent to which dialect interferes with reading is a complex question, but this is at least some suggestion that if teachers do not make dialect speakers feel rejected and if dialect readers are provided with meaningful contextual materials, the language differences will have minimal or no effect.

Because auditory discrimination is dependent upon both sensation and experience, either factor my contribute to a discrimination problem. Children with severe speech defects may also have severe problems with auditory discrimination. Both problems may reflect a sensory (hearing) loss. On the other hand, it is quite possible that a child who has never heard the words "vow" and "thou" before will not hear them as being different. The more experience children have with language, the more facile they become in responding to its likenesses and differences.

As with hearing loss, it is often said that children with auditory discrimination problems will have substantial difficulty with methods of teaching reading which place great stress on phonics. Though this is largely unverified, it would seem a reasonable proposition.

MEASURES OF AUDITORY DISCRIMINATION. Probably the most widely used measure in this area is the Wepman Auditory Discrimination Test. There are two forms of the test, and each consists of 40 pairs of words. Some pairs consist of two identical words (boy, boy); others of two similar sounding words (vow, thou). The examiner pronounces each pair of words and the child must indicate whether the examiner said the same word twice or two different words. A somewhat newer, more elaborate test of auditory discrimination is the Goldman-Fristoe-Wordcock Test. Most measures of reading readiness also include a subtest which requires some form of auditory discrimination.

EDUCATIONAL IMPLICATIONS. Though there is general acknowledgment that both auditory and visual perception factors can be important contributing factors to reading achievement, the relationships need much more study. Two general approaches can be taken with children who are diagnosed as having problems in this area. The first, which might be called an underlying skills approach, suggests that perception and discrimination skills are prerequisite to learning reading and other academic subjects and, therefore, should be taught before reading is taught. A good example would be training a child with visual perception problems using the Frostig-Horne program for the development of visual perception before beginning reading instruction. The underlying skills approach has become popular with a number of learning disability specialists. The approach often uses materials other than letters and words as the vehicle for training the skill.

The second approach, the one favored in this text, is to begin reading instruction, capitalizing on areas of strength and trying to overcome areas of weakness. Words and letters are used to train the skills as reading instruction proceeds. In extreme clinical cases, this may require a slow-paced, multisensory approach, but the difficulty of transfer of skills to reading is avoided. Working with geometric figures to develop perception skills appears far less desirable than working with letters and words. The letters can be widely different in shape (e.g., X vs. O), they can be large in size, they can be traced, there can be much needed repetition, but children can learn to make the necessary discriminations. A similar approach is recommended for auditory work. Using words (e.g., asking for rhyming words and for words that begin alike) appears a far sounder practice than having a child listen to a series of taps made by a teacher and then imitating the pattern.

Neurological Factors

Teachers and reading specialists will not be involved in administering neurological examinations to children with reading disabilities. Specialists and teachers will sometimes be involved in the process of referring children for a neurological examination.

If a child attending school shows prolonged difficulty in learning to read, a psychological evaluation can provide important clues as to whether or not the child needs to be referred for a neurological examination. Data from the WISC—R and Bender Gestalt can be used to suggest the need for such an evaluation. Teachers and specialists can assist in the referral processes by looking for a number of activities associated with neurological difficulties. If the child has extreme difficulty attending, is easily distracted by peripheral stimuli, has gross or fine motor coordination problems, or continuously shows perceptual confusion, in addition to failing to learn to read, such a referral may be in order.

EDUCATIONAL IMPLICATIONS. As indicated in Chapter 2, which deals with diagnosis, there appear to be few direct educational implications stemming from the conclusion that a child has a neurological problem. A child who is distractible may need individual help and a study place that has a minimum amount of stimulation, regardless of whether her or his distractibility is due to neurological or psychological factors.

If a child is given medication because of a diagnosis of neurological dysfunction, the teacher or specialist should be asked by the child's pediatrician to assume responsibility for monitoring the behavior of the child. The effects of drugs are difficult to judge. If no improvement or more disruptive behavior appears consequent to the child's being given medication, this information should be communicated to the pediatrician by the teacher or through the child's parents. A responsible neurologist will always seek information regarding a child's behavior in school and at home in an effort to determine the effect of the medication.

CONCLUSIONS

Determining the cause of a reading problem is often an essentially impossible task. In many cases it appears that a combination of factors contribute to a child's difficulty in learning. If serious vision, hearing, or neurological defects exist, they will certainly become stumbling blocks if not absolute barriers to learning. However, even when these areas of malfunctioning are corrected, teachers and reading specialists are faced with the responsibility of providing a sound program of instruction.

The results of a carefully conducted psychological evaluation can also yield information that can be useful in providing insight about the nature of a reading problem, but again the need remains for effective educational planning. The results of an intelligence test can be used to establish some initial hypotheses about areas that need to be further developed in order for progress in reading to take place at an acceptable rate. Intelligence test scores should not be viewed as an excuse for not planning an effective program of reading instruction. The basic thrust must remain helping a child to move to the next stage of achievement. In essentially all cases, children are capable of making some progress in reading and learning. It is necessary to constantly maintain an optimistic outlook and to avoid constantly looking for justification for failure.

BIBLIOGRAPHY

1. Blankenship, E. "A First Primer on Visual Perception." *Journal of Learning Disabilities,* 4 (1971): 39–42.

2. Bond, Guy, and Miles Tinker. *Reading Difficulties: Their Diagnosis and Correction.* Englewood Cliffs, N.J.: Prentice-Hall, 1967.

3. Boring, E. G. "Intelligence as the Tests Measure It." *The New Republic,* 35 (1923): 35–37.

4. Carroll, John B. "Language Development," in Chester W. Harris,

ed., *Encyclopedia of Educational Research*. New York: Macmillan, 1960.

5. Church, M. "Does Visual Perception Training Help Beginning Readers?" *The Reading Teacher,* 27 (January, 1974): 361–364.

6. Cleland, D. "Seeing and Reading." *American Journal of Optometry,* 80 (1958): 467–481.

7. Dykstra, R. "Auditory Discrimination Abilities and Beginning Reading Achievement." *Reading Research Quarterly,* 1 (Spring, 1966): 5–34.

8. Ebel, R. "Educational Tests: Valid? Biased? Useful?" *Phi Delta Kappan,* 57 (October, 1975): 83–88.

9. Flax, N. "The Eye and Learning Disabilities." *Journal of Learning Disabilities,* 6 (May, 1973): 329–334.

10. Freeman, F. *Theory and Practice of Psychological Testing.* New York: Holt, Rinehart and Winston, 1962.

11. Frostig, M., and D. Horne. *The Frostig Program for the Development of Visual Perception: Teacher's Guide.* Chicago: Follett, 1964.

12. Glasser, A., and I. Zimmerman. *Clinical Interpretation of the WISC.* New York: Grune & Stratton, 1967.

13. Green, R. "Tips on Educational Testing: What Teachers and Parents Should Know." *Phi Delta Kappan,* 57 (October, 1975): 89–92.

14. Groff, R. "Reading Ability and Auditory Discrimination: Are They Related?" *The Reading Teacher,* 28 (May, 1975), 742–747.

15. Hammill, D. "Training Visual Perceptual Processes." *Journal of Learning Disabilities,* 5 (November, 1972): 552–559.

16. Hammill, D., L. Goodman, and J. Wiederhold. "Visual Motor Processes: Can We Train Them?" *The Reading Teacher,* 27 (February, 1974): 469–478.

17. Hammill, D., and S. Larsen. "The Relationship of Selected Auditory Perceptual Skills and Reading Ability." *Journal of Learning Disabilities,* 7 (August–September, 1974): 429–436.

18. Harris, A. *How to Increase Reading Ability,* 5th ed. New York: McKay, 1970.

19. Harris, A., and E. Sipay. *How to Increase Reading Aibility,* 6th ed. New York: McKay, 1975.

20. Olson, A. "Relation of Achievement Test Scores and Specific Reading Abilities to the Frostig Developmental Test of Visual Perception." *Perceptual and Motor Skills,* 22 (1966), 179–184.

21. Pikulski, J. "Assessing Information About Intelligence and Reading." *The Reading Teacher,* 29, 2 (November, 1975): 157–163.

22. Pikulski, J. "The Validity of Three Brief Measures of Intelligence for Disabled Readers." *Journal of Educational Research,* 67 (October, 1973): 67–69.

23. Rodenborn, L. "Determining, Using, Expectancy Formulas." *The Reading Teacher,* 28 (December, 1974): 286–291.

24. Rosen, C. "The Status of School Vision Screening: A Review of Research and Consideration of Some Selected Problems," in *The Psychology of Reading Behavior: 18th Yearbook of the International Reading Conference.* Newark, Del.: International Reading Assoc., 1969, pp. 42–49.

25. Rosenthal, R., and L. Jacobson. "Teacher Expectations for the Disadvantaged." *Scientific American,* 218 (April, 1968): 19–23.

26. Smith, P., and R. Marx, "Some Cautions on the Frostig Test: A Factor Analytic Study." *Journal of Learning Disabilities,* 5 (1972): 357–362.

27. Wechsler, D. *Manual: Wechsler Intelligence Scale for Children —Revised.* New York: Psychological Corp., 1974.

28. Williams, R. "The Silent Mugging, The Black Community," *Psychology Today,* 7 (May, 1974), 34.

29. Woodworth, R. *Psychology.* New York: Holt, 1929.

30. Zach, L., and J. Kaufman. "How Adequate Is the Concept of Perceptual Deficit for Education?" *Journal of Learning Disabilities,* 5 (June–July, 1972): 351–356.

CHAPTER 7

An Ego Approach to the Study of Reading Disability

It was stated earlier that we view the child as a physical organism, functioning in a social environment, in a psychological manner. Reading is a complex intellectual process involving a total individual, and may invoke any or all of these aspects, with cause and effect being closely interwoven. Learning is a dynamic process. To understand what happens in the process, attention must always be focused on its comprehensiveness and on the whole individual involved in the process.

Throughout this book we have emphasized the importance of knowing the child. We have spoken of the factors which play a very important role in determining how well a child will learn. We have discussed the various methods utilized to assess and evaluate these factors. Prevention and diagnosis have been stressed but always in the context of determining the best possible way to help the child.

Yet all our "scientific" and sophisticated techniques are of no great value unless the child is approached through a sound conceptual framework. There are many possible pitfalls in the evaluation of any youngster with a learning problem. It is certainly important that the observations and testing be perceptive and accurate; the interpretation of both clinical and test findings depends to a great extent upon the competence of the diagnostician. Most essential, however, is that the evaluation not be done mechanically. It is unfortunate when test patterns are memorized and used rigidly with little understanding of the functions that account for these test patterns. There should always be some underlying rationale which is brought to the interpretation of test findings. While an eclectic approach may appear to be objective and nonbiased (and, therefore, devoutly to be desired), it can become a way of hedging to hide the fact that there is no clear-cut understanding of the nature of the problem.

Through the years, there have been innumerable shifts of professional opinion concerning the vital issues of etiology, diagnosis, and remediation in reading and related learning disabilities. Twenty years ago, if youngsters had severe reading disabilities and were referred to a clinic or to a private practitioner, the chances would be very strong indeed that following a careful evaluation of their problems, they would be recommended for psychotherapy. There was absolutely nothing in the psychological literature which could not account for children's having difficulty in learning to read. Thus we heard such terms as unresolved Oedipal strivings, guilt feelings, conflict over aggression, and overly dominant mother figure as explanations for severe reading difficulties. Unfortunately, all too often after two or three years in therapy the children would be discharged with some of their problems resolved but their reading problem still intact. Psychotherapy may be helpful to some youngsters whose learning problems are directly the result of emotional disturbance, but psychotherapy never taught anyone how to read.

Approximately fifteen years ago, the pendulum shifted. Slowly, like a sleeping dragon that had been awakened, this basically amorphous but powerful concept of organicity reared its ugly head. Almost before they knew it, teachers and other professionals were enveloped by such terms as minimal cerebral dysfunction, dyslexia, minimal brain damage, strephosymbolia, maturational lag, developmental discrepancy, and the most flowery of all, minimal cerebral desynchronization syndrome. In other words, the clinical situation had been reversed: organic factors overpowered functional factors and emerged as the most common single cause of behavioral disorder in childhood.

We begin with the axiom that there is no one single etiology for all reading disabilities. Rather, reading problems are caused by any number of factors, all of which may be highly interrelated. Frequently children who are experiencing a reading or learning disability are approached with a unitary orientation; consequently, extremely important aspects of their problems may be ignored. The tendency of each professional discipline to view the entire problem "through its own window of specialization" often obscures vital factors which may contribute to, or at least exacerbate, the basic difficulty. It is just as invalid to conceive of one cure, one panacea, applied randomly to all types of reading problems. Not every reading disabled youngster requires a special school or psychotherapy or kinesthetic techniques or perceptual-motor training or, for that matter, a regression to crawling along the floor.

To return to the organic-functional controversy, what is clear is that we do not fully understand the relationship between neurological impairment and reading disability (or between neurological impairment and behavioral disorder). We can recognize that there are certain physical and psychological conditions which may predispose a youngster to meet with learning difficulty, but we certainly do not know why. We are aware that environmental conditions may have a profound effect upon even constitutional factors, but the quality and quantity of that influence remains obscure. Thus an approach to the disabled reader that takes into consideration the unique interaction of functional and organic factors would be most desirable.

An ego orientation with its emphasis on the developmental-interaction approach seems most viable. In this way the *interaction* of both neurological and psychological factors can be studied extensively; the factors are not regarded as isolated units. It is true that in other approaches many ego functions—such as perception, concept formation, and language development—have been utilized in diagnosis and remediation. But with an ego orientation, with the constant emphasis on developmental interaction, we are provided the opportunity for treating the child more effectively as a whole person. The ego approach to the study of reading disability provides the conceptual framework that is so sorely needed in a field that has become so often fragmented.

CONCEPT OF EGO DEVELOPMENT

A unique approach, then, to the study of reading disability is found in the tenets of ego psychology. The center of attention is upon the ego functioning of the disabled youngster. In line with the pioneer efforts of Hartmann, Kris, and Loewenstein (4), the basic functions of the developing personality are referred to as the functions of the developing ego.

It is important that the reader understand the global meaning of the word *ego* as it is used here in the context of psychoanalytic ego psychology. It does not refer solely to the way people feel about themselves. (In common parlance, we say that people have good egos, or weak egos, and so forth; basically we refer to their confidence or lack of it.) In ego psychology, the ego is essentially a hypothetical construct which allows us to deal with very important psychological and physiological functions in a unified rather than piecemeal fashion. The ego is not to be thought of as an anatomical section of the nervous system. As a matter of fact, the ego carries out all of its important functions through the central nervous system. The neurological substratum of the ego is the central nervous system (this is why any insult to the central nervous system constitutes a severe threat to the integrity of the organism). In a very real sense the ego is the central executive and directing force of the mind. It is to the mind what the executive branch of the government is to the country. Utilizing an ego orientation, we need not be primarily concerned with determining if there has been any injury to the brain or some physiological dysfunction or some environmental deprivation. What we focus our attention on are the ego functions of the disabled youngster, the ego functions which are so necessary for learning. What may have interfered with their development is certainly of academic importance, but with any specific youngster, our concern must be on how to remove the interferences to the ego functioning in order to allow the child to learn more effectively.

Primary Ego Apparatuses

None of us are born with an ego, merely with the physical apparatus (the brain and the various sensory and motor systems) which provides the potential for developing one. Rapaport (5) has referred to this potential as the "natural endowment" which unfolds in a process of maturation and experience. This natural endowment may be thought of as the source for the initial development of the primary ego apparatuses. These apparatuses consist of such basic skills as perception, concept formation, motility, and language development. These fundamental ego skills represent a potentiality for development—a potentiality which ultimately develops into the secondary ego functions that are so vital to the learning process—sublimation, delay of impulse, reality testing, synthesis, analysis, integration, and so forth.

For example, children are not born with the ability to *perceive* but with the physical apparatus which gives them the opportunity to develop that ability. From the time of birth, however (and perhaps, even prenatally), there is increasing neural differentiation and maturation, as well as stimulation from the environment. Even when infants do not "know" their mothers and cannot recognize them on sight, they are receiving an infinite number of impressions through physical contact that gradually lead to the formation of their image of what their mothers are like.

One of the infants' first *concepts* may be related to the fact that mother brings about relief from hunger, which in turn is tension-reducing and gratifying. Initially, of course, the infants' smile of gratification will be in response to the simple fact that they are being fed. Again in the course of maturation and experience the infants establish an association between nursing and the human face. What is even more important is that the satisfactions of being fed become associated with the mother figure. Ultimately, at about seven or eight months, there is sufficient development of the primary ego apparatus to allow children to differentiate one human face from another and to show the well-known fear of strangers. That is, babies may smile and coo while their mothers are holding them, but begin to cry when they are turned over to others. With the return of the mothers, infants revert to their initial state of quiescence and pleasure.

Motility is another rudimentary ego skill which develops through a process of maturation and experience, and which plays a major role in subsequent ego development. We are obviously not born crawling or walking, but with the potential to develop those abilities. Once children have sufficiently matured and there is again proper stimulation from the environment, their ability to move around and to explore brings about changes in their personalities. The world becomes their oyster, and although their mastery of motor skills is accompanied by a certain amount of anxiety, it is at least the beginning of a sense of autonomy. (Notice, for example, how children of 10 to 15 months practice separating from their mothers by moving more and more away from them and yet at times having to return for "emotional refueling.") It is at this stage, too, that children develop a sense of being "people who can rather than people who cannot."

Language is perhaps the most important primary ego skill, particularly as it relates to reading and reading disability. Language originates in a kind of magic; sounds are uttered for pleasure and employed indiscriminately to bring about a desired event. Gradually children realize that their words are truly powerful: they may cause the appearance of the invaluable person who ministers to their needs. As time goes on, language begins to bring new meaning to the children, as they learn to use it to transform action into thought. Words substitute for human acts and set the stage for important secondary ego functions, such as delay, postponement, and even renunciation of gratification. Without language the important faculties of judgment and reasoning could not occur.

Secondary Ego Function

As we have indicated above, the fundamental ego functions begin to be crystallized and differentiated in a spiraling process of maturation and experience. They necessarily begin in a primitive way and develop only gradually as the infant grows. With every interaction of children with their environment (usually the mother in the initial stages), there are stimulation, tension, and relief-of-tension situations. Thus the ego and the mental organization of the infant begin to develop. Ultimately, as there are greater and more varied experiences, the secondary functions of the ego also develop. Secondary ego functions are learned and include defense mechanisms such as repression, isolation, and reaction formation. The defenses of the ego serve the very important purpose of adaptation and learning. Some of these defenses deal mostly with the external world, while other defenses deal more with the internal world of drive, conflict, tension, and emotion.

Of utmost importance is the ego's ability to maintain *relative autonomy,* that is, to exercise a healthy balance between the demands of the world around it and the strivings and desires from within. Thus, if for any reason (organic, physiological, psychological) there is too much unsatisfied instinctual tension, children may not be able to postpone gratification long enough to learn. Children must be able to attend and to concentrate in order to profit from instruction. The ability to delay or to channel their impulses in a way that allows them to distance themselves from the press of the internal stimuli is an absolute prerequisite for learning.

It is vitally important that we focus our attention on the developmental-interaction approach through our study of primary and secondary ego functioning. Child development is a complex network involving both constitutional factors and environmental input. Even in the first year of life, as the primary ego apparatuses mature, we see sensory-motor development, the beginnings of autonomy, the emergence of the ability to relate, and the laying down of memory traces. Later we observe the progress in vocalization and language, the ability to delay and control impulse, and further development and definition of the ego. What is most important is the continuing dynamic movement and simultaneous interplay of all developmental levels. It is in fact a three-ring circus!

RELATIONSHIP OF EGO FUNCTIONING TO READING DISABILITY

We may conclude that anything which interferes with the development of the ego and any of its functions will undoubtedly influence children's adaptation to life, including one very particular adaptation, namely their capacity for learning. There is not a single aspect of psychological development, structure, and dynamics that does not relate very directly to some aspect of learning. And it is axiomatic that a knowledge of normal development is vital to the understanding of children with reading-learning disabilities. To evaluate children with reading problems, it is essential that we know what constitutes normal growth and behavior.

Our emphasis on ego functioning avoids an all too common pitfall for those who work with retarded readers. That is, the tendency to speak of certain cognitive factors as if they were divorced from affective ones. Most teachers have been alerted to cognition, perception, and language development, and know their importance in the reading process. Educators are besieged with "innovative" methods for both assessing and remediating specific deficits manifested by the disabled reader. They are taught to teach to the "auditory sphere" or through the "visual receptive mechanism." The Frostig technique (2), which was originally devised for certain youngsters with precisely defined perceptual weaknesses, is now adopted by school systems for the entire first- and second-grade classes. Children are asked to walk on balance beams in the belief that this will magically help them learn to read. (It might prove helpful indeed if children were required to read books as they engaged in some of these perceptual-motor activities.)

If some of the things that are done in the name of innovation seem bizarre, what is perhaps more tragic is our tendency to forget that we are indeed teaching the whole child. The educator, along with many other professionals, has all too often given only lip service to this basic concept. In our zeal to develop more refined and sophisticated methods of diagnosis and remediation, we sometimes forget that we cannot separate feeling from cognition, emotion from perception, affect from concept formation. We argue endlessly about the relative influence of genetically determined factors and environmental ones. Yet we all too often ignore the most important factor, the interaction of all these influences.

It is in this area that ego psychology can make its greatest contribution. The very nature of ego functioning focuses our attention not on the organic child, not on the functional child, but on the unique interaction of both functional and organic factors which always are operative in any youngster. Further, we cannot ignore the significant contribution made by Erikson (1) who spoke of the "epigenesis of ego functioning." Through this concept we recognize that it is not only the factors which operate on children which are important in shaping their adaptation to life, but the timing of the events, as well.

As children develop, they acquire an increasing array of actions to deal with problems. As the organism evolves through a process of maturation and experience, children become "ready" at different stages for further input from the environment. If that stimulation is not received when children are biologically ready, the stage may be set for problems which will not only affect the development of the primary ego functions but will undoubtedly affect the children's capacity to learn, as well. The converse is also true. If the children are not physically or physiologically ready for the environmental input, then the organism in a very real sense is overwhelmed. The desired learning does not take place; instead there is only frustration, withdrawal, and a resultant aversion to the whole learning process.

Informal Learning

Learning is an integral part of all development. It is certainly not something which begins with the formal entrance into school. If we view learning in the context of ego functioning, we must recognize that most of the organization of the ego has taken place long before children start kindergarten. While most teachers do not have the professional responsibility for guiding children during early infancy, the first few years are vitally important, because during that time is laid the groundwork for both the rudimentary and secondary ego functions.

At birth human infants have only a few of the inherited patterns of adaptive behavior that can contribute to their survival. They do have inherent rooting, sucking, and swallowing reflexes, which enable them to find and take nourishment, provided the breast or bottle is within the range of their movements. They learn to get the nipple end of the bottle to their lips and suck it for pleasure. They are capable of vocalizing relatively undifferentiated cries of distress, thereby unwittingly signaling that they are in need. Within a period of days they can make cooing noises and other facial expressions which evoke feelings of tenderness and warmth in mothers. The ability of the mothers to respond to the early cues sent out by infants plays a significant role in how well children will make their initial adaptation to life. In turn, as has been discussed earlier, the proper crystallization of percepts and concepts, the fundamental building blocks of thought, must take place if the children are to achieve readiness for formal reading instruction.

Children's endowment in the more complex behavior patterns, such as the ability to track objects with their eyes or to coordinate visual perception with reaching for and grasping an object, is in terms of potential rather than immediately useful skills. This is even more true of the higher mental abilities, such as conscious memory, anticipation, speech, abstract reasoning, and communication by spoken and written language.

In summary the capacity to initiate motor and mental activity is partly determined by the intactness of the central nervous system. In addition this capacity is influenced in very important ways by environmental conditions that impinge upon the children. There is the continuous interaction of innate and experiential factors. Children who from the beginning of life are enabled to develop the primary ego apparatuses (perception, concept formation, motility, and language) will be less vulnerable to problems later than children who are impaired in one or several of these areas. The corollary of this is that disturbances in early ego development that can be detected early (perhaps in infancy) can respond to methods of intervention much better than those which are detected once the ego has already been largely developed.

INTERFERENCES WITH EGO DEVELOPMENT

We have pointed out that anything that interferes with the proper development of the ego may influence children's capacity to learn. It is therefore not surprising that any classification of learning disorders would double equally well with a classification of types of emotional disturbance or disturbances interfering with basic ego functions.

Hartmann (3) felt that it was necessary to assume that children are born with "a certain degree of preadaptiveness," meaning that they are at birth equipped in a rudimentary way with the primary ego apparatuses and thus prepared for dealing with reality even before they have experienced it. Deficiencies in the primary autonomous ego functions render children vulnerable to some form of aberrancy, perhaps a mental disorder or a reading disability.

Disorder in the Organic Substratum of the Ego: The Central Nervous System

When children suffer brain damage, prenatally, perinatally, or postnatally, they have experienced an insult to the very matrix of the crucial organ of learning, the brain, and its sensory and motor systems. There is a defect in their primary ego apparatuses, which, in turn, interferes with their ability to interact with their environment in an adaptive manner. Defect in the ego apparatus in some cases may result solely from a situation where the children are completely deprived of intellectual and/or emotional stimulation. In any event, in order for the ego to develop properly, there are two basic requirements: (1) the primary apparatus, that is, the neurological substrata of the ego, the central nervous system, must be intact; (2) and there must be a proper degree of stimulation in the environment.

Rappaport (6) has pointed to three major areas of difficulty in children who have suffered an insult to the central nervous system. Under the broad heading of inadequate integrative functions, he discusses problems in perception and concept formation. We may speak about children who are able to take in stimuli, but who have trouble fitting them appropriately into things they already know. For example, children may learn how to climb on a jungle gym, but when they are out in the woods and faced with the possibility of climbing a tree, it might not occur to them that the climbing skills they have learned in one area can be applied to another. This is illustrative of children's likely difficulty in making any kind of generalization. They can deal with that which is specific and concrete; they cannot engage in the kind of active mental manipulation that is such an essential aspect of abstract conceptualization or generalization.

Children may have trouble pulling out of their storehouse of knowledge things that are related to something that is introduced in a class discussion. This is a cognitive disorder. Although they may be able to deal successfully with that which is rote and represents simply an acquisition of information, they have difficulty in applying that information to different functional situations. It is no surprise that their score on a test assessing their judgment is often far inferior to their score on a test measuring their fund of general factual knowledge. To apply information requires the kind of mental manipulation and freedom of psychic energies that is so antithetical to the types of ego functioning so characteristic of this disability.

These children also have a great deal of difficulty in manipulating verbal concepts. If they are asked how a peach and a plum are alike, they may very well deny that there is any similarity whatsoever. If they are given the aid of external structuring, they will most likely respond in terms of functional or concrete properties of objects. This kind of youngster finds it quite impossible to make generalizations from one specific learning situation to another.

A second area of disruptive ego functioning is that of inadequate impulse control or the control of ideas and feelings. It is well known that youngsters with this problem tend to be highly narcissistic, disinhibited, hyperdistractible, hyperactive, and impulsive. These symptoms should, at all times, be related to the deficiencies in normal ego development, because there is no conclusive evidence that hyperactivity or distractibility are related to defective neural transmission or specific brain cell malfunction. All the symptoms mentioned above represent rather the ego's method of defending the rest of the personality from awareness of its defects. Thus children who have had a basic deficiency in the primary ego apparatus of perception or motility have been hampered in their ability to explore the environment adaptively and cannot acquire a sense of mastery.

Our third area of concern is the defensive maneuvering on the part of the ego in coping with the anxiety brought on by the very intense feelings of inadequacy and defectiveness. Children who have experienced early insult to the central nervous system feel a severe threat to the integrity of their organism. They feel helpless in the face of their own intense handicap, and when they feel this way, they become more frightened and anxious. As a result, they tend either to be more aggressive, more hostile, or sometimes withdrawn. They also become highly egocentric and show feelings of omnipotence which, of course, represent their defense against strong feelings of defectiveness. Their egocentricity reveals itself in their need to relate all objects to themselves before they can relate them to others. (Perhaps this plays an important role in their difficulty in generalizing.)

The majority of children who suffer with this malady do not experience severe reading disorders although, of course, they may have many problems in learning generally. Nevertheless, there is a small percentage whose perceptual and conceptual deficiencies, derived from the early insult to the central nervous system and exacerbated by the reaction of the environment to the defective ego, will cause severe problems in reading, particularly in reading comprehension. The etiology, therefore, of this type of reading disorder is not defective neural transmission or specific brain malfunction; rather, it is related to the abnormal development of primary functional ego apparatuses.

Maturational and Developmental Problems

Even when no specific insult to the central nervous system has occurred, disturbances can arise from some interference with or delay in the maturation or development of the ego apparatus and its functions which are necessary for formal academic learning. Certainly there are some children who, for one reason or another, are not prepared for formal learning at the typical age assigned in our culture. It must be emphasized that just because neurological or biological difficulties exist in children, it does not necessarily indicate that they will develop serious learning problems. It may well be that, in order for youngsters to develop into so-called dyslexics, they must have this predisposition; but simply because the tendency is present, it does not mean that they must develop the disorder.

Most teachers today recognize the fact that some children are maturationally unprepared for learning to read when they are first introduced to the printed symbol. A small percent of these children may not have mastered certain ego functions which are basic to reading. Children's problems in perception may especially be evident in associative learning difficulties. Because reading, in the broad analysis, is a process of association, trouble in this area presents a major problem for students.

If youngsters are initiated into reading at a time when their ego deficiencies do not allow them to profit from the normal methods of teaching reading, they almost inevitably experience failure. It is no wonder that secondary emotional problems may then ensue; the children may feel discouraged and develop negative attitudes toward reading.

CONCLUSIONS

An ego approach to the study of reading disability provides a conceptual framework by means of which children can be studied in a comprehensive fashion. Rather than fragmenting our approach, we view children as physical organisms, functioning in a social environment in a psychological manner. This is essentially a developmental-interaction approach. We recognize that every individual is born with a potential to develop the primary ego apparatuses. It is the interaction of this native endowment with the environment which subsequently leads to the development of secondary ego functions and which, in turn, determines the ultimate fate of the child, insofar as adaptation to life is concerned. It is never just the neurological or physiological status; it is how these predisposing conditions are ultimately influenced by the nature of the environmental stimulation.

Injuries to the central nervous system (the neurological substratum of the ego) can effect serious problems in the unfolding of the primary ego apparatuses. These delays in the development of primary ego functions can bring about altered responses from the environment, which in turn may affect the development of secondary ego functions. What has often been considered neurological impairment may really be the result of a unique interaction of both organic and functional factors. This has important implications regarding the kind of intervention employed to alleviate the problems. In essence, our attention must always be upon the current ego functioning of the child, no matter what the original etiology may have been.

BIBLIOGRAPHY

1. Erikson, E. *Childhood and Society.* New York: Norton, 1950.

2. Frostig, M., and P. Maslow. *Learning Problems in the Classroom.* New York: Grune & Stratton, 1973.

3. Hartmann, H. *Essays on Ego Psychology.* New York: International Universities Press, 1964.

4. Hartmann, H., E. Kris, and R. M. Lowenstein. "Comments on the Formation of Psychic Structure." in *The Psychoanalytic Study of the Child,* vol. 2, pp. 11–38. New York: International Universities Press, 1948.

5. Rapaport, D. *Diagnostic Psychological Testing,* vol. 1. Chicago: The Yearbook Publishers, Inc. 1946.

6. Rappaport, S. R., ed. *Childhood Aphasia and Brain Damage: A Definition.* Narberth, Pa.: Livingston, 1964.

CHAPTER 8

Physiological Development

In our last chapter we cautioned strongly against a fragmented approach to the diagnosis and remediation of reading disabilities. Inherent in the ego orientation is the recognition that mind and body do not function as separate entities, and that the interaction of physical, physiological, psychological, and social factors must always be emphasized. In fact there is a rapidly growing accumulation of evidence that mental states can affect bodily processes. A corollary to this is the awareness that heredity and environment also cannot be viewed as discrete entities in studying the causes of reading and related learning difficulties. The continuing and often painful question of nature versus nurture is essentially a superficial one. There is no doubt that both hereditary and environmental factors work together, in differing proportions under different circumstances, to determine the ultimate adaptiveness of children. These factors influence the way children will respond to both informal and formal learning tasks. To say that a human trait is inherited does not imply the absence of environmental influences but merely the presence of genetic ones.

Let us illustrate by offering one hypothesis concerning the possible etiology of severe reading disability. There is increasing evidence that at least one type of rare and severe reading disability (developmental dyslexia) may have a genetic etiology. Nevertheless, the validity of this concept would only postulate that there is a genetic predisposition. Because this predisposition to difficulty exists in children does not necessarily or usually mean that children will develop dyslexia. That is, for children to have this problem, they must have the genetic predisposition; simply because they have this predisposition, however, does not mean that they will develop dyslexia. Probably a very important factor in determining the ultimate outcome would be the environmental influence, that is, the nature of the children's earliest learning experiences. Thus, if we had the techniques to determine the presence of the genetic predisposition at a very early age, we could probably be much more effective in preventing the child from actually becoming dyslexic. As is so often the case, the teacher who is responsible for the children's first formal introduction to reading activities may play a very influential role in determining the effect of the genetic factors.

NATURAL ENDOWMENT

Any discussion of genetic factors must be tempered by a consideration of the broader concept of *natural endowment* (Rapaport, 8). We pointed out earlier that this represents merely a potential for development, a potential that unfolds in a process of maturation and experience. It can also be thought of as the inherited constitutional pattern, but a pattern which can be modified by events which occur after conception. In other words the constitution or native endowment ultimately is the inherited pattern as affected and altered by prenatal, perinatal, and postnatal factors.

This is not an issue to be passed over lightly. If, for example, infants have suffered overt brain damage, it is abundantly clear to the parents or to the teachers that their native endowment has been altered. Their subsequent devlopment will be evaluated in this light, with obvious allowance made for deficiencies resulting from the injury to the central nervous system. In addition, if the brain damage has been identified, effective plans can be made to establish the proper social and educational intervention to allow children to function optimally. However, if there is alteration in hereditary endowment without clearly demonstrable clinical manifestations, children may not be recognized as constitutionally handicapped. In such cases, appropriate allowances may not be made, and the children may be looked upon by both parents and teachers as simply not measuring up to expectations. (This is seen quite commonly in those youngsters who later are diagnosed as having minimal cerebral dysfunction.) One interesting phenomenon related to this is the tendency of parents of cerebral palsied children to be less threatened and wounded by their children's overt handicap. On the other hand, when the "insult" is more subtle, the parents are even more greatly confused. Fantasies emerge; the parents wonder, "Just what is wrong with my child?" As the anxiety of the parents is aroused, negative emotions begin to have a marked effect upon their attitudes and behavior toward the ambivalently perceived children. These, in turn, create further disruption in the parent-child relationship. Ultimately this may result in a disorder in the children's learning process and, sometimes, specifically in their ability to learn to read and/or to use their reading skills effectively.

Intrauterine Factors

The most rapid and crucial period of growth in the human being occurs in the nine months before birth. The uterus provides the required environment for different organ systems to develop harmoniously. There is increasing evidence that the uterine environment may wield as great an influence as does genetic endowment in determining how well the fetus may develop before birth. Dudgeon (2) has pointed to a number of intrinsic and extrinsic factors to which the fetus may be exposed and which may affect its subsequent development. He classifies the environmental factors causing fetal damage in three categories: physical agents, such as radiation trauma; chemical agents, such as the noxious effects of drugs; and biological agents, such as infections.

Pasamanick and Knobloch (7) have coined the term "reproductive casualty" to account for the sequelae of harmful events during pregnancy and the birth process; most of the resulting damage to fetuses and newborn infants is in the central nervous system. Because fetal and neonatal deaths are largely associated with complications of pregnancy and/or prematurity, these potentially brain damaging events might result in children who do not succumb, but go on to develop a series of neuropsychiatric disorders. Depending upon the specific nature and extent of the insult to the brain, the disorders might range from gross neurologic impairment to the more subtle specific and nonspecific disabilities labeled as minimal brain dysfunction and dyslexia. It may well be that the greater vulnerability of the male fetus and neonate may account for the higher incidence of reading problems among boys. (This is in no way is meant to minimize the importance of social, emotional, and cultural factors in effecting more reading problems among boys.)

Throughout the country, intensive studies of neonates are being made, many of these dealing with those infants who fail to grow to normal size before birth. The survival of infants seems to be profoundly affected by the birth weight; the lower the weight of newborn, the greater the danger they face. At the same time, an important distinction is being drawn between premature infants and those infants whose growth has been retarded in their intrauterine life. As a matter of fact it may be that intrauterine growth retardation, not prematurity, may account for one-third to one-half of all low weight newborns.

Probably the greatest culprit contributing to low birth weight in both the premature and the growth-retarded baby is a poor nutritional status of the mother. What is most important is the nature of the mother's long-term diet before pregnancy. This is even of greater consequence than the nature of the expectant mother's food intake during pregnancy. It may be of some help to improve the quality of the diet of the expectant mother, but unfortunately, this does not compensate for the nutritional deficiencies of a lifetime.

It should be pointed out that what might be considered a psychophysiological etiology (poor nutrition) may indeed be a sociopsychological etiology. That is, if we consider the possible reasons for the nutritional deficiencies of the mother, we find that we are actually enmeshed in a wide variety of sociological and psychological factors that ultimately manifest themselves physiologically. This is another example of the continuous interaction of both organic and functional factors in the development of most learning disorders.

In any event there seems to be little doubt today that there is a significant correlation between premature children (or low-birth-weight children) and some forms of aberrancy later in life. Usually this will take the form of some sensory defect, school problems (the most common of which is reading disability) and cerebral dysfunction. A thorough history of the child with a severe reading problem would therefore be extremely helpful in determining some of the factors that may have contributed to the reading disability.

Perinatal Factors

If, as reading diagnosticians, we must be concerned with the prenatal history of the youngster, then we must at some time direct our attention to the birth record. Birth trauma of one form or another is a process that may cause severe damage to the central nervous system and lead to heavy neurological and psychological sequelae. Of utmost concern is any report of *anoxia,* or sustained oxygen deprivation, at the time of delivery. Although much has been said about the significant role this may play in the etiology of reading disability, the actual research has been somewhat ambiguous. According to Graham et al. (4), anoxia does not appear to have an all-or-none effect. Rather the concepts of minimal brain dysfunction and of a continuum of reproductive casualty appear reasonable. Corah et al. (1) also saw that the effects of anoxia were not absolute. Perinatal anoxia is related to deficits evident at seven years of age, but it is also evident that such deficits which do occur are reasonably minimal for the group as a whole. While there is some tendency for the degree of impairment to be associated with newborn criteria of severity, the association is a weak one. Prognosis for any given newborn would be very difficult to make except when there are very severe or numerous complications.

There are other traumas that can accompany the birth process and that should be of interest to the reading diagnostician. One might almost wish to have a detailed obstetrical history in making an initial assessment of possible brain lesions in the full-term newborn. Our experience has been, however, that hospital records are practically worthless in yielding information which may be of some value in determining whether indeed there was birth trauma. The birth all too often is recorded as normal unless there was a very serious complication. It is probably more valid to rely upon the retrospective report of the parent. Even though this may be distorted by events which have occurred after the birth, it is very often a truer depiction of what really transpired during the birth process.

There is also conflicting evidence concerning the effect of prolonged labor, precipitous delivery, and intracranial pressure at the time of birth, caused by forceps delivery or a narrow pelvic arch in the mother. One must seriously question, too, the procedure of inducing delivery, especially when this is done artificially for convenience sake. (One can sympathize with obstetricians in their desire not always to be called away for a delivery; whether this justifies increasing the risk of injury to the neonate is another matter.) There certainly is consensus, nevertheless, that birth trauma, whether mechanical or anoxia, is inescapable in the separation process of childbirth.

Postnatal Factors

Postnatal factors can also affect the developing child in an adverse manner. Much has been written about severe nutritional deficiencies. Malnutrition apparently can affect the development of the central nervous system by the direct influence on the intersensory organization. In turn this is caused by the fact that poor nutrition adversely modifies the growth and biochemical maturation of the brain. Despite all this, however, one must not forget the environmental influence. There is evidence that, in the first months and years of life, these environmental factors effect anatomical, physiological, and maturational changes, which might ordinarily be regarded as exclusively genetically determined. Thus, different forms of stimulation, primarily derived from the multiple interactions of mother and child during the early months, may actually trigger off neural modifications and affect the basic equilibrium of the child. This is just one more example of the continuous interaction of constitutional and environmental factors. Again we are simply implying that children whose basic endowment has been weakened as the result of poor nutrition are youngsters who are then more vulnerable to environmental stresses. In other words, they do not have as many options in their efforts to adapt to their environment. Optimal development is hardly likely to occur when there is an interaction of a weakened constitution with a faulty environment. Although problems may not be evident at an early date, children may succumb to the total weight of the various pressures, once they must meet the demands of the school situation.

Other factors may be of vast importance during the period from birth to approximately the age of five or six. We are speaking, of course, about the period of ego development. It is axiomatic that the earlier traumas occur in the life of children, the more likely the negative effect on the proper crystallization of ego functions. For example, in terms of psychopathology, psychoses, which are the most serious emotional disturbances, are related to traumatic experiences occurring in the first two years of life; neuroses originate from traumas that occur subsequently.

But let us return to the more "organic" trauma that are characteristically associated with postnatal factors. Although there is no definitive research, we have been impressed with the rather frequent history of very high fever in children with serious reading disorders. Sometimes it is just as significant when children have experienced low fevers over a prolonged period of time. Head trauma or brain insult resulting from an accident may have serious sequelae. One must also explore the possibility of lead poisoning or oxygen deprivation due to suffocation. Rappaport, in his discussion of children with perinatal types of brain damage, finds the following manifestations of inadequate impulse control or regulation:

1. A deficient, or even absent, sucking reflex at birth. In some cases the child actually has to be taught to suck.

2. Lack of a rooting reaction; that is, searching for the nipple.

3. Sucking too briefly, taking perhaps only an ounce, then falling asleep. Such a condition may spark the beginning of a conflict between mother and child to induce him to eat.

4. Early vomiting, where the child, who cannot hold much, will throw-up right after eating. Projectile vomiting, like a high-pressure stream, sometimes occurs.

5. Chewing difficulties, in which the child may spit out or reject lumpy foods or meats, which require chewing. He may stay in baby foods up to school age, because these require no chewing and are easy to swallow.

6. Hyperactivity, hyperirritability, and destructiveness often become suddenly and strikingly evident with the onset of motility. The child never walks—he always runs!

7. Lack of coordination. Because of difficulties in handling eating utensils, the child often uses his fingers. He does not dress or button himself, or tie his shoelaces—at first because of physical inability. Later he

can learn such tasks if each is analyzed into its components, which are taught in absolute sequence, allowing him to succeed at one step before the next is introduced. (9, p. 52)

BIOLOGICAL MATURATION

All the constitutional (including genetic) factors which have been discussed continue to operate after birth. It is true that to a very large extent, the time of the emergence of the capacity to walk, of puberty, and of the ability for abstract reasoning is biologically predetermined. Because the children's psychological and personality development is so closely associated with the development of their mental abilities (see the chapter on intellectual development), we must take special note of the biologically predetermined maturation of the nervous system.

There is a sequence that is followed in the maturation of nervous system pathways. This maturation proceeds gradually and sequentially from the autonomic level, to the spinal cord level of the sensory and lower motor neuron reflex arc, to a subcortical level, to the level of the upper motor neuron and cerebral cortex. Thus at birth (except in the case of prematurity) the autonomic nervous system, which participates importantly in the homeostatic regulative functions, normally is functional and reasonably well integrated. Similarly, the lower motor neuron reflex arcs also are functioning, as is evidenced by response to stimuli. The integration of sensory-motor reflex pathways with other sensory and motor pathways and with the higher centers is dependent upon continuing maturation of the central nervous system and upon experience.

The innately predetermined individual pattern in the timing of sensory-motor maturation is therefore affected by environmental input. Ilg and Ames (5) point out that this interaction becomes evident from the moment of birth. As hard as a mother may try to impose a rigid schedule on some infants, she is not successful unless she responds to their individual demands. The demands are most marked in the first 12 weeks. The success of feeding in this period depends upon the environment's capacity to accommodate itself to the children.

The impact of emotional deprivation during infancy has been studied extensively during recent years. Healthy infants living in institutions fail to develop normally. Our experience has been that early severe deprivation is significantly related to psychological disturbance or deviant impaired development. This is revealed frequently in learning disorders of a wide variety, not the least of which is reading disability. It is probable true that children who have suffered this kind of trauma are scarred

214

for many years to come. The cognitive deficits that appear at a later date and that markedly operate against their ability to profit from normal reading instruction are extremely difficult to overcome. However, this is not to suggest that children are doomed inevitably to failure and/or maladjustment. Unforeseeable events during important later phases of development will often determine the resolution of earlier conflicts and imbalances, or the failure of such resolution.

In summary, we might say that the capacity to initiate motor and mental activity is partly determined by biochemical and structural elements of the body, especially of the central nervous system. This capacity is influenced in myriad ways by environmental conditions that impinge upon the children. Thus the interrelationship between innate and experiential factors determines activity, as well as other aspects of the developmental process. When we talk about optimal ego development, we refer to the opportunity for the children to be active motorically, socially, verbally, and intellectually. If there is impairment or delay in any of these areas, children are more vulnerable to stress. While symptoms may be masked for a long time, entrance into school may constitute the ultimate pressure to which the children no longer can adapt. It is true that some children may manage to get by in the earlier grades through the use of their capacity for rote memory work, so that they may be able to "read" (recognize words), and "spell" (remember sequences of letters). But when called upon to exercise the capacity for comprehension and understanding, to see relationships, or to conceptualize, such children's underlying vulnerability—leading to the reading difficulties—becomes all too evident.

Maturational and Developmental Problems

Even when no specific insult to the central nervous system has occurred, disturbances can arise from some interference with or delay in the maturation or development of the ego apparatus and its functions, which are necessary for formal academic learning. We should differentiate a maturation delay from a developmental delay. The maturational lag may be thought of as specifically distinguished from a delay in progression derived from the influence of experience. Developmental delay would refer to an interference with developmental progression in which the experiential factors play a predominant role. The two are practically inseparable, because they constantly influence one another. The stage and rate of physical maturation undoubtedly influence and probably also are influenced by the nature of the children's experience. However, just as it probably is very difficult for seven-month old children to establish voluntary control over bowel functions (they are neurologically incapable of being trained), so there are probably varying degrees of biological maturational preparedness required to undertake learning. De Hirsch is perhaps today the most prominent representative of the theory of maturational and developmental delay. She states:

> Specific dyslexia constitutes a developmental lag belonging in the general category of developmental language disturbances and as such often has significant familial aspects. Both the strephosymbolic and the speech-defective child, as well as other members of his family, frequently reveal difficulty with handling of all verbal symbols, spoken, written, or printed.
>
> Both dyslexic children and those with severe speech defects tend to show immaturity of their central nervous systems. They are often clumsy and awkward in their fine muscular coordination. They are frequently late in establishing cerebral dominance and usually have trouble with organization and spatial relationships, above all with left to right progression. Their perceptual organization is sometimes primitive, their visual motor Gestalt immature. They find patterning of any kind difficult. The question is raised whether the dyslalic youngster's difficulty in imitating auditory sequences and the dyslexic youngster's trouble interpreting visual sequences are not related to some more basic difficulty in differentiating foreground from background. (3, p. 110)

Certainly teachers today recognize that differences among individuals exist not only in generalized intellectual ability, but also in other facets of intellectual endowment. Children simply do not develop different capacities at the same time. Ilg and Ames (5) advocate that all children be given an individual behavior examination and that their particular levels of performance be determined at the time they are being considered for school entrance, and if possible, whenever promotion to a succeeding grade is being considered. Unquestionably there are differences in the so-called readiness skills, such as auditory discrimination and visual discrimination. Similarly the ability to learn to read, write, and do arithmetic develops as part of the maturational process.

The whole developmental-interaction approach that we have repeatedly emphasized here strongly indicates that children cannot be taught to read until they are ready. (One cannot help but comment on the increasingly popular idea today to begin to teach the child at a very early age. Parents are inundated by recommendations in popular magazines and books to begin to teach the child to read at age three or two. The obvious next step will be to introduce reading in the delivery room!) Physiologically the assumptions we make about readiness for learning are based upon the fact that only when certain associational pathways have become myelinized, and therefore usable, is the ability to learn to read possible.

It remains an axiom that the best single indication we have of readiness for reading is adequate language development. Other developmental irregularities are less reliable predictions of cognitive deficits.

But everything we know about the sequence of language development (experience, listening, speaking, reading, and writing) indicates the importance of good oral language development as an essential readiness skill. It appears safe to speculate that the child who fails to achieve normal development in the use of language will have reading disabilities in school. (Of course, no general rule is inviolate; there are always the exceptions. Newman et al. (6) discuss a fascinating group of youngsters who are clever, articulate, accelerated in language development, and who nevertheless experience difficulty in learning, including problems in reading.)

DRIVES AND EGO FUNCTIONING

In addition to native endowment and biologic maturation, one must also consider the role of drives in any discussion of physiological development. One's drives or energies are utilized in two related but different ways. On the one hand, they are used for the growth of the child, for the various physiological functions which are necessary for sustaining life. On the other hand, the energies are used for mental and physical activities that are not directly related to the viability of the individual. The basic function of the ego is to be aware of external reality through the perceptive system, to be aware also of the presence and nature of the drives and to synthesize these in such a way that there can be some harmony between one's drives and the demands of the external world. In order to do this, the ego has to develop an elaborate and complicated system of mechanisms of defense, mechanisms by which the drives can be controlled and redirected, so that there can be gratification without risking rejection from the environment. In other words, the ego defenses allow children to have sufficient mental energies—ego energies— available for the learning process.

To illustrate this, let us consider youngsters who experience difficulty in handling their aggressive impulses. No children will find the demands of reality always to their liking; nor are they readily able to meet and master these demands. Thus, in spite of the inevitability of biologic maturation and the strong innate tendency toward achievement and mastery, children will at times temporarily retreat in the face of difficult problems and tension, thereby creating conflicts. As long as their egos are basically intact (i.e., as long as the executive force of their personality, which controls their drives and reacts to the external world, is healthy), they ultimately can move forward once more. Thus, youngsters faced with the problem of channeling their unacceptable anger may erect ego defenses, which will operate to make them feel less anxious. For example, they may repress their anger or change it into its opposite, so that they now feel conscious affection toward the very persons with whom they are unconsciously angry. Or, they may discharge their anger at a target that is less likely to bring about the rejection they fear (they may tease and taunt their sibling). On the other hand, if the ego is unable to develop the defenses to cope with the threatening impulses, the children may act out aggressively or withdraw, or expend so much energy in keeping the feared feelings under control that they simply do not have enough left for learning activities.

Reading has been defined as the reconstruction of the facts behind the symbols. This definition points out very clearly that reading involves much more than simply the ability to recognize words; it also entails the ability of the readers to bring their experiences to the printed page and to interpret the symbols (i.e., the words) in the light of these experiences. The process of visual perception is one in which stimuli are taken in by a complicated receiving system; this receiving system is structured by basic needs and interests of the organism, modified by experiences long past and set by experiences of the recent past. Therefore, it should be quite clear that the availability of the ego energies must play an important role in influencing children's ability to read with comprehension. The supply of ego energies varies in accordance with changes in physiological functioning. But there is also the question of psychoeconomics. If too much of the mental energies is bound up in defenses, children will have little left for the external learning situation. Even the specific defense utilized by the individual plays a paramount role in influencing learning. (This is discussed in greater detail in Chapters 9 and 10.)

CONCLUSIONS

Our focus on ego functions as related to learning and adaptation in general, and to reading, more specifically, inexorably directs our attention to the unique interaction that exists between organic and functional factors in each child. We have continuously emphasized the developmental-interaction approach; mind and body cannot be viewed as separate entities but rather as dynamic processes that affect one another in myriad ways. At the root of all physiological (and psychological) development, is the native endowment: a potentiality unfolding in a process of maturation and experience. Certainly the early formative years, beginning with infancy, are the most crucial in determining the direction (or misdirection) of development. We are beginning to become acutely aware of the many pitfalls that can occur prenatally, perinatally, and postnatally: trauma that can have a profound effect upon the child's ability to learn and to adjust to the demands of school. We are learning much more about the specific factors associated with the early years, factors that can directly affect the child's capacity to learn to read. But we are just as aware that development is a continually evolving process, and that later experiences can do much to offset or compensate for the traumas that occurred earlier. We have the capacity to alter our environment and adapt it to our needs, instead of having to adapt to it. This should be most encouraging to our teachers, who must deal with children who come to school not as a *tabula rasa* but as people who have already experienced a great deal that affects the very foundations of their ability to learn, and upon which subsequent development must be built.

BIBLIOGRAPHY

1. Corah, N. L., E. J. Anthony, P. Painter, J. A. Stern, and D. L. Thurston. "Effects of Perinatal Anoxia After Seven Years." *Psychological Monographs,* 79 (1965).

2. Dudgeon, J. A. "Breakdown in Maternal Protection: Infections." *Proceedings of the Royal Society of Medicine,* 61 (1968): 1236–1243.

3. de Hirsch, K. "Specific Dyslexia or Strephosymbolia," in G. Natchez, *Children with Reading Problems.* New York: Basic Books, 1968.

4. Graham, K., C. B. Ernhart, D. L. Thurston, and M. Craft. "Development Three Years After Perinatal Anoxia and Other Potentially Damaging Experiences." *Psychological Monographs,* 76 (1962).

5. Ilg, F. L., and L. B. Ames. *School Readiness.* New York: Harper & Row, 1965.

6. Newman, C. J., C. F. Dember, and O. Krug. "He Can but He Won't." *The Psychoanalytic Study of the Child,* 28 (1973): 83–129.

7. Pasamanick, B., and H. Knobloch. "Epidemiologic Studies on the Complications of Pregnancy and the Birth Process," in G. Caplan, ed., *Prevention of Mental Disorders in Childhood.* New York: Basic Books, 1961.

8. Rapaport, D. *Diagnostic Psychological Testing,* vol. 1. Chicago: The Yearbook Publishers, Inc., 1946.

9. Rappaport, S. R., ed. *Childhood Aphasia and Brain Damage: A Definition.* Narberth, Pa.: Livingston, 1964.

CHAPTER 9

Intellectual Development

The ego orientation to the diagnosis and remediation of reading disability is best illustrated in its application to intellectual and personality development. In this chapter we will demonstrate that intelligence, like any other psychological function, should not be perceived in a static fashion, but should always be considered as a dynamic process. Intelligence is one aspect of the total personality; it is shared both positively and negatively by all of the things that we ordinarily believe influence emotional development. We no longer believe that psychological theory divides the mind into sensory, cognitive, and affective spheres. Yet, although most psychologists and educators would agree that this trichotomy is outdated, a review of the articles in both psychological and educational journals would reveal that we are still thinking in basically mechanistic terms. And at a meeting of the Joint Committee on Learning Disabilities, almost two days were spent in discussing the competencies necessary to teach children with learning disabilities (along with the characteristics of these youngsters); not once was there any mention of affective qualities or dynamic considerations. How one can speak of doing a comprehensive evaluation of a child with reading difficulty and ignore the emotional factors is beyond our understanding.

Probably one major reason for the tendency of too many professionals to be overly mechanistic in the diagnosis and remediation of reading disabilities is the frequently felt inadequacy on the part of the clinicians and teachers. If all that is required for a valid diagnosis is the administration of various standardized tests and the plotting of strengths and weaknesses, then there is less burden placed upon the talent and experience of the clinician. This is probably one reason why the Illinois Test of Psycholinguistic Abilities (3) became so popular among the reading and learning disability "experts." All too many people assumed that what was required was to compare the interrelationships of the various functions tapped by each of the subtests, delineate the specific deficits, and teach the child in such a way that these deficits could be compensated for. We find the same problem in the area of remediation. Many teachers are prone to rely completely upon the teacher's manual, following it precisely, and not recognizing that modifications must be made to fit the individual situation. We feel that occasionally this is a reflection of the insecurity on the part of teachers, their own doubts and lack of confidence in their ability to be intuitive and creative in meeting the individual needs of their students.

Just as we value the immeasurable contributions made by Grace Fernald to the field of specialized reading instruction, we look upon David Rapaport as a giant among the psychologists who have explored the thinking process. In the 20 years that we have been engaged in clinical practice, no single individual has influenced us more in our understanding of the psychodiagnostic process. Even though Diagnostic Psychological Testing (5) was published almost thirty years ago (and met with a polarized reception, clinicians hailing it as a most important and valuable book, and statisticians criticizing it severely because of research deficiencies), it remains the most influential and significant book of its kind even today. There is hardly a psychologist who does not in some way or another make use of Rapaport's concepts (perhaps without knowing it). To attest to the importance of Rapaport's original tome, 20 years after the initial publication an edited revised version, prepared by Robert R. Holt (2), has met with great critical acclaim. Much of what is developed in this chapter regarding intelligence and the factors which affect the thinking process is derived from Rapaport's magnificent contributions.

INTELLIGENCE: THE SOCIAL APPLICATION OF EGO FUNCTIONS

What has been discussed so far regarding ego development will apply equally well to our discussion of intellectual development. Ego functions such as perception, concept formation, analysis, synthesis, and language development are certainly very closely related to what we call intelligence. It can be seen that the factors which facilitate or retard ego development are the very same factors which facilitate intellectual development. In a very real sense, intelligence may be looked upon as the social application of ego functions. Rapaport (5) discusses in detail some basic assumptions regarding the factors which determine the nature of intelligence.

We must abandon the idea that people are born with fixed intelligences that remain constant throughout life. Intelligence tests* measure people's *functioning intelligence,* that is, their efficiency of functioning right then and there. Thus the IQ that is obtained on an individual intelligence test and that may be looked upon as immutable by the school system, may or may not be an adequate sample of children's general efficiency, or, in other words, of their potentially intellectual assets. For example, if a child were to obtain a verbal IQ of 125 (the superior range), and a noverbal IQ of 99 (normal range), the overall IQ would be 114 (bright-normal range). Another child with an overall IQ of 114 may obtain both a verbal and nonverbal IQ of 114. One does not need to be very sophisticated psychologically to recognize that there is a significant difference between the intellectual functioning of these two youngsters.

It is extremely important for the classroom teacher and the clinician to recognize this discrepancy, as well as others, and to be aware of the limitations of the functioning intelligence level (the IQ). Children's current life situation, their home environment (especially the degree of cognitive stimulation during the early formative years), emotional factors, and cultural influences may be among the manifold variables which can be operating to yield a specific IQ. If teachers are to be more sensitive both to the strengths and weaknesses of intelligence testing, they should try to differentiate these variables as much as possible.

NATURAL ENDOWMENT AND ITS CRYSTALLIZATION

Every individual is born with a potential for intellectual development; this may be referred to as the *natural endowment.* This potentiality unfolds through a process of maturation, within limits set by the natural endowment. In other words, we can look upon the endowment as a kind of upper limit of potentiality. It is hardly likely that any of us reach that limit; we are concerned with those individuals who function intellectually far below the limit because of some interference to develop-

---

* We refer always to individual intelligence tests. We feel that group intelligence tests are of little value, particularly in cases of reading difficulty.

ment. Again, if a youngster were to obtain a nonverbal IQ of 130 and a verbal IQ of 95, it would be quite proper to assume that her or his endowment is superior, and that some factor or combination of factors (organic, functional, or cultural) have acted to depress the verbal functioning.

The maturation process is fostered or restricted by the wealth or poverty of cognitive stimulation in the environment during the early formative years. (If this is beginning to remind the reader very much of what was written concerning ego development, let us reiterate that intelligence can be looked upon as the social adaptation made by the ego to the environment.) For example, within the limitations of the native endowment, maturational and developmental factors play an important role in the acquisition and accumulation of percepts (certainly a vital aspect of intelligence).

At birth infants are completely dependent upon the mother figure. The functioning of their undifferentiated perceptual apparatuses enable them from the beginning of life to signal and summon their mothers to minister to their needs. At about the age of three months, children gradually become dimly aware of the fact that satisfaction is dependent on a source outside of their bodily self. Thus they gradually come to recognize an orbit beyond their own body. By the end of the third or in the fourth month, the infant's reactions gradually become less diffuse, and their activities seem more goal directed, usually specifically toward the mother figure. They follow the mothers' now familiar preparation with their eyes. However, even at this stage, mothers are not perceived as specific whole persons. This is why mothers can be replaced by equally mothering substitutes.

By the eighth or ninth month, infants have begun to perceive themselves as separate individuals. They may pull alternately on their own and their mothers' hair, ears, and noses. They may also begin to put food into their mothers' mouths. It is also at this time that the children evidence their fear of strangers. In this way, they demonstrate their perception of the difference between familiar persons and strange persons, which seems to be spontaneous for nearly all children. Although there is no definitive evidence, it would seem quite likely that the reaction to strangers cannot be accounted for on a conditioned response basis. It is not that children have had unpleasant experiences with strangers; rather, it is simply that they have begun to perceive a distinction between the familiar and the unfamiliar.

The next stage, which occurs at approximately 11 to 12 months of age, is what Piaget (4) has defined as "the means-end relationships." At this point children are beginning to use what they have already learned in searching for objects, as well as repeating patterns of behavior. Then, between the ages of 12 and 16 months, they begin to experiment and search for other ways to solve problems; they also begin to become quite excited about novelty for its own sake. And finally, at approximately two years of age, they may begin to show the capacity for primitive symbolic representation. That is, they may invent solutions mentally—symbolically—rather than by trial and error.

As we pointed out in the previous chapter, the long-term significance of physiological and psychological development from birth to five years still requires careful investigation. The implications are indeed tremendous. The rate of change in many different physical and psychological areas of the developing infant during the early months and years of life must be considered. We must also take into account the complicated interrelations of the many different areas with one another and the critical role of environmental interaction with the children during this time. We know that both deficiencies of basic requirements and noxious influences on the complex, interdependent unfolding of the children's many maturational and developmental potentials have a much more damaging effect on the very young child than at any time later on. The results of early faulty development are unfortunately compounded geometrically, with great changes in a short period of time. Traumatic influences at one month are difficult to remove at three years. Missed opportunities for fostered development of intelligence through a supportive mother-child relationship at five months may not be replaced at age five years. In short, once the dough is mixed, one cannot substitute a better grade of eggs; and once the cake is baked, one cannot add more sugar. It may very well be that children coming from culturally deprived or disadvantaged homes have difficulty later on in school because of the fact of inappropriate cognitive stimulation during the earliest years. Interestingly enough the Get Set and Head Start programs, which proved to be somewhat of a disappointment to many people, may have failed simply because they did not start early enough. The intervention required to compensate for early and severe cognitive deprivation may need to be commenced during the first two years of life (perhaps by working directly with the mother of these infants and teaching them how to respond to their offspring).

SELECTIVE NATURE OF INTELLECTUAL FUNCTIONING

As we have stated earlier, intelligence is one aspect of total personality development and is fostered or restricted by the timing, intensity, and variety of emotional stimulation and by the resulting course of emotional development. In the total process of maturation and experience (environment input) a differentiation occurs (ego development). In the normal process of crystallization, some personalities may maintain balance and adjustment by tending to avoid acquisition of new knowledge. As Rapaport points out:

> Where a "see no evil, hear no evil, speak no evil" make-up characterizes the whole personality, it will be reflected in the "function" underlying intelligence. . . . The psychological concept of "repression" refers to the submergence in the unconscious of information or knowledge already possessed because of the danger hidden in that knowledge for the psychological equilibrium of the individual. Knowledge cannot be assimilated unless it is assimilated with other freely available knowledge; and once repression plays a pathological role, it tends to become ever more extensive, and with it, the accumulation of knowledge is limited. Thus, we deal here with a type of function which will tend to assimilate and accumulate less information, less cultural wealth, less vocabulary. (p. 89)

A case in point is that of a nine-year old female who had basically superior intellectual potential but who was showing definite impingement to her intellectual functioning. In school she was considered to be experiencing severe difficulty in reading. The problem she manifested was not in decoding; as a matter of fact she could recognize words quite well. Nevertheless, she had a great deal of difficulty in reading comprehension. Her major problem here was in conceptual thinking, specifically in the ability to engage in any inferential reasoning and to organize material successfully. This youngster's problem in thinking basically stemmed from her need to engage in massive repression. This in turn was stimulated by her need to remain a baby and her unwillingness to learn. To her, learning was dangerous because it unconsciously was equated with the act of growing up, and she was terribly afraid of this. Because of her massive repression, she would be expected to do poorly on any intelligence subtest that tapped memory functioning.

In essence, then, in the normal course of development, the natural endowment differentiates into various functions that can be measured by intelligence tests in which these functions underlie achievement. Some individuals find it necessary to acquire knowledge as their way of coping with new problems encountered in the process of unfolding. When the personality make-up is such that intellectual knowledge becomes the most important conscious weapon against the onslaught of the feared unknown, we are dealing with individuals who will do well on any of the subtests of an intelligence scale which tap the accumulation of information.

Clinically, one is apt to find the intellectualizing person experiencing difficulty in differentiating main ideas from supporting details. Intellectualizers tend often to be plagued by compulsive perfectionism. They are unable to see the forest because of the trees. They find it necessary to read every word and to chew and devour every single detail. Nothing can escape their attention; they simply get bogged down in trivia. (Sometimes these people have a great deal of difficulty with multiple-choice tests, because they just never can feel comfortable choosing one answer.)

Some personalities tend, as a result of a variety of personality influences, to try to acquire concrete knowledge, while others are drawn to that which is more abstract. These are just a few examples of the vicissitudes of natural endowment in the course of the maturation and development process. We can only speculate as to the degree to which the superiority of one function over another is primarily because of genetic factors. Is there a constitutional tendency to repress in some individuals, while in others the innate tendency is to intellectualize? Whatever the answer, there can be little doubt that there is an interaction process that operates between the natural endowment and the maturation-experience factors.

> The maturation process should be viewed as guarded, restrained, or fostered, by the environmental conditions—natural, cultural, and interpersonal "wealth" or "poverty"—which may be justly called "educational environment" in contrast to formal schooling. But educational environment crystallizes into schooling and the influence of schooling is, in some individuals, sustained in above average cultural interests which in turn, like schooling, contribute to a systematic crystallization of intellectual assets. Endowment, degree of maturation, educational environment, schooling, cultural predilection, are those factors whose influence on intelligence must be assessed. . . . But this is not all. [One] must know whether, maturation once achieved, there has come about an arrest of development or a setback; and, if not, whether there is present a temporary inefficiency encroaching upon and impoverishing the subject's test performance. (5, p. 39)

We are aware, of course, that children's concepts do change with increasing age, and that experience plays a very important role in the modification of concepts. The educator must always be alert to the fact that children's concepts must be judged with a yardstick quite different from that of adults. What may appear to be extremely illogical and irrational to adults may be quite acceptable from children's experience orientation. For example, a five-year-old child becomes terrified, while in the bathtub, that she will be swept down the drain. The adult, in all his wisdom, explains patiently to the child that the drain is much too small, and that the child's toe is just able to fit the drain. The child, however, responds: "But all the water, which is much bigger than me, goes down the drain!"

There are certain basic propositions to keep in mind in understanding the rationale proposed by Rapaport to delineate the dynamic factors which shape intellectual development. It may have been sophisticated at one time to say that "intelligence is what an intelligence test measures," but we have come a long way since someone made that world-shaking comment. A good clinician uses the results of an intelligence test in much the same way as a detective uses clues to solve a mystery. Nothing is left to chance or just considered an anomaly. The basic principle is determinism; the working assumption is that little if anything occurs by chance. Every subtest score, every single response, and every part of every response must be viewed as significant and as representative of the subject. When a response deviates greatly from what is conventional, this means something much more than the fact that an error has been made. If, for example, one child says: "Columbus discovered America," while another child of the same age responds: "I know you expect me to say Columbus, but actually it was Leif Ericson and his Vikings, while more recently there has been considerable evidence suggesting the Japanese came even earlier," both responses would be scored as correct. Nevertheless, it is clear that we are dealing with two different kinds of personalities.

Individual variations reflecting on the personality of the child are manifested on every subtest of an individual intelligence scale. Let us examine, for example, three different responses to the question: "What is the thing to do if you cut your finger?" (Each of the following responses earn the maximum number of points for a correct answer.) (1) "I would put a band-aid on it." (2) "I would wash it off; I would then put on mercurochrome or iodine; I would get a band-aid and then a bandage; and maybe I would go to the doctor." (3) "How big a cut is it? [Said with intense affect.] Was my finger cut off? I guess I would get a bandage or a band-aid, but is it really bad?" These responses reveal unquestionably important personality factors of each child. The first child answers the question immediately, exercising good judgment and experiencing no difficulty in making a decision. The second child, less decisive, must consider many different possibilities; there is almost an obsessive-compulsive quality to the response. The third child shows perhaps an excessive fear of bodily injury (some question of bodily integrity?)

Let us consider one more example of how verbalizations may be utilized to tell us something about the individual child. The following series of responses by one youngster of 10 years of age is of considerable interest in that it reveals a quality of the personality which could be deleterious to the child's ability to function effectively in school. To the question, "What is the thing to do if you cut your finger?" the response is given: "I would go home and tell my Mommy so she could put a band-aid on it." To a second question, "What is the thing to do if you are sent to the grocer to buy a loaf of bread, and he says he doesn't have any more?" the response given is: "I would go back home and tell

Mommy so she could send me to a different grocer." And to a third question, "What should you do if you lose one of your friend's balls?" the answer is: "I would tell my Mom so she could go out and buy a new one." None of these responses is wrong; each earns at least partial credit. But they are certainly suggestive of a youngster who has difficulty in assuming the initiative and in reacting autonomously. The kind of dependency on the mother-figure may be of sufficient intensity to preclude this child's being able to muster the assertiveness necessary to compete in the normal school situation.

The relationship of the score of one subtest to the scores of other subtests also tells much about the qualitative nature of the intellectual development of any individual. For example, one might oversimplify things somewhat by saying that the information section of the Wechsler Adult Intelligence Scale measures the ability to acquire facts; the comprehension section, the ability to utilize facts; and the similarities section, the ability to see relationships among facts. Thus children obtaining high scores on the information section and low scores on the comprehension section may be showing that selectively over the years they have developed the kind of intelligence that allows them to accumulate an extensive background of experience, but that they are unable to utilize this information in common sense situations. Or a child doing well in comprehension and poorly in similarities would suggest a worldly wise individual who perhaps has difficulty in concept formation and abstract reasoning.

There are many variations on this theme. However, our purpose in this chapter is not primarily to discuss the diagnostic aspects of an individual test, but to show the selective nature of intellectual development. As we have pointed out before, intelligence must be viewed as a dynamic process. In a sense what people do on an individual intelligence test (including their verbalizations) tells us where they have been (figuratively speaking). The many influences that have acted on them since birth—and particularly during the early formative years—will be manifested in terms of the selective impairment of the relatively autonomous ego functions measured by each subtest.

INTELLECTUAL DEVELOPMENT AS RELATED TO READING DISABILITY

Throughout our discussion of the selective nature of intellectual development, we have occasionally referred to certain characteristics which could play a part in bringing about reading and related learning difficulties. We would like now to consider this in a more formal way.

Specifically, with regard to intellectual processes, two very important functions are attention and concentration.

Attention may be defined as a relatively effortless, passive involuntary, free receptivity to environmental stimuli. On the other hand, concentration involves an active focusing of attention, that is, a deliberate, effortful, voluntary, and selective channeling of one's attentive energies. We have all had the experience of "reading" a book, reaching the bottom of the page and then suddenly realizing that we have no comprehension whatsoever of the content of the selection. When we accept the reality of the fact that it is vitally important that we do understand the material, we make a deliberate effort to put everything else out of our mind and to focus our attention on the selection. In a word we concentrate, while previously we were only attending.

Rapaport (5) points out that attention suffers first under the impact of stress, anxiety, and/or overvalent feelings of inadequacy. As long as individuals have at their disposal a reserve of mental energies not specifically tied up with these affects and anxieties, they are able to call upon this reservoir, as it were, and to concentrate. Even at this time, of course, the process is effortful, and individuals may evidence a high degree of stress by the reduction in their spontaneity and creativity. In actuality, their energies are bound up in their defenses and therefore not available for free, passive attending. Nevertheless, they are able to concentrate and still function, albeit in a somewhat impaired fashion.

If the stress situation continues beyond a certain point, people are inevitably forced to exhaust their reserves; they use up the energies that were not intimately associated with conflict and anxiety. It is at this point that concentration, too, becomes impaired. No longer can individuals force themselves to function. It is as if now they are exceedingly vulnerable to the stresses of the environment and the concomitant anxiety.

For many years both psychologists and educators have searched for certain patterns of intelligence which would differentiate achieving readers from children with reading difficulties. We see this as a fruitless task. Our understanding of the nature of intellectual development directs our attention not to patterns per se but to a rationale that will help in understanding the functions which underlie achievement or lack of achievement.

From our previous discussion on ego development and its relationship to intellectual development, we may now be able to understand Abrams' (1) contention that the child with acquired dyslexia differs strikingly from the youngster with ego disturbance related to early brain damage. The acquired dyslexic invariably has a significantly higher performance IQ, as compared to the verbal IQ. This is the result of the general retardation in the verbal area with practically all of the verbal skills at a low-average to less-than-average level. The notable exceptions are relatively (but only relatively) higher scores on the tests of attention and concentration, for language ability is only a minimal requirement. As might be expected, nonverbal functioning is generally excellent and may be anywhere from average to a very superior level.

The child whose ego disturbance stems from early brain insult will usually show a higher verbal IQ than performance IQ. The kind of ego skills (perception, visual organization, analysis, and synthesis) measured on the performance section have simply been too greatly impaired or delayed in development. In addition, secondary ego functions such as delay of impulse and regulation of impulse are much more vulnerable on the subtests of the performance section.

CONCLUSION

Although some diagnostic aspects regarding intelligence testing have been discussed, we have only touched the tip of the iceberg. Our primary purpose has been to acquaint the reader with the dynamic considerations regarding intellectual development. As in earlier chapters, we have emphasized the interaction of the sensory, cognitive, and affective spheres, demonstrating ultimately that intelligence is nothing more than the social application of ego functions. All that has been written concerning ego development must certainly apply to the development of intelligence, as well.

For too many years educators have been subjected to outdated mechanistic intelligence models. It is no wonder that so many teachers complain about psychological evaluations and state that this kind of testing is of little value in helping the child. The search for pathological signs has increased but is essentially fruitless (a cookbook approach); the validities of isolated scores and indicators have proved low, fluctuating, and of no practical usefulness. There is no easy way to do a responsible job. The understanding of what has led to specific thinking processes requires an investment in comprehending all aspects of the child in an integrated fashion. Nothing can substitute for a professional, responsible approach, executed in a dynamic and informed way. Nothing else should be acceptable.

BIBLIOGRAPHY

1. Abrams, J. C. "Minimal Brain Dysfunction and Dyslexia." *Reading World,* 14 (March, 1975): 219–227.

2. Holt, R. D., ed. *Diagnostic Psychological Testing.* New York: International Universities Press, 1968.

3. Kirk, S., J. McCarthy, and W. Kirk. *Illinois Test of Psycholinguistic Abilities.* Urbana, Ill.: University of Illinois Press, 1965.

4. Piaget, J. *The Child's Conception of the World.* New York: Harcourt Brace Jovanovich, 1949.

5. Rapaport, D. *Diagnostic Psychological Testing.* Chicago: The Yearbook Publishers, Inc., 1946.

CHAPTER 10

Personality Development

In previous chapters we have pointed out that the focus of psychodynamic psychology has shifted from the emphasis on unconscious wishes, strivings, and impulses to the relatively autonomous functions of the ego. This is not to say that the influence of the unconscious is ignored; it is simply put into a different perspective. Basically it is a recognition of the fact that there are primary functions, which develop relatively free of conflictual problems. Of course, this orientation is much more consonant with the needs of the educator who must be concerned with the relatively autonomous skills which are closely associated with learning such skills as perception, concept formation, and language.

Psychologists have long recognized that emotional factors are often closely related to the learning process. These factors seem to affect not only what children learn, but how they learn, when they learn, and even whether they learn at all. Yet there as those who tend to rule out almost completely the idea that emotions affect children's reading. These people show a flagrant disregard for the evidence that emotional behavior is closely interwoven with other factors in reading ability.

The major controversy, of course, is concerned with the chicken-or-the-egg proposition: what is the cause and what is the effect? There is no question that youngsters who have suffered with reading disability over a period of time are going to have serious questions about themselves and their abilities. Constantly frustrated, besieged with intense feelings of defectiveness, it is no wonder that they often react with hostility and various forms of acting-out behavior. Youngsters whose instructional reading level is primer and who are taught at the second-grade level are being compelled to climb over a 10-foot wall every day without anything to hold on to.

Perhaps it is fair to say that most children with severe reading difficulties have emotional problems that resulted from the constant failure to acquire a very important skill. Nevertheless, this is not to imply that the converse is not also true. That is, there are emotional conflicts, too, which may result in reading problems. For example, children may bring so much conflict to the learning situation that they cannot readily accept instruction. One boy had so much hostility within him (which was really directed toward the mother figure) that he perceived the teacher as hostile to him. The child was so hostile, and yet these feelings were so unacceptable and disturbing to him, that he necessarily had to project them onto others, in this case, the teacher. Still other children bring so much anxiety to the learning situation that it becomes almost impossible for them to focus their attention upon the teacher (or the book) for more than a short period of time.

Blanchard's (1) main thesis is that there is a need on the part of the retarded reader to inflict self-punishment to relieve anxiety and guilt feelings. In many instances the reading disability is a disguised expression of hidden motives, satisfying the need for punishment and relieving guilt by exposing the child to a situation of failure in school and to criticism. Blanchard elaborates on her point still further, attributing many reading disabilities to difficulties in establishing masculine identification and in handling aggressive impulses, together with excessive anxiety and guilt of a destructive, hostile nature, as well as sadistic feelings. The signs of emotional conflict appear chiefly in the reading disability and overactive fantasy life.

Pearson (8) discusses disorders of the learning process in terms of two major classifications: (1) when the learning process is not involved with the neurotic conflict, and (2) when the learning process is involved with the learning conflict. It is important to recognize that in both cases Pearson is discussing examples of children whose learning problems stem from emotional conflict. In the first case, he refers to the problem of deflection of attention. The children's conflicts, whether they are perceived consciously as worries, guilt, or shame and embarrassment, or whether they occur in the unconscious portions of the ego, attract the children's attention to themselves and deflect it to a greater or lesser extent from all other external considerations. To put it in a slightly different fashion, the children simply do not have sufficient mental energy available for learning.

When the learning process is involved in the neurotic conflict, we have a more insidious and complicated situation. Now it may be that the children have a positive motivation not to learn. The nature of the children's emotional conflicts are such that it becomes dangerous for them to learn. In one instance, it may be that learning to read becomes equated in the unconscious with growing up. If children feel for any reason that to grow up is undesirable and perhaps even dangerous, they will unconsciously resist developing the skills (i.e., reading) that represent in some way becoming independent. For another example, children may resist learning because it puts them into a situation in which they must be competitive. If, for any reason, they fear their aggressive impulses, and indeed cannot differentiate between destructive hostility and acceptable self-assertiveness, they may assume a radically passive posture, almost precluding any possibility of their being sufficiently aggressive to learn.

Klein (6) speaks of bright pupils' narcissistic maintenance of their status in their need to succeed without further effort or study. Some, whose narcissism has been fed throughout childhood by the realization that they are so bright they do not need to work, experience a great blow when this is no longer true. The inability to endure relative failure with subsequent restriction of ego activity is not due to narcissistic factors alone. Klein also discusses in detail failure in learning resulting from intense castration anxiety. Other narcissistic children withdraw from competition because they cannot bear to have their performance compared unfavorably with someone else's. Some children experience learning difficulties because of a fear of their own curiosity, which inhibits them from exploring the environment and accumulating knowledge.

Daniels (2) modifies his psychoanalytic position to some degree and focuses his attention primarily on the concept of *morbid envy*. He relates certain psychodynamic aspects of this concept to parental attitudes toward children's efforts to learn. Daniels also draws attention to the ways in which children use their school failure in dealing with parents and teachers.

Clinical experience has alerted us to the possible effect of a personality problem in the etiology and development of a reading disability. On the other hand, as was pointed out earlier, if children are constantly exposed to a milieu in which they cannot compete successfully with their peers in relation to learning activities, then it will not be surprising that the children develop intense feelings of insecurity and inadequacy. Children who are tense, worried, and fearful cannot focus their minds on intellectual pursuits any more than can adults who are in similar emotional states. What we have is a continuing series of interactions between the insecurity generated by the lack of success in learning on the one hand and any emotional instability which may be independent of the learning failure on the other.

Let us provide one example of a youngster whose emotional conflicts were caused by the reading failure:

Johnny was an eight-year old youngster who was referred because of a severe reading disability. In a conference that the parents had with the teacher, they were told that Johnny had a lazy mind and that he should be taken to a psychiatrist.

Both parents had tried to help Johnny with his homework; when he was quizzed on the work at home, he knew the answers. But when he was in class, he failed the tests. Recently he had brought home a test paper in which many of the questions were unanswered.

Johnny had done appreciably better in his schoolwork when he had material read to him, rather than when asked to read it for himself. Johnny had felt badly that he had to read a first-grade book through the third grade.

There had been much discussion, both in the immediate family and when other relatives and friends came to visit, about Johnny's poor work. Often he was told to show how well he could do. More frequently he was chided for not being able to read or being dumb in school. His siblings particularly criticized him about this. Johnny had never been openly defiant, negativistic, or hostile at home concerning his school work or anything else. He had never presented a behavior problem at school. His teacher was dissatisfied with Johnny because he daydreamed and seemed not to be working.

A psychological evaluation was administered to Johnny; the following is excerpted from the report of that evaluation:

> Johnny shows considerable anxiety connected with feelings of inadequacy. He does not see himself as an effective individual capable of manipulating the environment in order to achieve his goals. He is afraid of being hurt and for this reason does not feel free to invest his emotions in interpersonal relationships. One means of defense he uses is to wall off his emotions so that they are not expressed. Johnny shows considerably less affective responsiveness than is typical of his age. What affective responsiveness he does show is narcissistic and not channeled in a productive fashion.
>
> Another defense Johnny employs is to limit his attention primarily to the obvious aspects of situations or to tiny, inconsequential details of the situation so that he might feel safe. He does not invest as much energy as he should optimally in goal-directed strivings. Because he invests considerable energy in the defense of isolation, he does not integrate elements

of a situation into more complex organizations, which process is necessary for higher levels of achievement.

It would seem that one reason why Johnny cannot allow himself to be more productive—in addition to his fear of wounding his pride—is fear of his own hostile impulses. He handles these unacceptable impulses primarily by repression and, as already indicated, isolation.

Even though the nature of his defenses does not allow Johnny to be as productive as he might be, he compensates for this in fantasy. His fantasies are highly aggressive, and replete with demonstrations of masculine prowess and authority. The nature of these fantasies is not pathological or even atypical. He shows the aggressive fantasies typical of his age. Indeed, if he could implement these fantasies in realistic endeavors, he would be much more productive and successful than he currently is.

Johnny shows no disturbance in ego functions. His defenses operate efficiently for him, so that unacceptable impulses break through only rarely. When they do, they are aggressive in nature, just as his constructive fantasies are, and are most likely in response to feeling he is being made even more inadequate than usually. Most of the time Johnny shows no difficulty in delaying or mediating the expression of his impulses. His ability to perceive situations realistically also is very good. Johnny is interested in who other people are and how they think and act, and has no difficulty in reacting to situations appropriately. Although Johnny shows some conflict concerning hostile impulses, and resultant defenses which impede his efficiency, there is reason for his hostile feelings, for his feelings of narcissistic wounding, and for his feelings of inadequacy, all in his current life situation.

Because Johnny's parents had not understood the reading difficulty, he had not gotten the love, protection or support from them which he had sorely needed. He also had been chided and criticized by his siblings, as well as by many other people who came into the household. In other words, there was nothing either in his basically obsessive character structure or in his current mode of handling his conflicts which seemed sufficient to have caused such a severe reading difficulty. In fact, the evidence was just the other way: his reading difficulty with its resultant environmental stresses had caused his present emotional conflicts.

NORMAL DEVELOPMENT

Although there is certainly no question that prolonged difficulty in learning to read often results in emotional disturbance, there is also little doubt that psychogenic difficulties may bring about reading failure. A discussion of the basis for functional reading disorders would entail the entire fields of child psychology and psychiatry. But in order to understand child psychopathology, one must first be cognizant of those factors which are important in normal development.

In the usual course of growing up, children learn to fear certain of their impulses. They come to anticipate that discharge of these impulses will result in their losing the love of important persons in their life and possibly being punished by these persons as well—punished in the form of deprivation, physical attack, or moral condemnation. The pressure of the unacceptable and intolerable impulses and the prospect of discharging them stimulates reactions of anxiety. In order to defend against this anxiety, the ego builds up defenses which help the child to deal with the threat of the disturbing ideas and feelings.

This can happen for realistic and for unrealistic reasons. Let us consider one example of a realistic reason. A child engages in thumb-sucking, an action which is intolerable to the child's mother. In one way or another, she forces the child to relinquish the gratification obtained from the sucking. Yet because the thumb-sucking satisfies an instinctual urge on the part of the child, it is very pleasurable. Thus, he or she develops unacceptable hostile feelings toward the mother.

An example of what might be termed an unrealistic reason is the "normal sleeplessness" of the two-year old. Children at this age are beginning to establish some independence from the mother. They have discovered the world, and they fight relinquishing those activities which bring them gratification. They become more and more people in their own right, as they find that they can do certain things and create certain effects. Increasingly, they are operators of a growing concern. When they have to be put to bed—and thereby give up their recently acquired and tenuous sense of identity, they fight this and become negativistic. They do not want to relinquish control and be left helpless. Because they want to hold on for dear life, they resist sleep, much to the consternation of their mothers. They become negative and hostile toward the mothers, whom they feel are trying to rob them of the gratification they greatly deserve. We believe that it is the children's struggle with their need to be independent versus their need to remain dependent that accounts for the so-called terrible twos.

Essentially children need to develop a personality that can control their drives and, at the same time, obtain sufficient satisfaction in keeping with the requirements of social living. The work of the ego is extremely important in this regard. As Erikson (3) has pointed out, there is a certain predominant ego quality which normally is acquired during each stage, and results from mastery of the challenges presented to children and from resolution of the resulting conflicts. For example, at the close of the oral phase, infants normally should have acquired feelings of trust as a result of their various experiences with their mothers. This includes the experience of being weaned, from which infants should also gain ego strength in having been able to give up the pleasure in sucking the breast or bottle. The children, therefore, should have the sense of ego mastery over the various challenges and conflicts presented to them by their own biologic maturation and by their environment.

Long before children develop the ego defenses necessary to cope with their anxieties, they are dependent upon their parents to satisfy their needs, to relieve them of tension, to anticipate danger, and to remove the source of a disturbance. Normal ego development is dependent upon adequate early environmental stimulation of infants, as well as on the presence of a single consistent mothering person in their lives. The children need to know that they can depend upon these people to relieve tension. To a large extent, the children's later ability to tolerate tension and actively deal with anxiety situations will be determined by the experiences of the early years. And much of how the children perceive the school and the teacher will be a displacement from what has happened in the crucial early stages of ego development.

The Separation-Individuation Process

The biological birth of the human infant and the psychological birth of the individual are not coincident in time. The former is a dramatic, observable, and well-circumscribed event; the latter a slowly unfolding intrapsychic process. (7, p. 3)

In this very profound statement, Mahler summarizes the significant contributions she has made to our understanding of child development in general and the separation-individuation process more specifically. The latter is seen as the establishment of a sense of separateness from, and relation to, a world of reality, particularly with regard to the experiences of one's own body and to the principal representative of the world as the infant experiences it, the primary love object. *Separation,* then, is children's emergence from a symbiotic fusion with their mothers, while *individuation* consists of those achievements marking the children's assumption of their own individual characteristics.

Mahler (7) structures a series of developmental steps beginning at birth and concluding at approximately the fourth year of life. It is during this extraordinary period of physical, mental, and emotional development that children struggle to establish a certain degree of independence from the mother figure, and at the same time adapt to the rigors and vicissitudes of the external environment. It is a struggle which only begins during the first years, to continue through the course of life.

At the time of birth, children's basic needs center around the mouth. Even prior to the actual need for food, the desire to suck is manifested.

For example, X rays have shown intrauterine sucking. Also, children demonstrate the sucking need at birth, although they have the resources to live for a few hours. Sucking gratification is usually first felt in contact with the mother. Children begin to focus on stimuli from the outside world; they begin to be aware of themselves and of the discrete objects outside. There is no visual memory yet, but the physical intimacy of mother and child is already producing reactions which will lead to the association of mother with pleasure, satisfaction, and protection. Any failure in these requirements, whether due to circumstances around the children or to accidents of "fate," such as prolonged physical illness, may result in conditions which are associated with learning disability.

When children reach the age of two or three months, they show their first social response to the outside world. Children may smile because they come to associate this image with the visual image they have developed of something which gratifies them. But at this point the children, even though they have made their first human connections, do not yet discriminate their mothers' faces from other human faces. At seven to eight months of age, the generalized social response becomes more specific. Infants will now begin to show what might be described as a fear of strangers. It should be kept in mind that this is a healthy sign, because it is indicative of the ego's differentiation. Children are now recognizing the mother as a separate entity.

With each advance in development, there are concomitant dangers. For example, when children reach the point of physical development where they are able to differentiate themselves from external objects, they become terribly afraid of desertion or separation. In the face of this threat, children desire to incorporate their mothers, so that their mothers will not be able to leave them. *Incorporation* is very important to children, because the process gives them the opportunity to imitate mother, to absorb her characteristics, and to feel safe.

At approximately 10 to 15 months, the practicing period begins. Children now have the capacity to be more active in separating physically from the mother and to use motility as a means of beginning to establish an incipient form of psychological independence. It is during this practicing period that one may see vividly some of the earliest antecedents of the independence-dependence conflicts to be discovered later. This is a period of great joy for children; the discovery of independent locomotion ushers in a new phase of personality development. But, as before, the new advance brings with it a concomitant danger. Even though the world is their oyster, children's continued dependency upon the mother is evident in their need for "emotional refueling." The youngsters must periodically establish some physical contact with the mother figure, touching base as it were, in order to venture forth again. By the time children have reached the age of three, they have begun to establish patterns for themselves, which will allow them to move out into the world and simultaneously to deal with the part of themselves which always wants to stay dependent.

It is also at this point that children reach a stage in their development where they realize that their mother's not being in the room with them does not necessarily mean that she has deserted them. They are now no longer fearful of loss of the love object (of separation), but they are fearful of the loss of mother's love. This, of course, is associated with the fact that this is the time when they are first beginning to be disciplined and have to begin to exert some control over their aggressive impulses.

At the age of four or five, the children become especially fearful of some injury to their bodies. This particular fear arises because of the stage the children have reached in their continuous physical development. The major point, however, is that preschool children are under tremendous pressure as the result of these conflicts. Much of their mental energy is tied up with their need to control ideas and feelings which are quite frightening to them. It is very difficult for many youngsters of this age, therefore, to become really involved in formal learning procedures. These children primarily need to be given the opportunity to gain mastery by working with a great deal of make-believe.

The rub in all this, of course, is that so much depends on what happens at the start. The basic personalities of children, their egos, are established by the age of five or six, that is, before they start school. All children bring to their school experience their own unique set of problems. It is the children's methods of meeting and solving problems that indicate their level of emotional maturity. But we have emphasized that the pattern of personality functioning has been set prior to school entrance, simply because we feel that too many teachers grow frustrated and guilty when they cannot instill in children a sense of security and well-being.

In adolescence children are confronted with another crisis in the process of separation-individuation. They must now separate themselves from the fusion of the family, just as before they had to separate themselves from their mothers. Now, as before, we see the manifestations of the internal conflict over independence-dependence. Educators are familiar with the seventh- and eighth-grade slump. This may be seen partially as the result of anxiety around separation, which interferes with school performance. The difference in the separation-individuation phases in infancy and in adolescence may be summed up by stating that in the earlier separation phase real physical autonomy gives rise to psychological differentiation, while in the later phase separation must be achieved on an intrapsychic level.

Of necessity, this has been merely a sampling of the normal vicissitudes of child development with the focus on the separation-individuation process. In summary, normal development implies that there is sufficient gratification of children's basic needs, both physiological and emotional. There must be a gradual presentation of the society's demands (usually as represented in the wishes of the parents), but this must be done gradually, in keeping with children's rate of biological maturation and ego development. Youngsters must be given the opportunity for ego mastery. That is, they must have ample opportunity to practice: to learn techniques of managing themselves and of gaining feelings of competence and self-confidence. This is akin to the whole concept of readiness in education, as well as to some of the ideas we have discussed in Chapter 7.

Interference in Personality Development

The same factors which account for children's flexibility and adaptiveness also account for their susceptibility to possible problems in emotional development. This takes place after birth; it is determined by the interaction of the children with their environment. It has already been pointed out that the so-called intellectual factors are considerably influenced by the children's conflicts, attitudes, interests, and anxieties. This really is not surprising, because learning is such an integral part of all development; there is not a single aspect of psychological growth, structure, and dynamics that does not relate to it.

Perhaps the most important contribution made by psychology to the field of education is the knowledge that mutual love between teacher and child—a positive object relationship—plays an extremely important role in influencing any learning situation (8). This interpersonal relationship between teacher and child is the first step in the use of the mechanisms of identification and incorporation. It is through these mechanisms that all learning actually takes place, whether it is the parent or the teacher who is communicating the learning. The corollary is that feelings of hatred and fear, whether one-sided or mutual, interfere with the learning process. Children who learn incorporate not only what the teacher teaches but all aspects of the teacher's personality. Because the relationship between the teacher and the child forms such an important part of the educational procedure and of the character development of the child, it becomes very evident that the teacher must have an adequate personality. The qualities of an adequate personality are extremely beneficial in developing a quick, positive relationship to a child.

Nevertheless, even with an excellent teacher, occasionally perplexing problems will arise. We have spoken of all of the influences that operate on children before they enter school. There is to be discovered in each child a definite constellation of hopes and fears, dislikes and preferences, a particular kind of jealousy and tenderness, and a particular need of love or rejection of it.

PROBLEMS IN PERSONALITY DEVELOPMENT AS RELATED TO READING DISABILITY

Some children enter school so emotionally disturbed that reading failure is almost inevitable. For example, children who come from homes in which there is continuous and intense marital disharmony may be constantly preoccupied with questions concerning the basic security of their family life. They may even feel themselves responsible, to some degree, for the constant conflicts that they perceive between their parents. It is not at all surprising that such children are unable to focus their attention on the tasks presented by their teacher. The children have become so invested in their own problems that they can no longer concentrate on the learning situation. Their mental energies are so tied up in their conflicts that they have little energy left for the outside world.

Jarvis (5) has pointed out that, because of the "fear of looking," some youngsters experience extreme difficulty in learning to read. He says that it is the active part of looking necessary to establish the automatic skill of reading, rather than the reading content, which is felt to create the major difficulty for the retarded reader. It is possible that some so-called nonreaders have a greater reading vocabulary than is suspected, but that alphabetical letters and words lend themselves to a quick association with the underlying fantasies related to reading and make it necessary for the retarded reader to resort to the mechanism of denial to keep these fantasies repressed.

Another possible interpretation of this is not a fear of looking, but rather a fear of exploration. Some children may be brought up in an environment that leads to their feeling that acquiring knowledge is the same as the learning of intolerable ideas and feelings. If this is so, they will not learn, since "knowing" becomes equivalent to finding out about these unacceptable impulses.

We have seen that a small group of children will experience difficulty in reading primarily as the result of faulty personality development. In many cases of this kind the basic problem in reading is not one of word recognition, but essentially one of inefficient learning. More specifically, the problem is not one of acquisition of skills, but the proper utilization of these skills in the school situation. One example of this is Perry.

Perry is a 10-year-old who was referred because of continuing difficulties in school, as well as recurrent asthmatic attacks. In the first grade, Perry had no apparent difficulty. In second grade, the teacher felt Perry was not giving his best. Despite his other allergies, Perry had not experienced food allergies. He had been a good eater, and with the exception of milk, he had not been finicky about foods. Perry also had slept well. He had not had nightmares but had been a restless sleeper. He never had to share a bedroom with anyone else. Whenever his mother put Perry to bed, she always put his hands above the blankets so that he would not masturbate; she did not think that he ever did masturbate.

However, one of the chief complaints which the second-grade teacher had was Perry's excessive masturbation in class. Apparently, when Perry's mother conveyed to him the prohibitive attitude toward masturbation, instead of doing it in bed as most children do, he did it at school.

A psychological evaluation was administered to Perry; the following is excerpted from the report of that evaluation:

> Perry is rather completely overwhelmed by his environment and is exceedingly vulnerable to the concomitant anxiety. He tries to cope with his anxiety by either drawing away from the environment or else trying to hang on to small, very familiar aspects of it. He does not seem to be at all confident that he can meet a new situation adequately.
>
> Perry appears to be a child whose fearfulness permeates every action and every thought, so that he literally dares not try out various modes of behavior that would lead toward growing up and being at ease in the world. Such behavioral constriction hampers learning processes since the necessary self-assertion is lacking. Perry finds it necessary to filter his ideation through a series of defenses before it becomes overt. The most habitual defense he uses is to separate his thought from his feeling. He is much better able to express aggressive or hostile thoughts if the concomitant feeling is repressed. In this sense he is able to intellectualize his hostility, or to play around with it verbally. However, at times the underlying hostile impulse is too strong to allow him to play around with it verbally. If he did, it would break through into behavioral expression. Perry's conscience, which really is an internalization of parental teachings (primarily his mother's, it would seem), has become so overly strict and constricting that it allows for very little expression of aggressiveness. His conscience is so despotic that it makes no differentiation between constructive and destructive aggressiveness, simply forbidding any such expression. As a result, he often needs a second defense. In this defense he completely denies any aggressive wishes within himself and also any external stimulus which could arouse such aggressiveness. Then, he could have everyone, including himself, believe that all was sweetness and light. Similar to this last defense is another one in which he finds it necessary to turn everything into its opposite. He shows this a great deal where his parents are concerned. If he thinks his parents are mean to him, this idea is immediately converted into the idea that his parents are the best in the world.
>
> When it comes to expressing actual feelings, Perry is very much constricted. He is afraid of his feelings and emotions. Hence, if he expresses them at all, they are quite arbitrary and superficial. He gives lip service to emotion rather than experiencing it. This is highly deviate for his age. At his age children are usually very emotional. What they feel, they feel intensely, although it might be short lived. Perry is too fearful to allow himself this very important experience. In a sense he is denying the exist-

243

ence of an integral part of himself, his feelings. He thereby is also denying the driving force with which he could instrument wishes and make them achievements.

Perry's case is illustrative of a youngster whose difficulties in school are symptomatic of an underlying emotional difficulty. Perry never had the opportunity to learn how to channel his aggressive impulses successfully. The outcome was that Perry had a great deal of conflict concerning hostility and guilt; he had built up a system of defense which was to his detriment. In a very real sense, he had not moved through the separation-individuation process successfully. He was overly dependent upon the mother who had kept him in emotional infancy.

Nature of Ego Defense

The type of defense employed by the ego to cope with unacceptable ideas and feelings may be of significance in the learning process. One defense that an individual may use is that of *repression:* the expulsion from consciousness of ideas and feelings that are intolerable. If children, for one reason or another, find it necessary to engage in massive repression, then a situation may be created where they may actually become afraid of absorbing knowledge. They become afraid of assimilating facts. It is almost as if any fact, even though it may be only distantly related to the originally repressed material, has to be kept out of mind. These are the youngsters who may learn how to recognize words but who have serious difficulty in reading comprehension.

A defense which we frequently see in youngsters who are experiencing difficulty succeeding in school is that of reaction formation. Children who use this defense extensively are often described by their teachers as being too passive. Reaction formation involves changing an unconscious impulse into its opposite at the conscious level. These youngsters may feel a great deal of unconscious hostility, but at a conscious level, all is sweetness and light. If they have the feeling that their parents or teachers have been mean or cruel to them—if they do not like their parents or teachers for whatever reason—they consciously become the best people in the world. These children characteristically are well-behaved in class, but they simply do not work. They appear to be lazy, to dawdle, and to have difficulty getting their assignments in on time. Their teacher and parents become discouraged by the wasted potential.

Another defense frequently used in conjunction with reaction formation is that of isolation of feeling. Children may be able to intellectualize their anger, but they must keep their emotions stifled. They are always very fearful of their feelings. They cannot allow themselves to have any real feeling. They cannot invest their energies into striving for success, because this involves a desire, an emotion. It is as if they feel that if they were to allow any feeling to break through, all of their emotions would rise up and overwhelm them. Most youngsters who rely heavily upon this defense do not have difficulty in the acquisition of skills, but in using those skills.

Another defense that may hamper learning is that of compulsive perfectionism. This is illustrated by students who cannot see the forest because of the trees. In reading material, these students have to read every word; they must be certain that they chew up every single detail. They are unable to differentiate between the main ideas and supporting details in a selection. They feel compelled to learn every single thing in the material. Compulsive perfectionism characteristically is rooted in children's need to defend against the wish to be careless, disorderly and impulsive.

Parental Reactions to Children with Disabilities

In most instances children with severe reading disabilities are products of adults who, because of their insensitivity, act before understanding, impose rather than guide, and punish; as a result, gentleness goes begging. At crucial points in their lives—in fact, throughout their early years—children with severe learning problems are forced to realize that their desperately needed mentors and guides—parents and teachers—are so unaware of their problems that they hinder rather than help. Histories have further shown us that children's constant exposure to a world ill-equipped to aid them makes them turn against their erstwhile helpers and to view them as enemies. As time passes—and especially as these children reach school—they frequently begin to distrust those who set themselves up as friends, mentors, and teachers. We have seen that this attitude is a serious hindrance to academic, social, and emotional growth.

During the pregnancy period, expectant parents develop a glamorized image of what their children will be like. The psychological preparation for expectant children normally involves the fantasy of a perfect youngster, a kind of ego-ideal. More specifically, the parents may long for, either explicitly or implicitly, offspring who possess all the characteristics they admire in themselves, and who will not have any traits they dislike in themselves. Probably there always will be some disparity between the parents' dream child and the actual child. To accept and resolve this discrepancy becomes one of the developmental tasks of parenthood. It is an aspect in the evolution of a healthy mother-child relationship. Nonetheless, when the disparity is too great, as in the birth of a baby with some handicap, or where the parents' wishes are too unrealistic, a trauma may occur.

In normal children, the acquisition and mastery of certain basic skills during infancy and the first few years of childhood evoke a maternal responsive joy and pride in the children's development. The children are frequently perceived by their mothers as the wished-for extensions of themselves and represent a personal accomplishment and achievement. But when the children are "defective" or seem to be lagging behind in developing normal functions, they may elicit a different response from their mothers. A mother may think: "How could I have produced this defective, unappealing child?"

It seems to us that the process of learning to accept and to cope with the child's condition is somewhat analogous to the process of grief and mourning that sets in when one learns that a loved one is near death. Upon being informed that the child is in some way impaired, the parents suffer a sense of loss of the fantasied perfect child. First there is a denial that it is so; the clutching at straws, the shopping around for a doctor who will give them a more favorable diagnosis and prognosis. When the handicap is confirmed over and over, the anger sets in. Agitatedly, the mother may query into space; why did this have to happen to me? Is this a kind of punishment for some real or imagined transgression on my part or my husband's? Infinite fantasies and frustrations dart into consciousness as the mother struggles with her mixed emotions toward the child and her fury at God, the doctors, and other less specific forces.

Next there is the attempt to bargain with the powers that be, to promise to behave in a certain way if only the child will somehow be made well and whole. But this too is a futile quest. Only when the remnants of the wished for child can be buried and mourned, can the real, defective child be allowed to live and develop to her or his fullest capacity with acceptance and encouragement, even love, from the parents. The acceptance of the child for what he or she is and can become is essential if parents and child are to make progress.

In the early stages after a diagnosis of minimal brain dysfunction of reading disability has been made, there is bewilderment over causality. The parents feel extraordinary ambivalence, which arouses intolerable and unacceptable feelings of guilt and shame. The fury and hostility which they almost inevitably must feel toward the child cannot be tolerated by their consciences, and barriers against acknowledging these impulses are erected. The parents, in an attempt to at least partially compensate for their intense guilt over their hostility toward the child, often become overprotective and overindulgent. Their defensive strategies, in turn, deprive the child of opportunities for growth and development of adaptive secondary ego functions. Instead, the child becomes adept at using his or her handicap as a way of controlling and manipulating the parents. In a very real sense the child becomes the dependent despot. It is this manipulative dependency that plays a very large role in the power struggles which are set up between parent and child. And it is the very same struggle that will confront the teacher in any attempt to get the child to adapt to the classroom setting.

CONCLUSIONS

In all of our chapters on development, we have stressed the fact that children are physical organisms functioning in a social environment in a psychological manner. We have repeatedly emphasized the dangers inherent in a static, mechanized approach to the diagnosis and remediation of reading disabilities. A psychodynamic, affective approach to children must replace the more traditional orientation, which has separated the cognitive from the emotional realm, a dichotomy which is superficial to say the least.

Any discussion of both intellectual and personality development is closely associated with ego development. All of those factors which are important in the study of ego functioning are involved in our understanding of how children adapt to their environment so that they can be receptive to the learning process.

The question of differential diagnosis in reading and emotional disability has always been a knotty one. Certainly a very definite relationship exists between reading failure and emotional maladjustment; the question is primarily one of cause and effect.

In our attempts to focus on the ego functioning of children, we have found that a study of the separation-individuation process is invaluable in understanding the vicissitudes of early child development. The struggles waged by the children as they attempt to establish some independence from the parental figures have important implications for the learning process. Ultimately the reactions of both parents and teachers to children who are adapting and to children who are not adapting become extremely significant.

BIBLIOGRAPHY

1. Blanchard, P. "Psychoanalytic Contributions to the Problems of Reading Disability." *Psychoanalytic Study of the Child,* 2 (1946): 163–187.

2. Daniels, M. "The Dynamics of Morbid Envy in the Etiology and Treatment of Chronic Learning Disability." *Psychoanalytic Review,* 51 (Winter, 1964). 45–56.

3. Erikson, E. *Childhood and Society.* New York: Norton, 1950.

4. Freud, S. *The Problem of Anxiety.* New York: Norton, 1936.

5. Jarvis, V. "Clinical Observations on the Visual Problem in Read-

ing Disability." *Psychoanalytic Study of the Child,* 8 (1958), 451–470.

6. Klein, E. "Psychoanalytic Aspects of School Problems." *Psychoanalytic Study of the Child,* 3–4 (1949), 369–390.

7. Mahler, M. S. *The Psychological Birth of the Human Infant.* New York: Basic Books, 1975.

8. Pearson, G. H. S. *Psychoanalysis and the Education of the Child.* New York: Norton, 1954.

CHAPTER 11

Remedial
Instruction [I]

Anytime anyone succeeds in doing almost any task there seems to course through the veins a chemical that causes a swelling of pride. The elation experienced, though of only fleeting duration, rouses a spirit of glory. Even among the most modest there may be a momentary show of arrogance. Successful people take credit for themselves, sense their self-esteem being bolstered, and above all feel spurred to try again and even better their efforts.

Every golfer knows the expression, "That's the shot that will bring you back." It seems that almost regardless of the round one has been playing, hitting one superior shot produces strong feelings of joy and pride and motivation to try again.

It is the joy of success, the recognition of achievement that provides the highest form of motivation in any endeavor, but particularly so in the case of a nonreader or a partially disabled reader who achieves. Without a doubt all teachers who have successfully worked with folks in need of highly specialized remedial reading instruction will agree on the potency of success. The old cliche that "nothing succeeds like success" is an unquestionable truth.

THE FERNALD TECHNIQUE

In my 25 years as director of the Reading Study Center at the University of Delaware, during which time I have worked closely with innumerable children and some adults in need of specialized and personalized instruction, I have found myself most indebted first to Grace Fernald (4) and second to Emmett Betts (2, 3). To the latter I am enormously obliged for directing my attention to Fernald and demanding that her recommendations be thoroughly studied and mastered.

To Grace Fernald I am inordinately grateful, not only for the remedial techniques she described in detail but also for her unquestionable belief that most all children of extreme and partial disability could be taught to read at a level almost in keeping with their expectancy. It is for this reason that over the years I have continued with my graduate students the practice initiated by Betts of requiring them to study Fernald closely. To the best of my knowledge no other technique has been introduced that could supplant hers.

Lewis M. Terman, a widely known and respected scholar, wrote in a foreword to Fernald's text,

> If educational methods were more intelligently adapted to the idiosyncrasies of the individual child, all children would achieve up to their mental age level in all the school subjects. It is largely for this reason I believe this book is one of the most significant contributions ever made to experimental pedagogy. (4, p. *ix*)

This is high praise from a highly respected professional. In his enthusiasm even Terman is carried away when he says, "all children would achieve up to their mental age level in all school subjects." His is a loose use of the logical qualifier "all." By and large, though, he is right insofar as reading failures are concerned. Most reading disabilities stem from pedagogical failures. The next chapter in this text reflects a careful look at what Fernald activated and a marked departure from her practices to others found more fruitful.

Terman also refers to the work of Anne Sullivan in training Helen Keller to read and to speak, even though she was blind, deaf, and mute from early childhood. This unbelievable success story should be sustaining to teachers at all times. All remedial teachers should read *Teacher: Anne Sullivan Macy* (6) and *The Story of My Life* (5) by Helen Keller. One is impressed by Anne Sullivan's untiring effort at coping with the thwarted desire and the distemper of Helen Keller. One is equally as impressed by Helen Keller's boundless gratitude to her teacher. By far the most priceless return one can obtain from helping failing children is the immeasurable psychic reward. Undoubtedly this is what Anne Sullivan Macy must have experienced.

A first requisite attribute of a successful remedial reading teacher is faith. One must believe sincerely that children, and others as well, can be helped. Faith is not enough, though, just as "love is not enough" (1). Conjoint with this must be a sound grasp of pedagogical practices, a penetrating appreciation for therapeutics, and an untiring determination. These are the qualities that compass an able teacher.

Terman says:

> It is my considered judgment that Fernald's conquest of word-blindness is an achievement comparable with that of Miss Sullivan. . . . Dr. Fernald was the first to demonstrate beyond possibility of doubt that the most extreme cases of word-blindness are quickly and completely curable. (4, p. *lx*)

The praise lavished on Grace Fernald seems merited indeed, even though again Terman appears overenthusiastic when he says "quickly and completely curable." Experience with extreme disability readers has taught me that while progress may be steady and at times astounding, in no instance has achievement been accomplished either "quickly or completely."

There is no quick panacea and in our clinic we have always been quite cautious about making a prognosis that would suggest "quickly." We have been equally as guarded about saying "completely." After all there is no measure to determine complete attainment. Most of the children referred to our clinic are about nine years old. On occasion we may see a child of seven, but this is the exception. By the time children are nine years old they have had at least three years in school, have been exposed to different teacher attempts at instruction, including special help either after school, Saturdays, or summers, and have begun to doubt themselves most seriously. By the time a program of instruction is introduced, the teaching must cope with the emotional involvement of the child, as well as the inability to read.

It is true, too, as Terman says, that in many ways the predicament of the extremely disabled reader is more tragic than that of the deaf or the blind. The handicaps of deafness and blindness are so apparent that most folks make some allowance. On the other hand, the plight of nonreaders is quite different. They have no readily observable physical defects and as a result people, including teachers, expect achievement similar to that of typical children.

Terman also refers to a certain amount of skepticism voiced by teachers and psychologists concerning the kinesthetic-tactile aspects of Fernald's technique. How and why should the employment of such procedures prove effective? While explanation or rationalization could be offered, it is a fact that Dr. Fernald and others who have used her technique succeeded where others failed. Throughout Fernald stresses the flexibility of what was done in adapting her techniques from case to case. At the same time she avoided saying that her techniques were the only ones that could produce results. What she did do, though, was to document her claims with case records supporting them.

STAGES OF PROGRESS: TOTAL DISABILITY

Fernald devotes chapter 5 in her text, *Remedial Techniques in Basic School Subjects* to explaining the four stages of her method which she labeled the kinesthetic-sensory method. The essential of her technique consists in having children learn to write words correctly and in motivating them to do so. The method initially involves the use of the children's sense modalities of seeing, hearing, speaking, and touching to focus on word forms. The children progress by stages from having to trace each word they provide and learn to the point where they are able to read materials other than their own.

The practice of writing and tracing, which Fernald advocates, has been used on many occasions in many different eras. This attention to word form can be found in Plato, Horace, Seneca, Quintilian, St. Jerome, Charlemagne, Locke, Brinsley, and Montessori. Of Montessori she says, "Whatever criticisms one may have of the 'Montessori method' as such, its effectiveness in the development of letter and word forms cannot be questioned by anyone who has seen a good Montessori school in operation" (p. 29).

It seems fitting to pause at this point and comment on Maria Montessori and her practical application of the action-type activities she developed and the intellectual stimulation they provided. Her "exercises of practical life" (8, 9) not only utilized sensory training designed to make tactile (touch), thermice (heat), baric (weight), and muscular (motor) senses more acute but also resulted in intellectual development. Because the key to her exercises was action, the self-activity strength resided in its power to motivate. In turn the teacher became, first, a designer of activities and, second and perhaps more important, an observer of actions. Montessori's "didactic activities" based on "real life" activities, were designed not only to provide the stuff of experience, but also to support the ordering of that stuff. As Lavatelli says, "the interest of a child could be better explained not so much by the satisfaction in being able to button a button . . . but by the satisfaction of his intellectual curiosity about how buttons 'work' " (7, p. 14). Thus Montessori reflects activities of Froebel's "gifts" of 100 years earlier. In her preface she says, "I therefore recall here, as an eloquent symbol, Helen Keller and Mrs. Anne Sullivan Macy, who are, by their example both teachers of myself—and, before the world, living documents of the miracle in education" (9, p. 25).

Fernald's citing of scholars across the centuries in conjunction with Montessori's concepts should give credibility to the kinesthetic-sensory method. It has been tried many times under varied circumstances and has been productive. In brief, it has the sanction of tradition and precedent.

Fernald also refers to the method as being eclectic, meaning that it utilizes different practices in a flexible way. Thus, her kinesthetic-sensory method enables a teacher to use phonic methods (even though Fernald does not), whole word practices, alphabet method practices, and semantic practices, and to adapt the method according to what works best with any particular child.

The contents of chapter 5, which Fernald refers to as an outline, give the stages through which her cases of total reading disability moved to develop reading skill. She distinguishes between cases of total disability and partial disability. The stages outlined in chapter 5, however, are from the former population.

After years of working with her techniques and her text, I prepared an outline of her proposals that has proved helpful to students. The outline provides an organization that is quite similar to her accounting as provided in chapter 5. On the other hand, it pulls together details and recommendations that she has scattered throughout her book. That I have done this should not be interpreted as a reflection on her text. She wrote in detail about the first-hand circumstances of cases with which she was involved, and it seems likely to conclude that whenever one writes in this way ideas are apt to lie scattered about.

To provide a basis for comparison, Fernald's outline is presented first in a very abbreviated form to which I have added a summary of the major characteristics of each stage. This may prove helpful to the reader before examining the detailed and organized outline and discussions of the four stages presented on pages 255–279.

> *Stage 1: Child Learns by Tracing Word.* This stage is in large measure the heart of her technique and is distinguished by children learning to write correctly words they wish to learn, by first tracing the written form of those words with their fingers, as they say each syllable. This continues until the children can write the word correctly without looking at the copy.

> *Stage 2: Same as Stage 1, Except That Tracing Is No Longer Necessary.* In this stage of development children learn the word by looking at the word written in script by the teacher, saying it,

and then writing it without looking at the copy. This stage is also characterized by more extensive writing on various subjects of interest to the children.

Stage 3: Same as Stage 2, Except That Child Is Able to Learn from the Printed Word by Merely Looking at It and Saying It to Himself Before He Writes It. It is during this stage that children also begin to read materials other than their own written stories.

Stage 4: Ability to Recognize New Words from Their Similarity to Words or Parts of Words He Has Already Learned.

Another way to record the differences in the four Fernald stages is to use the first letter of each of the following basic distinguishing features: visual, auditory, kinesthetic, and tactile. This results in a label known simply as V-A-K-T (3). Fernald says, "Our study seems to show that normal perception, retention, and memory for these same visual symbols could be developed by individuals whose failure seems to be due to inability to learn through visual and auditory channels, if tactual and kinesthetic experiences were involved in the learning process" (p. 167). She states too that perception is a complex process but that through many experiences a simple sensory clue may result in instant recognition "a simple sensory cue, as visual, tactile or auditory" (p. 181). Hyphenating the letters V-A-K-T as Betts did suggests that each of the sensory modalities functions in an interrelated manner and not in a discrete way. Tactile means touch. When children trace words as Fernald describes, they use each modality. They touch the written word by finger contact; they move their lips and throat when they say the word as a unit and by syllables; and they see it. Thus V-A-K-T can refer to Stage 1, V-A-K^1 to Stage 2, V-A-K^2 to Stage 3, and V-A to Stage 4. Notice that V-A-K is used twice and is distinguished by the exponents 1 and 2. Even the brief description of the four stages as provided thus far reveals that pupils use all three modalities in Stages 2 and 3, whereas in Stage 4 they use visual-auditory procedures largely.

Stage 1   V-A-K-T
Stage 2   V-A-K^1
Stage 3   V-A-K^2
Stage 4   V-A

As previously stated, in chapter 5 of her text Fernald outlined in detail the recommendations of instructional techniques used in each of the four stages. In each instance an outline point is elaborated by a paragraph or two of explanation, with the exception of Stage 3, for which she provided an 11-page discussion. Readers tend to find this inconsistency in outline form puzzling. In part this is true, too, of the reading of the detailed explanations. The details are helpful but, because of the rambling manner of their presentation, add a complexity to the comprehension of the whole. The following organization of her recommendations should prove more functional, because the continuity of her ideas is more discernible. At the same time various items from parts of her text other than chapter 5 have been added, because it is felt these points add clarity and are necessary for an understanding of her technique.

At a glance the reader can tell that the outline of Stage 1 that follows is lengthy, documented, and provided with subheadings that do not appear as such in the Fernald text. The reader is urged to examine carefully and thoughtfully each detail, remembering that the quotes are all Fernald's.

Stage 1: Children Learn by Tracing Words

A. General Procedures of the Technique
   1. "The essentials of our technique consist in (1) the discovery of some means by which the child can learn to write words correctly; (2) the motivating of such writing; (3) the reading by the child of the printed copy of what he has written; (4) extensive reading of materials other than own compositions." (p. 33)
   2. "The only thing that will result in a real change of attitude is to show the child that he can learn as well as anyone else and then make it possible for him to continue to master new words until he writes as easily and correctly as other children his age." (p. 194)
   3. "These methods allow each child to learn in the manner that is most satisfactory for him." (p. 32)

B. Motivation
   1. "Our method consists in starting the child off on his first day with an activity that will result in successful learning." (p. 14)
   2. "We start by telling the child that we have a new way of learning words, which we want him to try. We explain to him that many bright people have had the same difficulty he has had in learning to read and have learned easily by this new method, which is really just as good as any other way." (p. 33)
   3. "His attention is not called to the words he does not know but to the fact that he is capable of learning any words he wants to learn regardless of their length and complexity." (p. 15)
   4. "A positive reaction was established the first day and care was taken not to allow any situation to arise that would bring to life old negative reactions until the new attitude had been fixed." (p. 15)

C. Procedure
1. "We let him select any word he wants to learn, regardless of length." (p. 33)
2. "The word is written for the child with crayola on paper in plain black board-size script, or in print, if manuscript writing is used." (p. 35)
3. "The child traces the word with finger contact, saying each part of the word as he traces it." (p. 35)
4. "He repeats this process as many times as necessary in order to write the word without looking at the copy." (p. 35)
5. "Finger contact is important in tracing." (p. 35)
   a. "The word should always be traced with the finger in contact with the paper." (p. 35)
   b. "The child uses either one or two fingers for tracing, as he wishes." (p. 37)
   c. "The child then traced the word with one or two fingers of the right hand (or the left, if he was left handed)." (p. 105)
   d. "Care was taken in the beginning to be sure that the tracing was correct in general direction, for example, that the child followed the proper course in making *a*'s, *d*'s and other letters." (p. 105)
   e. "The learning rate is much more rapid with finger contact than when a stylus or pencil is used." (p. 37)
6. Points to be noted
   a. "The individual must say each part of the word either to himself or aloud as he traces it and as he writes it." (p. 40)
   b. "It is necessary to establish the connection between the sound of the word and its form, so that the individual will eventually recognize the word from the visual stimulus alone." (p. 40)
   c. "It is important that his vocalization of the word should be natural; that is, that it would be a repetition of the word as it actually sounds, and not a stilted, distorted sounding out of letters or syllables in such a way that the word is lost in the process. . . . The sound for each letter is never given separately nor overemphasized." (p. 40)
   d. "In a longer word like *important,* the child says, *im* while he is tracing the first syllable, *por* while he is tracing the second syllable, and *tant* as he traces the last syllable." (p. 40)
   e. "In writing the word he again pronounces each syllable as he writes it." (p. 40)

7. Tracing

"He repeats this process as many times as necessary in order to write the word without looking at the copy." (p. 35)

8. Writing
   a. "As soon as the child thought he knew the word, the copy was covered and he wrote it. If there was any difficulty in writing the word, he went back to his copy and traced it as many times as he wished." (p. 105)
   b. "The child should always write the word without looking at the copy." (p. 37)
   c. "When the child copies the word, looking back and forth from the word he is writing to the copy, he breaks the word up into small and meaningless units. The flow of the hand in writing the word is interrupted and the eye movements are back and forth from the word to the copy instead of those which the eye would make in adjusting to the word as it is being written." (p. 37)
   d. "This writing of the word without the copy is important at all stages of learning to write and spell. The copying of words is a most serious block to learning to write them correctly and to recognize them after they have been written." (p. 38)
   e. "The word should always be written as a unit." (p. 39)
   f. "In case of error or interruption in writing the word, the incorrect form is covered or crossed out. The child then starts the word again and writes it as a whole. In many cases it is necessary for him to look at the word or even to trace it again before he can write it correctly. The word is never patched up by erasing the incorrect part and substituting the correction." (p. 39)
   g. "The reason for this procedure is that the various movements of erasing, correcting single letters or syllables, and so forth, break the word up into a meaningless total which does not represent the word." (p. 39)

9. "Words should always be used in context." (p. 39)
   a. "It is important that the child should know the meaning of all words that he learns. It is also important that he should experience the words in meaningful groups." (p. 39)
   b. "Even if his vocabulary is somewhat limited, it is better for him to start his work with the learning of words he already knows how to use in speech." (p. 39)

10. "He writes the word once on scrap paper and then in his story." (p. 35)

11. Story writing
    a. "As soon as the child has discovered that he can learn to write words, we let him start 'story writing.' " (p. 33)
    b. "Each word is written for him and learned by him before it is written in his 'story.' At first we leave him quite free to write anything that is of interest to him." (p. 33)
    c. "The learning of new words is so easy that there is nothing to keep the child from writing any word that is a part of his spoken vocabulary." (p. 46)
    d. "At first their stories were very short. . . . The stories kept getting longer and more complicated as the mechanics of writing became easier." (pp. 109–111)
    e. "As his skill increases, we let him work up projects in his various school subjects, write about them, and read what he has written after it has been typed for him. He asks for any words he wishes to use but does not know how to write. Each word is written for him and learned by him before it is written in his 'story.' " (p. 33)
    f. "The most surprising thing to most people who saw the work of these children was the complexity of content in their stories and the difficulty of the words used." (p. 111)
    g. "The children wrote stories of events both real and fanciful." (p. 111)
12. Story typing
    a. "After a story has been written by the child, it is typed for him and he reads it in print." (p. 35)
    b. "Whatever the individual writes must be typed for him and read by him before too long an interval." (p. 41)
    c. "Whatever he writes is typed for him within 24 hours so that he may read it while the original is fresh in his mind." (p. 33)
    d. "Since the individual is able to recognize words in script or print after he has written them, it is essential that his recognition of words in print be established by having him read the printed form of what he writes." (p. 41)
    e. "Any errors in his writing are corrected when his story is printed but attention is called to a few principles [of grammar] at a time." (p. 97)
    f. "At first, the stories were written without any attempt at punctuation, capitalization (except in case of proper names) or paragraphing." (p. 113)
    g. "As the writing progressed, the child began to use periods, commas, and question marks. Then he learned to begin a sentence with a capital letter, to write a title for his story and

do various other things required for good form." (p. 113)

    h. "The children's stories were always typed in correct form. Capital letters, punctuation, and paragraph divisions were used in the typewritten copy even though they were omitted in the story as written by the child." (p. 112)

13. Word file box

    a. "After the story is finished, the child files the words under the proper letters in his word file." (p. 35)

    b. "Each child had his word box and filed each word he learned after the word had been written in his story." (p. 198)

    c. "The natural result of the use of these early alphabetical word lists is the dictionary habit." (p. 198)

    d. "This takes some extra time at first, but children become quite skillful in identifying the first letter of the word with the same letter in the file and enjoy putting the words in place." (p. 35)

    e. "In this way they learn the alphabet without rote learning of the letters as such and without too much emphasis on letters in words. This practice with the word file is excellent training for later use of the dictionary and for the use of the alphabet in organizing and filing away material in connection with any subject." (p. 35)

    f. "It is to be noted that, in using the word file, the child picks up the succession of letters in the alphabet and develops habits that make use of the dictionary natural and easy as he progresses." (p. 109)

    g. "If he wanted to use the word later and was not sure that he could write it correctly, he found it in his file and relearned it." (p. 109)

14. Spelling

    a. "No special period is set aside for spelling." (p. 197)

    b. "It is made possible for the child to learn any new word he wishes to use in his written expression whenever he is ready for the word." (p. 197)

15. Interests

    a. "If the child's interests are to be used as a means of motivation, it is necessary to know not only his general interests but also his immediate interests." (p. 111–112)

    b. "One very simple way of discovering what interests a child at a particular moment is to let him tell about it in spoken or written language." (p. 112)

    c. "The technique we have described allows free expression of whatever happens to be at the focus of the child's attention at a specific time." (p. 112)

  d. "The child is much more interested in writing and reading fairly difficult material that is on the level of his understanding than simple material which is below his mental age level. In fact the child who has never been able to read or write anything takes delight in learning difficult words." (p. 44)

D. Transitional Steps

  1. "The child stops tracing when he is able to learn without it. If left to himself he discovers that he is able to learn without the tracing that was so necessary at the start." (p. 41)

  2. "In all cases the tracing drops out gradually. There is first a decrease in the number of tracings necessary to learn a word, then certain words are learned without tracing." (p. 41)

  3. "At first a few words are learned without tracing and on the same day other words are traced. A child will often trace all his words one day, trace none of them the next day, and trace again the following day." (p. 41)

  4. "The average tracing period is about two months, with a range of from one to eight months." (p. 41)

  5. "Eventually tracing disappears altogether." (p. 41)

  6. "After a certain period of tracing, the child develops the ability to learn any new word by simply looking at the word in script, saying it over to himself as he looks at it, and then writing it without looking at the copy, saying each part of the word as he writes it." (p. 39)

DISCUSSION. It would be wise if at this point the reader turned to the Fernald text and made a comparison between the text presentation and the outline presented in this text. This would help the reader understand the degree to which the outline reflects Fernald's text, not in mirror form but in quotations that are assembled in a sequential order. It is apparent that quotations are scattered from page 14 to page 198 and that they are not grouped under such headings as motivation, interests, transition, and the like.

Stage 1 is in large measure the heart of the technique Fernald labels the kinesthetic-sensory method. A number of conditions distinguish this method. First, if the material or words to be used are selected as she recommends, then the children already "know" the word. They do not necessarily know the full meaning. What is known is that the words the children give are in their speaking vocabulary. On one occasion a child asked to learn "demolish" and when asked what it meant replied, "I don't know. Last night I heard my father say "demolish." Second, the word form is presented to the children. They do not recognize but are about to learn that this written form is also a symbol for the concept.

Third, the kinesthetic-sensory method involves movement of eye, lip-throat, and hand. This gives the word form a visual, auditory, and kinesthetic content. Fourth, to use and coordinate the sensory pathways the child must give close attention to the object at hand or to the word form. This causes them to focus on that which they do not know: the word form.

The Fernald method is on occasion referred to as the "writing approach to reading." Rereading the general procedures section of the outline supports such a labeling. The essential of her technique consists in having children learn to write words correctly and to motivate them to do so. Success undoubtedly is the best way to change children's attitude. Even so, it has been our experience using her technique that seldom if ever does a child learn to write "as easily and correctly as other children his age."

It seems true in part that there is some variance and flexibility in the way different children use the tracing technique. By and large though, the adaptations are within the technique rather than the use of distinctly different methods. Some children trace only a small number of words and move readily to the next stages. Others require many contacts to fix and retain words. Still others revert frequently but are not totally dependent on tracing. It is only in this sense that her technique and its use is "eclectic." All the children taught by her method follow identical steps, but can do so at different rates.

The motivation aspects she details largely hold true. Children start with a word of their choice and learn to write it. On the other hand it seems patronizing to say, "many bright people." By the time children are nine-years old, as most of her cases were and as most of ours are before they reach a clinic, the self-image of each is so tarnished that they are convinced they must be dummies. They are poignantly aware of their failure and seriously question their ability. As a result they are sensitive about and resentful of the hypocrisy of flattery.

Experience has also shown that almost all of the extremely disabled readers do not learn easily. She indicated that some traced a word as often as 50 to 100 times before writing it correctly. While this represents an extreme, it suggests that many tracings are usually needed and this requires a great deal of persistence. Particularly difficult is the coordination of tracing and saying of a syllable at the right moment and without distortion. Much the same difficulty is experienced when children try to write the word in a similar manner.

Care is also taken to be sure the children follow the proper course in making letters. No copying is permitted, and while this is as it should be, it exacts a high price. A word is always written as a whole and no patching or erasing is allowed. This is a highly commendable procedure, but exacting.

These stipulations reflect Fernald's belief in the efficacy of meaning and her grasp of the semantic significance of word unity. A whole word provides the perceptual unit for representing a concept. It is the whole word that represents and not a letter or a syllable or an inflectional or a derivative change or a root word.

Her devotion to the power of meaning is exemplified, too, in her insistence that the words used should appear in a context. Not only does she want pupils to use words for which they know meanings, but also she insists that the pupils must experience these words in "meaningful groups." The use of words the children know and can use orally is endorsed even though their vocabularies are somewhat limited.

> Words are of interest to the individual when they express ideas. Word lists, as such, are disconnected and lacking in interest for the intelligent individual. To get a maximum of attention to a word, it must not only be one in the child's vocabulary but it must also be one used to express an idea that is of interest to him at the time he is writing it.

In addition, as soon as children have learned that they can write words, they are asked to start story writing. This procedure has both assets and liabilities. Much effort is made to capitalize on pupil interests and permit their language facility to dictate the complexity of the content. Both immediate and general interests are utilized and material is written that is both real and fanciful. On the other hand, each word is learned before it is written in a story. Sometimes this requires the learning of each word and imposes a dilatory pace. As a result stories are very short and become longer only as the word learning becomes easier.

It is an excellent idea for children to trace words as often as they wish or until they think they know the words and can write them without looking at them. The children sense that they are being trusted and realize that their decisions are honored. If they have any difficulty, they are free to go back to their copy and trace again. Probably equally as important is the fact that at no time is copying permitted. Copying is a serious block to learning. Paralleling this is the regulation against erasing or patching.

Experience has taught us at Delaware that when tracing was found useful, teaching the technique and assuring its correct usage (blending pronouncing of a syllable with writing without distortion; not permitting copying, patching, or erasing) required very close teacher supervision. One pupil to one teacher was the best we could do, especially during the early phases. Later, when tracing was giving way to Stage 2 or teacher writing of a word in normal size, we found we might work with two or three pupils, but not with more.

Highly commendable, too, is Fernald's use of story writing and the writing of anything that is of interest to the children. This does encourage them to produce and motivates them to try and try again. Again, they are being respected. It is their interests that are accepted and attended to and prove useful. Working up projects in various areas of the curriculum is praiseworthy. This helps learners realize functionally or in a working situation that one does not read "reading" but one reads about persons, places, things, and events. In brief, one uses the reading process in each area of the curriculum.

Fernald is attentive to ways to facilitate fixation, retention, and memory. Children must, she says, reread what they wrote before too long an interval, certainly within 24 hours.

The word file has much utility value. It is a personal file. It can be used at any time. It is alphabetically organized and thus resembles a dictionary. It can be referred to later if a word needs to be relearned. On the other hand a word file can be a frustration and an embarrassment. Words added hastily, without being well fixed in the mind, are forgotten. The learners' bonus may not be determined by quantity of words in the box, but by quality or number of words that are known and remembered.

Because the procedure is used in a flexible way, adapted to and by individuals at their own rates of assimilation, the transition signs, while similar from child to child, are individual in nature. Some children do catch on in a short time (maybe two months), others may require eight or more months. Some seldom if ever return to tracing once they reach her so-called V-A-K^2 or V-A stage, others do. Individual differences dictate the learning rate and not lock-step practices.

Stage 2: Same as Stage 1, Except That Tracing Is No Longer Necessary

Now we may move on to Stage 2. Again, the reader is urged to do two things: turn to page 253 and read the digest statement of Fernald's reporting in her chapter 5; and turn to her text and read the full account provided.

The following outline is considerably shorter than the one provided for Stage 1. This is because Stage 1 is by and large the heart of her method, and because Stage 2 is built upon Stage 1. There is no unwarranted repetition.

A. Motivation
   1. "The child continues to write freely and to read the printed copy of what he has written. Writing is now so easy that the child's stories are much longer and more complicated than they were at first. The child writes about everything that interests him as well as about all his school subjects." (pp. 40–41)
B. Procedure
   1. "Same as Stage 1 except that tracing is no longer necessary." (p. 39)

    a. "It is now only necessary for the teacher to write the word in ordinary script for the child." (p. 50)

    b. "He learns the word by looking at it, saying it and writing it." (p. 50)

    c. "After a certain period of tracing, the child develops the ability to learn any new word by simply looking at the word in script, saying it over to himself as he looks at it, and then writing it without looking at the copy, saying each part as he writes it." (p. 39)

  2. "When tracing is no longer necessary, a small box word file is substituted for the larger one used up to this time." (p. 50) "The child writes the word on a card for his word file." (p. 206)

  3. "From the beginning of the remedial work with children of normal or superior intelligence, no attempt is made to simplify the content that they write or read. This applies both to vocabulary range and to complexity of subject matter." (p. 44)

    a. "All the children write books about subjects that interest them, including stories about their own interests and the material connected with projects that are essential for their school work." (p. 46)

    b. "The only limit to what they can write is what they know." (p. 46)

C. Transitional Steps

  1. "Because the children always write about things that interest them . . . they develop a reading vocabulary not only of the more commonly used words but also of words connected with particular subjects." (p. 49)

  2. "Finally, the children want to find out more about these topics and begin to read." (p. 49)

  3. "He learns the word by looking at it, saying it, and writing it. He is now ready for Stage 3." (p. 50)

DISCUSSION. Once again Fernald stresses the fact that children write "freely" and that writing becomes so "easy" that their stories are longer and more complicated. Once again, this has not been our experience, even though great effort was made to follow her precepts to the letter. Children do learn to write words correctly with very few tracings or no tracings. They do learn to write words by studying the writing of a word that a teacher has done in ordinary script on a 3″ × 5″ card.

The procedure now being used is quite similar to the practice endorsed when learning to spell a word. On pages 199–201 Fernald details eight steps. Her steps are similar to those widely endorsed and practiced for decades. In brief, they are to look at the word, to speak it distinctly without distortion, to study the configuration and letter order of the word in order to develop a memory image, and to write the word twice correctly.

It is our experience that, while this method of learning to spell a word is useful for the great majority of children who experience little if any difficulty in reading, this is not necessarily true for those children who experience extreme disability. A difficulty encountered is the natural vocalization of the word and at the same time establishing the connection between the articulation of a word by syllables and the hand movements involved in writing it. As a result children have a marked tendency to use the learning-to-spell technique and do not write a word saying it by syllables as they write. Consequently word learning for these children is neither easy, nor rapid.

The use of a small file box and the filing of words the teacher has written in ordinary script on a 3″ × 5″ card has not proved to be the boon Fernald attributes to it. Seldom do the children turn to the box to relearn a word or to reexamine it. The word cards are not used in any other way, as for instance for construction of ideas or for phonic activities.

Not placing any restrictions on vocabulary does prove to be heartening. Children are encouraged to use more fully the range of their vocabulary, to acquire the nomenclature of the different content areas, and to single out unusual words. As she points out, the longer, more difficult words are the more readily recognized at later presentations than are the so-called easier, shorter ones.

Her records show too that she is attentive to the need for recontact with words learned. She describes how words are recontacted 24 hours after learning, three days later, one month later, and again three months later. Not only does she reexpose the children at intervals to words learned, but also she says, "they were given out of context." This increases the demands on the readers because they are denied the recall cues, the use of the semantics, or meaning provided by the context.

Stage 3: "Same as Stage 2 Except That the Child Is Able to Learn from the Printed Word, by Merely Looking at It and Saying It to Himself Before He Writes It."

A. Procedure
1. "The child learns directly from the printed word without having it written for him." (p. 50)
2. "The child, who had to trace each word many times at first, eventually developed the ability to glance over words of four or five syllables, say them once or twice as he looked at them, and then write them without the copy." (p. 50)
3. "This occurs at a stage when the child still reads very poorly and fails to recognize even easy words after he has been told repeat-

edly what they are. He, however, recognizes even quite difficult words almost without exception, after once writing them." (p. 51)

4. "At this stage the child begins to want to read from books." (p. 51) "He is allowed to read as much as and whatever he wishes. He is told words he does not know. When the reading of any particular thing is finished the new words are gone over and written by the child as described above. These words are later checked to make sure they have been retained." (p. 51)

B. Transitional Steps

1. "Soon after the child is able to learn from the printed words, he begins to generalize and to make out new words from their resemblance to words he already knows." (p. 51)

DISCUSSION. Careful examination of what is done shows that the principal difference between Stage 2 and Stage 3 is the fact that in Stage 2 the teacher writes the word on a 3″ × 5″ card, whereas in Stage 3 the child writes the word. At this point in progress pupils are reading from books and encouraged to read whatever they wish. As a result they tend to encounter a sizeable number of words they do not know. These words are told to the reader and studied after the reading is done. Unfortunately the list of unknown words can become quite burdensome if the "read ability" or "reading ability" of the pupil is too far below the readability or the complexity of the material.

Again our experience has shown that extreme disability children do not reach this stage readily and when they do they experience difficulty if the vocabulary load of material selected is burdensome and every unknown word is "gone over and written by the child as described above." Much caution must be exercised in that movement from stage to stage, which must reflect pupils' attained progress and must not tarnish their self-confidence and ambition.

This, we discovered, is extremely important, because a shift in ability is occurring. Gradually attention is shifted from focusing on words and the learning of words to focusing on content. At this stage children want to read from books and by so doing avoid the writing process. No longer are the pupils subauthors writing what they read. Now they are supposed to be able enough and secure enough to read what others have written.

Stage 4: "Ability to Recognize New Words From Their Similarity to Words or Parts of Words He Has Already Learned." (p. 51)

We now turn to Stage 4. This is the ultimate goal, the V-A stage, and it reflects the fact that pupils can generalize their word knowledge and make out new words readily. Because this is so, readers are urged once more to read the original (pp. 51–55) and compare it with the outline that follows. If this is done, the reader will sense more clearly the cautions voiced by Fernald. For instance, children are never made to sound a word not recognized instantly, nor is it sounded out for them. They may, though, write the word. In addition, she cautions that Stage 4 level achievement may be attained if pupils are "handled skillfully."

A. Motivation
    1. "At this stage the child delights in the learning of new and difficult words. He recognizes many new words without being told what they are." (p. 52) "This recognition is immediate and not a slow sounding of the word." (p. 52)
    2. "The child is now eager to read. He is allowed to read as much as he wants to and about anything that is of interest to him." (p. 51)
    3. "It is essential that the content of the reading material be such that the child will continue to read what he starts in order to find out what he wants to know." (p. 51)

B. Procedure
    1. "Soon after the child is able to learn from the printed word, he begins to generalize and to make out new words from their resemblance to words he already knows." (p. 51)
    2. "He is told words he does not know." (p. 51)
    3. "When the reading of any particular thing is finished, the new words are gone over and written by the child as described. These words are later checked to make sure they have been retained." (p. 51)
    4. "The child is never made to sound the word when he is reading nor is it sounded out for him by his teacher." (p. 53)
       a. "He points to the word and is told what it is." (p. 53)
       b. "Any detail that he needs is given him by letting him write the word by the method already described. This writing of the word is merely for the sake of developing word recognition and is done only as often as is necessary to accomplish this end. If the child recognizes the word in print, the writing has served its function, insofar as reading is concerned, and is not repeated." (p. 53)
    5. "When the child reads stories, we let him read along as he wishes, asking any words he needs to know to get the meaning of what he is reading. He is told what the word is, and it is recorded for later reference if it is common enough to be important." (p. 52)
    6. "The meanings of words he cannot get for himself are told to

him by someone who is on hand to help him. At this stage it is particularly important that the child be given sufficient help to make reading fast enough and easy enough so that the mechanics involved in the process of word comprehension shall not distract his attention from the content of what he is reading." (p. 52)

7. "Eventually the child is able to retain the meaning of the word if he is simply told what it is." (p. 52)

8. "In reading scientific or other difficult material, it is often desirable to let the child glance over a paragraph and make a light mark under any word he does not know." (p. 53) "These words are pronounced for him." (p. 73)

9. "If he can look over a paragraph before he starts to read and clear up the meaning of the few new words, he then reads easily and with the word group as his unit." (p. 52)

10. "The only exception to the foregoing occurs in certain cases in which a child wants to sound the word out. He may be allowed to do this provided he points out the word before he starts to read the paragraph and not in the course of reading it." (p. 53)

11. "The amount of reading the individual must do before he is considered a completed case will depend upon the educational age he must reach. The younger child who will continue his reading in connection with regular school and home activities needs only to reach the reading achievement level of the class in which he will be placed at the end of his remedial work. The older subject must give much more time to this last stage if he is to go back into his normal group." (p. 53)

C. Transitional Steps

1. "If the child is sent back into a regular room before this remedial work has been completed and is forced to use methods that block learning, the old negative emotional reaction will be reestablished." (p. 17)

2. "It is essential that he should acquire sufficient skill to keep up with children of his age and intelligence before he is sent back into a regular schoolroom." (p. 18)

3. "In any case in which the subject is to be returned to any upper reading group, the following things must be accomplished:" (p. 53)

   a. "Sufficient reading to develop concepts that will make it possible to recognize new words from their similarity to ones that have been experienced in many different combinations." (p. 53)

   b. "A reading vocabulary adequate for the comprehension of

such materials as the individual will be expected to read."
(p. 53)

c. "The complex concept development, which makes it possible for a person to apperceive the meaning of word groups
in any new content." (p. 53)

DISCUSSION. It can be said with considerable confidence that when
children reach the level of capability as defined in Stage 4, and do so
after having been zero readers, they are eager to read. When this occurs,
the students should be allowed to read as much as they want about
anything that interests them. New words become an intellectual challenge and no longer are the block to understanding that they were at
an earlier time. Again, however, it has been our experience that few
if any zero readers ever reach what appears to be this idyllic level. Word
recognition does not become as immediate as is implied and neither do
the far more demanding cognitive actions of concept development.

It is a truism of almost all instruction that reading content be such
that students will continue to read what they start. This is more likely to
be the case, and a sustained effort is more likely to be maintained, if the
reader is finding "what he wants to know." The sustaining power that
springs from the seeking of answers a student wants to know is almost
inestimable. The secret, of course, is to use the pupils strongest interests
as the well-spring of motivation. This does require skillful handling.

The writing of many words does promote a certain degree of skill in
seeing how words or parts of words resemble words already known and
facilitates thereby some generalization. This generalization does prove
useful in making out new words. No systematic instructional effort is
made, though, to assure that such generalizations are made and acquired.

Far more questionable is the advice that a child is "never made to
sound the word when he is reading nor is it sounded out for him by his
teacher." The only exception to the foregoing, she says, occurs in certain cases in which a child wants to sound a word, but this he may do
only if he points out the word before he starts to read and not "in the
course of reading it." In brief, the only phonic word attack generalization that children may make must result from their simultaneous saying
of a syllable as they are tracing it or as they are writing it. The writing
of a word "is merely for the sake of developing word recognition and
is done only as often as is necessary to accomplish this end." Again, it
has been our experience that this method of teaching configuration or
form clues as visual discrimination generalizations and this method
of teaching phoneme-grapheme or phonic clues or sound clue discrimination generalization is just not enough.

Once again there is much to be said for Fernald's desire that the learners make a relentless pursuit of meaning; those helping the learners should assure them that this is the goal. Fernald seems to have grasped very well the fact that to say "reading comprehension" is to be redundant, because "to read" means "to comprehend." It is the aid that she provides the learner, particularly at the Stage 4 level, that comes into question. The reader is told the word and its meaning by "someone who is at hand to help him." This is done to "make the reading fast enough so that the mechanics involved in the process of word comprehension" do not detract from his comprehending the content.

Stage 4 achievers are not taught to use a glossary of terms, a dictionary, or even the semantics of a context by means of interpolation or closure. At all times words are pronounced for them and meaning help is provided. The only departure she allows she attaches to the reading of scientific or other difficult material. She says that often it is desirable to let children glance over a paragraph and mark words they do not know. These words are then pronounced for them and the meanings are cleared up so that they can then read the paragraph easily.

Words that are told a reader are recorded for later reference if the words are common enough to be important. This emphasis on concept development is praiseworthy. Once again, though, the burden of responsibility is largely the instructors, and no effort is made at controlling the number of words to be assimilated other than to say if they are "common enough to be important."

What are the instructional limits to be attained by each student? This Fernald answers in two ways, by dividing pupils into the younger and the older subjects. The former she says, "needs only to reach the reading achievement level of the class in which he will be placed at the end of his remedial work." The latter subject, she says, must be given much more time "if he is to go back into his normal group." As stated earlier, most of the children she wrote about were nine years of age or older before they were referred to her clinic. Apparently, then, the nine-year olds represent the younger population. If most of these children managed to make the needed progress after only two years of instruction, it is a matter of simple arithmetic to conclude that these zero readers would need to make six years growth in two years. Again, experience has taught us that this kind of growth is much more the exception than the rule. Even so, it seems puzzling that Fernald would now measure achievement by a class or age-grade norm rather than by an individual's expectancy as suggested by capacity. This is questionable because, as she says, she worked largely with children whose intelligence quotients were in the normal range and above.

It is true, of course, that if children were to be returning to a regular room before their remedial work were completed and then forced to use methods that might block learning, most likely the old negative emotional reactions would be reestablished. To avoid this she spells out three conditions, each focused on pupils' acquiring competency in "complex concept development." Again this is a most praiseworthy competency to focus on, but again she does not spell out how this is to be done or how such competency is to be determined. This is understandable, though, because to acquire an adequate reading vocabulary and complex concept attainment, competency is the goal of all instruction and this in large part is a lifetime goal.

Summary Discussion

At this point the reader may be curious about the fact that so much space and thought has been devoted to Fernald's accounting of her four stages for coping with extreme disability cases. An examination of the voluminous writings concerned with extreme reading disability reveals readily that the majority of it is devoted to testing or to telling what is wrong, with a disproportionately small amount of writing done to tell one what to do about correcting the disability. Yet, as any remedial reading teacher can vouch and as any child with extreme disability will support, it is the latter that is paramount.

Not only does Fernald outline stages and provide instructional specifics, but also she tells how what she advocates is reflected across the curriculum. As was said earlier, there is no such subject as reading. Reading is a process (10, 11), a dynamic way of dealing with ideas that are transmitted by writing. The reader must determine the value of the facts and ideas recorded and their likely consequences. In brief, reading is a process that is used in coping with all areas of knowledge.

The stages as defined reflect first-hand experience. After years of devotion to instructing children with extreme disability in reading, she observed degrees of progress that seemed step by step in nature. To provide an order in a quantified manner required close study over a period of time. It seems hardly necessary to belabor the difference between examined first-hand experience marked by objectivity and armchair speculation.

The widespread use of the tracing idea, or the Fernald technique as it is commonly referred to, suggests at least that many people have searched for workable instructional techniques and have turned to her for help. The degree to which the use of her recommendations has been successful depends largely upon how her ideas were interpreted and applied. On occasion children referred to us for help show that they have been exposed to some type of tracing instruction. In these instances we have found that failure to achieve could be attributed primarily to rather gross misinterpretation of Fernald's recommendation or inability on the part of teachers to give students the close skillfully managed attention required.

Fernald's sensitivity to the affective aspects characteristic of children burdened by extreme disability in reading earns for her high regard by anyone who has tried to teach such victims. Her recommendations have merit in a number of ways. Invariably children who are failures respond to the fact that the techniques as used in each of the four stages represent a clear-cut, discernible way of acting. The instructions are definitive and concise. To know exactly what to do promotes confidence. To follow the instruction to the letter yields results. To promote self-assurance and the calmness resulting from presence of mind, nothing succeeds better than success.

In addition, she repeatedly emphasizes the fact that her measures are adaptable to individual rates of learning and capacity and maturity. Instruction can be paced as is reflected in each of the transitional phases described. But as pointed out (p. 261) the adaptations are within the technique rather than in the use of different procedures for different children. In brief, it is the pace of learning that is varied and not the procedure. Each child must cope with the same tasks.

This close study of her recommendations should help the reader compare and contrast the recommendations that follow in Chapter 12. The reader can better understand the modifications experience and knowledge has taught me to make over a 30-year period. The perspective provided should permit the reader to apprehend more fully why, how, and to what degree modifications have been found necessary and useful.

STAGES OF PROGRESS: PARTIAL DISABILITY

Fernald's account of so-called partial disability children stresses two possibilities: obvious causes and faulty conditions. The former tend to refer to physiological and psychological conditions that are inherent in an individual and derive from the mind or the constitution. The latter, faulty conditions, derive from faulty experience, either in the home or the school.

When obvious causes have been dealt with and eliminated, she says there remains an appalling number who fail because of faulty school conditions. She singles out for special comment the school practice still common today of passing students on through the grades and graduating them from high school with some sort of certificate.

In either instance she applied much the same method as described for total disability cases to the partial disability children. This she did by "determining the point to which they had developed reading skill and then treating them like cases of original total disability that had developed to that point."

She classified cases of partial disability into three main types. One type was poor reading due to inability to recognize certain words. Another type was slow reading and poor comprehension due to the fact that the individual reads word by word. The third type was poor reading due to failure to comprehend content read.

The first type she dealt with much as she described procedures in Stages 3 and 4 of her outline for total disability. She attributes the failure to an escalation of negative emotional conditioning intensifying over a period of years until the pupils literally panic when they encounter an unknown word. The treatment she recommends is to provide the "uptight" student with "reasonably difficult material" selected for reading. The subject matter reflects either a pupil interest or "something connected with his schoolwork."

Students look over the selection and make a light line under any word not recognized. This is done without any effort at reading the content. These words are then pronounced for them. As with total disability children, they may need to have the word written for them so that they can look at the written copy, pronounce the word, and if necessary trace the word. Eventually they will be able to write the word after just a brief glance at it, provided they pronounce it as they look at it. At this stage it is no longer necessary that the word be written for them. At last it is necessary to only pronounce the few words asked for. To determine at which level individuals are subjects need only to be "taught diagnostically" for a short time with careful records maintained.

At this point readers might refer to the comments made regarding the recommendations for Stages 3 and 4. In brief, Fernald continues emphasis on the writing of a word and asks only for a somewhat loose control over the association of the pronunciation of a part of a word as the part is written. The pronunciation is to be done without distortion. Even so this is the only attempt at teaching phoneme-grapheme relationships and generalizing thereby to new word situations. In short, there is very little phonic training provided. It is readly evident, too, that teachers must be constantly at hand to pronounce the underlined words, to supervise the writing-learning act, and to select material of "reasonable difficulty." Ths means material in which the number of unknown words will not be overwhelming.

For the second type, in which individuals read slowly, she rules out word recognition difficulty. These are the people who can read but proceed word by word and usually have to "go over the content several times to get the meaning of the thing as a whole." One of her students referred to this disability as a translation liability whereby the child would in a sense translate each word and then sum the translations.

The instruction she prescribes to break the word-by-word habit largely utilizes what she calls informal methods. The formal methods she labels as the various forms of mechanical pacers designed to increase speed and comprehension, such as the tachistoscope, the metronoscope, and moving picture devices. A *tachistoscope* is a flashmeter-type device whereby words or numbers can be flashed upon a screen for timed intervals ranging from a fraction of a second to a second or longer. The intent of the timed exposure is to develop rapid perception and to increase span of recognition from a word at a time to a phrase or more at each exposure. The *metronoscope* is a triple-shutter device for exposing in succession from left to right three segments of a line of print. The lines are printed on something resembling a player piano roll and appear line by line at the triple shutter apertures. The readability of the material can be controlled from simple to complex, the nature of the content can be controlled as can the rate at which the three shutters move. Not only does the machine control the rate of exposure and the phrasing of each line, but it also prevents readers from making regressive eye movements: from rereading. It also prevents them from reading ahead. *Moving pictures* are designed to achieve similar ends. By means of a motion picture technique, lines grouped in phrases appear on the screen in successive presentations, thereby showing as much as a page at a time.

By contrast to the above, the informal methods she advocates depend "on the initiation of the natural learning process." Her techniques focus on the subjects' interests and their conscious efforts. In addition she recommends a *pacing device,* using a plain card to control exposure of groups of words. When reading material they are keenly interested in, either for information or entertainment, students are likely to proceed as rapidly as possible, in order to get to the outcome. By so doing they develop "the necessary apperceptive and physiological adjustment" to overcome the word-by-word habit. Final success, though, is attainable only if it includes "much reading in which interest in content is the pacer." The interest factor capitalized upon is supposed to reflect pupils' intense desires to learn the outcome.

To obtain a "conscious effort" on the part of students, they are told why people read slowly, shown how the eyes move in slow and rapid reading, and alerted to the differences between phrase reading and word-by-word reading. This done, they are taught by controlling two factors; readability level of materials and time. At first they are given material of low readability and then asked to read against time. Questions are asked to check comprehension. The number of words read are counted and used as the "measure of improvement." This can also be done by timing students while they read a fixed number of pages. The latter tests are made only periodically, because the focus must always be on speed with comprehension.

Fernald's pacing method consists of "giving a brief exposure of words in meaningful groups by using a plain card to control exposure." The card is readily manipulated, and its manipulation requires the eye to follow in the same direction.

> The card is held under the line with the left corner indicating the beginning of a group of words. . . . [A]fter an exposure of not more than 0.5 of a second the card is slipped over these words. . . . The process is repeated until an entire paragraph has been read. The subject is then allowed to read the paragraph silently and tell what he read.

A training period is no longer than 15–30 minutes. Again, the material selected is something of keen interest to the pupil. It is essential, she says, that the subject read extensively. Boys read books of adventure, aviation, animal stories, and so on, while adults read detective stories, autobiographies, novels, and the like.

The word-by-word habit is probably the most difficult habit to overcome. This is so largely because it requires a determined effort over a long period of time. The newly acquired habits must be firmly established so as to permanently replace the old habits. Fernald's "informal" methods merit a certain amount of commendation. Unquestionably, it is wise to capitalize on students' interests. They provide an immediate and sustaining motivation. Undoubtedly, too, it is wise to consciously involve the students by helping them understand the word-by-word circumstances as clearly as possible.

Varying the readability of material from simple to complex is a good practice. Any horserider knows the best time is run on a dry track. Utilizing material that ranges across the curriculum is a good idea, because by so doing the status of knowledge is capitalized upon, as well as the students' interest.

To time students is commendable. The procedure does spur pupils on to greater effort. Using time and material as measures, as well as conscious effort, should result in the acquisition of new habits.

Fernald's use of the labels formal and informal is much to be questioned. Why she should name proven classroom practices as informal is a perplexing curiosity. Formal habits or practices may be characterized as old fashioned or traditional, even ceremonial. In a sense formal is also synonymous with conventional, in the sense of "governed by established conventional meaning or governed by established conventions. Classroom practices which time and experience have shown to be functional merit the attributes declared for formal and should, therefore, be labeled as such.

On the other hand, labeling machinery such as tachistoscopes, metronoscopes, moving picture projectors, reading rate accelerators, reading rate controllers, rate readers, and reading boards as informal does seem fitting. To be informal means to be new-fangled, unorthodox, unnatural, strange, and unceremonious. It is probably because of the latter term that Fernald wrote as she did. To use the gadgetry requires a ritual. Her labeling would not merit these two paragraphs if others had not used them also and by so doing given them unmerited credence.

On the other hand the method of pacing she devised has highly questionable features. To move a card as she recommends is difficult indeed. The content must be selected very carefully. There must be a series of acceptable phrases so that the card can be moved fittingly from left to right, revealing in appropriate succession acceptable, unwarped phraseology. In addition, to time the holding of a card close to the precision of 0.5 of a second and to do so repeatedly is almost an impossibility. Then, too, her recommendation that the phrases be seen repeatedly if necessary, and not really read, is questionable. She wanted this phrase recognition to be largely mechanistic in nature rather than cognitive, because, as she says, when the pacing has been done "the subject is then allowed to read the paragraph silently."

Fernald gives only a brief treatment of the third type of partial disability, in which the individual fails to comprehend the content read. She intends that this rather universal dilemma be resolved in two ways. First, she recommends that material such as projects be used whereby subjects cannot finish the project unless they properly use knowledge gained by reading preceding passages. Second, subjects can be required to answer questions requiring data from what they read.

Both recommendations are good and can be productive. However, there is a great likelihood that both have been used repeatedly by teachers and parents and that the subjects have acquired strong dislikes for the techniques. Fernald makes no recommendations about how to deal with this perplexity. Undoubtedly though, if she had been asked she would have suggested once again to capitalize to the utmost on the pupils' keen interests.

Fernald deals with the partial disabilities due to obvious causes by a discussion on eye conditions and eye movements. In essence what Fernald says about physiological disability is to urge eye examination and correction. She does point out, however, that "we find individuals with monocular vision, nystagmus, spastic imbalance, and so forth who read with a high degree of speed and comprehension provided the mechanism of the eye is such as to give a clear retinal image." In short, vision problems can result in faulty seeing which in turn hinders learning to read. On the other hand subjects with varied vision problems learn to read even without correction. As she says, "There is no mystery about the matter." Expert and reputable help should be obtained to correct the vision needs but skillful teaching is still required.

She also advances the point and wisely so, that reading clinics and reading diagnosticians need not purchase expensive apparatus. Screening tests that any trained clinician can learn to administer will be sufficient. Needed is referral to an expert.

Her examination of the eye movement effort and its likely consequence is timely and most insightful. She points out that, "except for its significance for research the main point of such a study is not to determine how well a person reads but rather to give the teacher and pupil an idea of the type of adjustment that accompanies proper reading in the case of the average individual." Eye movements are but a symptom, an observable manifestation of what is most likely occurring in the central nervous system. In other words, eye movements are dictated by the brain and reflect adequate or inadequate use of the brain. Eye movements do not dictate the mind. Eye movements are symptoms of cognitive efficiency and are not determiners of it. This is what led Miles Tinker to discover that eye movements take only about 6 percent of the entire reading time, whereas fixation pauses (the period of clear vision) average about 94 percent of the time (12).

A superficial observation of slow readers shows their eyes stopping many times, regressing and the like. On the other hand the superior and efficient readers eyes make only a few fixations. The work of Javal at the University of Paris in 1879 concerned with eye movements of readers revealed this. Even though early means of measuring eye movements were crude, (a cup attached to the cornea of one eye recorded by means of a bristle pointer writing on a smoked surface) they revealed that good readers made three to five pauses per line of standard book size. Subsequent refined eye-movement cameras merely confirmed these findings.

Fernald, as do others, points out that training in eye movements is training concerned with symptoms. As a result it is unproductive mechanistic training. Needed is a treatment—by sound pedagogical procedures—of the underlying causes of reading inefficiency. As she indicates, people who know about eye movements are more likely to be cooperative, understanding subjects, who will work diligently to overcome the fundamental causes and by so doing improve their efficiency.

It seems timely to add that Fernald provides a chapter devoted to group work. She says that most satisfactory results have been obtained working with groups of 12 to 20 children per teacher. Tests are used to determine "the proper starting point" and "learning technique." Group work is done by means of the project method, with subjects learning words according to the stage they happen to be in—Stage 1, 2, 3, or 4. Children work alone and prepare material to be shared by presenting it to the group. "The teacher gave the child any help for which he asked, including the proper form of words." She supports her recommendation with illustrations. For instance, as she says, a child of 12 who is totally unable to read can make maps by tracing and can then label parts, and in this way acquire a reading vocabulary. She stresses the project idea constantly, because of the likely intrinsic motivation which results.

In summary, Fernald's cases of partial disability are handled in much the same way as those of total disability. The difference seems to reside in the degrees of achievement already acquired and manifested by a subject. This means testing to determine the stage in which subjects are and the nature of their needs at that stage. Throughout she gives repeated emphasis to the project method, the sharing of ideas, individual pacing, and intrinsic motivation.

CONCLUSIONS

It is good to keep things, beliefs, and ideas in perspective, because doing so increases one's insight and understanding. Fernald did just this when she gave credit to and in turn credence to the tactile-kinesthetic-sensory method. She gave credit to thinkers from Plato and St. Jerome to Montessori. This should instill confidence.

Grace Fernald wrote about practices and procedures she had personally examined carefully and used many times. Her declaration of four stages reflects her use of a technique. Even though her stages are determined largely by the use or disuse of sensory gateways rather than cognitive development, they are useful. Stage 1 is the tracing or tactile-kinesthetic stage; Stage 2 is the kinesthetic-sensory stage; Stage 3 is a form of Stage 2, and Stage 4 is largely the visual-auditory stage. Each of these stages have also been classified by letters: Stage 1 (V-A-K-T), or visual-auditory-kinesthetic-tactile; Stage 2 (V-A-K^1), or visual-auditory-kinesthetic; Stage 3 (V-A-K^2), or visual-auditory-kinesthetic; Stage 4 (V-A), or visual-auditory.

Fernald provides detailed explanations and useful specifics. Even though they are scattered about in her text, they have been grouped and arranged in this text. This should prove helpful to a qualified teacher trying to understand the technique. In addition, she shows great sensitivity to the stresses and strains endured by people who fail. Her humaneness is strikingly apparent and serves as a beacon.

Some of her instructions are indeed questionable. One such instruction is the writing of so many words. Another is the advice that children are never made to sound words, nor are words sounded for them by their teachers. This seems almost incredible. It could very well be that this reflects her reaction to the tyranny that so-called kinesthetic or blending or sounding out methods have held for so long. Regardless, she has overlooked what appears to be a more or less natural approach to speech and writing and communication. It develops from the oral level to the print level.

Most people who write about the so-called Fernald technique do not write about her work with partial disability children. Again Fernald's insights are keen and forthrightly stated. She refers to those disabilities resulting from obvious causes and those resulting from faulty conditions. The former refers to physiological and psychological conditions inherent in an individual. The latter derives from faulty home or school experience. The former is concerned with dyslexia, or related brain damage, with visual and auditory disability. The latter are those who are failing because of faulty experiences, whether in the school or in the home.

Fernald classifies the partially disabled into three types: the poor reader whose problem is lack of word attack skills; the slow word-by-word reader; and the reader who does not comprehend. For the first type she prescribes practices declared under Stages 3 and 4. For the second type she recommends focusing on interests and conscious effort. For the third type she recommends use of projects and questions.

In brief, Fernald's cases of partial disability are handled in much the same manner as those of total disability.

BIBLIOGRAPHY

1. Bettelheim, Bruno. *Love Is Not Enough*. New York: Free Press, 1950.

2. Betts, Emmett A. *Foundations of Reading Instruction*. New York: American Book, 1946.

3. Betts, Emmett A. *The Prevention and Correction of Reading Difficulties*. New York: Harper & Row, 1936.

4. Fernald, Grace M. *Remedial Techniques in Basic School Subjects*. New York: McGraw-Hill, 1943.

5. Keller, Helen. *The Story of My Life*. New York: Doubleday, 1954.

6. Keller, Helen. *Teacher: Anne Sullivan Macy*. New York: Doubleday, 1946.

7. Lavatelli, Celia Stendler. *Piaget's Theory Applied to an Early Childhood Curriculum*. Cambridge, Mass.: American Science and Engineering, 1970.

8. Montessori, Maria. *Dr. Montessori's Own Handbook*. New York: Schocken Books, 1965.

9. Montessori, Maria. *The Montessori Method*. New York: Schocken Books, 1964.

10. Stauffer, Russell G. *Directing Reading Maturity as a Cognitive Process*. New York: Harper & Row, 1969.

11. Stauffer, Russell G. *Directing the Reading-Thinking Process*. New York: Harper & Row, 1975.

12. Tinker, Miles, and Constance McCullough. *Teaching Elementary Reading*. Englewood Cliffs, N.J.: Prentice-Hall, 1962.

CHAPTER **12**

Remedial
Instruction [II]

One cannot help but sense the spirit of faith and devotion, the sensitivity and thought, and the value and significance of Grace Fernald's inspiring attempt to overcome the total and partial disabilities of children who failed to learn to read as and when society expected. Regardless of the labels applied to her approach, some of them ignominious, she sought for a means that would utilize assets the children brought with them; perceptually, intellectually, linguistically, and culturally. She searched the annals of pedagogy to determine what the historical sages might teach. Then she devoted years of tireless effort to reclamation and restitution of the unfortunate. It is on this zealous vitality that we built and shaped the limits and confines of our practices and procedures.

Beyond question the vast majority of the children and young people who come to us for help do so with the dulling tread of captive beings reflecting the ugliness of their numerous undistinguished days. The acuteness of their problems, their struggles, anxieties, and defeats, has left them blighted and depressed. School learning-reading was not an inspiring panorama but an overpowering and often treacherous immensity. No thinking, sensitive person can escape these sour realities. Yet, one senses among the afflicted a vitality, a desire to achieve, an almost indescribable independence of spirit that can be harnessed. It is this consciousness, this determination, this will that takes on an influential reality and can give substance to motives and ends posited by pedagogical norms.

How to build a viable psychology and pedagogy upon such contingencies is the imperative. The undeniable rule of cause and effect must be recognized, and we must concede the shaping influences of heredity, environment, indoctrination, and circumstance. All partial or totally disabled readers can think and this is what gives them identity with their peers and with mankind in general. Their world is just as much a medley of sights, sounds, pressures, temperatures, tastes, smells, and feelings as that of the more successful achievers. They all can and do think of themselves and mold a "for-itself" image. Doubtlessly, it is their past, their environment, and their circumstances that enter into determining their actions. Behind and beneath their actions is a feeling of shame, a sense of guilt, however silent the accusations of others; but also there persists a will to achieve, to dignify their lives, to have noble and redeeming goals.

It behooves us, therefore, to use to the fullest those powers and acquisitions that the "disabled" bring with them. It has been said that by the time children are six-years old they are graduate students in the world of experience. It is experiences that provide the most immediate of all instructional realities, obscure at times, but undeniable and real. People are the sum of their past, and this can give instruction-learner boundaries and character. It is these bountiful "sums" that, when utilized, can yield curriculum potentials for instruction and learner catharsis.

These needy people are not a mess, a nuisance, a mutiny, or a blighted hope. They are a delight. Invariably they bear their semipoverty with a sense of humor. They are young, strong, and they still feel that the world is theirs to study, to enjoy, to overcome. A program of instruction that builds upon these assets can be absorbing and gratifyingly successful.

The pedagogy and therapy used largely in the Reading Study Center at the University of Delaware and developed over the past 25 years reflects in good part practices and convictions garnered from Fernald and modified by years of devotion to the more typically progressing developmental child and to differentiating instruction (not a single method) individually. The former provided a base for remedial actions and clarity as defined in the previous chapter. The latter supplied a foundation for understanding instruction geared to a learner's rate, capacity, and maturity, and for making viable adjustments in those individuals who had been violated by inappropriate instruction. Whether the causes can be traced to rate of learning, or capacity, or maturity, whether the causes are neurological or pedagogical in nature, whether there are a constellation of causes, early diagnosis can be made, and then instruction and expectancies can be adjusted. The progress of the many developmental children for whom instruction represents at least a fair degree of adjustment testifies to this. Above all, though, our clinical instructional program reflects not only the need for intensified individualized instruction, but also the need for warm, sympathetic understanding of emotional needs and instruction that is firm but fair and sober, and yet humorous.

OUR CLINICAL CIRCUMSTANCES

In many respects our clinical program is unique. Its primary justification is as an adjunct to the teacher education program, in general, and to the master's and doctoral program, in particular. Members of our staff who teach the undergraduate reading courses participate in the clinical program by supervisory effort, research, and attendance at the twice weekly staff sessions. Undergraduates observe in the clinic, and on occasion teach. Graduate students, particularly the full-time students, test, teach, counsel, and do research. All our faculty, even those primarily engaged in the clinical program, also teach developmental reading courses, consult in public, independent, and parochial schools, and do research. Thus the children who attend the clinic benefit by the broad spectrum of professionalism made available through this arrangement.

Children are not admitted to the Laboratory School Division of the Center unless they have been tested as described in Chapters 2–7. The testing is done to determine likely causes and teaching adjustments, in addition to the children's levels of expectancy and indices of their current achievement. It is the ratio of achievement to expectancy that provides some measure of degree of retardation expressed in years. For instance a child's reading age could be 6–0 and expectancy age 9–6, suggesting a three-and-a-half year retardation. The testing also provides clues to likely neurological, psychological, or emotional impairments and the need for referral to neurologists, ophthalmologists, optometrists, general and specialized medical and surgical doctors, psychiatrists, psychologists, counselors, and the like.

Both parents are required to attend three interview sessions, unless of course death or separation precludes. Parent accounts of the prenatal, birth, infancy, family, preschool, and school history of the child usually contribute vital information helping us understand the child's heredity and environment. Interviews with the child, as well as reports from the various examiners, provide insight into the child's successes, failures, interests, ambitions, fears, anxieties, and conduct in general.

The findings are shared with the parents, the school, and to a considerable degree the child. Children do not leave the clinic after the approximately three days of required testing without learning something about how they fared and what their prospects are for achievement. This is a crucial aspect of our testing program and reflects our concern for individuals' pressing anxieties about their prospects.

Children are admitted to the Laboratory School only after approval and understanding has been obtained from parents and schools. If neurological or psychiatric referral is required, approval must be obtained from these sources.

Two probationary periods must be completed before full acceptance. At the end of two weeks of instruction a child's achievement and general performance are evaluated in a staff meeting. If, in the judgment of all those assembled, it is thought that the teaching program is being helpful, then the child is continued for another four weeks. Both parents are called in after the two week staffing and are informed of our findings and prognosis. At the end of the sixth week of instruction the child's case is discussed again, and another prognosis is ventured. Even though a prognosis of likely achievement rate and level is offered at the end of the three-day testing period it is most guarded. By the end of six weeks of instructional diagnosis and two staffings, our prognosis usually can be more substantial. Always, though, in cases of extreme disability our prognosis is quite guarded. We do not want to mislead parents about the likely rate of progress and the level of achievement. If, at the end of six weeks, it is felt that we can provide the kind of psychopedagogical help that seems warranted, we do two things. First, we accept the child into the program on a long-term basis. Second, we meet with the child's teacher, principal, and counselor and give an account of the circumstances and solicit their cooperation in making the child's program a three dimensional thrust involving the home, the school, and the University Clinic.

Each child's progress is reviewed at a staff meeting approximately once every eight weeks. The parents, as well as the child's teacher, are seen once every six weeks. On occasion, as circumstances may suggest, more frequent parent interviews are scheduled. On occasion, too, the clinic instructors and the director meet with the parents, the school people, and the child in an effort to plan and attain the most effective program possible.

The clinic schedule during the academic year (September to May) provides for an hour a day contact, four days a week, Monday through Thursday between 8:00 and 10:00 A.M. This schedule was arranged for three principal reasons. First, the children should come to the clinic when they are likely to be rested and agreeable. At the end of a school day, when they have paid their penalty to a society that has failed them, they are likely to be irritable and anxious. They are much more likely to respond to motivation in the morning. In addition, by seeing them on four successive days we can better offset forgetting and influence retention and recall. At no time has the clinic operated evenings or Saturdays. The former arrangement involves too great a fatigue factor, and the latter too great a forgetting period (168 hours). On occasion some children attend both morning sessions (two hours) depending on their age and extent of disability.

Second, children should not become school isolates. A school curriculum is designed to provide learning and growth opportunities in each of the knowledge areas: literature, humanities, mathematics, and science. In addition, the school day provides many other opportunities on the playground, in organized group activities, in the cafeteria's food-for-the-body program, and the library multimedia centers' food-for-the-mind opportunities.

Furthermore, being an isolate promotes labeling and name calling, usually of a negative kind. Accordingly we want to do all we can to offset such practices. The prestige factor of coming to the university helps greatly to avert name calling. Invariably the children consider it a privilege to come to the campus and this helps thwart feelings of discomfort and embarrassment.

Third, because all the students commute, schedules are arranged according to the distance and time required to travel from the child's school. In almost every instance schools have been most cooperative and have arranged a child's schedule in such a way that the only classes missed were reading or language arts or both.

The open Friday serves a dual purpose. The children can spend an entire day in school and the graduate students have consecutive time for library work, research, or study. The former can participate in group reading instruction or in inquiry-style individualized instruction (3) sometimes as a guest member of a group and on other occasions as a full member.

The pupil-teacher ratio is seldom higher than two to one, although on rare occasions it is three to one. More often the ratio is one to one, especially for the first-year graduate students. Graduate students do not teach until they have completed the two basic courses: foundations of reading instruction and diagnosis of reading retardation. In addition, they serve a two month preparation period while taking a course in clinical procedures. During this time they meet with the clinic director to learn about instructional techniques, pedagogical and therapeutical, that are used in the clinic. By the time they are assigned a pupil, they have had a minimum of 48 hours of intense lecture-demonstration sessions, have observed the clinic in action, and attended staff meetings. We want to be quite certain that the teachers are prepared to cope with the complex task of dealing effectively and humanely with daily instructional demands and that they do so in an able, realistic manner. They need to know specific skills, the minute-to-minute kind of psychological and pedagogical didactics that succor and sustain, encourage and recruit, quicken and interest, temper and conduce, ally and mediate, credit and accrue.

Our instructional quarters consist of a large area that can be subdivided into three classrooms. This open-spaced arrangement allows for mobility, for teacher-pupil pedagogy, for cohabitation, for multimedia enterprises, and the like. Eight-year olds mingle with 10-, 12-, 16-, and 18-year olds. There is a quick realization by new pupils that they are not the only ones to need help. Pupils get to know and work with each other, to share, and to know other teachers. One child remarked recently on his third day in the clinic, "Gee, everybody says 'good morning' to me." Across the corridor is a materials center filled with books, periodicals, and so on. This is where graduate students gather, where coffee and tea is available, and where children and adults come for informal chats or to locate materials. This center is an invaluable adjunct for promoting good will.

This is a brief accounting of our circumstances at the University of Delaware. It is provided to give perspective to our endeavors and background to the procedures about to be detailed. We do not mean to imply that ours is the utopian arrangement, either physically or pedagogically. Rather it is meant to provide others with a description that possesses enough fullness to serve as a sound base on which to make judgments.

OUR INSTRUCTIONAL PROGRAM

It seems timely to reiterate that what is to follow reflects careful examination of Fernald's recommendations, plus years of working with children with reading disabilities. Children society has failed, and above all so-called developmental-type achievers, among whom the underachievers abound. Time and again Betts has stated, "There are more children achieving above the mean for their age group who are retarded in reading than there are achieving below the mean." By this he meant that bright superior children seldom achieve at their level of expectancy. This is so because instruction is geared to the average, thus penalizing the pupils at the extremes. As a result many bright people are underachievers.

Fernald declared stages of progress in perceptual terms: tactile, kinesthetic, auditory, and visual. Levels were determined by progress across and beyond reliance upon any one perceptual avenue. Even so, transition phases are allowed for and described showing that movement from stage to stage was not unadulterated. As a matter of fact it is fitting to say that almost all achieving readers use kinesthetic-auditory-visual means to a large degree in learning to read. This is why the last two stages of her approach fuse as they do and are not as distinctly different as the tracing stage, or the kinesthetic stage.

We, too, have noted stages of progress and see three stages as rather distinct levels of accomplishment, which mark a widening horizon in terms of attitude and skills. Stage 1 has been attained when a pupil can read material with a readability level most teachers would recognize as equal to a typical 2^1 reader. This means the acquisition of a sight vocabulary of at least 500 words; the ability to attack an unrecognized word systematically, whether in isolation or in context; the ability to recognize the need for help, the ability to read meaningfully, using the value of facts to predict outcomes, so that children will turn to books and the like without coercion or undue anxiety, and so that they respond to spelling instruction. For extremely retarded readers, attaining Stage 1 is the most difficult phase. It requires a sharp change in attitude and conduct, both personal and scholastic in nature.

Stage 2 is attained when a pupil can comfortably read material at a so-called 4^1 reader-level readability. This means excellent command of word attack skills, including the ability to use a glossary or dictionary to clarify both meaning and pronunciation needs: ability to predict, read, and prove; ability to do inquiry reading (4); ability to do some creative writing; ability to respond to spelling instruction; and a continuous willingness to turn to newspapers, magazines, and books for pleasure and for study.

Stage 3 is attained when pupils can comfortably read material at or about a so-called seventh reader-level readability. This means excellent command of word attack skills, including the ability to conceptualize; the ability to use facts and their value to verify or refute reader summations or predictions and to a fair degree determine author intent, as well as authenticity; a strong positive attitude toward reading materials of all kinds, in particular and the seeking of knowledge in general; a versatility that commands a fair control over change in rate of reading either to skim, to scan, to study, or to gain an overview; the ability to do research-type inquiry reading and the preparation and staging of reports; and the ability to engage in creative writing and related editorial work.

Admittedly this account of stages is skeletal. This chapter and the next will enlarge on each stage. Because this text is aimed primarily at remedial instruction, more detail will be given for Stage 1 than for Stages 2 and 3. It is apparent that the criterion stated at each stage are general. Even so they represent truths which I have tried to apprehend and fix. In a sense these truths are discrete and insular, but not mutually exclusive. By and large they are manifold or multifaceted in nature and develop in some constellation or other. The rate and degree of achievement of these truths varies from pupil to pupil and to some degree from teacher to teacher. Generally speaking these are the crucial points. Because one sees strikingly similar changes occurring from pupil to pupil, the concept of stages seems appropriate.

Through the years I have found it fitting to refer to the peak point of a stage or transition as "clearing a hurdle." When pupils reach a peak, it seems that new vistas or capabilities open to view. They show a new sense of confidence and security and are more cooperative and eager. There are times when a marked change in attitude is apparent. Usually, too, the vistas and reactions are quite uniform in nature from pupil to pupil, thus reinforcing the use of the concept of stages.

The best way to understand the stages, their specifics, transitions, and peak, is to work with children. This is why clinical experience, attained under the wardship of qualified people, is most valuable. There is no substitute for this kind of experience and no better way to remove the quackery from remedial instruction.

Obviously progressing through the three stages defined with achievement peaks at levels roughly defined as Stage 1, or 2^1 reader level; Stage 2, or 4^1 reader level; and Stage 3, or seventh reader level depends upon a pupil's age and degree of disability. In other words, a nine-year old might by age and capacity achieve through Stages 1 and 2, but most likely not Stage 3. In brief, the stages as declared are reflections of skill achievement and attitude and not limited to progress across perceptual changes.

In developmental programs, or in the typical school circumstance, rate of progress is geared to grade-level annual promotions. Stated differently, a typically developing child is expected to achieve a year's growth in a year and then be promoted to a next higher grade level. This arrangement, geared as it is to the typical child, does not allow for the atypical at either end. Very bright children could frequently make two years growth in a year. On rare occasion some bright children do skip a grade. At the other end, less bright children—the slow developers who do not make a year's growth in a year—are labeled. If they are retained a year, they are flunked and live with that disgraceful label the rest of their school days.

What then is a sane expectancy for 9-, 10-, and 11-year olds or older who are four and five years behind their likely expectancy in reading achievement and three and four years behind their grade level? Even though it seems the height of the ridiculous to expect them to make a year's growth in a year, frequently in the first and second stages they make more than a year in a year. Invariably years are required to overcome a four-year lag. Even if children make two year's progress in

REMEDIAL INSTRUCTION (II)

their first year of clinical instruction, they have in the meantime matured another year and thereby extended the gap. As said earlier, remedial instruction is a demanding, steadfast task that seldom results in miracle cures. It is damnably misleading to either state boldly or imply subtly that rapid progress will result. There are no magic wands. There are no substitutes for good teaching and paced learning. Rate of intake and assimilation of skills and knowledge will not exceed the human ability to learn, retain, recall and use; and it is highly unethical to even imply that this could occur. Remedial instruction and learning is invariably complicated by the emotional circumstances that have accumulated, and this influences pupils' rates of learning proportionately. This pragmatic declaration of prospects is not meant to be negative but to be forthright and thereby positive.

OUR ADJUSTED READING INSTRUCTION

Before children begin instruction their test results are carefully examined by the Laboratory School supervisor and the Reading Study Center director. With evidence at hand they decide what instructional procedures are to be recommended to best meet the child's specific needs. These are discussed with the chosen instructor, who has also carefully studied the findings of the child's extensive testing.

Because the children were tested in the clinic, coming to the Reading Study Center is a revisiting. Most children respond favorably to the testing, the attention they receive from the different examiners, the briefing given at the end of the testing, and the grandeur of the university. In brief, their attitudes toward the Center are favorable.

Upon arrival children are greeted by their instructor and introduced to the other children, the other instructors, the secretaries, and other staff members they may not have met. They already know locations of the rest rooms, the materials center, and the offices. Then, without either hurrying or dilly-dallying they are shown to the area where they will be instructed. Here they will find a desk or the equal, a clipboard, a dictionary, and paper and pencil. They are seated and instruction is begun immediately.

The discussion of procedures that follow is aimed primarily for children severely retarded in reading. A typical case like this is a boy, nine years old, enrolled in a third or fourth grade and unable to read at even a so-called preprimer level. He recognizes only a few words. (See Chapters 2–3.)

The moment the child is seated he is told, "We have a new way of learning to read, which we want you to try. It is just as good as any other way. Many people have had the same difficulty as you have had learning to read, and they have learned with this new method. Give me a word that you would like to learn." This statement contains only 56 words and requires about 23 seconds to deliver. Thus in a very short time instruction is activated.

This short statement is carefully worded and positive. The instructor speaks it with quiet confidence in an unhurried way. In a matter-of-fact way this matter-of-fact statement, untarnished by flattery or exaggerations, commands the attention of children almost as much as the words of a hypnotist. Certain words are especially commanding: new, way, just as good, many people, give, you would like.

Most children trust the circumstances and respond with a word they cannot read but would like to. Some are hesitant and ask if any word is acceptable; they need to be assured. Some select a word they think they can read, fearful of taking another chance of failure. Sometimes a reassuring, "any word" from the instructor proves helpful. Immediately the students are involved. They are asked to give any word. They can think, "The instructor respects me and asks me for a word." Whatever the word given, it will reflect the students' free choice, their experience, their vocabulary, or their level. "Start at the level of the learner" is a teacher admonishment of long standing.

If a child responds with "triangle," for example, the following dialogue may occur between the instructor (I) and the pupil (P):

I: "Triangle," what do you mean by "triangle"? (Already the teacher knows that the pupil remembered the word and produced it orally. Now what is sought is the likely meaning the pupil associates with the word.)

P: A triangle is a figure. It has three sides.

I: Triangle, how many syllables (or parts) do you hear in triangle? (As shown, the word is spoken twice by the instructor. It is pronounced without distortion.)

P: Two.

I: Let's look (or check) in the dictionary.
(The instructor is skilled at opening a dictionary, turns to the *T* section and rapidly locates the word.) Here it is (pointing to the entry word). It has three parts. (Then, pointing to each part the instructor pronounces the word by parts, "tri an gle." Thus it was the dictionary that indicated three parts and not the instructor. If the pupil had said three parts, the instructor would have said, "You are right; it has three parts" and then pointed to the parts as above.)

I: Now, watch what I do and listen to what I say. Ready! (The instructor writes the word with black crayola in chalkboard-size script on a piece of paper 2½" wide and 11" long. First, the word is spoken as a unit—"triangle"—then it is written as a unit but each syllable is spoken without distortion as the first letter of the syllable is started. When the word is written it is spoken again as a unit. Then it is underlined by syllables and again each syllable, or sound unit, is spoken without distortion. After the underlining is done, the word is spoken again as a unit. In brief, the word is spoken three times as a unit and twice by syllables. The paper is so positioned that the pupil can see the writing being done. This usually means seating the pupil to the instructor's left, slanting the paper toward the pupil and placing it in the pupil's clear view.)

I: Again, watch what I do and listen to what I say. (Now the instructor traces over the word using either one or two fingers. The tracing and pronunciation are coordinated as for the writing. First, the word is spoken as a unit. Second, it is traced as a unit but pronounced by syllables. Third, it is spoken as a unit. Fourth, the underlining is traced and each syllable is spoken. Fifth, it is spoken as a unit. This tracing-speaking action is demonstrated twice. Each time the pupil is asked to watch and listen.)

I: Now, you do what I did and say what I said, until you think you can write the word as you learned it and without looking at it. (Each of these actions requires mental alertness of a visual perceptual and aural perceptual nature. The pupil must grasp the coordination of phoneme (sound) and grapheme (letter) and produce it without distortion. Every pupil, at this phase, experiences difficulty. Usually a first error is lack of coordination of sound without tracing. The instructor must remain very alert, so that the instant an error occurs the pupil is stopped. The stopping is done by gently moving a hand over the paper.)

I: Watch again what I do and listen to what I say until you think you can write the word as you learned it and without looking at it. (Again the instructor demonstrates. The child is not admonished, merely stopped. Each time the procedure is redemonstrated until insight is acquired by the pupil. Once the pupil catches on, the tracing-learning proceeds more readily. The pupil knows when he or she has done the tracing correctly because the instructor has not intervened. Then the instructor continues.)

I: Trace the word as often as you wish until you think you can write the word as you learned it and without looking at it. (Some pupils wish to try immediately, others repeat the tracing four or five times more. The instructor stays constantly vigilant to be certain the phoneme-grapheme relationship being acquired is accurate. This is a first measure in phonic discipline and sets the stage for later skill refinement, for skill generalization, and for adaption of skills acquired to other words or different words. When pupils decide they can reproduce the word, they are given a sheet of paper and a pencil and are reminded to write the word exactly as they learned it.)

P: I can write it.

I: Be sure to write the word just as you learned it. (Different errors occur at this point. Usually the pupils are so eager to proceed that they forget to say the word as a unit, or forget to say a syllable, or forget to dot an *i* or cross a *t*. Each time they start to make an error they are stopped instantly. Sometimes the instructor demonstrates again and sometimes not. Sometimes pupils revert to tracing again and sometimes not. Instructor judgments and pupil judgments occur. Each wrong writing is folded over so as to be out of sight. Also, before the writing is done the tracing form is turned over so that no copying is possible. As Fernald stated, copying is futile. It requires no thinking and fails to establish the word in the central nervous system.)

A record may be kept of the number of tracings required, as well as the number of writing attempts. This record provides a measure of learning that can be graphed or plotted for the child to see how many tracings were required, how the number of tracings decreases, how a relearning of a word may require vastly fewer tracings, and so on.

Because the instructor is so busy, the record keeping is best done in code, so as to be brief and readily done. Thus a *T,* or simply a line 1, may be used for each tracing, a *D* for each demonstration, a *W* for each wrong writing, and a *C* for each correct writing. By way of illustration the following record shows 6 demonstrations, 11 tracings, 3 wrong writings, and 2 correct writings *C:* (D D T D T D T D T D T T T T W T W T W T C C). Only two correct writings are needed to establish proof of immediate retention and reproduction capability. A principal reason only two correct reproductions are needed is because copying is not permitted.

In addition, note may be made of the nature of the error. For instance, a tracing error may have occurred with the syllable *gle,* or a writing error with *tr,* or a writing error omitting the final *e,* and so on. Such an account keeping helps the instructor, as well as the pupil, focus on specific needs.

When a word has been correctly produced, a pride of achievement is sensed immediately. Even though in some instances as many as 20 or more tracings are required to establish the needed insights and phoneme-grapheme coordinations, achievement makes it all worthwhile. No artificial tokens or rewards are necessary. Success is the highest reward.

Now the instructor starts the process anew by saying, "Give another word you want to learn to read" and the process is repeated. Usually on the first day only two or, at the most, three words are learned. However, for a pupil who has a very small reading vocabulary, this represents a sizeable growth. In making judgments of progress and achievement, one must always make certain that they are made relative to a particular child and her or his circumstance and not relative to a mythical age norm or class norm. Instruction is being geared to individuals' needs, their capabilities, and their levels; and the measuring rod must be so geared, too. In brief, only gradually over a period of teaching days, may an index to growth rate be determined for a pupil.

The next day pupils proceed directly to their particular instructional areas. They are greeted there by their teachers and are shown a clipboard with their name on it and attendance sheets. They are taught how to keep an attendance accounting. Then they are shown the two words learned the day before. They have been typed in primer-size type and appear as if in a column order.

triangle

thermometer

They are permitted to examine both words and then asked to speak them. In most instances the words are recognized and spoken. This is true even though the words were learned in cursive writing and produced that way. For now, the words appear in type, with each letter a discrete unit. The recognition requires a transfer of knowledge from a word learned in cursive to a typed word, and this utilizes perhaps the most important principle in learning.

On rare occasion a pupil does not recognize and recall a word in type. Then they are shown the original cursive crayola-produced writing. This usually is all that is necessary for the word to be recalled.

After the children have identified the words learned the first day, new words are learned, using the same procedures. Again the pupils are asked to suggest any words they want to learn. Again the execution of the tracing and writing, and the blending of phoneme-graphemes is carefully marshalled by the instructor. Usually two or three words are acquired on the second day. The boy we mentioned earlier added "cardinal," "nuthatch," and "frog."

Usually, too, on the second day systematic visual-auditory discrimination skill training (phonics) is introduced with integrity and thoroughness, and with a first-hand pragmatic immediacy. The latter is accomplished by using phoneme-grapheme conditions that appear in the words the children have learned to read.

To return to our example, the word "triangle" is used as the visual base, and the boy is asked to focus on it. He is then asked to tell whether a word now spoken (oral) by the instructor begins, or does not begin like "triangle." Words like the following are useful because they are frequently occurring words and because they are one syllable:

tree (yes), try (yes), trap (yes), train (yes), blue (no), trick (yes), trail (yes), true (yes), snow (no), and so on.

Notice that four or five words are used in which the beginning phoneme-grapheme *tr* agrees with the key word selected and learned by the pupil. This affirmation of sounds and letters helps fix them for the pupil. The ones that disagree are distinctly different, *bl* and *sn*. Thus, very early in the pupil's program systematic phonic training is activated, using phonic conditions available from the pupil's choice of words.

The next day the hour is started by checking the attendance chart and by examining the three words (typed) learned the day before ("cardinal," "nuthatch," "frog") and producing them orally. Then the first words learned are presented ("triangle," "thermometer").

By this time the tracing idea has been quite well acquired. The pupil has had experience coordinating sound-sight when tracing and when writing. Now, rather than asking for other words the instructor suggests that the pupil say something about one of the words learned, or about two or three combined, or about something new. Usually the pupil offers to enlarge on some of the ideas represented by the words learned. The pupil dictates and the instructor records.

BIRDS

> We have a bird bath in our yard. Birds come there to drink and to bathe. Yesterday I saw a cardinal and a nuthatch. In the bath we have a rubber frog.

The recording can be done in either cursive or manuscript. At this point of progress manuscript is recommended. The dictation is read back to the student and changes made if they are suggested. The student does not read along with the teacher but is devoted entirely to listening. On occasion the pupil notes that some word or expression doesn't sound right and thus early begins making editorial suggestions. Now the pupil, instead of being asked to select any word to learn, is asked to select one from the dictation. In this instance "bird" and "rubber" were chosen and learned by tracing.

Again some visual-auditory discrimination training is done. Then another instructional feature is introduced, teacher reading. A selection about cardinals has been located by the instructor in the magazine *National Wildlife* and is read aloud to the student. This results in a brief discussion of birds in general, and the article contents in particular.

In addition, the child is asked to prepare an illustration to accompany his dictation. He draws a picture of the bird bath and the frog. The illustration helps firm up word associations and facilitate retention.

The next day activities are started by presenting to the pupil a typed copy of his previous day's dictation. He is urged to read as much of it as he can and underline any words he knows or recognizes. The words "bird," "cardinal," "nuthatch," "frog," and "rubber" are readily underlined. In addition he underlines "birds," "bath," and "yesterday."

Then he is asked to read the entire selection orally and is reassured that the instructor will assist. In the oral rereading the pupil also "reads" or speaks: "we," "yard," "a," "drink," "and," and "the." This recognition is facilitated most likely by the flow of ideas, the oral rhythm engendered, and the aided recall resulting from the fact that the pupil has produced the concepts (semantics), dictated the words (vocabulary), and established the word order (syntactics). Each of these avenues facilitates recall and recognition, and will in turn aid retention.

Now a new learning phase is introduced. Already the boy has shown that he can make the transition from recognizing words in cursive writing to recognizing them when typed. This day, instead of reading he is asked to locate the words "triangle," "thermometer," "cardinal," "nuthatch," "frog," and "rubber" in other printed materials, such as a book, a newspaper, or a magazine. The article in *National Wildlife,* which was read by the instructor the previous day, proved useful.

The words "we" and "yard" are added to the list of words traced and correctly reproduced in writing. In both instances the words are readily learned, requiring only a few tracings for two perfect written productions. These 12 words are then placed in a word bank where they will be readily available.

It is fitting to pause at this point and take a backward look at the substantial elements of pedagogical empiricism evident in and the influences resulting (skills acquired) from these four sessions that may be most enduring. This lad has had a capital experience. He has achieved success over a period of days. He has mastered 12 words and retained them for days (memory). He has recognized the words in different contexts (transfer of knowledge)—books, newspapers, magazines— and is able to cope with the different type faces and sizes (visual perception) both for upper and lower case letter structure. Thus, he has accrued an enormously psychological benefit from transfer of knowledge to new situations.

The words were of his choosing (personal involvement). The ideas and the syntax of the recorded dictation were his and thereby represent his experience, knowledge, and language power. Not only has he recognized the words in varied contexts, but also he has written each word (written recall) and produced each time the accepted letter order (spelling), as well as made appropriate phoneme-grapheme associations (phonics).

In addition he has made a reassuring discovery. When asked to "read" what he had dictated and underline any word he recognizes, he has readily spotted the words he had traced. But, he has also underlined three words he had not traced: "birds," "bath," "yesterday." So a question is raised in the boy's mind, "Can I learn words I dictate even without tracing?" and already he has a partial answer, "I can." It is this recognition of success and insight into his own capability that builds confidence and in turn motivates renewed effort. This kind of self-knowledge is priceless.

Phonic instruction has been introduced using words he has produced and learned. Visual-auditory discrimination is done, with attention focused on beginning or initial word sounds. Again, he has achieved success.

The teacher has read to him a fascinating article on cardinals and now he knows more about them than at any time before. He has actually shared some of the ideas with his parents, particularly his mother. His knowledge has been augmented and his interests extended and refined.

He has started a file, called a *word bank,* for his new words. The idea of words in a bank, like money in a bank, has impressed him and suggested a kind of knowledge security. He knows each word by its syllables and can blend the pronunciation of a syllable with the writing. The teacher called this phoneme-grapheme, or sound-letter, association.

He has met the other children who attended. Some are about his age, some younger, and some older. They accepted him, and he thereby not only responded kindly but also realized quite poignantly that he is not the only person experiencing difficulty and seeking help. All the instructors know him and greet him daily, as do the school supervisor and the director of the Center. The climate in the Center is warm and accepting, and the mood is one of confidence, friendly persuasion, and positive expectations. He shares with others and they share with him.

Instruction has been started by focusing on one word (a concept) and tracing and writing it until it is remembered. However, he has sensed that instruction is also focused on ideas, his ideas (semantics). The shift that has occurred is from one word to ideas. As a result he recognizes words he has neither traced nor written.

Instruction in sounds or phoneme-grapheme relationships has focused on sounds as they occurred in a word or syllable context, or, in brief, a *sound context.* Letters are not dealt with in isolation but only in a sound context (syllable) where their sound value can be determined.

The following week instruction is similar to that already activated. Additional dictation is obtained, other words are mastered, some are traced and some are not, phonic analysis skill training is continued, words are located in different sources, teacher oral reading and talking is done. New activities are introduced.

The instructor bears in mind the fact that a word bank could readily be stuffed with counterfeit coin. Words placed into the bank should always remain functional, in the sense that the pupil remembers them permanently and can read (recognize) them anywhere. Certain phoneme-grapheme relationships that are useful in attacking other words should also be retained. A good way to achieve such high order functional retention is through recontacting the words in the context in which they were learned, as well as in different contexts, and do the same with the phonic skills being acquired. Functional reuse at frequent intervals and in new situations is the answer.

Monday of the second week is a challenge for our pupil. Will he remember (retain) and produce (read orally) the 12 words he learned the previous week, after a forgetting period that extended from Thursday morning to Monday morning (approximately 94 hours).

The instruction hour is started by marking a new weekly attendance form. Then he is asked to reexamine the account about birds which he dictated the previous Wednesday and again underline words he knew then. Here is what he does:

BIRDS

We have a bird bath in our yard, Birds come here to drink and bathe. Yesterday I saw a cardinal and a nuthatch. In the bath we have a rubber frog.

He double underlines the 12 words he recognized the week before. He had traced none of these. Three he knew when he studied his account. He also underlined "a," "and," "we," "yard," and "drink." These are words he seemed to know when he and the instructor "read" the account jointly. The only word he did not mark was the word "the."

The instructor comments favorably about the word underlining and then they read the account jointly. Again the pupil produced each underlined word, as well as the word "the." Even though his oral reading is halting, in an even monotone, and with a raised voice, some expression attends his reading of "a cardinal and a nuthatch."

Now the instructor, using a 3″ × 5″ card with a small "word window" cut into it, has the lad produce the underlined words by reading them orally. This is done by exposing the different words, one at a time, through the opening in the card. This procedure isolates the word and cuts off the likely use of context clues.

Each word recognized when isolated by the card-window is then typed on a small card approximately ⅜″ wide and 1¼″ in length.

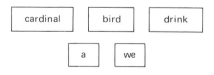

Thus, a second word bank is founded. This bank contains all words mastered, whether or not they are acquired by tracing.

These words are available for use in different situations, to promote retention, and above all to promote functional usage. The instructor produces an 8″ × 11″ card holder which consists of a cardboard covered by a piece of colored felt. On it she arranges and rearranges words the boy knows, organizing them into different idea units (semantic units). Some of the units are complete sentences, but some are not. Regardless, the units can be read by the child.

the	cardinal	and	nuthatch	drink
the	birds	and	frog	drink
the	rubber	triangle	and	thermometer
we	drink			

The instructor also arranges them in random order column units to promote recognition of perceptual differences.

bird	and	thermometer
yesterday	rubber	birds
we	the	drink
bath	a	frog
triangle	yard	nuthatch

Each arrangement, whether semantically or perceptually organized, requires the student to recognize, recall, and produce the words, and reconstruct the ideas the syntactically organized words created. These functional (working) arrangements facilitate fixation and retention.

This day's session ends with some teacher oral reading. The instructor has found a delightful editorial on birds in the Sunday *New York Times*. The student has experienced a full measure of success and converted what might have been another blue Monday into a successful "ego trip." The climb out of the failure abyss has been started, and a first plateau reached.

The next day the bird dictation is read once more and this time with greater ease. Then another dictation is obtained.

CARDINALS

Yesterday I saw a male and female cardinal. The male is very red and very pretty. The female has some red but not much. They both like sunflower seeds, and so does the blue jay.

Then, proceeding as before, the instructor reads back to the pupil all he has dictated. This serves two purposes: First, to be sure the recording is what the student said and what he wishes. As the student attends to the oral reading of his dictation he does so in an editorial way. He decides whether or not what he hears is as he wishes. Second, this activates auditory retention of words and ideas. Again an illustration is requested. This time a male cardinal is drawn.

Phonic skill training is activated and extended. This time there is visual-auditory discrimination. The instructor places the word "bird" on the word card holder. This supplies the visual perceptual part. Then she *says* words like "boy," "book," "bake," "sun," "be," "by," "barn," "man," "ball," "bend," and so on. This provides the auditory perceptual part of the visual-auditory discrimination decision making. Each time, a pupil judgment has to be made: Did "boy" and "book" begin like "bird"? Did words like "sun" and "man" did not start that way? After dealing intensively with the sound that the letter *b* represents in such sound contexts as "bird," "boy," and "book," a point is made of the fact that the name of the letter being used in these many sound-contexts is *b*. Thus the name of the letter is distinguished clearly from the sound it represents. This is a prime distinction.

Then the instructor places two words on the word card holder:

bird

rubber

This time the phonic decision is altered and made slightly more complex. The instructor says a word, "run," and the student has to decide which of the two words begins the same ("rubber"). Other words used are: "rain," "ring," "ball," "boy," "rice," "rib," "big," "ban," and so on. Always, the spoken word has the same beginning sound as one or the other of the two printed words.

Through this procedure, not only is the student we have been considering discovering that he can read and remember words, but also that he has a mind capable of making formalized decisions. He is learning, actively and aggressively, that he can think. He is acquiring a new awareness of himself, his capacity to learn; and these discoveries are having an impact on his motivation, his relationships with others, and his concentration of effort.

Twenty-four hours later the second dictated account is presented to the student for studying and for underlining words. This is done prior to the oral reading of the passages. This time the boy underlines words as shown:

CARDINALS

Yesterday I saw a male and female cardinal. The male is very red and very pretty. They both like sunflower seeds, and so does the blue jay.

The instructor paces the oral rereading by readily supplying words that are not rather immediately recognized. Again the oral reading results in additional words being recognized: "red," "pretty," "like." The window card is used and underlined words are recognized in isolation.

Again transfer of knowledge to a new situation is achieved by having available books about birds. One book, entitled *A Field Guide to the*

Birds (3) has been obtained and words are identified, notably: "cardinal," "nuthatch," "male," "female," "blue jay."

Again, teacher reading is done, but first the picture is examined. Here it is learned that the cardinal belongs to the finch family. Finches are compared. Then they learn that the cardinal is the only all-red bird with a crest and that it has a black throat. Both the words "finch" and "crest" are added to the word bank by tracing. "Finch" requires four tracings and "crest" only one. The latter name is also the name of the child's toothpaste.

The following day the account is reexamined, and the words "red," "pretty," "like," and "very" are also underlined. The account is then read orally and done on a steady and fairly even word-by-word basis.

Two other actions are introduced. First, instructor and pupil count all the running words in the account. The total is 36. Then they count the number of different words, and the total is 27. Next they count the number of different words underlined and known. This total is 16. These numbers and these labels are added as a footnote to the account.

Total words (TW): 36
Different words (DW): 27
Known words (KW): 16

Each total is impressive. This kind of log keeping shows clearly the number of words learned and the progress being made. Each is a token of success. No token buttons or coins are needed as extrinsic bribe-type rewards.

Then the instructor produces three columns of words. The words are the *Cardinals* story arranged in column order.

Cardinals	very	much
Yesterday	red	they
I	and	both
saw	very	like
a	pretty	sunflower
male	The	seeds
and	female	and
female	has .	so
cardinal	some	does
The	red	the
male	but	blue
is	not	jay

The student is asked to recognize as many words as possible in the first column, then the second column and the third. Even though the words are thus disconnected from the typical left-to-right syntactical order, the student can revert to the logical systematized semantic order if he wishes and thus use context clues to recognition. At first this discreet arrangement proves challenging, but as the student proceeds he senses the meaning value and uses it. Response to this challenge is spirited and lively. Thus ends a second week of instruction on a challenging and rewarding note.

Again it is fitting to pause and take a look at what has been done thus far both pedagogically and therapeutically. First, though, a note of warning. It must not be thought that the weekly account thus far provided is typical and that all children disabled in reading will progress in a similar way. This is not true. All children are different, and it seems that their differences are accentuated when they have experienced extensive failure. The account is representative and suggests an order of instructional events and learning that is likely to occur from child to child. The difference will be the rate at which individual children progress.

For instance, some children learn only one word the first day and add only one or two the second day. Even though this is the learning rate, the child can be led to dictate on the third day. Children respond to the dictation most favorably. By the third day it represents a change of pace and the novelty of the procedure is enhancing. Eight-, 9-, and 10-year olds (age does not really matter) are filled with experiences and often times unique interests and knowledge and are delighted and flattered to talk to a receptive listener.

Most children are brief. They voice three or four ideas and stop. When this occurs, the teacher capitalizes on the stop by commenting favorably and writing the pupil's name at the end. A short account is more likely to be remembered as dictated, when the rereading occurs the following day. This oral recall facilitation is highly desirable; it should be utilized wisely.

Sometimes, however, a child gushes a torrent of ideas, and dictates 10 or more sentences. When this occurs, it should be recognized as an instructional bonanza. Apparently the pupil-teacher rapport is such that the outburst results. Apparently pupil confidence and security is at a desirable level and mounting. The following day the typed account may prove rather formidable but nevertheless useful. At such times the instructor needs to be very ready to supply words, in order to pace the student through the oral rereading.

In many ways, therefore, it would be helpful to disregard the day-by-day idea and think of each description as an accounting of instructional-learning steps. As such the steps represent a sequence that has occurred with such frequency clinically that it can almost be said, "this is the order." Such instructional procedures as having children reread their dictated account the first time within a 24-hour period have been found to be pedagogically sound; it is recommended they follow the prescribed outline. It is to be noted, however, that assimilation and accommodation do occur in a pattern geared to each individual's rate of internalization.

Pedagogical skills activated—and in some instances acquired—thus far are as follows:

1. Pupil decision making to select words, to determine reproduction time, to dictate ideas, and so on.

2. Ability to trace a word written cursively; this involves a coordination of the oral phoneme and written grapheme, a crossing of *t*'s, a dotting of *i*'s and *j*'s, and so on.

3. Ability to recognize words learned even though the word configuration has been altered from cursive formation to discrete letters and different type faces.

4. Ability to remember on immediate recall and after a day or a week or more.

5. Ability to transfer word recognition power to new situations, such as books, magazines, papers, signs, store windows, and the like.

6. Ability to respond to auditory-visual discrimination of beginning word-sounds, as represented by a single consonant, blends, diphthongs, vowels, and the like.

7. Ability to deal with words by syllables or sound units.

8. Ability to recognize words in isolation, as well as in context.

9. Ability to use semantic or meaning clues to aid in word recognition.

10. Ability to listen attentively to material being read orally and to utilize the ideas attended to.

11. Ability to attend to an oral reading in an editorial manner.

12. Ability to keep words in a file box or word bank.

13. Ability to keep a dual file: one consisting of the tracings and the other of words learned without tracing.

14. Ability to keep a word log on dictations: total words (TW), different words (DW), and known words (KW).

15. Ability to keep an attendance record.

16. Increased confidence

Case staffings are done on a regular six-week period except for new students, as indicated earlier, who are staffed at the end of the second week and at the end of the first six weeks. Accordingly, the student we

Case Staffing Form — Individual

Case No.: 3146   Date: 2/18   Instr.: M. Wilson
Date Tested: 11/26-11/28   C.A.: 9-5   Present Grade: 3
Adm. to RSC: 2/3   IQ: F.S. 116 (WISC-11/26)
Total Inst. Time: 2 weeks   V.S. 131
Inst. Level: Then - Exp.   P.S. 96
          Now - Exp.

Etiological Factors:

1. Youngest of 4 children — 1 brother and 2 sisters.
2. Somewhat slow learning to talk.
3. Unhappy in kdg. and 1st grade.
4. Parents noted reading difficulty in first grade; teacher urged promotion.
5. Retained in 2nd grade.
6. Likes 3rd grade teacher.
7. Parents cooperative but seem overanxious.
8. Recent change in school attitude; rebellious, unmotivated.

Current Instructional Program:

Activities	Assets	Liabilities
Planning:	Cooperates, is interested. Selects teacher reading.	None.
Dictation:	Does readily.	Tension evident. Tries hard to do well.
Rereading dictation: silently— orally—	Proceeds very cautiously. Getting some expressive interpretation.	Perhaps too cautious. Voice high, tense.
Phonics training:	Quite attentive, catches idea readily.	Reluctant to start.
Word Attack: in context—	Uses meaning clues, looks ahead	Reluctant to use phonemegrapheme clues.
in isolåtion—	Will try.	Frustrates easily, gets blank look.
Structural analysis:	Responds eagerly.	Hears syllables, does well on endings.
Teacher reading:	Selects, enjoys, attentive.	None.
Word bank:	Eager and orderly. Responds well to phonic instruction using bank.	Too eager.
Locating words elsewhere:	Especially responsive.	Prefers newspapers and reluctant about books.
Reading dictation in column order.	Proceeds very well.	Too much word by word.

Needs:
    None really. Might get more attention from other instructors and perhaps
        more sharing with other students.

have been discussing is staffed at this point. The case staffing form shows the manner in which data, practices, and judgments are entered.

Notice that the top section provides timely data about admission, instruction, and expectancy. Almost at a glance one can tell that this student is in the bright normal class with considerable verbal facility. It is evident, too, that he most likely has repeated a grade, because a child with a C.A. of 9–5 is usually in fourth grade.

The etiological factors are informative. Family position could suggest being babied and probably becoming dependent. School history shows a negative picture except for this year, but even now shows stress signs. The current instructional program defines activities and teacher judgments about the nature of his responses and his needs.

The Reading Laboratory School supervisor, usually a second-year Ph.D. candidate, conducts the meeting. Approximately one-half hour is allowed for questions and answers. All attending participate by questioning or commenting. Usually the instructor is asked to elaborate. The supervisor and the instructor sit at a center desk, and the staff personnel sit at tables arranged in a large square. The atmosphere is open, relaxed, and devoted. Each child's situation is viewed seriously. All full-time graduate students attend, as do the director of the Center and other Center faculty who are free at the hour. Student attitude toward the staff sessions is highly favorable. They are viewed as the culminating experience of their year or years of graduate study. This is where they can utilize all they have mastered about the pedagogy and psychology of learning in general and reading and the language arts in particular and about human adjustment.

At the end of the staff questioning period, time is allowed for each person attending to write recommendations. The staff recommendation form (page 304) is illustrative of comments that resulted from the staffing exchange of ideas. The following week the instructor distributes to each graduate student a copy of recommendations made and describes briefly recommendations, if any, that have been tried in that one week interim.

Now that two weeks of instruction have been accomplished a report to parents is necessary. The report indicates the progress made to date, words learned, dictations made, word logs, word banks, word attack skills, and so on. The report is prepared in consultation with the child. At no time is a report made to parents without first planning and discussing it with the student. The report is done in terms of assets and goals to be reached. On occasion the pupil may sit in on the interview. Both parents are summoned. Reports are not made by phone. Dealing with the life and future of an individual is serious business and requires the best of attention in the most honorable way. In this instance the report for the first two weeks of instruction is positive and encouraging.

University of Delaware
Newark, Delware

The Reading Study Center
College of Education
Curriculum and Instruction Department

Staff Recommendation

Student's Name ____John Doe_____ Date ___2/18____
Teacher: _____M. Wilson_____

Recommendations:

   Pedagogical

Teaching Reading: 1. The Silent Meow
                                2. The Glass Elevator

Free Browsing: 1. Book of riddles – have him choose a riddle a day.

Dictation Motivation: 1. Book of riddles.
                                2. Observing eggs in incubator.
                                3. Do experiments with lenses and light.
                                4. Do experiments with heat.
                                5. Make a bar–type diagram of DW, RW, KW.

Word Recognition: 1. Cut words from a catalog and mount on some
                                   science instrument picture.
                                2. Do consonant visual–auditory training with
                                   another student.
                                3. Try beginning sounds of syllables in polysyllabic
                                   words such as "yesterday."

Concept Development: 1. Do a concept model of a bird, labeling its
                                   attributes.
                                2. Keep a bird scrapbook.

Reading and Reorganizing: 1. Scramble sentences in dictated accounts and have
                                   him reorganize them.
                                2. Have him compose ideas on a word card holder,
                                   using words in word bank.

_____

   Therapeutical   1. More contact with other students.
                                2. Have other instructors be more attentive to him.

On subsequent days new actions are introduced and new adaptations are made of actions previously started. The following new dictation is obtained from the boy we have been discussing:

OUR BACK YARD

Our back yard has different trees. The biggest tree is a sugar maple. It is easy to climb and I set in the tree often. At the foot of the yard is a small stream. It starts from springs in my neighbor's yard. His yard is always wet.

Always the account is read back to the pupil immediately after dictation for editorial purposes. Then the recorded account is placed in a typing folder for the clinic typist to ready for the following day.

By this time the boy has mastered 28 words. He recognizes them in the accounts he has dictated. He has found most of them in other sources. He has used some of the words for phonic auditory-visual discrimination training of beginning sounds.

Now he is introduced to an alphabetized word bank. Dividers are prepared for each letter in the alphabet except *XYZ*. These three are placed on one divider card. Next he files each of the 28 words, placing words in 16 of the letter compartments. This is a task he accomplishes readily; he is quite pleased.

This new filing arrangement provides another means of phonic training, having nurmerous variations and requiring different refinements. The instructor says, "Find a word that begins like *b*arn." He recognizes readily that words starting with the letter *b* are in the front of the word bank. "Find a word that begins like *many.*" This letter clue is in the middle of the bank. "Find a word that begins like *wind.*" This time he looks to the back of his bank. "Find a word that begins like *tree.*" Not only does he need to decide that the *tr* beginning sound is filed under *t* but also he has to select the word "triangle" from among "the" and "thermometer." This requires a number of decisions, based on precision of sound and letter, or phoneme and grapheme, distinction and association. All in all this is a profitable day.

The next day is started by a silent reading examination of the "Back Yard" dictation, along with an underlining of known words. He underlines: "Our," "Back," "Yard," "trees," "the," "biggest," "tree," "a," "sugar," "maple," "climb," "and," "I," "sit," "in," "small," "stream," "springs," "neighbor's," "wet." Then the instructor paces him through the oral reading of the selection. This way he also produces the words: "easy," "often," "foot," "of," "is," "from," "my," "always." This oral reading is less word by word than previous readings. Now he is grouping words and changing expression on such phrases as "the biggest tree," "I sit in the tree," "of the yard," "my neighbor's yard," and "always wet." Again a number of forces are propelling. Because the boy has produced the ideas, the semantic or meaning clues are compelling. The syntactical word order is his coinage and this facilitates recognition. He now knows certain words and recognizes them almost instantly; this helps him bridge the gap to other words. The instructor's supplying him with the words he does not recognize keeps the idea of what he said viable and helps recognition. In brief, his language, his experience, his word recognition power are serving him well.

Again he prepared a TW, DW, and KW word log.

Total words (TW): 51
Different words (DW): 35
Known words (KW): 28

It should be noted that inflectional changed words such as "tree" and "trees" are being counted as different words and entered in the word bank separately. In the early dictation "bird" and "birds" were entered similarly.

Thus a number of *structural analysis* factors have been introduced and refined. The words that were traced were marked by syllables or sound units. Ability to cope with sound units is a skill useful not only for recognizing words, but also in establishing the understanding that each syllable has a beginning sound just as does each word, and in establishing basic phoneme-grapheme associations that will prove useful when attacking words or when, at some fitting future moment, creative writing is introduced. The syllables in "tri an gle," in "ther mom e ter," in "car di nal," in "nut hatch" each have beginning sounds and letters that represent them, just as the words "tree," "my," "from," "stream," "springs," "wet," and so on. Each situation provides opportunity for sound-letter (phoneme-grapheme) association instruction in decoding.

Again the new dictation was typed in column order. This arrangement provides a unique pattern for word recognition in semiisolation practice. Some of the words, particularly those identified during the paced oral rereading, are not as well established as those underlined during the silent reading. Because this is so, these words sometimes evoke a recognition challenge. For instance, the boy we have been following does not recognize "easy" at sight. This gives the instructor an opportunity to aid the student in beginning to develop sound word recognition strategies. She first proceeded by writing the word in syllables: "eas-y." When this does not help, she points to the fact that in the first syllable, "eas," the second vowel is silent and the first sounded as it did in "eat" (ēs). The moment he says "eas," he is able to bridge the gap to "easy." Such word attack teaching situations are priceless, because, although pupils recognize that at this point they can unlock words on their own, when given guided help, they see how functional these procedures can be. This kind of resolving of a word problem facilitates recall of what is done and the possible use of similar actions in new situations. In the case we are considering, because the procedures are successful and because the student is not overwhelmed or embarrassed but helped in a quite firm manner to determine the word himself, the entire teaching-learning episode proves highly motivational. Gradually fears and anxieties are being offset by security and achievement.

On a number of occasions he locates known words in books, newspapers, magazines, and the like. Now he is encouraged to browse in the clinic library or in the materials center. To browse means to try reading, to examine illustrations, to locate known words, and so on.

By now the instructional activities engaged in are of such a number that it is wise to enumerate them. Doing so serves a number of purposes. It helps the student recognize in a specific way the skill activities he is and can engage in. It also provides the structure for planning a daily and sometimes weekly program of activities. This introduces the student to *action planning* and gives him an opportunity to make choices regarding his instructional program. It gives the instructors an opportunity to see what preferences the student has, to see if he selects challenging tasks or is not secure enough to do so, to see how well he recognizes what he needs to work at in order to achieve at a higher level.

Activities performed to this point and listed are:

1. Selecting any word to trace.
2. Syllabalizing words and checking dictionary.
3. Dictating.
4. Rereading dictations.
5. Locating known words in books, etc.
6. Underlining known words.
7. Phonic training: visual-auditory discrimination of word beginnings.
8. Listening to teacher reading.
9. Illustrating dictation.
10. Filing words in word bank.
11. Using word bank for phonic training.
12. Sharing with others stories, word bank, illustrations, library books, etc.
13. Categorizing words in word bank.
14. Dealing with a column listing of dictated account.
15. Preparing a word log (TW + DW + KW).
16. Making new words by making inflectional changes.
17. Free reading.

Now each morning (or week) students start the day by planning activities to engage in for the day. Even though at this point in progress some of the activities are fairly well determined by the students' achievements and natures (dictation, marking known words, rereading, illustrating), other related activities can be selected. To facilitate matters each activity can be listed on a 3″ × 5″ card. Each card in turn is numbered. Students select certain activities and record the numbers on the planning sheet. On the other hand, the activities can be kept in a list as done above.

Students understand from the beginning that some decisions are made by the on-goingness of the program. Others are made by the teachers.

This latter is an option that is always kept open. But also many decisions can be made by the students. The students now discover that activities take time and that some take more time than others and that the planning done is governed also by the time factor. Invariably the reaction of students to the time awareness is astonishment that the time literally seems to vanish. They have been so busy—so fruitfully engaged —that only vaguely have they noticed that often the instructional hour has ended almost before it started. This regard for and attention to time is one of the best measures of the nature of the instructional efficacy.

Second, what to dictate about becomes a crucial factor in the instructional program. At the same time it can be the teaching bonanza. It is crucial in the sense that dictation, because it is so vital, must not be allowed to deteriorate into a "what do you want to talk about today" circumstance. This is one of the quickest ways to short-cut progress and undermine instructional success, as well as learner attitude.

On the other hand the question of what to dictate about is the instructional bonanza. In the first place it is a marvelous way to convey the idea that reading is a process and not a product. Reading is a way of getting information and acting upon it cognitively. Second, what-to-dictate-about is as rich in possibilities as the school curriculum, or better yet, as the world of knowledge. In brief, the entire curriculum is available for use, from social science and the humanities, to science and technology, to the exciting world of numbers, and certainly to the wide world of literature and drama. The question must never be, "What do I dictate about?" but rather, "How and what do I select from the enormous number of opportunities?"

Third, this is the time to utilize to as full advantage as possible, but without grinding it into the ground, the pupils' interests and tastes. Every student has preferences, likes and dislikes, aptitudes and abilities. Some of these are identified during the testing and are featured as highlights in the test results reports. Others, though, are learned about by talking with and listening to the students. Everyone, and especially a person who has experienced difficulty, wants a confidant, a person who listens attentively and not condescendingly, who asks insightful and thoughtful questions, who is sympathetic and compassionate without being solicitous or patronizing. So, during the instruction time that has thus far elapsed, the student and the instructor should become resourceful friends. Almost all the children we have seen through the years want to talk. They talk about school, home, neighbors, likes, and dislikes. Some use talk as an escape, but the discerning teacher knows how to avoid time exploitation by getting on to other things. Even so, this discerning teacher must still provide an attentive ear.

Fourth, because these students are unable to read or are extremely limited in what they can read, they are unable to benefit by either intensive or extensive reading. This inability limits their development of concepts and understandings. Accordingly, to pursue an interest or develop a curiosity in one or more of the many areas of knowledge yields a valuable return. Teacher oral reading is one way of obtaining ideas. Viewing film strips, doing science experiments, and discussing news reports, are all conducive to extending concepts and language. Because of the ensuing dictation, the ideas are likely to become a part of the children's wealth of knowledge. To organize one's thoughts clearly enough to speak about them requires a certain amount of refinement. In brief, this is an excellent way to help students become more sophisticated, while extending their concepts, language, and reading skills.

Some children are quite bitter and withdrawn and quite reluctant to share or air any personal feelings. For these children it is wise to arrange varied contacts. For instance, as stated earlier, the materials center is an informal gathering place where coffee or tea is available along with morning newspapers, current periodicals, and the like. People who gather there sit around four tables arranged in an L shape. This is sort of like a family table and the clinic director often is there, much as a father surrogate. The chatter is light and friendly and kept so by the adults present. But sometimes this is an excellent way to get children to open up. On other occasions instructors and children may leave the building and cross the street to a university-run cafeteria. This is an excellent place and way to provide a different setting and stimulate confidences or slowly put an end to reticences. There, in the presence of college students talking and studying, faculty, university maintenance people, children sense a new and different environment that seems to help them in dialogue. Instructor and child may sit side by side or across from each other; this kind of physical freedom promotes an openness that can be desirable.

In short, what to dictate about is indeed a question. But it is a question of deciding which of many persons, places, things, and events to select. It never deteriorates to a humdrum "What do you want to dictate about today?" situation.

In many ways it is difficult to say which curriculum area has most utility value: current events, such as space exploration, new inventions, holidays, national days, election days, birthdays, weekends, trips, sports, television, and movies; historical events, such as discoveries, explorations, epidemics, governments, heroes and heroines; the theater, and related events; literature and the like; or scientific discoveries and events, such as nuclear power plants, off-shore oil drilling, extensive pipe lines, rendezvous in space. All seem so rich. Yet of them all, it seems that the best criterion for selection is action. Whenever possible we involve children in things they can act upon or do, such as science experiments. Or, we get them to act upon ideas, either ones they are personally involved in or national concerns, such as medicare, Watergate, and no-fault insurance. To act upon either things or ideas, or both, is the most fruitful stimulus for dictations.

In the case of the student we have been considering, with the advent of a new week the instructor keeps the instructional procedures going by introducing a simple but interesting science experiment. She had placed this on the planning sheet early, as her way to keep the child interested and involved. The dictation that follows tells what the experiment was and how the student responded.

THE CHEMISTRY OF FIRE

First we took a deep saucer and melted the end of a candle to make it stick to the saucer. We put some water into the saucer. Then we lighted the candle. We put a glass quickly down over the candle. Water from the saucer rose up into the glass and the candle went out. This was because the candle had used up all the oxygen in the glass and no more oxygen could get into the glass.

The nature, quantity, and quality of the dictation is readily recognized. The orderliness of ideas is good. It is structured by the circumstances. This retelling of an action experiment is an excellent way to develop appreciation for and understanding of sequence. Sequence is indicated by consequences, and this is evident in the dictated account. The sentence length varies from some simple subject-predicate-object type simple T units to complex structures with qualifying and constraining clauses. The vocabulary reflects the nomenclature of what was done: "chemistry," "deep saucer," "melted," "oxygen," "candle." The idea density is considerable.

A word log reflected the change.

Total words (TW): 82
Different words (DW): 45

The next day when he rereads the typed copy, the number of known words underlined increases rather sharply. Of the 45 different words, 27 are underlined, and 8 more are added when the teacher paces his oral rereading of the account. Only 3 of the 35 different words are already in his word bank: "the," "a," and "and." These three are connectives of the kind that are likely to reoccur whenever one uses language.

Because so many new words are being recognized (32 words) they are not added to the word bank for three days. Each day the child rereads the dictation silently, then orally. Then he deals with it set up in column order. The reasons for doing this are discussed carefully with the student. It is of utmost importance that he understand as best he can why things are done as they are. On a close one-to-one basis this kind of teacher-pupil instruction-learning understanding can be rather readily accomplished. This kind of understanding is essential for all instruction, whether remedial or developmental. Pupils should always know why they are doing what they are doing. This is the best way to develop learner insight and cooperation. Proceeding this way makes the student an active participant.

This sequence of instructional activities is an outgrowth of the science experiment vitality and the resulting dictation. As a result certain actions follow almost naturally on each of the next three days: silent rereading, oral rereading, underlining words a second time, coping with words in column order, using words for phonic training, locating the words in other contexts. Each action tends to reinforce recall and retention.

A word bank can become a liability if words are added without making such efforts as described, to be certain that they are well established. The instructor should be careful that quantity of words does not take on a disproportionate value. It is not the number of words but the quality of retention that is important. If words are hastily added to the word bank, they may be just as hastily forgotten and thereby cause an anxiety about the efficacy of what is being done.

A new instructional task is introduced intended to be more demanding and to further facilitate recall and retention of words. The words in the dictation (82) are put in columns, but in random order. Thus the student has an opportunity to recognize the words in the semantic-syntactic order as dictated, in the semantic column order but not left-to-right syntactic order, and now in random order with semantic clues to recognition greatly reduced. Experience has taught us over a period of years that the random order arrangement has great utility value. The arrangement is just short of being a words-in-isolation test. Some semantic clues are still present. Words like "saucer," "candle," "oxygen," "water," and "glass" are nomenclature of the experiment and thereby help trigger recall of other related words.

As a result the activities for the daily planning are almost totally established by the needed order of events. Time is always set aside for dealing with student choice activities, too. The first of the three days he chooses to browse in a science-experiment book. The other two days he selects teacher reading. This opens a fine opportunity. On one day she reads about another experiment that could be done by hiding pennies under a glass of water. On the other day she reads about the chemical foam spray firefighters use to stop fires anywhere, but especially at airports, on aircraft carriers, and the like.

All in all this lad is so busy each day that time seems to vanish. Even so, instructor and pupil do take breaks of various kinds: a stroll down the corridor to the water fountain, a stop in the materials center, a sharing pause with a neighbor pupil, a visit to the college's science department with its laboratories and library, a chat with the head of the science department, and so on. These pauses are an integral part of the action. They provide a desirable change of pace, they help offset likely boredom before it originates, they provide informal get-acquainted opportunities that can be priceless.

The fifth and sixth weeks are similar in nature. The instruction pattern is now well established and promotes a cycle of events.

Two more dictations are obtained:

How I Go Through Life

When I grow up and go to college I will become a scientist. I am going to live in the country. I may get into television engineering. When I get old I will retire and go fishing like my grandfather does. I will get my wife to clean them like he does.

My Plant Project

We made a terrarium with rock, sand, charcoal, and earth. We got the terrarium box in the science department on the second floor. We got some seeds there, too. In the terrarium I have some grass seed, mustard, and radish seed. I water it every day. Soon I may need sticks to fix the plants on.

Word logs are prepared for each dictation. In addition bar graphs are constructed. The total words (TW) bar is colored green, because the student says, "It grows so much." The number of different words (DW) bar is colored yellow, because he says, "Yellow and green look good together." The number of known words (KW) bar is colored red, because he says, "That's the daily double, the big winner."

Then he is reintroduced to creating ideas by using words in the word bank on his word card holder. At first he responds to this practice hesitatingly and cautiously. But once he is started and grasps the idea and its possibilities, he approaches the "idea construction board" more readily. Ideas he constructs with teacher help are as follows:

He learns a number of interesting facts by doing this. First, he learns he can do this alone and create as he wishes. Second, he needs words like "melted," "drink," "was," "saw," and "made" if he wants to say all he wishes. He begins to recognize in a functional construction-type way that he needs action words or words that tell what happened. What he needs is verbs, of course, to tell what happened to the subjects "thermometer," "rubber birds," and *"I."* Third, he learns the need to check his alphabetized word bank to see what vocabulary is available. Fourth, he can see more strikingly than ever how words fit together syntactically, or on an idea order. Fifth, he discovers that he needs extra copies of some words, like "the," "I," "water," and "in." He is discovering in a functional way that our language is redundant and that words serve different communication purposes. Sixth, he discovers a need for words he did not have in his bank: "fish" and "aerial." Because the psychological principle of closure operates when such need occurs, recall and remembering of such words is greatly facilitated. Two days later, after recontacting the words and using them for phonic training and categorizing activities, he places them in his word bank. Seventh, he can have other pupils read what he has assembled. This works very well because he has to help some of them recognize words. One boy did not know "thermometer," so he gets out the original tracing form and helps him use the syllables. Another did not know "aerial." This time, to get syllable help, he turns to the dictionary at the instructor's suggestion. This helps him see how he can, on his own, use a dictionary. He marks the syllables, but still has to tell the word to the other pupil. Thus he has assumed an instructor role and established an interesting bond between himself and one of his peers.

Assembling ideas in this independent creative way using printed words rather than spoken words is a big step toward creative writing. He can put words together and form ideas that others can read, so that in a sense he is writing.

At the suggestion of the instructor, he puts together a thank-you note for the director of the college science laboratory. This, too, is a very functional use of printed or written language. When he finishes, the instructor types the letter for him and then together they put it in the college mail box. Once again he adds words to his word bank.

The "no secrets" understanding is proving its value. At the start the boy was told why and how each activity engaged in was helpful in the learning to read. At first he just listened and seemed not to react. It was as if he questioned the sincerity of the idea of keeping him informed. But because the practice continued with the introduction of each new activity and because the instructor asked periodically, "Do you know why you are doing this?" he began to be attentive.

Now that six weeks of instruction have been completed, they readied for another staffing. This time the staffing form is done jointly. The pupil is much interested in the form and its completion. He wants to know what the WISC scores mean and grins in a silly, reflective way when he is told again he is not a "dummy." The etiological factors provoke interesting reactions. "Was I slow learning to talk?" "Yeah, I didn't like school in the beginning." "What is 'rebellious' and 'motivated'?" A brief discussion leads only to an "ahmmmm."

Completing the current-instructional-program portion is quite revealing. The child knows well the different things he has been doing. He provides a few ideas to the assets column. For instance, he says he thinks he is doing much better at sounding out words, or decoding as the instructor calls it. Yes, he thinks alphabetizing the word bank was a great idea, and he likes referring to the dictionary. He has enjoyed finding "aerial" and trying to help Mike decode. He likes the column arrangement of the words in his dictations.

The liabilities column brings on an interesting reaction. He agrees that he likes attacking words in column order (really almost in isolation) better than when they are in a line. He at one point blurts out with, "It's too much like school." Most of the children we see in the Center have acquired strong negative feelings toward books and reading. It always seems extremely puzzling to think that teachers would year after year try with good intention the same basic books and the same isolated skill activities with which children have already had difficulty. Putting skill type materials on a screen or computer does not alter the circumstance. For a while a new gadget idea evokes some response, but it is soon realized that the same pointless tasks are being done.

The boy wants to know what is meant by saying his voice is high and tense when he reads orally. So they do some tape recording and allow him to hear himself. This does influence his oral reading positively.

Completing the case-staffing form takes a couple of days but is worth every minute of the time. It provides the vehicle for better understanding.

Perhaps equally as fruitful, if not more so, is the arranging and preparing of back-up data for the staffing. The dictations have already been assembled in chronological order in a loose leaf folder, as have the illustrations. To this the bar graphs on words have been added.

This leads to another discussion on the value of immediate recall-type activities and long-term recall. The former are double checks on the same day or the days after. The utility of this is readily recognized and brought on the suggestion that it might be good to end each instruction session with a short immediate-recall or retention session.

Long-term retention checks have been done, too. He has reread what had been dictated each of the six weeks. Then he double checked all the words in the word bank. This, of course, took time, but was well worth the effort. On a few occasions he needed to refer to the dictated syntactic context to recognize a word.

All of this retention-check business required another two days. In brief, this accountability check was pointed, timely, and highly motivating. The pupil feels very much a partner to the teaching-learning enterprise. He knows that if an activity is introduced it is done to help him with an immediate need. He knows what the need is because he knows when he encounters a word or an idea that he does not know. He knows which skills of word attack he is beginning to master. He knows how to check beginning sounds and how to look for syllables and their beginning sounds to decode words.

He has a tendency when reading silently and then orally to guess at words he does not recognize instantly, even though this distorts the meaning. When asked if what he just read makes sense, he answers no and exhibits two interesting signs of tension: rubbing his left leg, and twisting his hair. It seems that his early instruction has led him to conclude intuitively that he should say words and keep going rather than stop and face up to a need. Apparently, too, this kind of oral reading had taken on the characteristics of a test, and in tests one must show up well and not look for help or face up to a need. All of this evoked tension and anxiety, and his two tension signs become a ready cue.

Interestingly enough, when he deals with the same words in the isolation produced by a column order arrangement, he can identify some of the words correctly immediately and try attacking those he does not know. Those he does not recognize and need help with provide excellent "felt need" instructional cues. This led to introducing a WH (*w*ith *h*elp) sign for words. When words are checked in column order we note achievement in three ways: SW (*s*ight *w*ords, or words he recognizes at once); and AW (*a*ttack *w*ords, or words he unlocks by attacking them with skills he has mastered). Always the SW figure is highest, and in turn reinforces faith in himself. Typical scores are: SW—75 percent, AW—15 percent, WH—10 percent. Such sucess offsets frustration.

Word attack skills he is using now are consonant substitution, left-to-right blending, identifying syllables, and attacking by sound units, cutting off some common inflectional endings like "s," "ing," "ly," "ed," sounding out (or trying to) vowel sounds. His biggest problem is guessing and being deceived by misjudged configuration clues: "never" for "every," "from" for "floor," "big" for "box," "cloud" for "clean," and so on.

Consonant substitution is a profitable and engaging word attack skill to acquire. It is profitable because it leads to the construction of words such as: *r*ed, *b*ed, *f*ed, *l*ed, *N*ed, or *b*ack, *s*ack, *t*ack, *l*ack, *J*ack, and so on. In turn, when faced with a word attack problem, substituting a letter may help in the decoding. This is an engaging skill, because students rise to the challenge of creating words. In a sense it becomes a kind of Scrabble game.

From the beginning the boy we have been discussing his been reluctant to talk about personal concerns and feelings. This continues throughout the seven weeks. Even after he seems relaxed and comfortable and shows signs of being pleased with his achievements, he will not openly express annoyance or disappointment and unhappiness. Apparently he has learned not to be too expressive. This restrained, passive way seems evident in his planning. He is willing to plan but will not initiate planning. On no occasion has he come in at the start of the morning and begun to plan. Yet, once we start planning he is thoughtful about what he does and ready to insert activities that need more attention.

Again both parents attended the interview. Progress can be reported in his response to and production or reproduction of ideas (dictation); to the quantity and quality of his dictation, by sentence structure and length, by sequence of ideas, by use of nomenclature, by richness of vocabulary, by aptness of titles, by variety of interests and the nature of his curiosity, by silent reading and oral rereading performance, by word attack skill acquisition, by planning, by attitude and willingness to cooperate, by response to others in the clinic, by his ease in moving about in the clinic environs. The staffing response has all been favorable, and it is agreed that he can stay on in the Center, because we can see that we are able to help him.

At the end of the first six weeks and every six weeks thereafter, the Center instructors visit students' schools and report progress to the teachers involved and to the principals. Not only are reports made but also further understanding is sought. How are the children doing in school? Are any changes showing up? If so, what are their natures? By and large, teachers are cooperative and so are principals. We want to be as certain as possible that we work jointly: the Center, the school, and the home. Children are much aware of the united effort and are responsive. Parents are often bitter about school efforts, and this gives them an opportunity to acquire new understandings. Schools are concerned about instructional failures and need to be reassured. In the majority of instances, the joint meetings and efforts are quite fruitful. On occasion the Reading Laboratory School supervisor accompanies the instructors. At times teachers and principals come to the university Center. And on occasion, if circumstances warrant, the Reading Study Center director sits in on meetings.

For some children, and parents as well, this first six weeks period proves to be testing. Usually, by the time children are brought to the Center, other avenues of help have been tried and found wanting. So there is much concern about our ability to help and our readiness to accept children. At the end of six or seven weeks of teaching we are in a much better position to offer some prognosis. All our teaching is viewed as being diagnostic. By the end of six weeks we know better the nature and extent of the changes to be made and the likely rate at which the changes may be acquired.

The instructors learn an extremely important lesson about teaching: "If you cannot communicate with, understand, and teach one child, it would be foolish and unfair to attempt to teach a group of 8 or a class of 30." This is a priceless lesson to learn and should be the price exacted from all novice teachers. They also learn that the year-long apprenticeship in the Center provides enough time to try different techniques, to reflect over actions and performances, to consult with the school supervisor, and the Center director, to attend staff meetings, and to see other teachers in action, to understand the foundation processes and structures that ability to read require, to be versatile and creative in their planning. Above all they learn to avoid stereotyping the children; they learn that each child's capacity, social and emotional maturity, and rate and style of learning varies and must be understood.

It must be understood that the successes we have described in defining Stage 1 are generalizations derived from careful study of well over 2500 children, and that the case described so far is somewhat typical. This means, though, that there are many and wide variations among the children. Also, because the variabilities are so numerous, they cannot all be described here. Instructional resourcefulness in terms of knowing the reading process (pedagogy) and in terms of sound mental hygiene (therapy) is essential. To describe some variations seems fitting.

Ed was an outgoing lad who readily initiated conversation. He enjoyed relating anecdotes and usually started a tale with, "Do you know what?" These tales of his provided a fund of material for dictation. Many of them centered about projects he did at home and in the cub scouts. He seldom if ever spoke about school.

Rereading of dictation required considerable teacher pacing. His oral rereading was slow, word by word, and with an unnaturally high pitched voice. He would yawn frequently and rub his eyes. In the early phases his presilent reading and underlining of words was so slow and time consuming that instructor pacing of oral reading (an instructor-pupil effort) was done. Then on a second day he was asked to underline words. Usually, too, he acquired a word or two each day by tracing. The number of tracings needed was small (two or three), he blended phoneme-graphemes very well and was attentive to other specifics. Somehow he obtained a certain security and confidence from the actions.

In his oral rereadings his attack on a word not recognized at sight was to try a letter-by-letter sound-letter synthesis way of blending. Even though this approach is replete with pitfalls and inconsistencies, this was his in-school indoctrination and apparently was reinforced at home. To help Ed overcome this reliance on one quite untrustworthy technique, the rereading of dictated accounts provided an enormously priceless

opportunity to teach the most basic foundation skill of word attack—
the use of context clues, or the psychological principle of closure, or the
philosophical clue of interpolation—focusing on comprehension.

It seemed useless to ask Ed to skip an unrecognized word and read on
to the end of the sentence. It was necessary to occlude, or cover up, the
word. For this a reverse of the word window card was used. At the
end of a pencil was affixed a card about an inch in length and one-
fourth of an inch in width. Then the word in question could be occluded
while Ed read on. It took repeated opportunity plus teacher steadfast-
ness to get him to use the technique regularly. The advantages are with
the reader. He dictated the account, and the fact that he was the pro-
ducer and creator of the semantics helped. He had selected the word
order or syntax, and this facilitated recall. Once he began to see the
potency of meaning, he saw more clearly how and why phonic analysis
becomes a useful auxiliary aid in the search for recognition and meaning.

To help acquire the idea other instructional practices were used.
Sentences from a dictated account were redone and words were deleted.

We saw some men ——————— on Hondas. (working)
We saw where the shock ——————— things were. (absorber)

Another procedure was to delete a word and provide two words from
which to select.

$$\begin{array}{c}\text{gym}\\ \text{I was in the} \quad \text{show.}\\ \text{barn}\end{array}$$

$$\begin{array}{c}\text{straight}\\ \text{Rusty came off}\\ \text{strong}\end{array}$$

$$\begin{array}{c}\text{stuff}\\ \text{I had to} \quad \text{up my muscles.}\\ \text{tighten}\end{array}$$

Each arrangement provided a different challenge while focusing
on the basic task: the use of context clues. In some instances the words
deleted were varied grammatically. Sometimes only a noun or nouns
were deleted and at other times a verb or an adjective or an adverb.

Ed handled sequential lists of his dictation (column order) readily.
He liked the idea, because he responded so well to attacking a word. He
was introduced early to scrambled or random order lists. This is a
column order arrangement in which the words do not occur in the syntactic order in which they appear in the dictated account but in a scrambled arrangement. This proved a useful way of stressing again the power

of meaning. If Ed failed to recognize a word at sight, he would return to the dictated account and locate and recognize it in context.

This kind of instruction led to an interesting happening that persisted for a while. When Ed reread his dictation, he started making meaningful substitutions. Apparently two things were happening. First, his eye-voice span was increasing. In other words his visual intake or his eyes were running ahead of his oral output or pronunciation, but he had grasped the meaning. This is one of the most astounding skills of able oral reading at sight: the substituting of fitting words thus keeping the oral reading going. The substitution is undoubtedy intuitive, occurs rapidly, and is not premeditated.

Ed resorted to another attack device that had limited value. He would attend mainly to the initial letter or letters. Words he substituted reflected this. This proved an ideal opportunity to introduce Ed to vowels and vowel keys. Certainly he had heard about vowels and had apparently been drilled in the art of sounding vowels and trying to memorize regulations that influenced vowel sounds. He had not, though, seen how, when one reads for meaning in a meaningful context, unlocking or decoding a word by sounding it out served an immediate need. The teaching of phonic analysis skills in isolation and in skill books has been the ruin of innumerable children.

Up to this time Ed had been using the dictionary, as had the child we discussed earlier. He had seen phonetic respellings and diacritical markings. Now he was introduced to the vowel key at the bottom of each dictionary page. Then he was started on the construction of his own key. For this a 5″ × 8″ card was used. He started with the long *ā* sound and chose as his key word "dāy." Under the word "dāy" he put a small calendar to help remind him of "dāy." When he could identify readily spoken words that had a long *ā* sound, he moved on to the long *ē,* and used "mē" as his key word and a picture of himself as his picture clue. When he could readily decide that a word had either a long *ā* sound or a long *ē* sound, he added another vowel, the long *ī* sound. The key word chosen was "īce," and the picture clue was a cake of ice. In this way, step by step, he added the long and short vowels and the *r*-influenced vowels to the key. The vowel key then appeared as follows:

a	*e*	*i*	*o*	*u*
dāy	mē	īce	ōld	mūle
căt	nĕt	sĭt	cŏt	cŭp
cär	fërn	skïrt	scöre	spür

This was a long process but one that began to yield a good return. We selected one-syllable words as key words, so that attention could more readily focus on the right letter and the vowel sound being represented.

This also led to vowel substitution activities as follows:

	net	sin
	not	sen
cat	nut	sun
cut	nat	son
cot	nit	san

When he could shift vowel sounds and speak the newly created word correctly, he was well on his way to attacking words by using more than the beginning sounds only. At first the picture clues proved especially useful. Of course he encountered variations and soon saw the need to add words to the key for the double vowel situations.

bō/at bel/ēve again brĕ/ad

(agĕn)

The teacher oral reading and the use of pupil predictions at pauses in the reading book *How To Be a Nature Detective* (Milicent Selsain, Scholastic, 1966) proved most useful. The very design of the book prompted the eliciting of predictions. Prior to this Ed had predicted reluctantly. This book got him involved and was an impetus to his use of predicting in other books. Of course the pause to predict was all done to prepare him for the reading process of predicting, reading, verifying or anticipating selections evidence, and making decisions. These pauses to reflect on what was heard and to predict thereby what might follow was excellent preparation for later use of D-R-T-A or directed reading-thinking activities (4).

This D-R-T-A preparation was augmented by the use of sets of pictures in sequence. Using a sequence of four pictures, Ed was shown the first two and asked to predict what would follow. After he had told what he thought and why, he was shown the remaining two pictures and asked to select the one that best fit the circumstances as the next picture and of course to tell why. In other instances he was shown three of four pictures and asked to rough sketch what he thought would appear in the fourth. Each of these activities required a search for evidence, a discerning of the value of the evidence, and a confirmation or denial that the anticipations made were well founded or not.

Ed had expressed interest in constructing a radio receiver, stimulated by observing the project of another child. They pursued this by teacher reading of science materials on radio principles and construction processes. Diagrams were carefully examined, and parts identified. In so doing they were starting on the attribute and function level of concept attainment: in this instance, the building of a radio receiver. At every opportunity the instructor raised questions, trying to elicit logical and creative thinking, as well as predicting. The teacher raised the question, "How far away might the stations be that we can hear?" evoked much thought. This provoked a discussion of distances and how to measure them. This was approached through an examination of maps, looking at local areas and surrounding states.

Each day Ed devoted about twenty minutes to this project. Other activities were pursued constantly. Dictation resulted that was almost of the diary or log type. So to supplement this, pictures were taken of the step-by-step process.

A visit was made to a local radio station. Pictures were taken and explanations offered by the director. This time, rather than dictate about the visit, he did an interview-type accounting.

When the pictures arrived he assembled them in the order allowed by his dictations. Then he dictated captions for each.

This project spanned about three weeks and was highly productive. The different phases of the construction led to Ed's sharing other events that had been important to him. Each conversation, because that is what they developed into, became in a sense a catharsis for Ed, a revealing of interests and attitudes.

He also did chemistry-type experiments with colors, organized a slide show, wrote poetry, listened to records, did independent reading or free reading, a motorcycle series, constructed a spook house with mask making, formulated recipes, and made a visit to see a skeleton. At this point Danny, another lad in the Center, joined Ed. This was a marked departure for Danny, who had a reputation in school and at home for strained peer relationships. His conduct in the Center had been marked by short attention, frequent trips to the water fountain, and visits with others, largely to be annoying. But Ed's involvement crossed Danny's curiosity threshold, and the latter showed he was quite capable of a healthy, positive interaction with another child. As a result they joined forces on a variety of other activities, such as writing with invisible ink, a visit to the computer center, and a visit to the university's solar home.

The two did several joint dictations. Now an interesting discovery was made. Danny displayed for the first time a considerable skill with dictation. His dictated accounts were excellent, showing a marvelous flare for language.

Ed could not read all of Danny's dictation, but this didn't prove distressing. Danny sat by to pace him along. On the other hand, Danny could read all that Ed produced. So to vary the style and offer some challenge Ed would scramble by sentences his original dictations, and Danny would unscramble them.

Another activity initiated by Ed's instructor was the purchase of a pet rabbit. The instructor had reviewed this idea with the parents and obtained their approval. Ed's father helped Ed build a house and pen for it. In addition the instructor had loaned Ed her camera and supplied a roll of film. The resulting pictures led to spontaneous dictation and a picture book with picture captions. This resulted in his most comprehensive and productive enterprises. It led to the reading of *Rabbit Hill* (Robert Lawson, Viking, 1944), to a study of materials on rabbit care, and to a vocabulary of rabbit nomenclature, plus a modern version of the hare and the tortoise.

The instructor's comment on Ed after five months was:

> I have watched his confidence and self-esteem grow. He has shown increased willingness to create and share, to become involved in teacher read materials, to predict and comment. He is livelier, more out-spoken, shows more leadership and a readiness to make decisions about how he will spend his instructional time.

At the fifth staffing session (at the end of 27 weeks), a somewhat similar comment was made by the instructor of the child we discussed earlier. That child was more secure about his actions and in many ways had acquired a different posture. He was more erect and poised and ready to smile. His interests were varied and intense. He was very responsive to his growing sight vocabulary and delighted with his bar graphs. He was especially pleased to turn to magazines, newspapers, and encyclopedias and to "read." He was also greatly pleased with his increasing ability to attack a word not recognized at sight.

Other activities now introduced into that child's program were to read daily, and as he read to mark any word he could not get on his own. Later he would obtain instructor help. This led to a word-attack soul searching each time and became very pointed. Always the first question asked by the instructor was, "What part of the word is giving you trouble?" For instance, he was unable to cope with the word "practice" in the sentence "To be a good wrestler one must practice every day." He had trouble with the "ac" part, as well as "tice." First, they divided the word by syllables: "prac tice." Then a look at his vowel key, on which he now had long and short vowels, caused him to try the short $\breve{a}$ sound and come up with the first syllable. At this point the instructor had him turn to the context and read the sentence in which the word occurred, and he then suddenly pronounced, as if in exclamation, "practice." The fact that the final syllable was not a long $\bar{\imath}$ situation had also confused him.

The instructor made a record of such attempts and the following day presented the attempts again so that the student might recall what he did or what was done to decode the word. This reviewing of the steps taken to unlock a specific word not only aided recall but also retention and use of the skills.

Experiences like this, coping with actual first-hand need situations, always prove helpful. Students are unthreatened and are not frustrated. The instructor is not only helping them decode a needed word but at the same time is aiding them in the development of a sequence of skills that will enable them to become an independent reader.

In addition, attempts like this, whereby students deal with words in a context, provide priceless opportunities to show the interrelatedness and priority of comprehension and word attack skill command. Emphasis in reading is always first on comprehension, on understanding what has been written. In the instance cited, if the pupil had been more attentive to meaning and used context clues, he might have recognized the word, as well as used some phonic skill. When coping with words in context, the order for attack is:

1. Read to the end of the sentence. (This focuses on meaning, through the principles of closure or interpolation.)

2. Break the word into syllables and note structural and inflectional changes. (This results in reducing a word into phonic units that can be dealt with.)

3. Apply phonics (sound knowledge). (Now the sounds that letters are to represent can be blended together.)

4. (If the above three actions have been taken and one has not succeeded, then help is needed. However, the person seeking help should now know quite specifically why.)

By now the boy's vocabulary had increased to the point where he could handle first-reader level materials comfortably. So he was introduced to D-R-T-A procedures. Selections or stories were reproduced so that the likely onus of a first-reader book could in part be eliminated. Of course, the child knew that this was being done. On the other hand, more useful was the ability to deal with a page or two more readily because they were loose pages. Because John's sight vocabulary was not constricted to that developed by a basal series, other materials of a first-reader level could also be selected.

A D-R-T-A with only one person can be interesting and beneficial, but it lacks the give-and-take vitality of a group situation. So after the child had learned to use facts to determine their consequences (predict), to read on to determine the accuracy of the predictions, he joined two other students at his level for group-type D-R-T-A's. The first ones were done by the director of the Center, at a table in his office. This arrangement was used to impress the students with the value of and seriousness of such instruction in critical reading. To be a thinking reader requires mental alertness, creativity, decision making, and an open mind.

Each D-R-T-A session took about 20 minutes. Once the group sessions were started, one or two were done per week. Other instructors took over directing the process. But a major highlight was when one of the students took over. Before this was done, the student was readied to direct, by prereading the selection and then deciding on a course of action or the number of pauses and on where to make judgments.

Spelling was also introduced. At first the words were selected by the student from his dictated accounts. The vast majority of students instructed in the Center have an astounding aversion to writing and in turn to spelling. Without a doubt these are areas that have aroused deep-seated animosities. In brief, the children hate them. This is why both activities must be approached and introduced only after enough success has been realized in word recognition and in oral and silent rereading and reading at sight to foster and maintain the confidence required.

By this time, much word-attack training has been done, whereby students are asked to identify letters as they represent different sounds in different words. A good practice is to say: Name the first letter in "big," "fat," "hop," "rabbit," "number," "let," and so on. Or: Name the first two letters in "blue," "flip," "tree," "station," "print," and so on. Or: Name the first letter in "dog," then name the second letter, and then do the same in "not," "six," "go," "on," "it," "will," and "mole." Or: How many syllables do you hear in "number?" Name the first letter in the second syllable. How many syllables do you hear in "wonder," "people," "inside," "final," and so on. Name the last two letters in "slowly," "painted." Name the last letter in "toys," and "smiles." Name the last three letters in "walking," "running," "singing." Daily practice of this kind is productive, develops confidence, and prepares students for creative writing.

When formal spelling instruction was introduced to the boy we have been considering, he was asked to select the words from his dictated accounts and to decide on the number he would deal with. At first he selected only four or five. He marked the words, and then the instructor dictated them. Each word was spoken only once and without distortion. The first day he chose "box," "sand," "we," and "the" and produced each one correctly, but his handwriting was such that the *x* in "box" was almost unrecognizable and the *n* in "sand" was scrawled. Even so, no issue was made about handwriting. That could come later. Now the number one task was to develop spelling confidence.

Each day the child selected a few words. A log had to be kept of the words chosen so that replication did not occur. In addition a bar graph was maintained, showing the number of words tried, the number correct, and the number wrong. The keeping of a graph was a good way to maintain interest and to increase effort. He colored the number correct in red and he wanted no black (number wrong) to show.

He selected only 4 or 5 words each time for about four weeks. Then he upped the number to 10. This posed a word selection problem. So the instructor suggested using a Center spelling list. He agreed to this. First they always made certain he could read each word with ease.

In addition he always checked each spelling effort himself. This self-correction procedure helped him see instantly what errors he had made and their nature. His first error had been producing "dey" for "day." He recognized this as a vowel error and started an error form as a record sheet. He learned how to study a misspelled word by covering it up and focusing on the correct letter order. He learned to close his eyes and visualize the word. Then he covered both the right and wrong production and wrote the word at least two times correctly.

At the end of each week he had a weekly retention check. In the beginning he selected spelling on his planning form only twice a week when he discovered the need for a weekly retention check. Again the instructor reviewed with him the need for long-term retention. At the end of each three weeks an even longer-term retention check was held.

By this time it was apparent that he had cleared Stage 1 and had acquired enough confidence and competency to move on at a different pace and level. He had acquired a sizeable sight vocabulary; he knew quite well how to attack a word both in context and in isolation; he participated in D-R-T-A's individually and in small groups; he was involved in projects and activities that extended and refined his interest; he had read innumerable simple books found in the Center library; he had shared with others and attended to others; he listened attentively to teacher reading. He had experienced a marked change in attitude and confidence. He had always been cooperative in a way, but now he was far more willing. His need for breaks were less frequent, and the breaks he took were of shorter duration. All in all it was felt that he was turned around.

Stage 2 is a middle ground time and is characterized chiefly by a settling into the demands of a more rigorous development. It contrasts with the first stage in that the former might be described as the written-communication stage, during which the children learn that they can communicate using the printed word. In many ways, it is like the learning-to-talk phase of life. Now the children know they can read; they know they can think; they know they can do some spelling. Above all, they know when they do not know and are ready to face up to their needs. What they face now is coping with the spiraling reading demands of a spiraling curriculum. Even though Stage 1 achievements require attentiveness and cooperation, they seem not to require the calculated effort and cooperation of Stage 2.

For most of the children we see—those in grade level 4–6—Stage 2 represents a narrowing of the gap in that the instruction in the Center is honing in more sharply on the nature and variability of the curriculum demands they encounter daily in school. An analogy that can be made in this regard is the circumstance of the boy learning to high-jump. At first, once he masters the approach to the bar, his timing and his footwork, he makes easy progress until he begins to approach his limit, then raising the bar just a half inch may make unusual demands. Needed at that stage of jumping, as in almost any other achievement, whether physical or mental, is regular, determined, well-directed practice.

On the other hand students see with increasing clarity how the growth in reading competency is yielding a return in school. They can handle more of the reading demands and, above all, do so with greater self-assurance and determination. These realizations are priceless.

In Stage 2 the number of D-R-T-A's scheduled increases, as does the nature of the content. Perhaps most important is the constant discussion with the students about why instruction is varied. The students know that the procedure of a D-R-T-A is to predict-read-prove, but they do not know why the scholar always uses this procedure and how. Accordingly, each time a D-R-T-A is done, a different approach is used, along with a discussion of why.

For instance, a usual first-learned capability is to deal with a title and predict. Now the pupil needs to know with increasing insight why and how titles are useful to direct thought. It is as one bright nine-year old said when progressing through this stage: "A title is like a newspaper headline." Titles provide cues to the central theme of a selection or story; in a sense they represent a summary statement. Titles are plot binding in that they link beginning and end together. Titles usually are indicative of the nature of the content. Title use encourages divergent or creative thinking. Predictions should reflect this and do so with increasing capability.

Similarly, if schooled readers read a title and first pages in a selection, they know what kind of information they obtain and how to use it. Information obtained in introductory paragraphs, pages, or columns usually provides the setting or geography, the time or history, the characters or social aspect, and the plot direction or sequence. Repeated D-R-T-A's must help make the scholars articulate about the likely facts and their likely value in leading to plot outcome or experiment results.

So children are given different schemes for doing D-R-T-A's. This not only readies them intellectually but it also offsets the boredom resulting from always approaching a group D-R-T-A in the same manner. Ways that may be listed are:

Scheme 1.
 a. Title cues
 b. First two page cues
 c. All but last page cues

Scheme 2.
 a. Title and first page cues
 b. Half the selection cues

Scheme 3.
 a. Title and one-fourth selection cues
 b. One-half selection cues
 c. Three-fourths selection cues

Scheme 4. Title and one-half selection cues

Scheme 5. Title and all but last page cues

Other schemes for pauses to predict can readily be declared. What must be kept in mind is the mental processing of data that each scheme requires. For instance, Scheme I may require data processing as follows:

Scheme 1

QUANTITY	THINKING	RELEVANT DATA
a. Title cue	Divergent	3 facts
b. First two pages cue	Divergent	7 facts
c. All but last page cue	Convergent	16 facts

The reader referred to in this table needed to use the 3 cues in the title in a creative, divergent way and consider a number of plausibilities. The 7 facts on the first two pages were those relevant to the plot outcome and needed to be screened from those not relevant. Then they had to be weighed for greatest predictive value and for interrelatedness. At the same time speculations based on title cues had to be screened and firmed or rejected in light of the new information. The 16 relevant clues on the next pages placed an additional burden on the mind. The number of relevant facts alone totaled 26. To assimilate 26 discrete facts in rote manner would be overtaxing the mind. Accordingly, the reader needed to find generalizations and schemes in order to hold, manipulate, and make judgments based on the evidence.

327

Children need to be alerted to all this. They must learn to seek the truth by not overlooking the likely consequences of facts and by making sound decisions. The art of reasoning while reading is no more difficult to acquire but just as demanding as is the art of clear thinking. The printed word is merely a source of cues. It is true, of course, that clarity of writing, honesty of writing, and the nature of the context makes a vast difference. Graphs, charts, and maps, while very useful, can be highly misleading, as can illustrations. Similarly, oral presentations can be clear and unemotional or can be vastly distorted by tone and gesture.

Creative writing is a major part of Stage 2. Sometimes creative writing becomes a part of Stage 1, as the early transitional signs become evident. The most significant ready signs are: student willingness and aptitude at creating ideas on the feltboard holder, using word bank words; ability to deal with phoneme-grapheme relationships on both a decoding and encoding basis; and, ability and willingness to write.

It is the last item, ability and willingness to write, that poses the biggest hurdle. Literally every student we see has acquired such an intense dislike for writing that their feelings can best be described as a deep-seated hatred for writing. Invariably their handwriting is a warped form of scribble. It is this scribbled aspect of students' efforts that perhaps is most indicative of the degree of reaction to their inability to "measure up." In only rare instances does the handwriting inability result from a lack of dexterity. In only rare instances, too, does a child leave the Center having acquired excellent handwriting. These children know they cannot read, and they realize even more that they cannot spell. Yet they have been forced to copy words to learn handwriting, most often words they could not read, and they have been forced to try to spell words they could not read.

The hate these children have for spelling and writing reflects the deep-seated negative aversion they have acquired to reading in general and spelling and writing in particular. Any error made in writing is strikingly apparent, especially when they have been censored in red, or any color for that matter. Unless oral reading efforts are recorded, the errors vanish with the saying, but not so in writing. Even a cursory examination of writing efforts shows such children making endless erasures, along with undecipherable scribbling.

Creative writing must be defined to mean any writing that a pupil does. The meaning must not be restricted to composing a story. It means any writing, such as a note, a message, a memo, a question, a diary statement, an account, a poem, a letter, a recipe, a set of directions, a play, and so on.

Because the children feel so negatively about writing, we have found it necessary to use means for daily planning which would not involve writing. One of the ways devised was to put each instruction activity on a separate 3″ × 5″ card and number the cards. A pupil's planning sheet for the day might then show: 1, 3, 4, 10. Another scheme was to use abbreviations, such as D-R-T-A, Dict., V-AD, W.B., T.R., I.R. (meaning directed reading-thinking activity, dictation, visual-auditory discrimination, word bank, teacher reading, independent reading).

When children are urged to try creative writing, every effort is made to reassure them that what they try will be accepted. They are urged to encode as best they can, using the knowledge acquired about phoneme-grapheme relationships (auditory perception), or to spell a word as it looks (visual perception), or to try a combination (auditory-visual perception).

In the early phases and indeed for quite some time, we found it helpful, too, to prepare a typed copy of what had been written. The procedure for that is as follows: After a pupil has completed the writing, he or she reads it orally to the instructor, who is careful not to look over the pupil's shoulder, but to sit and listen, thus placing the emphasis on writing where it should be: on the communication of ideas. The instructor then makes a typed copy, not by copying what the pupil wrote, but by having the young author read orally what has been written. This approach frees the instructor from copying exactly what had been written and permits him or her to use accepted letter order encoding. The typed copy is then stapled to the back of the original. This is done at once and in such a way that direct comparisons cannot be made. It is interesting to observe that the pupil reads the typed copy with the correct encoding (spelling) with ease.

On occasion a pupil asks for help with encoding. Asking for help is not encouraged, yet neither is a request refused. The help sought gives the instructor a good idea about the skill or capability lacking. For instance a pupil who sought help with the word "covered" could be asked, "How do you think it begins?" If that does not help he could be asked, "Can you give another word that begins like "covered?" And if that does not help he could be told that "covered" begins the same as "cat." Then he could be asked, "What vowel sound do you hear in "cov," and proceed thus, by sound units or syllables. Help of this kind is useful, indeed, but it should not become crutch help. Instructor understanding and discretion is required.

No comparison is made by the instructor between the typed teacher encoded copy and the pupil's encoding. The child's effort is not only accepted but also quality performance (ideas presented, the way they are presented, phonological accuracy, and accepted letter-order encoding) is recognized. For example:

The rket   and the arpaln   bo   had   wngs.
  (rocket)   (both)

In this production "the" and "and" are encoded in the accepted letter order. The word "rocket" had the correct beginning letter and the last three letters. The word "arpaln" shows beginning letter accuracy and recognition of need for an *r* in "air," the second syllable has been started correctly, with a *p,* and also contains *a, l,* and *n.* The word "both" has the beginning consonant *b* and the vowel *o* correct. "Wings" is almost correct ("wngs").

Perhaps what is equally as important, if not more so, is the degree to which this encoding attempt shows a grasp of phoneme-grapheme relationships. For instance, a combination that could be singled out for study is the *pl* in "plane." Auditory and auditory-visual training can be done. Needs are strikingly apparent in such circumstances, perhaps even more so than in spelling instruction, when the pupil responds to a dictated word. The caution that must be exercised is that of not depressing the student by singling out too many needs to be dealt with at one time. It is far better to select only one or two. A positive attitude and a willingness to try must be maintained.

Auditory refinement is done first. Do "play" and "please" begin alike? (yes), "play" and "plow"? (yes), "play" and "boy"?(no), "play" and "plot"? (yes), "play" and "new"? (no), and so on. Because children often find it difficult to discriminate between a single consonant and a consonant blend, auditory discrimination exercises such as the following are helpful: Do "peace" and "play" begin alike? (no), "plow" and "price" (no), "plan" and "place"? (yes), and so on. Or: Which of the following words has the same beginning sound as "please": "pin," "play," or "print"? Required in these kinds of exercises is the skill of auditory (phonic or sound) discrimination.

This accomplished, proceed to visual-auditory discrimination. In this procedure the pupil is given pairs of words to read:

play	man	back
sun	please	plan
pan	prayer	plow
plane	ply	low

The instructor provides a cue word and the pupil underlines the letter or letters that represent the beginning sound. For instance for the first group of words the key word spoken by the instructor is "plenty." This requires the student to listen to "plenty," notice the beginning sound as represented by *pl,* identify and discriminate "play" from "sun," select "play," and underline the *pl.*

The biggest anxiety to overcome in creative writing is the fear of being wrong. Instructors must be most sincere when they say they will acknowledge any writing attempt and help identify successes and a need or two. Pupils are readily embarrassed by their inability to encode and by their handwriting. The trick is to get them to keep trying. If they continue to try—and do so preferably on a daily basis—they soon begin to see improvement. When the improvement aspect is recognized, then the belief in self is bolstered and greater effort is made. Here are some examples:

ALL ABOUT ME

i am Bill Spatz and i like to run and jump and red on lvator and i like to run on minebiks and i like to play basball.

John and Jimmy and Bill got in the amunition wagine and brote it up on a hill. They unhcht the horses and pusht it at the pirites bote. The pirites trid to stop it but thay count.

The first example shows repetition of "and i like to," a redundancy that seems to provide some security for the writer. Frequently, too, when this occurs ideas are connected by "ands." This may reflect inattention to punctuation and its value, but more likely is indicative of a willingness to go on. When marked encoding difficulty occurred with elevator ("lvator"), the struggle resulted in grammatical laxness "ride on elevator." Fourteen of the 17 different words are encoded in accepted letter order and that is a considerable success. The attempts like "red" for "ride" and "minebiks" for "minibikes" do show encoding power.

The second illustration reflects a different kind of effort and production. This was part of a creative story the student was doing. In it he had five episodes. This shows greater willingness to use a more polished language and a different kind of creative production. Spelling, when writing (*functional spelling*), frequently shows odd kinds of errors, such as "wagine" for "wagon," "brote" for "brought," "pusht" for "pushed," and "trid" for "tried." On occasion, and definitely at a different time, we ask students to spell "pushed," "wagon," "tried," and so on, and then in response to dictation almost always they spell the words correctly.

Another instruction feature of Stage 2 is an intensive use of inquiry reading practices (4). This is a procedure whereby a student selects a topic of interest and then examines it in some detail. One lad chose the Civil War. He did so because his great-great grandfather had fought with the Confederates. Dan pursued this topic for five months. He read or was read to from a varied supply of history books. First he read about major battles: Gettysburg, Vicksburg, Richmond, Atlanta, and so on.

He visited Gettysburg and constructed a model panorama of the battlefield. When he was finished, all the children in the Center gathered about and listened to his account. He also inquired into causes of the war and did a booklet filled with both dictated accounts and some creative writing.

Preparation for the exhibit and the booklet required a search for materials. Visits were made to the university library. One of the university professors was consulted. Letters were written to procure various pamphlets and brochures.

Usually, every six weeks a project-sharing time is planned in the Center. Pupils ready their projects for display and explanation. Then all the children in the Center go from project to project and attend to presentation. Questions are encouraged.

Much attention is devoted to concept development. Instead of word banks, as in Stage 1, concept notebooks are maintained. Concepts are usually dealt with in three ways: by concept (1) attribute, (2) function, and (3) class. Thus the concept of "right flank" was enlarged on by Dan. Attributes of flank were listed as: a cut of meat, a side, the right or left of a formation. Function was: to protect a side, to be at the side, to place something on each side. Category or class was described as branches, arms, wings, points of compass, border, moat.

This triple-pronged approach to concepts helps students immensely to acquire and fix an understanding and to make the concept's use more versatile. Dan knew what it meant to "protect a flank" to "out flank" to "turn a flank." The number of concepts thus entered in his concept book may have been small as compared to a so-called vocabulary list, but the concepts would most likely be retained and used.

For those children who come to the Center functioning at the beginning of Stage 1 level, progress through this stage will vary, as might be expected. However, most of them require about a year of intensive instruction before they can clear the hurdle and perform the kinds of tasks which are a part of Stage 2. Progress through Stage 2 also varies, but to a greater degree. Most children require two years, some require less, and others more. On occasion we have had children enter the Center at age 10 and attend until they are sixteen. It is Stage 2 achievements that are taxing. It is the time for steady, determined effort without some of the spectacular gains so strikingly apparent in Stage 1.

Confidence mounts, though, when students realize that they can read and that increasingly the number of books they can turn to grows. We keep many periodicals about, and pupils are encouraged to turn to them, and they do. Time for so-called independent reading increases and on occasion a Stage 2 student may devote an entire instructional hour to "just" reading. Another realization that proves ego-boosting is ability to write. Demands of the second curriculum usually require writing. Accordingly, instruction in the Center capitalizes on this demand by providing writing help and time. This kind of stand-by proves of high utility value. We help the students prepare booklets and the like and make the material as presentable as possible.

A Center newspaper is produced at least twice a year. An editor and two assistant editors are chosen from among the Stage 2 students. Preparation of a paper may require three to four weeks. This is so because the time at the Center is only an hour a day. The pupils are always quite responsive to this project. Dictations, creative writings, word game puzzles, picture captions, illustrations, and the like, are used. One of the best returns obtained from the newspaper production is the editorial effort. Grammatical changes are made, punctuation attended to, and spelling carefully scrutinized. It is always very reassuring to observe how sensitive the older Stage 2 students are about the nature and amount of editorial effort to make. An esprit de corps exists in the Center at all times, but seems to rise to new heights when they all team up on a Center newspaper.

CONCLUSIONS

The objective of this chapter was declared in the first few paragraphs: it is "to build a viable psychology and pedagogy" that may capitalize on the cognitive power and the will to achieve of every partial or totally disabled reader. To dignify their lives, to help them attain noble and redeeming goals, this is the imperative.

It should be apparent, too, the degree to which the psychology and pedagogy detailed is indebted to Fernald, Montessori, Herbart, Froebel, Pestalozzi, Rousseau, Comenius, John Dewey, and Jean Piaget. As Descartes said, "to converse with those of other centuries is almost the same thing as to travel." Above all, I believe, these people have taught us to speak with "an appearance of truth on all things." Like one who walks alone, I have gone slowly and used as much circumspection as possible. This was done so that the practices and procedures advanced and detailed might reflect sufficient planning and time in execution, in refinement, and in pure reason. All was done with the intent of guarding against any likely exploitation of the many young people urgently in need of remedial instruction.

There can be no disabled reader so remote that he cannot be reached. I have devoted much of my life to the investigation of the instructional practices and knowledge outlined here and feel confident that, if devotion is given to their study, any qualified instructor may by these means reach success. I have arrived at the causes by the effect, availed myself of many particulars, and must confess, have not sought out the rare or the recondite to be misled. As Rousseau said so wisely, every experience children engage in is a book that enriches their memories, that ripens their judgment, and that can be turned into a profit. Hence, what the practices defined here are intended to do is to preserve the talents and ambitions, the courage and open-mindedness of disabled readers, and to inspire them to produce the necessary intellectual energy to achieve. There is a natural aristocracy among these children, and this is our boon.

The quantity of the practices provided do make this a long chapter, but into the compass of things to do they represent but a portion of what might have been detailed. Each child is unique and each provides a different instructional history. It would have been ideal to provide a hundred or more case histories and to thereby allow the reader to generalize about the nature and quality of practices that seem both general in nature and most effective. Because this is not possible, the accounts provided are those which have most universality. The details provide sufficient base to permit the able, qualified, and humane teacher to adapt and succeed. It must be remembered that each child is different and that the best pedagogy is to be wise and discerning and never too solicitous and patronizing. True, love can be an exhalting influence, but love alone is not enough.

The fact that girls were not mentioned or used in a case history illustration reflects the fact, stated earlier, that the ratio of girls to boys runs about 1 to 36. This, in turn, is not a reflection on boys, because in my judgment, the great majority of the children we have dealt with come to us because of pedagogy failure rather than psychophysiological ineptitude.

BIBLIOGRAPHY

1. Betts, Emmett. *Foundations of Reading Instruction*. New York: American Book, 1946.

2. Fernald, Grace M. *Remedial Techniques in Basic School Subjects*. New York: McGraw-Hill, 1943.

3. Peterson, Roger T. *A Field Guide to the Birds*. Boston: Houghton Mifflin, 1947.

4. Stauffer, Russell G. *Directing the Reading-Thinking Process*. New York: Harper & Row, 1975.

CHAPTER 13

Partial Disability Children

The clearest distinction between persons of partial disability and extreme disability is that the latter people either cannot read at all or possess only a very limited sight vocabulary of about 20–30 words. Obviously one cannot make a rule-of-thumb generalization like this without providing elaboration. One must consider the rate, maturity, and capacity of the student being diagnosed. A six-year old, after a year in kindergarten and a year in first grade, may be proceeding at his or her rate, maturity, and capacity if he or she can read 30 or so words. On the other hand, the child might not, and then the need for specialized help should be readily recognized. Capacity scores, as determined by a competent school psychologist, maturity as recognized by teacher judgment, may show clearly that a child's rate of learning, even at this level, is not measuring up to expectancy.

On the other hand, if an eight- or nine-year old or older child has so limited a sight vocabulary (20–30 words), then the question of extreme disability is readily answered. These are the children who generally are classified as remedial. However, in many ways Fernald's labels of extreme or partial disability are much more pointed than the labels remedial or corrective. Both of the latter labels are applied according to the extent of disability (9).

As pointed out in earlier chapters, most of the studies in reading disability used as criterion for classification as remedial either one year below grade norm or at most two years below. The folly of this type of classification is readily apparent. If and when a grade norm is used, then the range of scores automatically places one-half the population below the norm and 30 percent or more a year or two or more below grade level. Such classification does not take into account how norms on standardized tests are obtained, nor does it take into account individual differences of rate, maturity, and capacity.

The folly is even more apparent when one considers the differences between an eight-year old who achieves two years below grade norm and a twelve-year old who achieves two years below. The former is a third-grade level child reading at about the level of a typical first grader, whereas the latter is a seventh-grade child reading at about the level of a typical fifth-grade child. Unquestionably, even though both children are two years below grade norm quantitatively, qualitatively the degree of retardation is vastly different. In brief, one cannot convert a grade norm into a grade standard. Neither can one ignore the range of scores or the accepted scatter of scores and the range of human variability. There is no such thing as a standard test, but there are such measuring devices as standardized tests.

Judged by the stages declared in the previous chapter, an eight-year old child in third grade might be in need of the special differentiation of instruction as described under Stage 1. On the other hand the 12-year old, although achieving scores two years below grade norm, is reading as well as a typical fifth grader, or ten-year old, and is attaining at the upper end of Stage 2. Obviously more precise measures are needed; rule-of-thumb classifications, such as two years below grade norm, are almost meaningless and will not do. The label remedial reader must be applied only with the greatest of caution and on a qualitative level.

On the other hand the label corrective reader also must be examined with great care and not be allowed to become a blanket label or become misleading. Generally, it might be said that the 12-year old who is reading quite well but not up to grade norm might be called corrective. But, if this label is used this loosely, then it could very well be that two-thirds or more of the children at any age level are either two years or more below their expectancy or two years or more below their grade norm. Thus, most children could be so labeled, and the label could become meaningless (9). It is far better to drop a label such as corrective and think of such people as developing at different rates, with varying maturities and expectancies. In brief, if instruction is differentiated and individualized, then there are only two classes: the range of developmental children and the extreme disabilities. The former

require typical differentiated instruction and the latter require specialized help.

SCHOOL OR CLINIC

Fernald divided partial disability children into two categories, according to two conditions: obvious causes and faulty conditions. The
obvious causes were the physiological and/or neurological causes and
psychological or emotional causes. The faulty conditions group derived
from faulty experiences either in the home or the school.

It is my experience, as it was that of Grace Fernald, that of the two
conditions the faulty experiences category is by far the largest population. I am convinced that most of the children in need of special differentiation of instruction are so because of pedagogical or social-cultural
failure. In most instances teachers per se are not primarily at fault. A
child who is not achieving well can be spotted readily at any grade level
and particularly at first grade. All one needs to do if there is doubt is
to ask the children who is the poorest reader in a class. They know.
All too often, though, it is a school policy not to act upon children's
needs until they are in third grade or are eight years old. On the other
hand it must be said, too, that in many schools instruction is adjusted
in grades one and two and sometimes in grade three, but beyond this
curriculum demands impose standards and the pupil whose rate, maturity, and capacity is different and atypical is asked to measure up to
curriculum standards or else. Unfortunately the recognition of and
provision for individual differences receives largely lip service beyond
grade three. It is a common cliché among teachers, "If we didn't get
you (pupils) by third grade, we will in fourth." This is the time, too,
when teachers of arithmetic, science, and social science begin to complain that the children cannot read. Invariably these teachers are themselves untrained in the art of teaching the reading of arithmetic, the
reading of science, or the reading of social science. In addition they
do an inadequate job of concept development in their areas. The concept "every teacher is a teacher of reading" is frequently voiced but
seldom dealt with in reality. It is disheartening indeed to know that
almost all states will certify teachers who have had only one course in
reading instruction and that in most states secondary teachers are not
required to take any courses in reading instruction.

Obviously, too, home and society conditions influence children's
attitudes and motivation. That many parents do not read is indeed unfortunate, but what is even more so is the fact that teachers do not.
Children in homes where there are no books or only a very few do not
readily acquire a favorable attitude toward reading. Not only are there

no books but also no magazines and only one or so newspapers. In this day and age, though, most homes have a *TV Guide* and its universality could have as bright a prospect and as wide an influence as the mail-order catalog of a century ago.

Yet schools need not let these circumstances be a total denial. Teachers and scholars have known for years that children are greatly influenced by teacher reading. Three recent studies provide at least a partial answer. In 1967 Dorothy Cohen, working in schools designated as special-service schools because of academic retardation, a low socio-economic population, and a high percentage of ethnic and racial minorities, used second-grade children in nine experimental classes and seven control classes, to study the effects of daily oral reading by the teacher. Besides being read to, the children in the experimental classes also reacted through discussion, drawing pictures, dramatization, and writing stories. Significantly greater gains in both reading and vocabulary were made by the experimental classes (2).

A second study was done by Dorothy Strickland (14), in an attempt to determine how a special literature program would influence linguistically different black kindergarten children. Her study demonstrated a successful method of expanding the language repertoire of linguistically different children to include more standard English.

A third study was done by Beverly Sirota in 1971 (8). She sought to determine the effect of a planned literature program of daily oral reading on the voluntary reading of fifth-grade children. The results of this study showed that a planned literature program could have a significant effect on the quantity and quality of children's voluntary reading.

In addition Richard Petre (5) introduced a program at the junior and senior high school level that spread across the state of Maryland and beyond and into the elementary schools. The idea is astoundingly simple and effective. The plan is to set aside one 30–40 minute period a day for everyone in a school to read. This includes all the teachers, the principal, the librarian, and the secretaries. It is a strange quieting experience to walk the corridors of a large junior high school and see everyone reading. The end result of this idea and of the school-wide follow-up activities Petre discusses is most fruitful. Students' attitudes toward reading and reading achievement are changed, and so is their regard for the school.

It is evident that, while the faulty experience of home and society can be a deterrent, it need not stifle children. Many actions can be taken by the school to offset such lags and, if programs to educate parents are added, progress can be made. Recent efforts in this direction are heartening. The state of Maryland has produced 30 half-hour TV shows aimed at helping adults in general and parents in particular improve their reading abilities, understand the reading process better, and in turn acquire a different attitude about and motivation toward reading (1). All of this is bound to influence the teaching of reading at all levels.

The other aspect of "faulty experience" is the school. Arthur Gates (2) said in the early 1930s that in his judgment most remedial instruction was no more than good first teaching. In brief he was saying that if good first teaching had been done, most remedial instruction would be unnecessary. The outcry against lock-step procedures strongly voiced in the 1880s by Preston Search was and remains an attempt to have reading instruction differentiated. Most of the reading failures stem from such practices. Children are different. They learn at different rates and in different styles. They have different degrees of maturity, different interests and values, and vastly different capacities. It is folly to try to lock-step them into any sort of cognitive-process program. Yet this is what most of the materials offered on the market have tried. The programmed, boxed, skill books, "individualized" efforts are all based on lock-step principles. Most basic reader programs provide similar lock-step recommendations and claim that their fixed skill activities and teacher-posed questions will fit indiscriminately to teach children anywhere. Teacher's manuals which can make slaves and puppets of teachers (13), recommend largely rote-type procedures that require little if any thinking of the children and by and large do not provide for differences in their thinking.

Many of the diagnostic procedures recommended in this text can be grasped and adapted to daily teaching. This is particularly true about measures related to informal diagnoses of oral and silent reading, of writing, and of oral communication. Every time a teacher instructs a pupil or a group she or he must recognize successes and needed areas of development, both collectively and individually. All good teaching is diagnostic.

In the last 20 years or more schools have been employing on an increasingly wide basis so-called remedial reading teachers. Usually the people so employed are teachers who obtained master's degrees in education with a major in remedial reading. Universities and colleges across the country have added such programs to their curriculums. State certification requirements for remedial teachers were declared.

In many states across the country a teacher can qualify to be a developmental teacher of reading and do so by taking only one undergraduate course devoted to the teaching of reading. In some few states, in very recent years, two and three courses are being required, but one of the three is devoted to reading diagnosis and remedial instruction. On the other hand, and in sharp contrast, remedial reading teachers are required to have four or more courses in reading, and three or four courses in the psychology of human adjustment. It is ironic indeed that this is so and as long as such regulations prevail, emphasis will focus on correction rather than prevention and on locking the barn door after the horse has fled.

Remedial teachers in a school usually serve two purposes: to test children referred by teachers and to teach those who seem to need special help. Teachers usually heartily endorse such arrangements, because they can have the disabled and the semidisabled readers, who are usually the behavior problems, out of the classroom for a while. The end result is a dumping of children, a negative labeling, and no prevention.

Gradually, though, alert principals and school executives are recognizing the folly of such a dumping approach and are instituting minor changes. For example remedial teachers in some schools are spending only half a day doing remedial instruction and the other half day collaborating with teachers to help them do a better job of differentiating instruction and improving teaching procedures. This kind of practice represents a gradual shift from correction to prevention. This has also led to a more careful screening of those children singled out for special help by the reading teacher.

In turn, because diagnosis is more meaningful, children of extreme disability are being referred to centers such as the one at the University of Delaware, at Temple University, and elsewhere. Not all schools employ a special reading teacher, and as a result children of the partial disability type continue to find it necessary to attend special centers or clinics for remedial help.

ADJUSTMENT OF INSTRUCTION

Remedial reading teachers usually work with groups of 8, 10, or even more children for 30–40 minutes at a time. It is an impossible task for any teacher to provide the kinds of individualized instruction these children so need. Their progress, therefore, is all too often negligible.

In some schools administrators and reading teachers recognize that such high teacher-pupil ratios are most unproductive and have tried to make some adjustments. Pupils are carefully screened in terms of achievement level and need and are assigned to groups of four to six which can be more effectively dealt with. However, this means that, if a special reading teacher meets with five different groups per day, the total number of children she can help is only 20 or 30. In a building with 20 classroom K–4 there are over 500 children. It is readily apparent that in such circumstances not many children can be "dumped." As a result more careful screening of pupils and their needs occurs, and greater effort is made to differentiate instruction in each class. Most children who are not reading up to a specific grade norm can be effectively helped within the classroom when their individual needs are defined and dealt with accordingly. Those children in need of more specialized instruction because of the extent of their disability will most likely profit from the smaller group size, which allows for more intensified, individualized instruction.

It is regrettable that most of the instructional practices resorted to in the special reading classes can be classified as more of the same. The special teacher engages in about the same type of instructional activities as does the regular teacher and all too often uses the same kind of basal readers in a way that has already proved to be unsuccessful with these children. Skill books are used to develop so-called word attack and comprehension skills. It is true, of course, that now the teacher can police pupil efforts more closely than could the regular classroom teacher. But instruction is not usually geared to specific pupil needs identified while reading, but is governed by the arrangement of the short, tenuous-type skill activities so typical of blanket-type skillbooks. A skillbook prepared to be used anywhere with all pupils can by no means be claimed a tool for adjusting instruction to individual needs. On occasion some teachers say the skill book activities are being used selectively and only if they fit a particular need. The likelihood of that really happening is very limited. Even so, some children do respond to the change of scene, physically and pedagogically, and show progress in response to this effort in their behalf.

The need to keep each homeroom teacher informed proves a demanding challenge. Keeping records of achievement and needs is no small task. Using regular classroom activities and skillbooks to structure remedial instruction also requires careful interaction between the special teacher and the regular classroom teacher.

In those instances when a special teacher individualizes instruction for the four to six children, progress can be made. To do this, language-experience-type activities much as described in the previous two chapters and in an earlier text (11) can be used. In many instances these specially differentiated practices, along with the use of a wider variety of materials such as newspapers, magazines, and library books, combined with the special teacher attention, turn children on, so to speak, and help them make quite commendable progress. It is the attitude and motivation change that a partial disability child may experience that is most fruitful. Such a change is achieved through recognized success, which is best achieved by creative teaching geared to individual needs and strengths without being patronizing.

In some districts pupil attendance is planned on a time basis. A selected group may attend specialized individualized instruction sessions for a period of six to eight weeks and then return to class full time. This procedure can have advantages. It can provide a shot in the arm for children, which may be all that they need to again function without stress in the regular classroom. This kind of procedure necessitates the regular teachers to be closely attentive to the instructional help their children have received and to ways they can best continue helping their children progress.

It is the view of this author that in order to accomplish the shift from correction to prevention, it would be profitable for the specialist to spend half a day teaching children and half a day consulting with teachers. This arrangement would be even more productive if one day a week is totally free for consulting. If children receive specialized instruction only four days a week they in turn can have a full day in their classrooms. This plan provides more time for teacher conferences to discuss practices and procedures and to coordinate effort.

STAGE 3 ADJUSTMENTS

The distinctions between a Stage 3 and a Stage 2 child are in some ways clearly definitive, but in other ways they are not. Almost the same can be said about the distinctions between a Stage 3 pupil and a typical developmental child who has not required intensified individualized instruction. This is so because the pupils are so close to being self-regulatory at their level. They know what to do to achieve the reading goals they have set, to command the skills needed to comprehend the material and make the most of the opportunity, to adjust their reading rates to the purposes for reading and the nature and difficulty of the material, and above all to respond to a situation, interact with it, and transact a course of action.

The teachers not only take on the responsibility for providing an environment and creating an educative experience, they also take into account the powers and purposes of those they are teaching. They are alert to the attitudes and habits that are being created, to understanding the individual as an individual, and to recognizing what experiences lead to growth. They either are articulate about or sense intuitively that the greatest of pedagogical gains are really collateral learnings or the formation of enduring attitudes and interests.

Pupils at this stage have acquired the practice of reading for meaning. If they encounter a term they do not know and cannot grasp from the semantic setting, they turn to a glossary or dictionary. They know the steps toward vocabulary development:

Step 1. Context clues
    A. Language clues (semantic, syntactic, grammatic)
    B. Picture, map, diagram, or graph clues

Step 2. Structural and phonic clues
    A. Prefixes and suffixes
    B. Syllables
    C. Phoneme-grapheme relationships

Step 3. The dictionary
    A. Syllabified word entries
    B. Phonetic respellings
    C. Definitions

Suppose, when reading, pupils encounter the line, "Thunderous applause and cheering greeted his arrival because he had won the exhausting Marathon." To grasp the meaning of "Marathon" and the reason winning it should merit such recognition, alert readers do not let an ignorance of the moment be a handicap. They turn to the dictionary and observe the entry word is capitalized and has three syllables. They check the word's correct pronunciation. A check on definitions provides some word history. The meanings are: 1. a seacoast town in old Greece; 2. the plain near the town; 3. a long foot race, usually over 26 miles in length, like that run in old Greece from Marathon to Athens.

In the process of conceptualization pupils now inquire into the Olympics and their function and into racing. Then they observe that the Marathan fits in a racing category such as the Indianapolis 500, the Triple Crown in horse racing, and the like.

Because of their increasing maturity and scope of interests and wide reading, the Stage 3 pupils question the value of facts in a more discerning manner than previously. Accordingly, when reading Edward Park's article, "A Single Shot on a Spring Day Starts the War" in the April, 1975, issue of *Smithsonian* in preparation for a school sesqui-centenial commemoration, one child comes upon the following, pausing to weigh the facts and their likely authenticity.

> Here in the half-light at Lexington, they saw a chance for it and mounted officers probably drew their pistols. How easy, then, to cock one, to grip it too hard as you yank it from its holster, to loose a harmless shot at the ground. Gunsmiths say that a well-worn flintlock could go off from the presumably safe half way position of the hammer. The war could have started by accident. (4)

This involves the reader in thoughts about pistols of the time and their flintlocks. It may involve him or her in some figurative language analysis for the meaning of, "Don't go off half cocked." Or in a search for a fuller meaning to "the war could have started accidently." Was this the straw that broke the camel's back? Was there really a miasma in the spring air of 1775?

Stage 3 readers have had their natural curiosity aroused, their appetites for knowledge whetted, their interests widened, and their tastes refined. Their minds have become inquiring minds. Questions abound in their thinking. The world is becoming their oyster. Their daydreams are curiosity dreams and increasingly reality is dominating. No longer do they seek escape, either mentally or physically. Their self-images are secure enough to permit them to seek, even to blunder, and to seek again. Not only do they roam widely, but also they are no longer reluctant to share.

Above all, though, they are learning to adjust their rate of reading to their purpose for reading and to the nature and difficulty of the material. Through the skill acquisition of D-R-T-A's, they have learned the art of asking questions, of speculating, of becoming personally involved according to their own experiences and knowledge. They are learning how to marshall their own abilities and curiosities and use them to provide and guide their thinking. They have learned how to use facts and ideas in a critical evaluative way.

Versatility in reading is in many respects the highest level of attainment in the total reading act, whereby printed words strung together syntactically and semantically provide the visual stimulus, and in a sense, the auditory stimulus, for activating the brain. The efficient, versatile reader is also the critical reader. It is naive to say that one set of capabilities (critical reading) develops prior to or is a prerequisite to another set of capabilities (versatile reading). Across the maturing years of a student intellectually, experientially, and pedagogically these skills are acquired simultaneously and are refined at each succeeding level of development. But in the final analysis the highly competent versatile reader is the one who commands all the basic skills essential to efficient comprehension. In brief, the term "efficient comprehension" provides the most distinctive name in that it embraces the concepts of versatile and critical reading (10, 12).

Rate adjustment is determined primarily by the purpose the reader wishes to attain. Usually the adjustment is referred to when a name is applied other than purpose. This results in a focus on rate rather than comprehension, hence the label speed reading or speed of reading. To name it speed of comprehension shifts attention toward the why rather than the how but still fails to do so in the same sense as the term efficient comprehension. In brief, efficient comprehension embraces each of the basic concepts.

Four adjustments of rate are commanded by the efficient reader and are commonly referred to as skim, scan, study, or overview type reading. To *skim* means to pass lightly and swiftly over the surface. Skimming is readily illustrated in two ways that stem from two distinctly different conditions. When people have studied a passage or selection and want to quickly locate a name, a phrase, or an idea, they go back and pass lightly and swiftly over the surface until they find that which they are looking for. Usually this skimming is facilitated by the readers' remembering to some extent where they read the idea. This could really be referred to as a rereading type skimming. By contrast, people may move swiftly and lightly over passages they have not previously read. Now they have no memory aid to help them converge on the specific word or passage. They may be searching for a name and address in a directory, for a title in a bibliography, for a word in a dictionary, for a name in a special listing. In either circumstance the comprehension purpose is to locate specific information that is limited to a point or two or a word or two. The efficient aspect is to proceed swiftly and lightly over the surface. The label commonly applied is *skim-type reading*.

To *scan* is to survey from point to point and sometimes refers to a cursory glancing from point to point. If again one focuses on the comprehension aspect, to scan agrees in good part with the meaning of "to scrutinize." Scrutinize means to look searchingly at minute details. Scanning contrasts with skimming in that the latter is always a swift searching for a point, whereas the former is a searching for related points needed for a specific purpose. It is this searching for points that causes efficient readers to proceed differently. First, they cannot be efficient if they skip points here and there or overlook some. Second, because they are searching for points, they must keep them in mind as they proceed. This requires the readers to give thought to retention and to association. This, in turn, influences their rate. Third, they may have to group the points under categories and this requires not only mental effort but time.

Study-type reading is reflective reading that requires quiet and serious consideration for the sake of forming and grasping ideas and of reaching conclusions. It requires the use of one's powers of discernment, organization, and judgment. Study-type reading may involve pauses to reflect, rereading to reaffirm, and decision making. Unquestionably the rate of reading is different; the pauses require time. Of the three degrees of comprehension, this in-depth achievement requires the most time, or, stated from a rate point of view, results in the slowest rate.

Overview-type reading implies no more than a careful looking over so that one has a picture or idea of the material as a whole. It is more than just seeing, because it involves the intellect and is done with a particular purpose. This is a remarkably efficient skill to command and one that should be acquired as early as possible in the life of a scholar. The able scholar is the efficient seeker of comprehension or understanding. The able scholar recognizes the intrinsic value derived from gaining an overview. It permits her or him to decide that the selection or book is worthy of study. If the book is reread, it is done with the perspective of the entire text. Obviously, overview reading is fast reading and as nearly approaches what is uncritically and commercially labeled speed reading as any of the four adjustments for efficient comprehension.

Each of these methods of efficient comprehension can and should be introduced in the early reading instruction life of any reader. Skim- and scan-type reading can and should be introduced to most children in first grade. This is readily done by having them relocate ideas after an initial reading. They may return to a selection to find a name, or a place, or an idea or a series of ideas. In a group D-R-T-A situation children can be learning to skim or scan as the need dictates when finding the necessary information to prove a point or back up a prediction. If the children are required to read orally the points they have located, the teacher notes the manner in which the information was located. Immediate feedback or affirmation is provided, and the teacher can determine how efficient the performance really was.

Study-type reading can be done quite early by some very bright children but is usually not specifically taught as a skill until a pupil is at about a fourth-grade reading level. Study-type reading should be most purposeful. Students must know how to declare their own purposes and how, when necessary, to internalize the purposes of others (10). They must know how to weigh evidence, screen the relevant from the irrelevant, and make sound decisions. At a later stage they must add to this the ability to determine author authenticity and/or author attempts at slanted writing. Obviously as the reader matures and grows into the intellectual age where logical reasoning is possible (6), the demands are greatly intensified. Wise judgments, even with all the evidence in, may be difficult to determine.

Overview reading can be introduced at about the same time as intensive study reading. Students must be taught how to pace themselves and be wholly attentive to the task at hand: to obtain an overview. Pacing can be done by hand for a while, but must be commanded by sheer will power to be effective. Overview reading is not a Sunday scholar's way of catching up without putting forth the usual effort. Neither is skill in overview reading the kind that can be peddled in the market place as a quick and ready panacea for lazy reading habits.

A good way to begin is to pace a group of children through a book that is easy reading for them. This is equivalent to creating a dry track effect. A dry track is a fast track and that is when horses establish records. Show children how to hold a book and pace their reading down a page to a count of 10 and so, continuing page-by-page counting to 10 for each page for about twenty pages. Pause briefly to reflect and then continue, and so on through the book. Then lead a discussion about ideas garnered on a recall pattern basis. Follow this with questions about the plot or the scheme, and then reread at an even faster pace. After a number of such practice sessions pupils begin to grasp the principle of proceeding by ideas and not word by word. They recognize that the sweep across and through a text does yield a huge return and can be done in a very short period of time. It does take determined concentration, however.

Let the measure of rate be by the number of pages examined per minute and not the number of words. This takes into account all sources of ideas, whether they be words or maps or graphs or charts. Words per minute is a very inadequate measure and for five good reasons. First, it does not allow for the reading of maps, graphs, charts, picture captions, and the like. Second, it equates all words by configuration and says that the eye and mind require the same recognition effort when attending to a two letter word like "go" as when attending to a 13-letter word like "circumference." Obviously this is not true. Third, it equates all words syntactically and says that position in a sentence makes no difference. Fourth, it equates all words grammatically and says that in each sentence each word, whether noun, verb, adjective, or the like, plays the same role. Fifth, it equates each word semantically or conceptually and says that the word "run," with its 103 different meanings, is no more complex than the word "dress" with its 5 meanings.

Pace the children through a textbook, particularly a social science book or a science book and have them reflect and question and reread to gain an overview. Then have them determine questions for skimming or scanning or study reading and observe how much more readily the answers are attained. The overview perspective does make a difference. The entire process prepares a reader to be versatile and efficient.

Of course such training sessions must be conducted across the years in order to be instilled. Maybe once every five weeks an entire week can be devoted to overview reading training. This repeated reinforcement across the years, using various content material at varying levels of difficulty, will prepare pupils to adapt their rate of reading to their purposes for reading and the nature and difficulty of the material.

Training in versatility will improve the quality of performance in so-called inquiry or research-type reading and is an essential adjunct to the skills of critical reading obtained in group-type directed reading-thinking activities. Pupils who master both sets of capabilities will be the efficient scholarly reader. They will know how to inquire into a topic or an area of knowledge such as rocks. They will know how to raise questions: How were rocks formed? How many different kinds of rocks are there? Why are some rocks harder than others? They will know how and why to speculate about likely answers. Rocks are formed by ice and earth and weather. There are thousands of different rocks, and so on. They will know how to search for answers, how to use versatile reading skills to make the search more efficient, and how to share their findings with their peers. This is the essence of inquiry reading and the course of an inquiring mind. Practically all children are curious, but few know how to direct their curiosity by inquiring deliberately and thereby frequently converting an interest into a taste. What is necessary is to provide them with the necessary skills and opportunities to use them.

CONCLUSIONS

Stage 3 children are students who are working almost up to their capability and are very responsive to instruction that accepts them where they are and moves on from there. As such, if they do attend a clinic, they are there for only a short time before returning to regular school attendance. They are responsive to individualized instruction that avoids lock-step skillbooks or boxed materials.

Probably the factor that best distinguishes Stage 3 pupils from those at the other levels and makes them most like the able developmental pupil is the students' attitudes. Not only are their attitudes toward themselves positive and confident, but their attitude toward reading in general and knowledge in particular is one of curiosity and inquiry. To attain and maintain this high level, students must acquire and refine over the years the skills of efficient comprehension. They must know how to ask questions, how to marshall their knowledge and experience, how to speculate, how to read efficiently and assemble authentic information, how to evaluate and interpret in light of the purposes that directed their reading, how to organize what has been learned so that it may be reported and shared clearly and concisely, and how to acquire and extend concepts.

To acquire these competencies will require instructional time. The time must allow for considerable practice under careful supervision. To maintain high level efficient performance requires reinforcement throughout an academic year and extension and refinement across the years. This is the only way for pupils to acquire a respect for accurate and effective use of reading-thinking skills, which govern achievement to such a great extent. Effective scholarly study is highly motivated and sharply focused by questions or problems or purposes the students have stated or helped to state. Furthermore, the student's abilities to declare purposes clearly are the best evidence that they are ready to read.

Finally, when instruction is differentiated, caring for the wide range of reading-thinking abilities within a class is done without the use of a label such as corrective. All students are developmental except for those few with extreme disabilities who are recognized as remedial and are in need of very special differentiated instruction.

348

BIBLIOGRAPHY

1. Cohen, Dorothy H. "The Effect of Literature on Vocabulary and Reading Achievement." *Elementary English,* 45 (February, 1968): 209–217.

2. Gates, Arthur I. *The Improvement of Reading.* New York: Macmillan, 1935.

3. Maryland State Department of Education, Division of Instructional Television. "Rx for ABC: Basic Education: Teaching the Adult." *Instructional TV Series.* Baltimore: Maryland State Department of Education, 1974.

4. Park, Edward. "A Single Shot on a Spring Day Starts the War." *Smithsonian,* 6 (April, 1975): 43–46.

5. Petre, Richard. "Reading Breaks Make It in Maryland." *Journal of Reading,* 14 (December, 1971): 191–2.

6. Piaget, Jean. *Six Psychological Studies,* trans. David Elkind. New York: Random House, 1967.

7. Sirota, Beverly. "The Effect of a Planned Literature Program of Daily Oral Reading by the Teacher on the Voluntary Reading of Fifth-Grade Children." *Dissertation Abstracts International,* 32 (November 5, 1971): 74.

8. Stauffer, Russell G. "Basic Problems in Correcting Reading Difficulties," in Helen M. Robinson, ed., *Corrective Reading in Classroom and Clinic.* Supplementary Educational Monographs, no. 79, pp. 118–126. Chicago: University of Chicago Press, 1953.

9. Stauffer, Russell G. *Directing the Reading-Thinking Process.* New York: Harper & Row, 1975.

10. Stauffer, Russell G. *The Language Experience Approach to the Teaching of Reading.* New York: Harper & Row, 1970.

11. Stauffer, Russell G. "Slave, Puppet or Teacher?" *The Reading Teacher,* 24 (1971): 24–29.

12. Stauffer, Russell G., et al. *Communications Through Effective Reading.* Haddonfield, N.J.: Learn, Inc., 1972.

13. Stauffer, Russell G., et al. *Rapid Comprehension Through Effective Reading.* Haddonfield, N.J.: Learn, Inc., 1972.

14. Strickland, Dorothy. "A Program for Linguistically Different Black Children." *Research in the Teaching of English,* 7 (Spring, 1973), 79–86.

15. Sutherland, A. H. "Individual Differences Among Children." *Adapting the Schools to Individual Differences: Twenty-fourth Yearbook of the National Society for the Study of Education,* part 2, section 1. Bloomington, Ill.: Public School Publishing Co., 1925.

CHAPTER 14

Prevention and the Role of Reading Specialists

No one quarrels with the idea that "an ounce of prevention is worth a pound of cure." It is in the nature of a homily and, as is so often true of preachings, "it goes in one ear and out the other." Even though preventive medicine has made great strides in recent years, most people continue to be negligent and careless. Because this continues to be true in matters of life and death, it is understandable why in such other areas as education, preventive measures are so little practiced.

Almost all qualified educators will tell you that children who are likely to experience extreme difficulty in learning to read can be identified early in first grade if not earlier, in the preschool years. Even though this is so, most schools continue to devote most of their funds and their energies to trying to cure or correct disabilities rather than to prevent them.

Perhaps, though, the most damaging circumstance is the degree to which sound instructional practices lag behind sound theory. Teachers continue to use practices that were resorted to in the dame schools of early New England and the one room schools of the nineteenth century. This was the time of the recitation school, when the teacher listened to recitals or oral readings that had been taught at home. If no home teaching occurred, as was often true, reading failures resulted. Recent social, cultural, scientific, and economic changes have made such practices obsolete and have required a reexamination of both theory and practice.

In 1922 the National Society for the Study of Education appointed a committee to do something about the great waste of time and effort in the teaching of reading. The committee was staffed by educators whose names have since become revered: William S. Gray, Ernest Horn, Laura Zirbes. They said, "The primary purpose of reading in school is to extend the experiences of boys and girls, to stimulate their thinking powers, and to elevate their tastes" (5, p. 9). They placed emphasis on reading as a thought-getting process, stressed speed of silent reading, and made a clear distinction between "training pupils to read well and preparing them for expert service as public readers or elocutionists." (p. 71). They spoke strongly against such unproductive practices as: round-the-robin oral reading, oral reading in concert, whole classes reading the same article, and using meager and insufficient materials. These procedures are so manifestly unsuited to the attainment of sound objectives and so obviously productive of poor attitudes that one can only wonder at their prevalence and persistence so far into the twentieth century. The committee also urged provision for individual differences, to grouping for instruction, to multiple assignments, and to making meaning and not word calling the primary focus.

In *The Teaching of Reading: A Second Report* the authors stress that intelligent reading not only stresses problems that are highly motivating and sharply focalized, but

> sets the pupils to work under the guide of specific purposes he has helped to state. . . . [H]e assumes responsibility for helping to state and organize the problems that are to guide his reading. (6, p. 154)

Today, a half a century later, not only are many teachers practicing the same procedures so heartily condemned then but also they have reverted to lock-step procedures that would utterly shock Preston Search, Frederick Burk, Carleton Washburn, Ernest Horn, William Kilpatrick, Laura Zirbes, and the like. Search protested vehemently against lock-step methods as early as 1888. In 1915 Burk produced his famous *Monograph C*. Later, 1925, the Winnetka plan directed by Washburn stressed individualization of instruction, as did the Dalton plan (16). Even so, these people thought that most likely their measures were "only halfway measures" and more needed to be done to improve reading instruction. This being the case, it seems a strange paradox indeed that in this day and age of computer capabilities, space exploration, biological advances, instruction in reading has not made comparable progress. In fact in many instances advocated procedures combined with the materials being used have resulted in the same kinds of teaching condemned a century ago. Prevention of reading disabilities does not lie in lock-step practices; and labeling programs as individualized or computerized or adding cassettes or games does not necessarily alter what in essence are the same kinds of lock-step procedures.

THE ROLE OF THE READING CONSULTANT

In the previous chapter the use of the school reading specialist not only for remedial instruction but also as a consulting "helping teacher" was discussed as one positive step schools could take toward shifting the focus to prevention. Another is the increasing use of the reading consultant or supervisor who has had special training in reading. This change in emphasis from remedial reading teacher to reading consultant has brought with it a careful look at the qualifications of a consultant. In October, 1963, over 120 carefully selected reading specialists, supervisors, and consultants convened at the University of Delaware for three days for the particular purpose of examining the role and qualifications of the reading consultant. The meeting resulted in the preparation of an extensive questionnaire. The returns obtained (14) permitted some generalizations which proved useful: (1) All respondents had undergraduate degrees and the majority were education majors. (2) Approximately half the number had master's degrees with majors in reading. (3) Some had doctor's degrees. (4) The average number of years of teaching experience was five years; all had at least two years. (5) The range in size of districts employing consultants extended from districts of approximately 500 pupils, grades 1–12 to districts of up to 185,000 pupils. (6) In a few instances the consultant's work was limited to one building, but usually responsibilities were for the entire district. (7) None of the respondents were engaged as remedial teachers. (8) All but four met the International Reading Association minimum standards for a reading specialist. (9) The majority engaged in in-service training, the writing of instructional aids, and individual teacher consultation. (10) All engaged in related community activities: PTA meetings, library boards, and the like. In brief, it could be said that consultants are experienced, specially trained, hard working individuals doing a big job but with too little help.

A decade later, 1973, the original questionnaire was modified slightly and mailed to specialists in Delaware, Maryland, New Jersey, and Pennsylvania. Approximately one-half replied. Only minor changes were noted. Now all the consultants had master's degrees in reading and this included six to nine hours of clinical laboratory experience. Most of them were engaged on a 10-month basis. They continued to prefer in-service meetings and regretted that more of their time was being devoted to the preparation of federal program requests and reports, because this curtailed their activities involving demonstrations for teachers and the actual working with children. Federal programs like Title I have supported teacher aides, and consultants have been called upon to train them. Sadly enough, although the number of reading consultants has increased over the past decade, they continue to be fewer in number than supervisors of art, music, or physical education (15).

In many districts consultants are merely that: people available for consultation to a building principal or a school superintendent. Too often school principals set the policy, purchase programs, and materials, and then ask consultants to implement. These same principals seldom if ever have taken more than one course in reading instruction. However, with this limited base and with a jaundiced eye on standardized test score norms, they dictate policy and procedure.

Two federal programs have spent huge sums intended to improve reading instruction: Right to Read and Title I. The former is aimed at in-service efforts, an excellent proposition. But with the effort being dictated by people generally unqualified in reading and not the reading consultant, the returns have been far less than they could be. Title I funds have a very strange limiting control. When a school's achievement scores reach the norm or exceed it slightly, then the funds are terminated. As a result districts receiving huge grants and cannot afford to loose them make certain the scores do not improve too much.

Some districts continue the service of a reading consultant but engage some person not qualified in reading to oversee the Title I and Right to Read programs. In turn these districts engage large numbers of remedial reading teachers who are all too often untrained in corrective or remedial practices and therefore engage in teaching procedures that have already failed to teach the pupils how to read when they were used in the regular classroom. Many worthwhile traditional classroom activities could and should be employed. These include: stress on purposeful reading, on group instruction to develop thinking readers, on differentiated instruction to develop resourceful self-regulatory students, on inquiry reading and the intensive use of multimedia centers, on libraries, on using pupil's language and experience power at all levels, on the functional teaching of word recognition skills, and on concept attainment. These are traditional practices that have proved fruitful for a century or more when and where used and therefore should be staunchly advocated. These are not the objectionable lock-step practices, the round-the-round oral reading practices, the use of teacher predictions and purposes, the teacher questioning seeking only simple facts and ignoring the value of facts and ideas, the teaching of phonics in isolation and on a lock-step basis, the word-by-word reading of all materials.

Consultants should be required by certification demands to have a minimum of nine credit hours of reading clinic laboratory school instruction under supervision, to have studied developmental reading programs carefully, to have studied the role of a supervisor in general and a reading consultant in particular, to have courses in the psychology of learning, in mental hygiene, in human growth and development, in personality, and in abnormal psychology. By and large consultants should be extremely qualified people. More important is that, as such, they should be granted authority to act in a district and not be the tool of persons not so qualified. Consultants can and should conduct in-service programs for teachers, teacher aides, and administrators; visit classroom and advise and demonstrate; help teachers coordinate their effort on an intragrade and intergrade basis; arrange and conduct workshops; advise in the purchase of instructional materials; stay posted on new materials and view them critically; protect principals from overzealous sales people; integrate library or multimedia center usage with instructional programs; attend P.T.A. meetings or their counterparts; prepare timely and warranted instructional goals; chart achievement progress; and counsel teachers and parents on disability cases.

THE REMEDIAL READING TEACHER

The remedial reading teacher contrasts quite clearly with the reading consultant, specialist, or supervisor. In most instances graduate course work requirement is much less and totals about twelve hours, consisting of a general foundations course, a reading diagnosis course, a reading analysis course, and a remedial reading course. In many instances remedial reading teachers are experienced teachers. In some few instances they have done only student teaching and taken the four graduate courses specified and then are employed as remedial reading teachers.

As stated in the previous chapter, the remedial reading teacher usually helps test children to decide those who need special help. On occasion this is done in collaboration with the school psychologist and the more recently federally created learning-disabilities teacher. The selected children are taught in groups of 10–20 by the remedial teacher, in a special room or area set aside for this purpose. Invariably the remedial instruction consists of more of the same kind of instruction and material as provided in the regular classroom. Skillbooks are dealt with page by page, regardless of what skill comes next or whether or not the pupil needs further instruction to master a particular skill. Basic readers are used for group instruction, with each child reading the same story and being asked the same questions by the teacher. Little if any teacher oral reading is done, because as most remedial teachers claim, they do not have the time. No creative writing is done, spelling is not taught, and little use is made of a wide variety of materials, such as magazines, newspapers, filmstrips, trade books, and the like. All too often these programs are primarily an undifferentiated dose of phonics and/or word attack skill building activities, a low level isolationist approach with the phoneme-grapheme patterns isolated from sound units or syllables and the words isolated from semantic contexts or meaning.

In some instances the language-experience approach is used. With its dramatic emphasis on utilizing the children's language power and interests, in developing concepts and vocabulary usage, in using a wide variety of materials and activities, the atmosphere and attitudes are different, as are the results. Because the language experience approach stresses differentiation of instruction geared to individual children's language power, their experiences and knowledge background, and their interests, pupil response is different. The children recognize that they are accepted as they are, regardless of their language patterns or enunciations, their social or cultural status, their reading abilities, or their appearance. This attitude of acceptance is not assumed but is augmented by the fact that the instructor is interested enough in his or her ideas and reactions to not only listen but also to use them for instructional purposes and in choosing materials to be read. No longer are they forced to memorize words, or to make strange noises by distorting their lips and mouths, and to then try to put the noises together when reading material that contains nothing of interest to them (13).

Children sense these changes in atmosphere and attitude intuitively and respond accordingly. They delight in the action activities that are planned: collecting things, growing things, constructing things, measuring things, and comparing things. Always they are doing things, talking about them and sharing with each other. In the meantime they are learning words regardless of whether they occur on a word list. They are learning words as they should: when words serve a purpose. If they speak about and study flowers, they talk about the stem, the pistil, the petals, the leaves, the stamen, the sepal, the stigma. These words serve a purpose: they identify a specific and they communicate about it. Words in a word list are placed there only because of frequency of usage and, as a result, often used words like "and," "the," "on," "an," and "so" appear at the top of the list rather than the functional nouns, verbs, adjectives, or adverbs. The latter are the core words used to talk about something, to tell what happened, how and why.

Remedial reading teachers in schools soon learn (or should) that what they do instructionally is a lot more than "good first teaching." The children they see are eight years old and older and possess more language and experience power than five- and six-year olds. In addition, they have anxieties and fears, negative attitudes and low motivation and require a different, more intensified personalized instruction, which is paced carefully to their particular needs and learning abilities.

If a group of slow achievers is dealt with early enough, in second grade or at the latest early in third grade, then a procedure that is quite fruitful is to have the special reading teacher come to the regular classroom and instruct a group. This does not remove the children from the classroom and avoids that kind of segregation stigma. It permits the classroom teacher to observe the many advantages of what is being done by the special reading teacher. The classroom teacher may observe actions and procedures that can be incorporated into her or his teaching. The two teachers are much more likely to coordinate their efforts. The remedial teacher may observe instructional practices that could be improved or changed. At times the classroom teacher can work with the slow group while the remedial teacher instructs the others. In brief, a coordinated instructional effort is much more likely to occur and be productive.

Teacher aides can be very helpful or they can be a deterrent. When funds are provided, as they are under Title I, then aides can be screened and selected. Usually this is done with the help of the remedial reading person. In turn, this person also does the instructing to prepare the aides for their role.

If aides know what to do and what not to do, they can be quite useful. Sometimes children are less reluctant to open up with an aide. Aides can assist the teacher by doing some carefully selected instructional tasks, help prepare instructional activities and materials, read orally, set up films and the like, escort children to the library, help the teacher be omnipresent in differentiating instruction, assist in spelling instruction, help monitor creative writing, and help plan sharing activities and the staging of sharing. Aides should not take over any group or level for special instruction. All too often uninformed teachers assign the slow rate achievers to an aide. This is unfortunate, because these children more than any others need the special insight, experience, and training the classroom teacher has. Teachers must also stay alert to not only what the aide is doing but also to the way in which children are reacting to him or her. Usually aides are attentive to instruction, are very willing helpers, and can be a great boon.

Volunteer aides can also be helpful; but they, too, need training and guidance. Mothers frequently volunteer to help and can be a great help if (1) they are trained to help, and (2) they are regular in attendance. A ready morale breaker is to count on the use of an aide who does not show up. This is discouraging to both the children and the teacher. Accordingly, while mother aides are not turned away, assurance is needed that they will be present when scheduled and will attend aide training sessions. It is most important, also, that the teacher not turn over to the volunteer aides only the slower achievers. Far too often this arrangement becomes a kind of baby sitting arrangement, from which the children do not obtain the help they really need. The teacher must never forget that she is the teacher and hers is the leadership role.

PREVENTION OF READING FAILURES

In the brief section that follows, ideas may be repeated that have been stated previously. It is thought though that singling them out this way under this heading may help focus more clearly on prevention.

The cliche, "If wishes were horses, beggars would ride," can be readily applied to the many who wish they could read but cannot. Wishing is not the answer. This is especially so for those whose learning pace is slower than the typical and who all too often, as a result, are faced with pedagogically created failure of varying degrees. To learn to be a competent reader requires of most people a disciplined effort. Such an effort cannot be effected by a so-called pouring in of phonic rules or of teacher fact-questioning and pupil parroting to develop comprehension.

By contrast, the notion of teaching as a drawing out represents a distinct polarization of teacher actions. This notion capitalizes on another often used pedagogical cliche: "Begin at the level of the learner." If to this is added the notion of pacing instruction, then teaching can do more than render lip service to differentiating instruction.

The fact that children differ from one another, most times distinctly so but sometimes quite subtly, can be both the boon and the bond of instruction. The range of differences when recognized and utilized are what make teaching and learning exciting and invigorating. Teachers exclaim about a spectacular pupil achievement and are thrilled by it. But when instruction is more truly differentiated, they can be constantly exclaiming about each child. Pupil differences make instruction vital, exciting, and stimulating and make learning functional (practical) and profitable (useful). It is the range of differences from pupil to pupil, in capacity, creativity, curiosity, physical stamina, and social and emotional adjustment that makes the wheels of society go around and can make instruction an inviting challenge.

Most children of three or four or more are already running over with all kinds of energies and curiosities. They are alert and responsive and especially so to the use of language purposefully. This is why John B. Watson is referred to as saying that, by the time children are of school age, they are graduate students in terms of learned responses. These learned responses of a sensori-motor nature, a linguistic nature, and an environmental-cultural nature provide a tremendous reservoir of potential that can be put to good use by any alert teacher. Some of these ways are described in much detail in another text (13).

Not only does every teacher know that children are different, but also that the differences exist at the preprimary level. In addition every teacher knows, too, that "good teaching increases individual differences." The gifted show their talents more bountifully. So do the average and those that are least fortunate. Some teachers realize too that intrapupil variance can be greater in terms of range of talent and potential than interpupil differences.

Interestingly enough teachers of preschool-age children are usually more attentive to individual differences than are teachers at any subsequent level. It is not uncommon to hear a kindergarten teacher say, "I teach in kindergarten. That is where the action is." There is much truth to what they say, but the statement is also a serious indictment of teachers at other levels. Nursery school and kindergarten-age children are active and doing, exploring their world on a sensori-motor level, a rapidly expanding conceptual level, and a steadily increasing sociocentric level. It could be because the various stages of maturity or immaturity are so striking that they compel teacher recognition of differences that teaching and learning are paced differentially at these early levels. On the other hand it could also be true that teachers of older children are obliged to see to it that the children master and acquire certain skills in arithmetic, science, health, social science, and so on. As a result these teachers become preoccupied with skill knowledge acquisition rather than with the motivation, curiosity, aptitude, security, and rate of learning of individual pupils.

In addition at the preschool level parents seem considerably more concerned about their children's transition from home to school than at any other level. This attentiveness and anxiety in turn can result in timely and desirable parent-teacher, home-school contacts. All in all, as a result, individual differences are given more attention and recognition than is usually true at higher levels.

At all stages of the learning process neuromotor, perceptual, emotional, and intellectual operations are closely bound. This interaction is a continuous process, and children's performance and progress reflect this, as well as their relationships with adults and peers.

At the same time it is abundantly evident that the lock-step practices of teaching are bonds of our own making. We are the cruel robbers. We build the Procrustean beds. We try to fit all children into skillbooks or learning boxes or rigidly defined teaching manuals and almost totally disregard the human and humane side. How unfortunate that instruction in reading is taught largely by the Procrustean tradition wherein, as Goodlad and Anderson so aptly state, we "trap school age travelers in much the same fashion as Procrustes's bed trapped the unwary" (4,

p. 1), by expecting all children to fit certain predetermined norms and patterns of thinking.

When to all this one adds the realization that reading is a process and not a product, then the teaching advice and the resultant teaching actions fostered on most teachers are almost unbelievable (12). Reading is a dynamic on-going process. It is a way of thinking ad acting. It requires the readers to know (1) why they are reading, (2) how to adapt their rate of reading, (3) how to determine the value of facts, (4) how to suspend judgment until all the evidence is in, (5) how to make sound decisions, and (6) how to relax and enjoy reading. Learning to read is a matter of acquiring cognitive-affective skills useful when reading in any area of the curriculum. Because reading has this universality and because no fixed body of "reading" knowledge must be acquired just to learn to read, it is puzzling indeed that the Procrustean reading instruction methods persist so universally and have been augmented in the past decade.

In brief, sound instruction practices must be built upon truths about individuals and their differences. First, differences among children of the same age are great and require recognition and attention. Second, it is unwise indeed to attempt to teach a skill that a child is unable to cope with. Third, boys and girls develop at different rates and in different ways. Fourth, teachers must take into account individual children's developmental ages as they grow physically, mentally, and emotionally.

THE TEACHER COORDINATOR

By now it may be judged that the teacher of children with reading disabilities must indeed be a specially trained person, and this is so. But it should be equally as apparent that the teacher of so-called developmental-level children must be equally as competent. Every teacher, regardless of the capability of the children they teach, the level at which they teach, or the skill or knowledge area in which they teach should have the experience of instructing only one child at some time. Every teacher should discover how difficult it can be to communicate effectively with one child and then realize thereby that to teach 30 children requires vastly greater acumen.

Teachers need to realize, too, that in reality they are coordinators of physical and mental actions. They create situations where actions can be accomplished, where purposes and goals can be set and attained, where structures can be discovered, where decisions can be made, and where cooperation becomes co-operation. Piaget said that the principal goal of instruction is to create men who are capable of doing new things, not simply repeating what other generations have done—men who are creators, inventors, discoverers. The second goal of education is to form minds which can be critical, can verify, and do not accept everything they are offered. . . . So we need pupils who are active, who learn early to find out by themselves, partly by their own spontaneous activity and partly through material we set up for them; who learn early to tell what is verifiable and what is simply the first idea to come to them. (10, p. 175)

In addition, if it is essential in remedial instruction that learners always know why they are doing what they are doing and what skill or knowledge they are to acquire, then it is equally as essential for developmental instruction. The teaching-learning situation is definitely a hyphenated situation in which the student is an active participant in setting objectives, determining ways to efficiently attain the objectives, and in determining how well acquired are the new learnings. In brief, the learning responsibility involves the pupil intimately. Where this is true, pupils become more self-regulatory, self-disciplined, and self-reliant scholars. Under such instruction one finds a certain serenity in the room, because learning is going on all the time (3). Pupils learn to think before acting, to plan before proceeding, to anticipate before quickening, to reflect before reacting. Pupils learn the value of actively pursuing a goal in a disciplined way, to show respect for the thoughts and deeds of others, and to appreciate the amenities that accompany the interchange of ideas. In the area of social learning and in putting reading into the context of the communication arts, the student is gradually gaining release from "the prison of his own perspective" (3). Undoubtedly there are age-dependent skills at work at the different maturity levels from kindergarten to high school. But above all, teachers must help students learn to examine their own interests and convert some of them to tastes, to gain increasing appreciation for a question well asked, and to realize that knowledge resides almost equally as much in the questions raised as in the answers found. By so doing students learn that the highest form of motivation is that of intellectual commitment.

OPEN-MINDED INSTRUCTION

Currently the popular notion abroad in education is that of the *open classroom*. In reality what is meant is not what American economy-minded school superintendents and boards of education have construed it to be: wall-less barnlike rooms—but open-minded instruction abounding in pupil-teacher open communication structuring. This is the kind in which teacher questions are largely open-ended, interpreting and inferring, and pupil responses are chiefly critical, representing higher levels of thinking.

What is different in these classrooms is "the approach, the motivation, the emphasis and the outcome" (1). In these schools children's interests and aptitudes are converted to use. Children have a natural urge to explore and enjoy doing so. Where these urges are wisely utilized, learning activities become self-perpetuating. This embodies the basic tenet of open-minded (open classroom) instruction. The boundless curiosity of children is directed flexibly and adroitly into the various areas of knowledge and their accumulated spiraling complexities. Teachers are willing to experiment, to innovate, to be inventive and to be forward looking. In a broader perspective children are no longer in schools; the world of knowledge and reality provide the dimensions. Regardless of all that has been said, the one feature that truly distinguishes open-minded instruction from any other methodology is "the nature of the teacher's questioning" (1).

LEADERSHIP

It would be helpful indeed if somehow the labels principal and vice-principal could be discontinued and some form of the word leader substituted. The concept of leader implies a capacity for guidance or direction and winning support. By contrast, Principal refers to a power structure whereby one person is given authority over and control of others. Successful schools, particularly open-minded schools, attain their status through superb leadership. What is needed is a higher level of communication and coordination of staff and administration.

Teachers must be led to realize that they have nothing to fear except "fear itself," as John Dewey once said (2). If teachers are fearful and anxious, they treat children that way. It is not only the way teachers view themselves but how they think they are being viewed by a power structure principal that makes a difference. If the leadership is positive, hopeful, supportive, and optimistic, the teachers and the children will reflect this.

Carl Rogers (11) built his theory of adjustment around the concept of self. He described self as a social product, developing out of one's actions and interactions with others. He also believed that there is a strong need for positive regard from others. Thus, a teacher's concept of self is much influenced by the nature of the interactions with the leadership in a school and the positive regard received.

SELF-CONCEPT

Much was said earlier about the self-concept or self-image or self-esteem of a child experiencing great difficulty learning to read. The point was made that frequently "therapeutical" instructional practices took precedence over pedagogical instructional practices. According to Edmund Henderson and Barbara Long (7, 8, 9), successful adjustment to one's environment requires ability to predict, anticipate, and direct behavior in relation to environmental events. This is equally as true of the so-called developmental child as of the serious disability child.

Henderson and Long also noted that successful readers are more socially oriented. From this they do some interesting speculation when they say,

> Such a pattern would be consistent with the theory of reading which holds that the process is in part a dialogue in which the reader experiences a continual social interaction with persons both real and imaginary. From this point of view social orientation should indeed facilitate achievement in reading. (7, p. 4)

In other words reading is in a sense a dialogue between readers and the authors. If the readers' self-esteem is untarnished they are likely to openly and freely challenge authors. This in turn clearly influences the reading performance. Secure readers, ardently seeking knowledge, will question and debate and will want to know how trustworthy are the authors and the ideas presented.

In the instructional practices described so far in this text, it is evident that three factors serve as mediators of self in a wholesome way: motivation, commitment, and sharing. Possibly the highest form of motivation stems from commitment, namely, intellectual commitment. It has been suggested repeatedly that pupils be urged to express themselves, to relate their experiences and knowledge to the event at hand, and to use it to predict, anticipate, plan, and evaluate. It is this honoring of a pupil's analysis of events and his judgments about them that develop confidence, poise, and the desire to seek and to know. Therefore, all learning should involve the development and refinement of decision making and the ability to weigh alternatives.

The best way to start to instruct at the level of the learners is by involving them intellectually and by leading them on to new insights and understandings. High-level motivation stems from the pursuit of objectives that students have helped declare because they become their commitment. The fulfillment that results not only from finding answers to one's own questions but also from sharing answers found with others provides reward and equilibrium. Such intellectual commitment, and sharing goes a long way toward fostering self-esteem. In the process, moreover, pupils learn that plaudits are not the sole key to motivation.

In the world of today one is constantly faced with many options. Accordingly, one must learn the responsibility of making choices. Sartre has said that one is the result of one's choices, and this is an apt summation. To learn to make choices in an educative environment appears to be ideal. Each opportunity pupils have to participate helps them cope with likely repressions or rationalizations and learn that strong self-esteem requires a consistency of esteem and a defense against anxiety.

To help pupils see options, make decisions, make commitments, and prepare sharings requires teacher know-how. As Edgar Dale says,

> We should give all students the opportunity to test their powers to make judgments and to draw inferences. They must be faced with problems, puzzles, dilemmas, and issues which cause them to "rack" their brains; too often, they begin to read instead of to think. (2, p. 72)

In short, all children must be made to feel that they are important, that their thoughts and ideas are of value, that they are wanted, and that they can do things and make decisions.

TEACHING-LEARNING STRUCTURALISM

If we keep all this before us, the initial teaching of reading becomes largely a matter of directing children's activities, of giving them exercise and freedom along certain lines, and of thereby leading logically to the goal to be attained: the recognition of printed words. Thus the children's impulse to find expression—in play, in movement, in make-believe— becomes more definitive as they shape ideas into spoken language and sees them organized into tangible form and permanent written embodiment. Children like to do things and to see what happens. And when these impulses are taken advantage of, as they are in the individualization that occurs in the eclectic language experience approach (13), then they are directed into ways in which their language power and curiosity give results of personal value. And so the recognition of the printed word grows out of the communication and constructive instincts of each child. By giving the construction adequate form, giving it a social motive, something to tell, the result is a work of art.

Thus, through individualization of instruction inaugurated by means of an integrated language arts approach, an instructor can capitalize on the four-fold interests of children. First is their interest in conversation or communication. Second, their interest in finding out things, in inquiry. Third, their interest in making things, or construction. And, fourth, their interest in artistic expression. This represents the uninvested capital upon which can be fostered the active growth of each child. This utilization of a child's potential represents a sharp change from recitation or rote memorization and affects and modifies all the language work of a school. So it hardly needs to be said that language is primarily a social device, a means by which we share our experiences with others.

Reading, as something to be taken up into a child's own communicating experience, should not be presented as lessons, as something to be memorized. It can best be learned through a child's own activities, whereby the intimate connection between knowing and doing are maintained and strengthened. The aim of reading instruction is not then to teach a set of discrete skills apart from life-like language usage and communication, but is rather a means of recapitulating a child's experiences and those of others. In turn these experiences are enlarged, enriched, and gradually better formulated. By so doing, language processes and social processes become cohesive realities. Moreover, through dramatic identification of each child, there intervenes an intellectual identification. Children learn to put themselves at the heart of problems that they meet and to discover ways of solving them.

In brief, the conditions of individualization of reading instruction in particular and all instruction in general may be reduced to two. The first is to provide each child with a variety of experiences with reality, both social and physical. The second is that, as a result, the questions, motives, and interests of each child produce a need for their pursuit and solution. It is possible in the early years to appeal, in teaching the recognition and production of printed symbols, to any child's power of production and creation.

Grouping for instruction is also an essential. The study of oral and printed language is a study in communication and must be placed in a human setting that fosters interaction. No separation should be made between the social or communication side of reading, with its concerns with people's activities and interdependencies; and the "science" side, with its regard for facts and forces. The learning environment is always social, and is, therefore, not to be thought of as isolated.

In addition, there is the question of interaction, not only of children within a group or class, but also with the various matters studied. Interacting minds foster ways of developing certain features or ideas to a more rounded and unified mental and emotional satisfaction and completeness. Interacting minds formulate different questions and varied responses and provoke a sharpening and intensifying of language usage, interests, and goals.

It is in a group situation that reality-adjusted thinking is intensified and sharpened. The opportunity to make inferences and the need to defend or reject them in the presence of a group is highly influential in provoking conscious behavior that is reality-adjusted. The group provides a means of testing the degree to which the scheme of things are anticipated. Many inferences, of course, remain untested, because they were not conceptualized.

In turn, the effectiveness of discussion helps students to discover unrecognized assumptions. They realize through repeated opportunity how many ways there are for looking at a problem or a schema. Gradually, they become aware of discrepancies between different peer reactions to the same schema and thereby learn to weigh alternative evidence. Gradually, too, they compare and contrast their own world of experiences with those of others and begin to modify their world. It is their interacting with the ways of thinking of the other members of the group that is fascinating. Thus the group members are continually learning to understand by the very process of acting on what they read.

This is decoding on an intellectual semantic level. Among teachers of reading that idea is invariably limited to decoding or unlocking a word by phonic analysis. It seldom embraces semantic decoding: interpolation and extrapolation. Of far greater significance is the degree to which thinking readers decode the ideas they perceive and the assumptions they make. They must learn to make verifiable assumptions on which they can base effective action. This is intellectual decoding of a high order. The aim of group instruction is to provide a medium in which individuals can learn about their own decodings.

It is not possible to protect students from making mistakes in judgment. What is vastly more important is that they recognize how they erred. In the process they realize, too, that no one is infallible. Thus a range of behavior is useful because it allows for analysis and comparison. In different ways it is as useful to criticize as to approve; to disagree as to agree; to speak in a straightforward manner as to listen. Often it is the so-called weak student who offers a common-sense analysis or who keeps a discussion on course.

The role of the teacher in a group situation is in many ways similar to that in an individualized circumstance. In both, the teacher's role is to make the student think. This is done by arranging the circumstance (the article, or selection to be read), by open-ended question asking, by asking for evidence, and by asking why and eliciting and honoring pupil purposes and predictions. In turn, because of repeated opportunities, the role of teachers can be taken over by various members of a group. Pupils become quite skilled at directing a D-R-T-A. In the final analysis, the aim of group instruction is to provide students with ways of behaving which are useful when the group is dissolved and when they are on their own in reading.

SUMMARY

Lock-step practices perhaps more than any other pedagogical procedure led educators to not only protest about such teaching actions but also to advocate procedures that would more appropriately differentiate instruction and develop competence. These protests and recommendations promoted the use of supervisors and consultants to help teachers combat inappropriate techniques.

The use of consultants and the like, in turn, led to a more concerted effort toward pacing of instruction in keeping with varying rates of maturation, intellectually and physically. This has resulted, at least in part, in a steady but slow shift from remediation to prevention of reading failure. A whole-hearted effort is required on the total pedagogical scene to keep remedial instruction functional while placing fuller effort at activating and pursuing preventive differentiation of instruction.

Emphasis on sound developmental teaching practices is essential. We know how to teach reading properly; what is needed is a wider dissemination of know-how freed from commercial exploiting of lock-step consumable materials and gadgets. In the process it must be recognized that differentiation of instruction involves both group and individual settings and that reading is a process applicable to all areas of knowledge.

BIBLIOGRAPHY

1. Brandt, Richard M. "An Observational Investigation of Instruction and Behavior in an Informal British Infant School." Paper presented at the meeting of the American Education Research Association, April 5, 1972.

2. Dale, Edgar. *Building a Learning Environment.* Bloomington, Ind.: Phi Delta Kappa, 1972.

3. Department of Education and Science, *Children and Their Primary Schools: A Report of the Central Advisory Council for Education,* vol 1. London: Her Majesty's Stationery Office, 1967.

4. Goodlad, John I., and Robert H. Anderson. *The Nongraded Elementary School.* New York: Harcourt Brace Jovanovich, 1959.

5. Gray, William S. "Essential Objectives of Instruction in Reading, in *Report of the National Committee on Reading: Twenty-fourth Yearbook of the National Society for the Study of Education,* part 1. Bloomington, Ill.: Public School Publishing Co., 1925.

6. Gray, William S. "The Nature and Types of Reading," in *The Teaching of Reading: A Second Report: Thirty-sixth Yearbook of the National Society for the Study of Education,* part 1. Bloomington, Ill.: Public School Publishing Co., 1925.

7. Henderson, Edmund H., and Barbara Long. "Self-Social Concepts in Relation to Reading and Arithmetic." Unpublished paper. Charlottesville, Va.: University of Virginia Library, 1970.

8. Long, Barbara, Edmund H. Henderson, and Robert C. Ziller. "Self-Social Concepts of Disadvantaged School Beginners," *Journal of Genetic Psychology,* 111 (1968): 41–51.

9. Long, Barbara, Edmund H. Henderson, and Robert C. Ziller. "Self-Social Correlates of Originality in Children." Journal of Genetic Psychology, 111 (1967): 47–57.

10. Piaget, Jean. "Development and Learning," in Richard R. Ripple and Verne N. Rockcastle, eds., *Piaget Rediscovered: A Report of the Conference on Cognitive Studies and Curriculum Development* (March, 1964). Ithaca, N.Y.: Cornell University, School of Education, 1964.

11. Rogers, Carl. *Freedom to Learn.* Columbus, Ohio: Merrill, 1969.

12. Stauffer, Russell, G. "Slave, Puppet or Teacher?" *The Reading Teacher,* 24 (1971): 24–29.

13. Stauffer, Russell G. *The Language Experience Approach to The Teaching of Reading.* New York: Harper & Row, 1978.

14. Stauffer, Russell G. "The Role of the Reading Consultant," in *Modern Educational Developments: Another Look: Report of the Thirtieth Educational Conference.* New York: Educational Records Bureau, 1966.

15. Stauffer, Russell G., Patricia Hodgson, and Mary L. Hutchison. "The Role of the Reading Consultant Reevaluated." Unpublished paper. Newark, Del.: University of Delaware, College of Education, 1974.

16. Sutherland, A. H. "Individual Differences Among Children." *Adapting the Schools to Individual Differences: Twenty-fourth Yearbook of the National Society for the Study of Education,* part 2, section 1. Bloomington, Ill.: Public School Publishing Co., 1925.

Index

78 79 80 9 8 7 6 5 4 3 2 1